OHIO REAL ESTATE PRINCIPLES AND PRACTICES

7th Edition

Hondros Learning would like to thank Jan Manila, GRI, RSD, SRES, DREI, for serving as project editor on this Seventh Edition of ***Ohio Real Estate Principles and Practices***, and the many other instructors for their contributions to the revision and editing of this text.

HONDROS LEARNING™
4140 Executive Parkway
Westerville, Ohio 43081
www.hondroslearning.com

Published 2006. Printed in the United States of America

10 09 08 07 06 1 2 3 4 5

ISBN-13: 978-1-59844-003-4
ISBN-10: 1-59844-003-9

For more information on or to purchase our products, please call 1-866-84LEARN or visit www.hondroslearning.com.

TABLE OF CONTENTS

SYLLABUS: DAY CLASSES
OHIO REAL ESTATE PRINCIPLES AND PRACTICES

COURSE DESCRIPTION: The course covers the theory and concepts of the field of real estate. Topics include property management, leasing, title closing, income analysis, license law, brokerage real estate transactions, property ownership and rights, marketing, land development, and building construction.

COURSE OBJECTIVES:
1. Demonstrate a basic knowledge of Ohio real estate principles and practices.
2. Demonstrate a basic knowledge of real estate terms.
3. Recognize documents used in real estate practice.

COURSE TEXTBOOK: *Ohio Real Estate Principles and Practices*, 7th edition, ©2007 Hondros Learning™

COURSE CREDIT HOURS: 40 clock hours or 4.0 credit hours awarded upon successful completion of the course. Attendance is mandatory to receive credit for the course.

INSTRUCTION METHOD: Lecture

DAY 1

Module 1 (a.m.)	Introduction and Overview Chapter 1 The Real Estate Profession Chapter 2 Getting a Real Estate License
Module 2 (p.m.)	Chapter 2 Getting a Real Estate License (*continued*) Chapter 3 Keeping Your Real Estate License Chapter 4 The Real Estate Industry

DAY 2

Module 3 (a.m.)	Chapter 5 Overview of Real Estate Law Chapter 6 Brokers, Salespeople, and the Agency Relationship
Module 4 (p.m.)	Chapter 6 Brokers, Salespeople, and the Agency Relationship (*continued*)

DAY 3

Module 5 (a.m.)	Chapter 7 Real Estate Contracts, Agreements, and Documents Chapter 8 Deeds and Ownership
Module 6 (p.m.)	Math Formulas Chapter 9 Real Estate Closings Chapter 10 Real Estate Practice

DAY 4

Module 7 (a.m.)	Chapter 11 Fair Housing Chapter 12 Overview of Real Estate Finance Chapter 13 Mortgage Basics Chapter 14 Overview of Real Estate Appraisal
Module 8 (p.m.)	Chapter 15 Property Valuation Review of Class Material Final Examination; Evaluations; Review of Final Examination; Distribute Certificates

GRADING: Final grade is based (25%) on classroom participation and attendance, and (75%) on Final Exam and Quiz grades. ***NOTE:*** Tape recorders are not permitted during class lecture sessions.

SYLLABUS: NIGHT CLASSES
OHIO REAL ESTATE PRINCIPLES AND PRACTICES

COURSE DESCRIPTION: The course covers the theory and concepts of the field of real estate. Topics include property management, leasing, title closing, income analysis, license law, brokerage real estate transactions, property ownership and rights, marketing, land development, and building construction.

COURSE OBJECTIVES:

1. Demonstrate a basic knowledge of Ohio real estate principles and practices.
2. Demonstrate a basic knowledge of real estate terms.
3. Recognize documents used in real estate practice.

COURSE TEXTBOOK: *Ohio Real Estate Principles and Practices*, 7th edition, ©2007 Hondros Learning™

COURSE CREDIT HOURS: 40 clock hours or 4.0 credit hours awarded upon successful completion of the course. Attendance is mandatory to receive credit for the course.

INSTRUCTION METHOD: Lecture

MODULE 1	Introduction and Overview Chapter 1 The Real Estate Profession Chapter 2 Getting a Real Estate License
MODULE 2	Chapter 3 Keeping Your Real Estate License Chapter 4 The Real Estate Industry
MODULE 3	Chapter 5 Overview of Real Estate Law
MODULE 4	Chapter 6 Brokers, Salespeople, and the Agency Relationship
MODULE 5	Chapter 7 Real Estate Contracts, Agreements, and Documents
MODULE 6	Chapter 8 Deeds and Ownership Math Formulas
MODULE 7	Chapter 9 Real Estate Closings Chapter 10 Real Estate Practice Chapter 11 Fair Housing
MODULE 8	Chapter 12 Overview of Real Estate Finance Chapter 13 Mortgage Basics
MODULE 9	Chapter 14 Overview of Real Estate Appraisal Chapter 15 Property Valuation
MODULE 10	Review of Class Material Final Examination; Evaluations; Review of Final Examination; Distribute Certificates

GRADING: Final grade is based (25%) on classroom participation and attendance, and (75%) on Final Exam and Quiz grades. ***NOTES:*** Tape recorders are not permitted during class lecture sessions.

PREFACE

Real estate education has changed dramatically over the past few years. Increased educational requirements in Ohio were passed to encourage a higher caliber of real estate professional. This text was written and revised with those requirements in mind—and the goal of preparing you to pass your real estate licensing examination.

Ohio Real Estate Principles and Practices is now in its 7th edition. This text has helped thousands of students become educated about the theory and practice of the real estate profession. This new edition has been revised to reflect recent changes in Ohio real estate law and to better reflect the world of real estate today.

Revisions to this 7th edition were both factual and organizational, and include:

ORGANIZATION:

Some chapters were combined, some split, and some rearranged to make for a more logical presentation of topics.

- *Chapter 2* Getting a Real Estate License and Keeping it has been split into two chapters: *Chapter 2* Getting Your Real Estate License and *Chapter 3* Keeping Your Real Estate License. This important topic of keeping your license now receives as much attention as how to get it and includes the discussion of ethics, formerly in the Fair Housing chapter.
- The discussion of ethics has been moved to *Chapter 3* Keeping Your Real Estate License, where it is highly applicable.
- *Chapter 9* Real Estate Closings, *Chapter 10* Real Estate Practice, and *Chapter 11* Fair Housing have been moved to follow *Chapter 8* Deeds and Ownership.
- Overview of Real Estate Finance is now *Chapter 12*, followed by *Chapter 13* Mortgage Basics, *Chapter 14* Overview of Real Estate Appraisal, and *Chapter 15* Property Valuation.
- *Chapter 14* Alternative Real Estate Careers has been combined into *Chapter 1* The Real Estate Profession to cover all career options early.
- *Math Appendix*: Percent formula is now presented first, as all others formulas are based on understanding this concept.

CONTENT UPDATES:

Chapter 1 **The Real Estate Profession**: General terminology and clarification updates

Chapter 2 **Getting a Real Estate License**: Terminology and license requirements updates

Chapter 3 **Keeping Your Real Estate License**: Complaint procedures and reasons for suspension/revocation of license; discussion of ethics now covered here

Chapter 6 **Brokers, Salespeople, and the Agency Relationship**: Agency law updates and addition of information on Limited Services Brokerage Bill (HB 491)

Chapter 7 **Real Estate Contracts, Agreements, and Documents**: Clarification regarding “consideration” and “Sherman Anti-trust Act”

Chapter 8 **Deeds and Ownership**: Clarification of “tenancy in common”

Chapter 9 **Real Estate Closings**: Clarification of RESPA

Chapter 11 **Fair Housing**: Terminology update: “handicap” replaced with “disability”

Chapter 13 **Mortgage Basics**: Clarification of ECOA

According to the Ohio Division of Real Estate, only 66% of Ohio's new licensees are in the real estate business after their first year. Survey results indicate that more than 91% of Hondros College's graduates are active in the industry after their first year. We directly attribute that success to the practical, comprehensive education provided through our program. Hondros Learning's course materials provide a full understanding of both the very basic and the very complex studies of real estate and their application to the real estate career.

Successful completion of this course is essential to your career as a real estate professional. To help you with that—and passing your licensing exam the first time—these additional real estate products are available from Hondros Learning/Hondros College:

EXAM PREPARATION

Ohio Real Estate CompuCram® Exam Prep Software

Real Estate Math Crammer™ Software and Workbook

Real Estate Vocab Crammer™ Audio CD and Dictionary Set

Real Estate Vocab Crammer™ Flashcards, 2nd edition

Real Estate Sales Review Crammer™ Course: National (book included)

Real Estate Sales Review Crammer™ Course: State Specific (Ohio; book included)

1 THE REAL ESTATE PROFESSION

CHAPTER OVERVIEW

Now that you've decided on a career in real estate, it's time to discuss getting started in your real estate career.

First, we'll talk about becoming a real estate professional, then real estate license categories.

Next, we'll explore personal considerations: the advantages and disadvantages of real estate sales, criteria to consider when choosing a broker, forms the broker-salesperson relationship can take, and different types of real estate offices. Finally, we'll look at professional considerations: areas of specialization in real estate sales, professional organizations, and professional designations you can attain.

KEY TERMS

Broker
Any person, partnership, association, limited liability partnership, limited liability company, or corporation who, for a fee, sells, lists, leases, exchanges, negotiates, or otherwise deals in the real estate of others or represents publicly that he or she does so.

Independent Contractors
Self-employed people paid based on jobs completed rather than hours worked, and responsible for setting their own hours and paying their own taxes.

Multiple Listing Service (MLS)
A service whereby local member-brokers agree to share listings and commissions on properties sold jointly.

Real Estate Licensee
A person licensed to practice real estate in Ohio. Ohio law requires that any person, partnership, or corporation who, for a fee, sells, lists, leases, exchanges, negotiates, or otherwise deals in the real estate of others, or represents publicly that he or she so deals, must be licensed.

Realtist
Any real estate licensee who is a member of the National Association of Real Estate Brokers.

REALTOR®
Any real estate licensee who is a member of the National Association of REALTORS® (NAR) and his or her affiliated state and local boards. Only members may use the term REALTOR® as it's a registered trademark of the NAR.

Salesperson
Any licensed agent who is associated with a broker and as such may perform most of the acts a broker can on behalf of the broker.

I. BECOMING A REAL ESTATE PROFESSIONAL

Ohio law defines a real estate broker as any person, partnership, association, limited liability partnership, limited liability company, or corporation who, for a fee, sells, lists, leases, exchanges, negotiates, auctions, **or otherwise deals in the real estate of others, or represents publicly that the person so deals, and who must be licensed.** Our focus is on obtaining a real estate salesperson's license. This license, along with broker affiliation, is necessary to sell real estate as well as act as an agent for someone who wants to buy or sell real estate. This license also covers people who wish to become commercial agents, property managers, or rental agents who negotiate leases with residential or commercial tenants.

There are *six exceptions to Ohio's real estate license requirements*. They are:

1. Persons dealing with **their own property**, including partnerships and corporations through **regular salaried employees**.
2. **Fiduciaries** who are duly appointed and acting in a fiduciary capacity, such as the executor of a will or the guardian of a minor.
3. **Public officials** acting in an official capacity, such as a sheriff.
4. **Attorneys-at-law** performing the duties of an attorney on behalf of a client, such as a probate attorney.
5. Persons selling **manufactured homes** or **mobile homes**, provided the sale does **not** include the real estate on which the home sits.
6. An out-of-state commercial broker may deal in commercial real estate in Ohio without an Ohio real estate license providing certain conditions are met. One is, he or she works with a broker who holds a valid active Ohio broker's license.

When most people think of the real estate profession, they think of brokers or salespersons. While the people in these careers have the highest visibility, there are many other aspects of real estate that one can choose to specialize in. Let's look at a few.

II. CAREERS IN REAL ESTATE

Although our primary focus is on real estate sales, there are a tremendous number of opportunities for real estate licensees to move into other related fields. In addition to the brokerage and sales side of the real estate business, careers are also available in finance, appraisal, property management, development, construction, title work, trade associations, education, and government work. While all of these do not require licensing, the most lucrative ones do. And a real estate license or an associate degree in real estate is an asset for all, as each is becoming increasingly competitive.

CAREERS IN REAL ESTATE FINANCE

Real estate finance provides excellent employment opportunities, particularly for those who are good with numbers and with people. Ohio ranks near the top of states with financial institutions including savings and loan associations, mutual savings banks, and commercial banks. These institutions have a constant need for highly trained people to fill real estate-related positions.

In addition to taking and approving mortgage loan applications, financial institutions need people who can help manage loan portfolios, appraise properties, and assess risk. There are also opportunities in banks for people with title experience and for people familiar with the national secondary mortgage markets.

Mortgage companies are also looking for people who have many of these same skills. Mortgage brokers, real estate trusts, endowments, private lenders, and government agencies devoted to real estate finance (such as FHA and VA) offer additional opportunities for interesting careers that involve real estate and finance. As with all real estate-related positions, a real estate license or real estate associate degree is an asset that shows potential employers you understand real estate licensing laws and how they affect real estate business.

CAREERS IN REAL ESTATE APPRAISAL

Real estate appraisal offers many career opportunities. Appraisers can work for financial institutions, developers, property managers, or government agencies. Eventually, as you gain experience, you can work for yourself by bidding on independent appraisals for these employers or private investors.

In addition to a good understanding of real estate, an appraiser must have a good understanding of the appraisal *methods*. Eventually, experience will be the appraiser's best asset. By working for an employer first, you can gain this experience working with other experienced appraisers. After amassing sufficient capital, competence, experience, and contacts, you should be ready to go out on your own as a fee appraiser. Now you'll know how to price properties and your services. *Note*: it's unethical to base your fee entirely on the amount of value you estimate for a certain building.

For an appraiser, a real estate license or a real estate associate degree is an asset. To become a licensed real estate appraiser in Ohio, a person must meet specific requirements such as age, reputation, experience, and education. These requirements periodically change, as do the requirements for most professions. You should inquire about the pre-licensing requirements when you decide you want to become a licensed appraiser.

Currently, certification for appraisers in Ohio is voluntary but required if you want to represent yourself as a state-certified or licensed appraiser. State-certified appraisers and all federally related appraisals must comply with the Uniform Standards of Professional Appraisal Practice (USPAP).

PROFESSIONAL ORGANIZATIONS AND DESIGNATIONS. There are a number of professional organizations that appraisers can join including The Appraisal Institute, the American Society of Appraisers, and the National Association of Independent Fee Appraisers. Professional designations that you can work toward include **Member of Appraisal Institute (MAI)** offered by The Appraisal Institute, **ASA Senior Member** offered by the American Society of Appraisers, **IFA** and **IFAS Senior Member** offered by the National Association of Independent Fee Appraisers,

Residential Accredited Appraiser (RAA®) given by the National Association of REALTORS,® (NAR) Appraisal Section to those with 1,000 hours of appraisal field work experience and 45 hours of course work above state mandates, and **General Accredited Appraiser (GAA®)** given by the NAR's Appraisal Section to those with 1,000 hours of field work experience and 60 hours of course work above state mandates.

CAREERS IN REAL ESTATE PROPERTY MANAGEMENT

Property management is a challenging real estate career. The property management company is in an agency relationship with the property owner and owes the property owner the same *fiduciary duties* of *obedience*, *loyalty*, *disclosure*, *confidentiality*, *accountability*, and *reasonable care* (OLDCAR) that are owed to all clients. Here, though, a property manager or property management company is a general agent because of the broad range of duties that must be performed under property management. A real estate salesperson is classified as a special agent because duties are restricted to one area of performance.

The property management relationship is typically governed by a management agreement. This agreement will detail the duties and responsibilities of each party as well as the compensation. Typically, the property manager is responsible for collecting rents, selecting tenants, renting and leasing units, maintaining and repairing the building, supervising all building personnel, tenant relations, and accounting for all income and expenditures.

Accounting for all income and expenditures is more involved than it sounds. The property manager is responsible for setting rents that cover all expenses associated with operating the building and still return a profit. The property manager must also develop and maintain a plan for the maintenance and rehabilitation of the building so it produces the greatest amount of rental income for as long a period of time as possible. Furthermore, the property manager must be skilled at risk management to protect the building from loss and insulate the owner from liability with appropriate insurance policy recommendations to the owner.

If the property being managed is residential and built before 1978, the property manager must abide by the Lead-Based Paint Hazard Reduction Act and provide the tenants with a lead paint hazard disclosure letter.

If the property manager has 20 or more employees, he or she must abide by the Americans with Disabilities Act (ADA) when hiring employees and screening tenants.

All brokerages who engage in property management activities may have an interest-bearing property management account for each property management job and shall provide an accounting to each owner of property managed on a regular basis but not less than on a quarterly basis.

PROFESSIONAL ORGANIZATIONS AND DESIGNATIONS. For those wanting to specialize in a property management career, a real estate license is a must, and a real estate associate degree is an added asset. Some professional designations that you can work toward include **Accredited Residential Manager**, **Certified**

Property Manager, and **Real Property Administrator**. **Accredited Residential Manager (ARM)** is given by National Association of REALTORS'® Institute of Real Estate Management (IREM) to those specializing in managing residential properties who complete an IREM management course, meet experience standards, manage a sizeable portfolio, and are endorsed by the local IREM chapter. **Certified Property Manager (CPM)** is also awarded by IREM to those who meet certain requirements. **Real Property Administrator (RPA)** is awarded to those completing training courses offered by the Building Owners and Managers Institute International, an independent institute affiliated with Building Owners and Managers Association.

CAREERS IN REAL ESTATE DEVELOPMENT

Real estate development offers a range of career opportunities. Land development is the process of acquiring large tracts of land at a low cost per acre, then subdividing and improving it with streets, sewers, and utilities so it can be resold at a higher cost per front foot (for lots) or per square foot (for buildings).

Land can be developed for residential, commercial, industrial, or other uses. Once the appropriate amenities are in place and necessary zoning obtained, lots can be sold as bare land ready for a structure to be built on it or with houses or buildings already in place. Most residential developments have houses built on them or vacant lots on which a buyer can choose to have a particular style of home built by the developer.

Typically, residential developers take the following steps:

- Make a feasibility study of the prospective development
- Execute an option or purchase agreement for a large tract of land
- Obtain any necessary zoning changes
- Obtain early financing from financial institutions or through syndication
- Install improvements, such as streets, sewer, water, electricity, gas lines, etc.
- Make arrangements for parks, playgrounds, golf course, swimming pool, etc.
- Take care of legal arrangements, such as deeds and title evidence for each lot
- Market and sell the individual lots
- Construct buildings

Any of these areas could become a career opportunity with a development company, and a real estate license or real estate associate degree can help.

CAREERS IN REAL ESTATE CONSTRUCTION

Real estate careers in construction are often entered through the real estate brokerage side of the business by selling homes or other buildings. Homes are built either on contract for clients who specify the type of structure and features they want, or on speculation ("spec") and a buyer is found for a home after it's completed. Builders can work as developers or with specific development companies.

In addition to sales help, companies that specialize in construction also have a need for appraisers, property managers, and finance people. People with a finance and real estate background can be especially beneficial to builders because large-scale financing is usually involved, and costs and profits are constantly monitored. Career opportunities with builders can be boosted with a real estate license or real estate associate degree.

CAREERS IN REAL ESTATE TITLE WORK

Real estate title work is a growing field. More and more brokers, banks, and lawyers are getting into this service area as profit margins are shrinking elsewhere. New regulations are making it easier for companies to provide homebuyers with more than one service as long as there's proper disclosure. Title work is a natural extension of many other real estate service businesses.

Within the area of title work, there are many functions that can offer a career. These include title research, escrow agent, and title insurance overseer. In fact, a person working for a title company may be asked to do more than one of these tasks. A real estate license or real estate associate degree can be a plus as you demonstrate knowledge of real estate transaction procedures and real estate law.

CAREERS IN REAL ESTATE TRADE ASSOCIATION WORK

There are numerous national, state, and local trade associations in real estate or related fields that offer career opportunities related to the real estate field. Staff positions usually offer day-to-day support to the mostly volunteer officer positions. The duties of the staff include education, lobbying, public relations, and member services. Additional positions may include computer work or work on one of the many publications and journals published by these organizations.

Again, a real estate license or real estate associate degree can be advantageous in demonstrating your understanding of, and commitment to, the real estate field. Also, association work can serve as a steppingstone to more knowledge and contacts as you begin your real estate career.

CAREERS IN REAL ESTATE EDUCATION

Ohio's license law educational requirements and continuing education provide ample opportunities for interested persons to get involved in real estate education. Qualified practitioners are in constant demand for teaching these courses.

As for teaching courses leading to an associate degree in real estate, part-time faculty members who teach college-level real estate courses in Ohio must generally have a bachelor's degree and/or the appropriate professional designation in that real estate discipline. Again, a real estate license or a real estate associate degree mark you as an individual who has studied real estate law and gained an understanding of how real estate practice operates in Ohio, providing you with an additional asset.

CAREERS IN REAL ESTATE-RELATED GOVERNMENT WORK

Real estate-related careers are available at all levels of government. At the federal level, agencies involved with real estate include FHA, VA, Fannie Mae, Ginnie Mae, Freddie Mac, EPA, and HUD to name a few. There are literally hundreds more with some connection to real estate—from the General Services Administration, which is a property management agency, to most branches of the military, like the Army Corps of Engineers.

On the state level, there are also numerous agencies involved with real estate in some way. From the Department of Commerce, which includes the Ohio Division of Real Estate, to the Ohio EPA, to the Ohio Department of Taxation, all of these and more benefit from people with a knowledge of Ohio real estate laws and procedures.

On the local level, departments of taxations and departments that oversee zoning regulations and enforcement are two of the more prominent agencies that are related to real estate.

Many of these careers can be rewarding careers in their own right or serve as good steppingstones to other real estate careers.

CAREERS IN REAL ESTATE OVERALL

Whether you choose to go into real estate sales or another real estate-related career, you'll find that the knowledge and insight you gain from studying for and obtaining a real estate license or real estate associate degree is worth the effort. You'll feel confident as you pursue your career goals, and demonstrate to your employer the ambition and foresight you have. In the end, you can feel good about choosing a career in real estate or another related field. Real estate is one of the few careers where pure ability is all that matters. Many brokers use performance as their only employment test and rate desire as their most important criterion. Your age, race, gender, and even a disability aren't important—if you are good with people and perform well, then you're a coveted individual in an industry where performance and personal service go hand in hand.

III. PERSONAL CONSIDERATIONS

There are a number of different factors to take into account when choosing the best path for a real estate career. After confirming your preference for a real estate sales career over a career in another aspect of real estate, you must then select a broker with whom you'll work.

There are many factors to consider when choosing a broker. There are different levels of training and staff support, as well as different compensation structures. You will see there are many forms the broker-salesperson relationship can take, as well as different types of real estate offices.

A REAL ESTATE SALES CAREER

The job of a licensed real estate sales professional begins by obtaining listing agreements from sellers and then searching for ready, willing, and able buyers for the listed properties. You can also choose to work with buyers and show them properties listed by other brokers. Your real estate education will explain real estate law, contracts, financing, and other important knowledge that you need to complete the process of selling a property.

Real estate sales professionals utilize various forms of advertising, information sharing, and people skills to find the right buyer. If successful, they present signed offers to the seller and are paid a commission when the transaction closes. There are some advantages and disadvantages to making your livelihood this way.

ADVANTAGES TO REAL ESTATE SALES

The advantages are:

1. Compensation is based on commissions, so earnings are only limited by your knowledge, experience, desire, activity, and hard work.
2. You control your time. Work as much or as little as you like to reach your goals.
3. Office time is kept to a minimum, as contact with people is the primary means of soliciting listings, showing properties, and making sales.
4. Owning your own brokerage is possible.

DISADVANTAGES TO REAL ESTATE SALES

The disadvantages are:

1. Since compensation is based on commissions, your income may not be steady, especially in the early stages.
2. Real estate sales are affected by seasonal and cyclical swings.
3. Most successful people in real estate need to work at least some evenings and weekends.

CHOOSING A BROKER

Choosing a broker is one of the most important decisions that you'll have to make after deciding on a real estate career. You will want to listen carefully and ask questions as you are talking with prospective brokers. The three main areas that you should consider are:

1. Level of training
2. Broker services (such as staff support)
3. Compensation structure

LEVEL OF TRAINING. The level of training offered by brokers varies greatly. We are talking about the help that you will be given as a new licensee. This help may be everything from assistance with filling in contracts, forms, and other documents, to how to close a sale.

Many large brokerages have standardized training programs that all new licensees must complete. These training sessions cover a broad range of topics including how to sell yourself and how to sell your company to prospective clients. This can be very helpful in attracting new listings. Some will assign you phone time, or even assign you a mentor to walk you through some of the processes and procedures.

Many smaller brokerages do not have formal training programs, but they still offer assistance. This type of arrangement usually gives you direct contact with your broker, allowing you to profit directly from your broker's experience. You need to know which level of training you are most comfortable with and which best suits your individual needs.

BROKER SERVICES. Broker services are those tools that are made available to you to help you do your job effectively and efficiently. These include stationery, staff support, and advertising of your listings. Many brokerages will supply these things; some will charge you a nominal fee; still others require you provide these things at your own cost.

Staff support can be important because you may not have your own resources for secretarial services. Furthermore, having someone answer your phone when you're out can project a level of professionalism that would require you to work harder to achieve on your own. Finally, advertising may be provided or costs reduced as your listings appear in large ads that your firm places showing many of their listings.

COMPENSATION STRUCTURE. Typical compensation splits range from 40%-60%, to 100%. The more common split is 50%-50%.

Some firms now offer commission-splitting arrangements as high as 80%-20%, 90%-10%, and even 100% to you. Of course, these arrangements often necessitate that you pay for your own costs—sometimes even those costs associated with the closing. And the 100% arrangement often means that you need to pay your broker a monthly fee for using the brokerage name, services, and facilities—even if you do not make a sale in a particular month. As you can see, there are pros and cons to both, and there are some places that offer choices in the middle. You need to do a lot of research and ask a lot of questions to find the situation that's right for you. Remember, a larger commission split may sound good, but paying for everything yourself can add up. Plus, the larger commission split doesn't matter if you can't make sales because you don't have the necessary tools or the proper training.

On the other hand, if you have access to services, a sales background, or experience in some area of real estate, this may influence your choice of a broker. Some salespeople like the image, prestige, and contacts they get by being associated with a large firm. Others like the opportunity to work with customers in servicing the niche market a smaller brokerage specializes in. Only you can decide what's right for you.

THE BROKER-SALESPERSON RELATIONSHIP

A salesperson can work as a personal assistant to another sales agent. In this case, the sales agent could hire the personal assistant as an **employee** and pay either a salary or hourly wages.

Salespersons are usually considered by their brokers to be **independent contractors**. Independent contractors are self-employed people hired to perform a specific assignment or complete a specific project but who are free to do that work as they wish.

Salespersons use the broker's office to conduct business activities but are often permitted to set their own hours. According to IRS rules, though, the ultimate test of whether salespeople are independent contractors has to do with how they're paid:

1. On success only
2. Paid directly by the broker

If a salesperson's compensation is based on commission for sales produced rather than a salary or hourly wage, then the salesperson is considered an independent contractor—as long as an independent contractor's contract is signed that details this independent contractor arrangement. Brokers prefer it because they don't need to withhold social security or income taxes—so ***it's important for salespersons to set aside a portion of commission checks to pay their tax obligations!***

Other important points of the broker-salesperson relationship are defined by the type and size of brokerage in which you choose to work. Such points may include, but not be limited to, designated phone time, customer referral policy, and chain of command.

IV. PROFESSIONAL CONSIDERATIONS

Again, there are a number of real estate career choices that can be made. Even if you have made the decision to begin your career as a real estate salesperson, your decisions do not end there. There are many specializations within real estate sales, as well as professional organizations you can belong to and professional designations you can achieve.

SPECIALIZATIONS WITHIN REAL ESTATE SALES

There are a number of different types of real estate that one can specialize in. These include single-family residential properties, multi-family residential properties, condominiums and cooperatives, commercial properties, industrial properties, and farm properties. For the most part, although there are a few laws that are specific to one type of property or another, the law is applied uniformly to all types of real estate. The main obstacles in moving from one specialization to another are the special terminology for a particular kind of real estate and finding a broker who is willing to act as a mentor in helping you learn the technical knowledge needed to be competent and succeed in a highly specialized area.

RESIDENTIAL PROPERTIES. Residential properties include single-family homes, multi-family residences, and condominiums and cooperatives.

SINGLE-FAMILY RESIDENTIAL PROPERTIES. The majority of new licensees begin their work in the single-family residential market. Buying and selling single-family homes is the typical entry-level position in real estate. Most brokers are recruiting for salespersons to work in this area since there are more single-family homes than any other type of property.

From the perspective of new licensees, beginning in single-family homes is a logical choice since they probably know at least a few people who may be in the market for a house. Furthermore, many people may have some familiarity with this area of real estate through personal experience. Finally, there's less technical knowledge required to become competent in this area.

MULTI-FAMILY RESIDENTIAL PROPERTIES. Multi-family residential properties can be anything from a simple twin-single (or double or duplex) to a large apartment building. The typical buyer in this category is an investor rather than a homebuyer. Much more technical knowledge about return on investment, occupancy rates, maintenance, and other topics relevant to investment properties is required and expected from this group of buyers.

CONDOMINIUMS AND COOPERATIVES. These types of properties share some aspects with single-family properties and some aspects with multi-family residences. There are special rules for how each type of property operates, and you should be familiar with these before working with them.

COMMERCIAL PROPERTIES. Commercial properties include offices, stores, hotels, and other buildings. Those dealing in commercial properties are usually involved not only in sales and other aspects of brokerage, but also in leasing and leasebacks, property management, appraisal, and even construction or financing.

PROPERTY MANAGEMENT. This area involves the operation of property as a business. Both residential and commercial properties can incur property management responsibilities such as renting, rent collection, and maintenance.

INDUSTRIAL PROPERTIES. Land and structures involved in the production, distribution, and storage of tangible economic goods are usually classified as industrial real estate. People involved with industrial brokerage must be familiar with many of the same areas needed for commercial properties. Typically a person will specialize in commercial *and* industrial properties because there's less demand for only industrial services, and a high level of experience and expertise is required.

FARM PROPERTIES. Specialization in this area has been declining due to the widespread sale of farmland for other uses and the smaller number of family-run farms.

PROFESSIONAL ORGANIZATIONS

The main organization that real estate licensees join is the **National Association of REALTORS® (NAR)**. Licensees may also join the state and local affiliated real estate boards. Any person who has a real estate license is called a real estate licensee and must abide by the Canons of Ethics. A licensee doesn't automatically become a REALTOR®. Only those who join the National Association of REALTORS® may use the term REALTOR® because it's a registered trademark of the NAR. Members agree to voluntarily follow a Code of Ethics. Membership is not mandatory unless your sponsoring broker is also a member. Most join to receive the benefits of membership.

The primary benefits are participation in the **Multiple Listing Service (MLS)** and the right to use the trademarked term, **REALTOR®**. Other benefits include a political and legislative voice at all levels of government for the interests of the real estate industry, education, and training that can earn you certain professional designations, real estate business publications, and standardized real estate forms.

The **MLS** is a service whereby local member brokers agree to share listings, and further agree to share commissions on properties sold jointly. The MLS generally consists of online computer services. A book published regularly, and updated to include new listings may also be available in some areas but is rarely used in today's computer world.

Another professional organization that real estate brokers can join is the National Association of Real Estate Brokers. Members of this organization use the term **Realtist**. This group is comprised mostly of minority brokers since it was initially formed as a response to minorities being excluded from membership in the NAR. Members agree voluntarily to follow an additional, separate Code of Ethics.

The Women's Council of REALTORS® (WCR) is another organization that licensees can join. The organization is devoted to addressing the issues, needs, and concerns of salespeople in the real estate profession. The WCR was originally formed as a response to discrimination that kept women from full participation in the NAR, but now the WCR is affiliated with the NAR.

Other professional organizations that real estate salespeople can choose to join include The Appraisal Institute, American Society of Appraisers, National Association of Independent Fee Appraisers, and Building Owners and Managers Association.

PROFESSIONAL DESIGNATIONS

There are many designations you can work to achieve as a means of keeping yourself and your education current. They mark you as a highly qualified specialist to other agents and the public.

NAR DESIGNATIONS. Those offered by the NAR include **ABR**, **ABRM**, **CCIM**, **CPM**, **CRB**, **CRE**, **CRS**, **GAA**, **GRI**, **LTG**, **RAA**, and **SIOR**. Most are available to residential or commercial real estate agents, except ABR and CRS (residential only), and CCIM and SIOR (commercial only). All require membership in the NAR.

ABR. **Accredited Buyer Representative** can be earned by a member of the NAR who completes an extensive classroom training program on buyer agency practices and procedures (offered by Hondros College), passes a written exam, and submits evidence of practical experience as a buyer representative.

ABRM. **Accredited Buyer Representative Manager** is geared to real estate firm brokers, owners, and managers who have or wish to incorporate buyer representation into their daily practice; designees have taken and passed both the ABR® and ABRM℠ course and provided documentation of past management experience.

ALC. **Accredited Land Consultants** are the recognized experts in land brokerage transactions of five specialized types: 1. Farms and ranches; 2. Undeveloped tracts of land; 3. Transitional and development land; 4. Subdivision and wholesaling of lots; and 5. Site selection and assemblage of land parcels. You'll acquire valuable skills through educational offerings leading to the ALC designation.

ARM. **Accredited Residential Manager** is given by the NAR's Institute of Real Estate Management (IREM) to those specializing in managing residential properties. You must complete an IREM management course, meet experience standards, manage a sizeable portfolio, and be endorsed by the local IREM chapter.

AHWD. **At Home with Diversity Certification** relays to the public that those certified have been professionally trained in and are sensitive to a wide range of cultural issues, inviting a wider volume of business from a greater variety of cultures.

CCIM. **Certified Commercial Investment Member** is awarded by the NAR.

CIPS. **Certified International Property Specialist** network is comprised of 1,500 real estate professionals from 50 countries who deal in all types of real estate but with one common element: they are focused specifically on the "international" market. Whether traveling abroad to put deals together, assisting foreign investors, helping local buyers invest abroad, or serving an immigrant niche in local markets, CIPS designees are consumers' best resource to ensure they are dealing with a professional skilled in the unique aspects of international real estate.

CPM. **Certified Property Manager** is awarded by the NAR's Institute of Real Estate Management (IREM) to real estate property managers.

CRB. **Certified Real Estate Brokerage Manager** is given by the Real Estate Brokerage Manager's Council to those who complete required coursework. Coursework varies by experience.

CRE. **Counselor of Real Estate** is given by the NAR's American Society of Real Estate Counselors for asset managers and others. Membership is by invitation only.

CRS. **Certified Residential Specialist** is given by the Residential Sales Council of the NAR to those who complete CRS courses and a certain number of transactions.

e-PRO®. **e-PRO®** is a revolutionary training program presented entirely online to certify real estate agents and brokers as Internet Professionals. The National Association of REALTORS® is the first major trade group to offer certification for online professionalism.

GAA. **General Accredited Appraiser** is given by the NAR's Appraisal Section to those with 1,000 hours experience and 60 hours of coursework above state mandates.

GRI. **Graduate, Realtor Institute** is given by state boards. In Ohio, 90 hours of coursework is required. This is often the first designation a REALTOR® achieves.

PMN. **Performance Management Network** is a new REALTOR® designation that's built from the ground up to bring you the real-world skills, the know-how, and the tools that will keep your business out front and on top of a lightening-fast market.

This designation is unique to the REALTOR® family designations, focusing on the idea that to enhance your business, you must enhance yourself. The curriculum is driven by the following topics: negotiating strategies and tactics, networking and referrals, business planning and systems, personal performance management, and cultural differences in buying and selling.

RAA. **Residential Accredited Appraiser** is given by the NAR's Appraisal Section to those with 1,000 hours of experience and 45 hours of coursework above state mandates.

RCE. **REALTOR® Association Certified Executive** is for association executives interested in demonstrating commitment to the field of REALTOR® association management. AEs are recognized for their specialized industry knowledge and their association achievements and experience.

REPA℠. **Real Estate Professional Assistant℠** is a comprehensive two-day certificate course that provides an intensive introduction to the real estate business and to the specific ways support staff can become valuable assets to their employers. Every administrative employee in the brokerage office, from listing secretary to the personal assistant, will benefit tremendously from this quick-start program

RSPS. **Resort and Second-Home Markets Certification** is a new certification offered by the NAR Resort for resort and second-home REALTORS® around the world. REALTORS® specializing in resort and second-home markets and interested in demonstrating their knowledge and expertise should pursue the RSPS certification. The RSPS core certification requirements include the NAR Resort and Second-Home Market Course and the RLI Tax-Deferred (1031) Exchange Course. RSPS applicants will also choose from nine different electives including courses from the NAR Education Matrix and the NAR Resort Symposium held every 18 months.

SIOR. **Society of Industrial and Office Realtors®** is a designation available to members of this NAR-affiliated organization, and is concerned primarily with the sale of factories, warehouses, and other industrial properties.

TRANSNATIONAL REFERRAL CERTIFICATION. The goal of this certification is to prepare real estate professionals to make and receive compensated referrals using the Transnational Referral system developed by the International Consortium of Real Estate Associations—ICREA. Students will learn how to integrate international referrals, resulting in increased income, into their business plans.

When you are involved in an international referral, as a referring or receiving agent, the Transnational Referral Certification demonstrates to other real estate professionals that you are well versed in the procedures of the Transnational Referral system, have pledged to follow a code of conduct in business dealings, and expect that compensation, paid in a timely manner, will be an integral part of the transaction.

Other Designations

Other designations offered in the real estate, appraisal, or property management fields are **ASA**, **CSD**, **DREI**, **IFA**, **MAI**, **NHSD**, **PMSD**, **RECS**, **RPA**, **RSD**, and **SRES**. (Some are available through Hondros College.)

ASA. **ASA Senior Member**, **ASR Senior Residential Member,** and **FASA Fellow** are offered by the American Society of Appraisers (ASA) to members who meet its criteria.

CSD. **Commercial Specialist Designation** is given to agents who successfully complete the coursework designed to give residential agents a look at the commercial side of real estate with special emphasis on learning unique aspects of commercial real estate so you will know what it takes to succeed.

DREI. **Distinguished Real Estate Instructor** is awarded by the Real Estate Educators Association (REEA). The DREI designation recognizes excellence among real estate instructors. It's awarded only to those who demonstrate outstanding knowledge of their profession, experience, and classroom performance. Successful applicants must also pass a Comprehensive Real Estate Exam and a Teaching Skills Evaluation (via submission of a video tape of an actual classroom session). Several Hondros College instructors have achieved this prestigious designation.

IFA. **IFAS Senior Member** and **IFAC Appraiser-Counselor** are designations offered by the National Association of Independent Fee Appraisers (NAIFA) to members who meet its criteria.

MAI. **Member Appraisal Institute** is the highest designation offered by The Appraisal Institute to members who meet its criteria.

NHSD. **New Home Specialist Designation** is given to agents who successfully complete the coursework designed for those who want to make their mark in the lucrative, but increasingly competitive, field of new builds.

PMSD. **Property Management Specialist Designation** is given to agents who successfully complete coursework designed to enhance property management skills and knowledge of acquisitions, financing, leasing, ethics, and legal issues.

RECS. **Real Estate Cyberspace Specialist Designation** can be earned by becoming a member of the Real Estate Cyberspace Society, taking a Selling in Cyberspace course, and completing an individual practicum. The designation distinguishes the person as a professional who is proficient in computer and Internet disciplines as well as one who stays current with industry advances and services.

RPA. **Real Property Administrator** is awarded to property managers for completing courses of the Building Owners and Managers Institute International, an independent institute affiliated with Building Owners and Managers Association.

RSD. **Residential Specialist Designation** is given to agents who successfully complete coursework designed to help new agents avoid many common mistakes.

SRES. **Senior Real Estate Specialist** is a designation of the Senior Advantage Real Estate Council (SAREC), aimed at those interested in the "over 55" client niche and those looking to enhance their status from "salesperson" to that of "counselor."

CHAPTER 1 SUMMARY

1. Ohio law requires that anyone who, for a fee, sells, lists, leases, exchanges, negotiates, or otherwise deals in the real estate of others, or represents that he or she so deals, must be licensed. *Exceptions to license law*: people and companies (or their employees) selling their own property, fiduciaries, public officials, attorneys at law, and persons selling manufactured/mobile homes without land.

2. Licensed real estate sales professionals obtain listing contracts from sellers, then search for ready, willing, and able buyers for properties they've listed. You can also choose to work with buyers and show them properties listed by other brokers. *Advantages* to real estate sales are unlimited compensation potential from commissions, controlling your own time, minimum office time, and potential to own your own brokerage with additional training, education, and experience. *Disadvantages* are possible non-steady income, seasonal/cyclical real estate swings, and need to work evenings and weekends.

3. Three main areas to consider when choosing a broker are *level of training*, *broker services*, and *compensation structure*. Training can include assistance with filling in contracts, forms, etc., phone time, and advice on how to close a sale. Services may include staff support, advertising, and staff to answer the phone. Commission splits vary, but can increase if you pay for your own supplies, services, monthly office fee, etc.

4. Most salespersons are hired as *independent contractors*. As such, they are self-employed people paid based on jobs completed rather than hours worked and are responsible for setting their own hours and paying their own taxes. An employment contract must be signed detailing this arrangement. Salespersons must set aside part of their commission checks to pay tax obligations because brokers don't withhold taxes from independent contractors.

5. Areas of specialization within real estate sales include residential properties (single-family residences, multi-family residences, condominiums, cooperatives), commercial properties (including property management), industrial properties, and farm properties.

6. Real estate licensees must join the National Association of REALTORS® (NAR) and affiliated state and local boards if their broker is a member. Benefits to joining include access to Multiple Listing Service (MLS) and use of the term REALTOR®. Only members may use the term REALTOR® because it's a registered trademark of the NAR. "Realtist" is the term used by members of the National Association of Real Estate Brokers. Professional designations can be earned by licensees who meet the requirements of different organizations.

7. People who enjoy working in real estate but desire a more steady income should consider one of the many alternative real estate careers, which can be less susceptible to real estate cycles.

8. Real estate is one of the few careers where ability is all that matters. Your age, gender, race, or disability aren't important—if you can perform well, and you're good with people, then you're a coveted individual in real estate.

CHAPTER 1 QUIZ

1. ***When may a person use the term REALTOR®?***
   a. Right away after passing the real estate license examination
   b. After closing a successful transaction
   c. After becoming a member of the National Association of REALTORS® NAR
   d. If his or her broker says it's okay

2. ***Advantages to real estate sales include all of the following,* except:**
   a. Setting your own hours
   b. Potential for unlimited earnings
   c. Possibility of owning your own brokerage with additional training, education, and experience
   d. Can double commission percentages during slow months

3. ***Most salespersons are hired as:***
   a. Employees
   b. Independent contractors
   c. Underlings or gophers
   d. Entry-level telephone solicitors

4. ***Areas of specialization within real estate sales include which of the following?***
   a. Commercial and industrial
   b. Cemetery sales
   c. The NAR listings only
   d. Line and staff organization

5. ***The professional organization new licensees must join if their sponsoring broker is a member is the:***
   a. National Association of Real Estate Brokers
   b. National Association of REALTORS®
   c. National Association of Licensees
   d. Franchise

6. ***A property manager is usually considered a:***
   a. General agent
   b. Universal agent
   c. Special agent
   d. Limited agent

7. ***A real estate property manager:***
   a. Must be licensed
   b. Must be certified
   c. Can be voluntarily certified
   d. Must join the Building Owners and Managers Association

8. ***Which of the following does not have to be licensed under Ohio law?***
   a. Real estate salespersons and brokers
   b. Foreign real estate salespersons and brokers
   c. Real estate auctioneers
   d. The sheriff handling a foreclosure sale

9. ***Which of the following people must be licensed to sell real estate under Ohio's real estate license law?***
   a. Personnel director who is paid a referral fee for a real estate transaction
   b. Executor of a will selling land for an estate
   c. Sheriff performing a sheriff's sale of real estate in foreclosure
   d. Lawyer performing the duties of a lawyer selling land on behalf of a deceased client

2 GETTING A REAL ESTATE LICENSE

Possible questions

CHAPTER OVERVIEW

Now that you have an idea of the path you'd like your real estate career to follow, you need to know the procedure for becoming licensed. We'll overview relevant topics and requirements for a real estate license: non-educational requirements, pre-licensing education, broker affiliation, submitting the test application, and the state licensing exam. License laws protect the public from fraud, misrepresentation, and deceit. We'll examine the Ohio Real Estate Commission and Division of Real Estate, who oversee licensees and implement license laws.

KEY TERMS

Ohio Real Estate Commission
Consists of five members appointed by the governor. They serve a five-year term; four are practicing brokers; one is a public member, and no more than three can concurrently belong to the same political party.

Ohio Division of Real Estate
Run by the superintendent who is appointed by the Director of Commerce.

Auctioneer
A person with an auctioneer's license as well as a real estate license and can sell real estate through an auction.

Foreign Real Estate Broker
Deals with real estate outside of Ohio and must be licensed if he or she engages exclusively in sales activity in Ohio.

Education and Research Fund
A fund designed to offer scholarships and loans to students who are taking real estate-specific classes and conduct real estate-related research for the benefit of licensees and consumers.

Reciprocity
The ability of a state department to give a real estate license to an applicant who received a real estate license in another state. Under certain arrangements, license testing, course study, or other requirements may be waived or modified.

I. LICENSE CATEGORIES

The two license categories are *broker* and *salesperson*. A **broker** is one who is licensed to represent a party in a real estate transaction for compensation. A broker's license can be held by an individual or a business (a corporation). The broker charges the fee, usually a commission, and the salesperson is paid from the broker's fee.

A real estate **salesperson** is a licensee associated with a broker and may perform most of the acts of a broker. A salesperson's license must be held by an individual.

Real estate salespeople must be associated with a broker. A potential salesperson must be sponsored by a broker before he or she can be seated for the salesperson license examination. A person must have worked an average of 30 hours per week for at least two out of the last five years, participated in at least 20 transactions (a listing or sale counts as 1/2, a rental as 1/4), and take additional education before being eligible to take the broker license examination.

Property managers or rental agents who negotiate tenants' leases, auctioneers who auction real estate, **foreign real estate brokers,** and **foreign real estate salespersons** (dealing with real estate outside of Ohio) must be licensed.

Other common terms heard in the real estate profession are *sales associate* and *REALTOR®*. **Sales associate** is not an actual license category but rather a title referring to any salesperson associated with a broker. The title is self-appointed and usually refers to a licensed salesperson but may also be used by one who's not actively using his or her broker's license and has it "on deposit," which we will talk about in the next chapter. The term **REALTOR®** refers to a real estate licensee who's a member of the National Association of REALTORS® (NAR), and their affiliated state and local boards. Only members may use the term REALTOR® as it's a registered trademark of the NAR.

II. REQUIREMENTS NECESSARY TO TAKE THE LICENSE EXAM

There are five basic requirements that must be met before a person can take the real estate sales examination. These are *non-educational requirements*, *pre-test education*, *broker affiliation*, *submitting the exam application*, and *scheduling the exam*.

NON-EDUCATIONAL REQUIREMENTS. Anyone wanting to become a real estate salesperson in Ohio must:

1. Be at least 18 years of age.
2. Be honest, truthful, and of good reputation.
3. Have any criminal record reviewed by the Ohio Division of Real Estate. As a part of this review, the superintendent has the authority to require a criminal background check.
4. Have no civil rights violations within the past two years.
5. Have no unsatisfied judgments from a court of law.
6. Have a high school diploma or its equivalent if born after 1950.

PRE-LICENSING EDUCATIONAL REQUIREMENTS. Before a person can apply to take the licensing exam, pre-licensing courses must be completed at an **institute of higher education offering at least a two-year degree program**. These courses must consist of 120 hours of classroom instruction covering the following real estate topics:

1. Principles and practices
2. Real estate law, civil rights and fair housing (waived for Ohio lawyers)
3. Finance
4. Appraisal

BROKER AFFILIATION. A prospective licensee must be affiliated with a broker *prior* to being seated for the examination. There is a space on the application for a sponsoring broker's signature.

SUBMITTING THE TEST APPLICATION. After the pre-licensing coursework is completed and a broker selected, the application for the licensing examination must be submitted to the Ohio Division of Real Estate with all essential parts:

1. Completed application
2. Application fee (check or money order to Ohio Division of Real Estate)
3. Copies of transcripts/certificates for all four completed pre-licensing courses

Incomplete application packages will be returned by the Division and delay scheduling for the examination. Rejected applications can be appealed to the Ohio Real Estate Commission.

SCHEDULING THE EXAM. Once the Division has reviewed the application and determined eligibility to test, the Division will notify the testing service, and it will send eligible candidates an examination eligibility letter and a *Candidate Information Bulletin,* which can also be found on the Division's web site. The candidate must then schedule his or her own exam by calling the Candidate Services Call Center (CSCC) using the toll-free number provided. Candidates may select the most convenient location, date, and time.

Bring a copy of the sales application to the next class.
Note: Always use the most updated forms which can be found on the Ohio Division of Real Estate's Web site, www.com.state.oh.us/real

TO DO FOR CLASS!

III. THE LICENSE EXAM

Real estate licensing exams for Ohio are administered at designated testing centers (for more information, call the toll-free number or visit the Web site listed in your eligibility letter). An additional fee must be paid to the testing center when scheduling. Exams are given on a computer similar to those in homes and offices. The system is simple to use and you are given extra time before the test to practice. All supplies needed for the test are provided at the test site. You may bring a simple calculator with standard functions (+,-, x, ÷) but you may **not** bring one with alphanumeric keys.

When arriving at the test site, you must present a photo I.D., such as a driver's license or state-approved I.D. You are allotted sufficient time for the three-hour test. You may leave when finished.

Test results are provided immediately. If you pass the test, the testing service transmits your score to the Division, and your license is issued within about three business days by the Division of Real Estate and sent to your broker. Although the broker's license must be displayed in a public area of the broker's main office, salespersons' licenses are kept on file by the broker at his or her main office and are available for inspection until license termination or disassociation with the broker.

Licensees may begin practicing real estate when their license has been issued. The best way to know if your license has been issued is to check the Division's Web site or check with your broker to see if it has been received. The Division strictly enforces its rules against unlicensed real estate practice.

TEST FORMAT

The sales exam is multiple choice, with two parts: a "*uniform*" part focusing on national real estate law, principles and practices, finance, and appraisal, and a "*jurisdictional*" part covering specific Ohio law and practices. The uniform part consists of 85 questions and has a two-hour time limit. The jurisdictional part consists of 45 questions, with a one-hour time limit. On the computer, you may "mark" a question you are unsure of, so you can return to it later, if time permits. If there is enough time, you may return to that question and review all answers.

On completion of the test, candidates receive a score report for each section. A scaled *score of 75 on each part is required to pass*, and *both parts must be passed to satisfy the licensure requirement*. If you do not pass, you are given a re-take application to submit, along with the fee. You may re-take the failed part as often as you like within the one-year eligibility period

TEST TOPICS

Topics covered on the licensing exam include:

1. Real estate and general law
2. Civil rights
3. Fair housing
4. Ethics
5. Finance
6. Appraisal
7. Principles and practice

Math questions involve basic functions (+, -, x, ÷) as well as fractions, percentages, and specialized math (prorations). Test categories include:

Uniform Portion

Business Practices and Ethics 20%

Agency 15%

Property Characteristics, Descriptions, Ownership, Restrictions. 15%

Property Valuation and Appraisal Process 8%

Real Estate Sales Contracts 15%

Financing Sources. 12%

Closing/Settlement and Transferring Title 10%

Property Management. 5%

Jurisdictional Portion

Duties and Powers of the Real Estate Commission 15%

Licensing Requirements 15%

License Law and Rules of the Ohio Real Estate Commission. 40%

Brokerage Representation (Agency Law) 30%

Math questions are mixed into the test. **The pre-licensing and review/crammer courses** are excellent reviews for the test. **Hondros Learning's *Real Estate Math Crammer*™ exam prep software and practice workbook are available for any additional study and practice you may need.**

OTHER LICENSE QUALIFICATIONS. Remember, a real estate sales license is only valid for conventional real estate transactions in Ohio. You must submit a separate application, meet separate requirements, and/or pass a separate test to auction real estate, sell shares in real estate investments, or sell foreign real estate located outside the state of Ohio as a foreign real estate salesperson or dealer.

Reciprocity of real estate licensing between states is not considered unless the licensing state has requirements similar to Ohio's. Students should refer to the Ohio Division of Real Estate's official Web site at www.com.state.oh.us/real for a current list of states with which Ohio has a reciprocity agreement. Under certain arrangements, license testing, course study, or other requirements may be waived or modified. **A licensee from one of these states might only be required to take the jurisdictional part of the Ohio real estate license exam.** These instances should be researched through the Ohio Division of Real Estate and the state authority where the candidate was previously licensed.

IV. OVERSEERS OF REAL ESTATE LICENSEES

The task of regulating real estate activity in Ohio has been assigned to the **Department of Commerce**. Within the Department of Commerce are the **Ohio Real Estate Commission** and the **Division of Real Estate**. You should understand the structure of the Ohio Real Estate Commission and the Division of Real Estate.

It's important to know how these bodies operate in setting and enforcing laws, including complaint procedures and suspension or revocation of licenses. This is important for license protection and the real estate sales exam.

THE OHIO REAL ESTATE COMMISSION

The **Ohio Real Estate Commission** consists of **five members** appointed by the governor with the advice and consent of the Ohio Senate. **Four members** are licensed real estate brokers, with at least ten years' experience before the appointment. The fifth member is a non-licensee who represents the public's interest. They all serve staggered five-year terms, so one appointment is made annually. No more than three members of the Commission may be of any one political party.

The Commission:

1. **Suspends and revokes licenses**
2. **Denies license applications**
3. **Promotes Canons of Ethics for the real estate industry in Ohio**
4. **Reviews any order issued by the Superintendent of the Division of Real Estate**
5. **Sets standards for licensing**
6. **Sets guidelines of suspension and revocation of licenses**
7. **Sets rules of conduct for hearings**
8. **Sets licensing exam standards**
9. **Sets criteria for continuing in business**
10. **Reviews all educational requirements for brokers and salespersons**
11. **Updates continuing education requirements**
12. **Publishes a newsletter**
13. **Oversees the Real Estate Recovery Fund**
14. **Administers the Education and Research Fund**
    - **$12 of each tri-annual license renewal fee goes into this account to provide need-based loans of up to $800 for education costs**
    - **Loans must be broker co-signed and are non-interest bearing if repaid in 1 year**

The Commission may levy fines up to $2,500 per license law violation, with no limit.

THE OHIO DIVISION OF REAL ESTATE

The **Ohio Division of Real Estate** is run by its **superintendent,** who is appointed by the Director of Commerce. The Ohio Division of Real Estate:

1. Issues licenses
2. Administers license laws
3. Issues Commission orders or other orders needed to implement license laws
4. Investigates written complaints against licensees
5. Places brokers' licenses on deposit
6. Audits brokers' records and trust accounts
7. May subpoena witnesses for investigations
8. Can apply to appropriate courts of jurisdiction for injunctions to stop activities that violate real estate law

The Superintendent may also issue citations up to $200 for violating advertising law, certain agency requirements, and fair housing language law. — $2500 cap

Chapter 2 Summary

1. A broker is one who is licensed to represent a party in a real estate transaction for compensation. A broker's license can be held by an individual or a business. A real estate salesperson is a licensed agent associated with a broker and may perform most of the acts of a broker on his or her behalf. The broker charges a fee and the salesperson is paid from the broker's fee. A salesperson's license must be held by an individual.

2. Real estate sales license exam requirements include *non-educational:* 18 or older, honest, truthful and good reputation; no criminal record, no civil rights violations in past two years, no unsatisfied judgments, and a high school diploma (born after 1950); *educational:* 120 hours of class work covering principles and practices, law, civil rights and fair housing, finance, and appraisal; ***broker affiliation*** must be secured before submitting application; ***completed application, application fee, and copies of transcripts*** for all four pre-licensing courses; ***additional fee to testing service*** to schedule test.

3. There are two real estate licenses—a **broker's license** allows a person to list, sell, negotiate, charge fees, and sponsor salespeople. A **sales license** allows a person to do most things in the name of the broker. The broker charges the fee, and salespeople are paid by their broker.

4. Licenses are issued by the Division of Real Estate and sent to the broker. A broker's license must be displayed; salespersons' licenses are kept on file. Salespeople cannot practice real estate in Ohio without a license issued by the Ohio Division of Real Estate.

5. Real estate activity in Ohio is regulated by the Department of Commerce through the Division of Real Estate and the Ohio Real Estate Commission. The Ohio Real Estate Commission consists of five members appointed by the governor. The Ohio Division of Real Estate is run by its superintendent appointed by the Director of Commerce. These bodies share responsibility for implementing and enforcing license laws.

Ohio Real Estate Commission Five members appointed by the governor		Ohio Division of Real Estate Superintendent appointed by Director of Commerce
Promote Canon of Ethics	Criteria/Continuing Business	Administers License Laws
Reviews All Acts of Superintendent	Audits Recovery Account	Investigates Written Complaints against Licensees
Set Licensing Standards	Review Education Requirements	Can Apply to Courts for Injunctions
Suspension and Revocation of License	Updates Continuing Education Requirements	Audits Brokers' Records and Trust Accounts
Rules Conduct Hearings	Publishes Quarterly Newsletter	May Subpoena Witnesses for Investigations
Sets License Exam Standards	Administer Education/ Research Fund	Issues Licenses Places Broker's License on Deposit Administer Recovery Fund
MAY FINE UP TO $2,500 PER LAW VIOLATION (NO LIMIT)		May Fine $200 for Certain Law Violations (maximum total $2,500)

CHAPTER 2 QUIZ

1. *When must you affiliate with a broker?*

a. When you begin your real estate education courses
b. After you pass the test
c. When you get ready to submit your first contract to list or buy
d. Before you submit your test application

2. *When may you begin practicing real estate?*

a. As soon as you learn that you pass the test
b. As soon as you learn that your real estate license was issued by the Ohio Division of Real Estate
c. As soon as you begin your real estate education courses
d. As soon as you affiliate with a broker

3. *Which of the following is true about the Ohio Real Estate Commission?*

a. It is run by its superintendent
b. It promotes a code of ethics
c. It consists of five members appointed by the governor
d. It investigates written complaints against licensees

4. *Which of the following is true about the Ohio Division of Real Estate?*

a. It is run by its superintendent who is appointed by the governor
b. It promotes a code of ethics
c. It consists of five members appointed by the governor
d. It investigates written complaints against licensees

5. *Ohio license law:*

a. Allows people to make a lot of money
b. Permits the Commissioners to pass laws in favor of their brokerages
c. Protects the public from fraud, misrepresentation, and deceit
d. Makes it easier to get listings

6. *The Commission does all of the following* except:

a. Promote the Canons of Ethics
b. Reject license applications
c. Publish a newsletter
d. Audit the broker's records

7. *The Division of Real Estate does all of the following* except:

a. Issue fines to licensees found guilty of misrepresentation
b. Issue citations for certain agency law violations
c. Issue the real estate license
d. Issue subpoenas

8. *A real estate salesperson may:*

a. Do most things a broker can do
b. Write contracts
c. Deposit earnest money into a personal checking account as long as it doesn't pay interest
d. Sponsor salespeople to work for him or her

3 KEEPING YOUR REAL ESTATE LICENSE

CHAPTER OVERVIEW

Now that you know what the real estate profession is about and the steps required to get a license, let's look at how to *keep* your license. It's important to follow all laws, rules, and canons of ethics established by governing bodies overseeing the real estate industry. We will review the **post-licensing education requirement, continuing education requirements,** the **license renewal process,** and **license statuses.**

We'll also look at the complaint procedures and reasons why licenses are suspended or revoked, as well as ethical issues. Finally, we'll focus on a few career tips to help avoid jeopardizing your license.

KEY TERMS

Inactive
License status of any licensee whose license is returned to the Division of Real Estate by a broker who does not want to maintain sponsorship of a licensee or by a licensee who no longer wishes to practice real estate.

On Deposit
A special license status available to brokers who wish to return their broker's license to the Division of Real Estate to reactivate their sales license. The licensee does not need a trust account.

On Deposit (alternate definition)
A special license status available to any licensee who enters the military or whose reserve military status is activated. Licenses may remain on deposit until the next renewal date following discharge from the military.

Revocation
The permanent withdrawal of a licensee's license by the Real Estate Commission.

Suspension
A real estate agent's license being temporarily withdrawn for a specified period of time and calling for performance of a condition prior to reactivation.

Real Estate Recovery Fund
The Real Estate Recovery Fund is used to satisfy unpaid judgments against real estate licensees for activities violating the license law that caused financial loss to the claimant.

I. POST-LICENSING REQUIREMENTS

Post-licensing Educational Requirements

After a license is issued:

1. Take an approved 10-hour post-licensing course within 12 months. You can take no more than 6 hours of post-licensing per day.
2. Provide evidence to the Division of Real Estate that you've satisfied this post-licensing course requirement. Failure to submit proof of completion for the 10-hour post-licensing course will result in license suspension.

CONTINUING EDUCATION

All licensees must complete 30 hours of continuing education requirements on or before their **third birthday after the date of initial licensure** and on or before their birthday every 3 years. In Ohio, the CE due date is now the same date the license renewal is due.

EXAMPLE Sally is licensed on June 30, 2006. Her birthday is November 15. Her CE is due November 15, 2009.

The 30 hours of continuing education (CE) must include:

1. Three hours on recently enacted real estate legislation and court decisions (referred to as core law)
2. Three hours of fair housing/civil rights updates
3. Three-hour course on "Canons of Ethics" per the Ohio Real Estate Commission

Classes must be approved by the Division of Real Estate for post-license or CE credit. Make sure the classes are certified for Ohio real estate CE credit because not all classes count. Only 15 hours of CE elective courses may be computer classes, and of those, a maximum of 6 hours may cover basic computer topics (such as Windows® or the Internet). The computer courses must be specific to real estate. All 30 hours of continuing education requirements may be satisfied through distance learning, online courses, or in a classroom. Licensees may take more than 30 hours of CE, but only up to 10 extra hours can count toward the next three-year period. No more than 8 hours of CE may be taken per day.

Licensees who are 70 or older need only complete the 9 hours of required CE classes every three years beginning with the three-year cycle in which their 70th birthday falls to keep an active license. The 9 hours must consist of 3 hours of core law, 3 hours of fair housing/civil rights, and 3 hours of canons of ethics. A licensee who is 70 years old and has a license on inactive status is not required to take continuing education.

Submission of Proof

The licensee is responsible for submitting proof of completed CE requirements to the Division of Real Estate. Licensees must wait until completing all 30 hours, then send copies of all certificates at one time (be sure to keep copies). Failure to submit proof of completion for the 10-hour post-licensing course or 30 hours of CE will result in license suspension. There's a one-year grace period for the 10-hour Post Licensing course and the 30 hours of CE. During the grace period, the license remains suspended until coursework is completed and application for reactivation is submitted with the appropriate reactivation fee and certifications.

II. LICENSE RENEWAL

All licenses expire every third year on the licensee's birthday. Licensees are mailed their own renewals, and each must renew his or her own license by filing a Certificate of Continuation on or before his or her birthday. Renewal is the licensee's responsibility.

Should a broker not wish to retain a salesperson's license, the broker will notify the licensee and return the license to the Division of Real Estate for inactivation, and send a notice of inactivation, within three days of the date of return of the license to the Division, to the salesperson via certified mail. A licensee may transfer his or her license from one broker to another at any time by delivering a written notice to his or her present broker of the intent to transfer and then completing a transfer application with the new broker.

Every license issued by the Division is valid until expired, revoked, or suspended. Specific causes of action for revocation and suspension of licenses are detailed later in this chapter.

Other License Statuses

Besides active licenses, other license statuses are **on deposit** and **inactive**.

ON DEPOSIT. **On deposit** is a special license status available to brokers wishing to return their broker's license to the Division of Real Estate to reactivate their salesperson license. A broker's license may remain on deposit indefinitely, as long as it is renewed, and the licensee keeps up with continuing education requirements. The licensee no longer needs to have a trust account.

Another definition for **on deposit** is a special license status available to any licensee who enters the military or is activated in the military reserve. The license remains on deposit until the next renewal date after discharge from the military. Remember, brokers or salespersons may put their licenses on deposit during military service; otherwise, only brokers can.

INACTIVE. **Inactive** is the term used for the license status of any salesperson whose license is returned to the Division of Real Estate by a broker who does not want to maintain sponsorship of a licensee or by the salesperson who, temporarily, does not wish to practice real estate. A license may remain inactive indefinitely as long as it is renewed and continuing education requirements are met.

III. COMPLAINT PROCEDURE

When conflicts arise between real estate brokers and/or salespersons and the public or other real estate professionals, resolution can be pursued. A complaint can be filed with the Ohio Division of Real Estate or with the state or local board of REALTORS®, if the licensee is a member. A civil suit can also be filed. Some of the more common reasons for complaints involve failure to remit earnest money, misrepresentation, conflict of interest, or other misconduct that will be discussed further in the next section.

ROLE OF SUPERINTENDENT IN COMPLAINT PROCEEDINGS

Complaints that involve alleged violations of license laws should be filed with the Ohio Division of Real Estate. The superintendent reviews all complaints to determine merit. A procedure exists to ensure equitable and expedient processing of complaints against real estate licensees.

A written complaint against a licensee can be filed with the superintendent by anyone. Upon receipt of the complaint, the superintendent notifies the licensee by regular mail and reviews the facts and supporting documentation for jurisdiction. If jurisdiction is appropriate, the law provides for a voluntary mediation to attempt resolution. If the parties fail to agree, the complaint is investigated by the investigations and audit bureau.

Upon completion of the investigation, the complaint is either dismissed or placed on the docket for a formal hearing. If there is a formal hearing, the licensee must be notified by certified mail. This formal hearing could result in suspension or revocation of the license, *and/or* a fine of up to $2,500 per violation, possible public reprimand (reported in the Commission Newsletter), and/or required completion of additional education courses. The licensee has the right to appeal to common pleas court.

The investigation and its results are confidential, as are all reports prepared by Division employees. Discipline imposed by the Commission is public record and reported in the Commission Newsletter. If a complaint and investigation are not initiated within three years after the alleged incident, no disciplinary action can be taken on that complaint.

Note: Remember that the superintendent may issue citations to a licensee instead of initiating a formal investigation for violations of:

1. Advertising law
2. Proper administration of the Consumer Guide to Agency Relationships
3. Agency/Dual Agency requirements
4. Fair Housing language

Citations may be up to $200 for each violation (up to a maximum total of $2,500).

Citations provide a quick way to handle infractions of license law. They avert the investigation and formal hearing process and allow all parties to move beyond the misconduct. On receipt of evidence of a violation of these laws, the superintendent has discretion to:

- Initiate a formal investigation: the superintendent must initiate a formal investigation if a licensee is cited more than three times within twelve consecutive months

- Issue a citation: gives notice to licensee of the alleged violation and the opportunity to request a formal hearing within 30 days of the notice
- Issue a fine of up to $200 per violation deposited in the Real Estate Recovery Fund: if no hearing, the citation becomes final on the 31st day after issuance. Failure to pay the citation within 60 days results in an automatic suspension of the license

IV. ROLE OF THE REAL ESTATE RECOVERY FUND

The Real Estate Recovery Fund satisfies unpaid judgments against real estate licensees for activities in violation of the license law that caused financial loss to the claimant. Up to $10 of each license renewal or transfer fee must go into this account when the fund falls below $1 million. If the fund is between $1 million and $2 million, up to $5 may be taken. If the fund is above $2 million, none of the fees will be deposited. Citation fines also go into the Recovery Fund.

For a claimant to use the fund there must be an unsatisfied judgment against a broker or salesperson from real estate-related activity. This judgment must represent a final order that cannot be appealed by a licensee. Furthermore, a claimant must show that a licensee failed to pay all or part of the judgment despite diligent pursuit of a licensee by the claimant in an effort to collect. Claims against the fund must be filed within one year of the date of final judgment against a licensee.

The payment ceiling is $40,000 for each licensee involved in a transaction. Note that the limit is *per licensee* not per violation. If more than one licensee is involved, the ceiling is multiplied by the number of licensees. If this sum does not cover the full amount of the claims from the transaction, then claimants shall be paid in proportion to their judgments.

When a payment is made from the fund in the name of any licensee, that person's license is automatically suspended and not subject to reinstatement until the amount, including interest, is repaid. A discharge in bankruptcy will not relieve the licensee of this obligation.

V. SUSPENSION OR REVOCATION OF LICENSES

Suspension means that a license is withdrawn for a specified period of time and calls for the performance of a condition prior to reactivation. Non-performance of a condition during suspension may result in license revocation. **Revocation** means permanently withdrawing a real estate licensee's license. Issuance of a new license to a person with a previously revoked license is by application (the pre-licensing certificates are good for 10 years), reviewed by the Commission, and may be denied. If suspension or revocation of a license is the result of a formal hearing, the licensee has the right to appeal to common pleas court.

REASONS FOR SUSPENSION OR REVOCATION

The law mandates the superintendent to investigate the conduct of any licensee against whom a written complaint has been filed. The superintendent may also initiate an investigation into the activities of a licensee. All licensees need to be familiar with the reasons licenses are suspended or revoked to avoid these problems. The Commission shall impose discipline against the licensee that may include suspension or revocation if a licensee is found guilty of any of the following activities:

1. **Making any misrepresentation knowingly**. Misrepresentation is defined as passing along false information. A misrepresentation need not be fraudulent, but it is false at the time you make the misrepresentation.
2. **Making false promises with the intent to influence, persuade, or induce.**
3. **Making a continued course of misrepresentations or false promises through agents, advertising, salespersons, or otherwise.** *Note*: "knowingly" is not part of this violation.
4. **Acting for more than one party in a transaction without the knowledge and consent of all parties involved.** This encompasses the problem of dual agency where an agent acts on behalf of both buyer and seller without consent. With proper written consent of all parties, however, this is legal.
5. **Failing to account for or remit within a reasonable time any money** coming **into his or her possession that belongs to others.**
6. **Dealing dishonestly, illegally, or with gross negligence or incompetence.**

7*A*. **A final adjudication by a court of law of any violation of any civil rights or fair housing law or any unlawful discriminatory act.** The law states that this must arise out of a *bona fide* purchase or lease attempt that would exclude actions by testers or checkers.

7*B*. **A second or subsequent violation of any fair housing or civil rights law regardless of final adjudication.** This violation carries a minimum two-month suspension with the possibility of license revocation. Any subsequent violations mandate revocation.

8. **Obtaining a license by fraud, misrepresentation, or deceit.**
9. **Disregarding this section of the law willfully.**
10. **Demanding unearned commissions from other licensees.**
11. **Dividing commissions with non-licensees**. It is clear, however, that you may pay non-licensees salaries or hourly wages as telemarketers, assistants, etc., as long as they do not enter the process of listing, selling, or leasing. You may not, however, pay a bonus for leads that become sales; this is commission splitting.
12. Misrepresenting **membership in a professional association.**
13. Accepting **a secret profit on money or assets provided by the principal.**
14. Offering **anything of value to get someone to enter into a contract**, known as an *inducement*, and not noting it in the contract. Included by special reference is the prohibition of using real estate as prizes in games of chance.

15. **Acting as an undisclosed principal**. This means that you are acting on your own behalf rather than as an agent. This is not a problem if disclosure is made immediately. The problem arises when an agent desires a property that he or she has listed. Without disclosure, it might appear that the broker or salesperson could under-represent the property to drive the price down.
16. **Guaranteeing future profits.**
17. **Placing a sign on any unlisted property.** This is a *blockbusting* technique designed to get the owner of the property to call, at which time the owner is told of the entry of certain elements into the neighborhood.
18. **Inducing the breaking of a contract to enter another.** This can happen when a buyer has entered into a lease extension. If the agent invites the buyer to enter into a purchase agreement before resolving the lease problem, the agent has violated the licensing law.
19. **Having negotiated the sale, exchange, or lease of any real property directly with a seller, purchaser, lessor, or tenant knowing that such seller, purchaser, lessor, or tenant is represented by another broker under a written exclusive agency agreement, exclusive right to sell or lease listing agreement, or exclusive purchaser agency agreement with respect to such property except as provided for in section 4735.75 of the Revised Code.**
20. **Offering real estate without the consent of the owner including offering unauthorized terms of sale.**
21. **Causing publication of inaccurate or misleading advertising**. All media are covered. Intent is unimportant and is routinely disregarded.
22. **Falsifying books of account.**
23. **Threatening competitors with unwarranted legal action.**
24. **Failing to keep complete and accurate records of all transactions for three years from the date of the transaction.**
25. **Failing to provide true copies of listings and other agreements to all parties at the time the documents are signed.**
26. Failing to maintain a trust account separate from broker funds. The account must be a *non-interest-bearing* account with a bank in the state of Ohio. The bank and account number must be provided to the Division as part of a broker application and kept for inspection by the investigations and audit bureau.
27. **Failing to deposit earnest money into the trust account when required by contract.** Putting earnest money into the broker's general account instead is called conversion (theft).
28. **Putting broker's money into the trust account (other than money required by the bank to keep the account open).** This is called commingling, which means failing to maintain a separate and distinct account for the deposit and maintenance of rents, security deposits, and other money received in the course of managing real property. This account *can* be an interest-bearing account with a bank in the state of

Ohio with interest paid to the property owner. The bank and account number must be provided to the Division as part of a broker application and kept for inspection by the investigations and audit bureau. Brokers not engaged in property management for others are exempt.

29. **Failing to put expiration dates on all listings and/or failing to obtain timely signatures on the Consumer Guide to Agency Relationships.**
30. **Having an unsatisfied judgment in any court against you arising out of conduct as a real estate licensee.**
31. **Failing to account on demand for funds placed into a licensee's hands by a party to a transaction.**
32. **Failing to pay a salesperson any due and earned commission within a reasonable time after receipt of funds.**
33. **Practicing law without a license.**
34. **Having an adjudication of incompetency.**
35. **Allowing a non-licensee to act on his or her behalf.**
36. **Knowingly inserting any materially inaccurate term into a document, including naming a false consideration.**
37. **Having failed to inform the licensee's client of the existence of an offer or counteroffer or having failed to present an offer or counteroffer in a timely manner unless otherwise instructed by the client, provided that the instruction of the client does not conflict with any state or federal law.**
38. **Failing to take the required continuing education.**
39. **Failing to renew the license regardless of its status (with the exception of military license on deposit).**

These reasons are important to know for real estate practice; plus, they're popular topics for test questions!

VI. ETHICS IN REAL ESTATE

Ethics in real estate can seem like a complex issue, but it really boils down to a few simple points: *fiduciary responsibilities*, *disclosure*, *don't take unfair advantage of people*; be honest with everyone; treat everyone equally and keep good documentation. If you do these things and follow the Canons of Ethics put forth by the Ohio Real Estate Commission (and the separate Code of Ethics if you are a REALTOR® put forth by National Association of REALTORS® and National Association of Real Estate Brokers that all members voluntarily agree to follow) then success should follow. **Take time to read the Canons of Ethics.**

Canons of Ethics for the Real Estate Industry

Pursuant to the requirement of ORC Section 4735.03 (A), the Ohio Real Estate Commission has promulgated the Canons of Ethics for the real estate industry. All Ohio licensees are bound by the Canons of Ethics. REALTORS® and REALTISTS, that is, members of the National Association of REALTORS, and the National Association of Real Estate Brokers, are further bound by separate Codes of Ethics. The Canons of Ethics are reproduced in their entirety below with emphasis added.

Section I: General Duties to the Public and Industry

Article 1. Licensing as a real estate broker or salesperson indicates to the public at large that the individual so designated has special expertise in real estate matters and is subject to high standards of conduct in the licensee's business and personal affairs. The licensee should endeavor to maintain and establish high standards of professional conduct and integrity in dealings with members of the public as well as with fellow licensees and, further, seek to avoid even the appearance of impropriety in any activities, as a licensee.

Article 2. It is the duty of the broker to protect the public against fraud, misrepresentation, or unethical practices in real estate transactions. The licensee should endeavor to eliminate in the community any practices that could be damaging to the public or to the integrity of the real estate profession.

Article 3. The licensee should provide assistance wherever possible to the members and staff of the Real Estate Commission and Division of Real Estate in the enforcement of the licensing statutes and administrative rules and regulations adopted in accordance therewith.

Article 4. The licensee should be knowledgeable of the laws of Ohio pertinent to real estate and should keep informed of changes in the statutes of Ohio affecting the duties and responsibilities of a licensee.

Article 5. A licensee should represent clients competently and should promote the advancement of professional education in the real estate industry through the licensee's conduct.

Article 6. The licensee should be informed as to matters affecting real estate in the community, state, and the nation so that the licensee may be able to contribute to public thinking on such matters including taxation, legislation, land use, city planning, and other questions affecting property interests.

Section II: Specific Duties to Clients and Customers

Article 7. The licensee should disclose all known material facts concerning a property on which the licensee is representing a seller or purchaser to avoid misrepresentation or concealment of material facts.

Article 8. The licensee should recommend that title be examined and legal counsel be obtained.

Article 9. The licensee, for the protection of all parties, should see that financial obligations and commitments regarding real estate transactions are in writing, expressing the exact agreement of the parties and that copies of such agreements, at the time they are executed, are placed in the hands of all parties involved.

Article 10. A licensee should not enter into an agency relationship with a party whose interests are in conflict with those of the licensee or another client represented by the licensee without fully disclosing the potential conflict and obtaining the informed consent of all parties.

Article 11. A licensee should not accept compensation from more than one party without the full knowledge and consent of all parties to the transaction.

Article 12. When acting as a seller's agent, a licensee should disclose to the seller if the licensee is the actual purchaser, or if the purchaser is another licensee affiliated with the same brokerage as the licensee, a business entity in which the licensee has an interest, or is a member of the licensee's immediate family.

Article 13. When asked to provide an appraisal (formal or informal), price opinion, comparative market analysis, or any other task that is intended to determine the value of property, a licensee shall not render an opinion without the careful analysis and interpretation of all factors affecting the property and should not mislead the client as to the value of the property.

Article 14. The licensee should not undertake to provide professional services concerning a property or its value where the licensee has a present or contemplated interest unless such interest is specifically disclosed to all affected parties. Nor should the licensee make a formal appraisal when the licensee's employment or fee charged for the appraisal is contingent upon the amount of the appraisal.

Article 15. The licensee should not attempt to provide an appraisal, price opinion, comparative market analysis, or any other task that is intended to determine the value of a property if the subject property is of a type that is outside the field of expertise of the licensee unless the licensee obtains the assistance of another licensee or appraiser who has expertise in this type of property

Article 16. The licensee should not advertise property without authority, and in any advertisement the price quoted should be agreed upon with the owners as the offering price.

Section III: Duties to Fellow Licensees

Article 17. A licensee should respect the exclusive agency of another licensee until it has expired or until the client, without solicitation, initiates a discussion with the licensee about terms upon which the licensee might take a future agency agreement or one commencing upon the expiration of any existing agreement.

Article 18. A licensee should not solicit a listing that is currently listed with another broker unless the listing broker, when asked, refuses to disclose the expiration and nature of the listing. In that event the licensee may contact the owner to secure such information and may discuss the terms upon which the licensee might take a future listing or one commencing upon the expiration of any existing exclusive listing.

Article 19. A licensee should not solicit a buyer/tenant who is subject to an exclusive buyer/tenant agreement unless the broker, when asked, refuses to disclose the expiration and nature of the exclusive buyer/tenant agreement. In that event, the licensee may contact the buyer/tenant to secure such information and may discuss the terms upon which the licensee might enter into a future buyer/tenant agreement or may enter into a buyer/tenant agreement to become effective upon the expiration of any existing exclusive buyer/ tenant agreement.

VII. A FEW CAREER TIPS

After working hard to get a license and fulfilling the ongoing requirements to keep the license active, be aware of all the ways that a license can be jeopardized. The lists in the preceding sections outline several simple mistakes that can cause suspension or revocation of a license. *Forgetting to put an expiration date on a listing agreement, failing to give copies of contracts to parties as soon as they are signed, and not submitting an agency disclosure form at the time an offer is presented* are three of the most common pitfalls. Follow the laws and procedures outlined in the coursework and you will have fewer problems.

CAREER TIP #1:

Pay attention to all procedural guidelines and rules, especially those mentioned as ones that can cause you to lose your license.

One of the fastest ways to lose a license is to violate fair housing laws. These laws are detailed thoroughly in this book. Pay close attention to them, not only because they can cause you to lose your license, but also because they can help you obtain a license since they factor into a large number of test questions.

CAREER TIP #2:

Treat all people fairly, equally, and with respect. You'll make friends, keep clients, get referrals, and be successful.

Finally, it's important to understand that when you are dealing with the single largest transaction that most people will make in their lives, there's always a chance for someone to feel dissatisfaction with the deal.

CAREER TIP #3:

Always keep detailed records of contacts with the public. Contracts and other paperwork must be kept for three years. Personal logs should be kept on record for a similar period of time.

We need to keep in touch with people, and we are constantly trying to contact new prospects. Remember that there are strict federal and state laws that dictate when and how we can contact people. Know the *Do Not Call* and *Junk Fax* rules. If you follow these guidelines and career tips, you should avoid some pitfalls and have the records, reputation, and other tools to make your career rewarding.

Bring a copy of the following to the next class. All can be found on the Division's Web site.

1. 2006 Combined Renewal Application with Education Compliance Form

2. Lead-Based Paint Disclosure

3. Lead Hazard Pamphlet

Chapter 3 Summary

1. *All licenses expire on the licensee's birthday*. **Post-licensing requirements**: 10-hour class within 12 months. All licensees must take *30 hours of CE every three years*, and submit proof on or before the licensee's birthday. Of the 30 hours required, 9 hours must cover core law, civil rights, and canons of ethics. Only 15 hours of the 21 CE electives may be computer classes, and a maximum of 6 hours may be on basic computer topics. Licensees who are *70 or older need only complete the 9 hours of CE every three years* covering core law, civil rights and canons of ethics to keep an active license.

2. Only a broker's license may be placed on deposit to reactivate a salesperson license. That broker's license may remain on deposit indefinitely. Either a broker or salesperson can place a license on deposit when entering the military or on activation in the military reserves. A salesperson may return his or her license to the Division of Real Estate indefinitely, as long as the license is renewed and the licensee's continuing education is kept current; the license status is inactive.

3. Common reasons for license suspension or revocation are detailed in this chapter. *Suspension* means a license is withdrawn for a certain and specified period of time and may call for a condition to be met before reactivation is permitted. *Revocation* means a license is permanently withdrawn, and an application for a new license must be submitted. If denied, the licensee may appeal to Common Pleas Court. All real estate licensees are bound by Canons of Ethics put forth by the Ohio Real Estate Commission.

4. The Real Estate Recovery Fund was established to pay unsatisfied monetary judgments from a court of law against a licensee found guilty of real estate activities that have violated license law. The fund is supported by renewal fees and citation fees. The amount of money put into this fund depends on the balance of the fund. No more then $40,000 can be paid out of the fund in the name of a licensee by court order. The license is suspended upon any payment from the fund.

5. The superintendent investigates written complaints against a licensee. A licensee is notified by regular mail if a complaint is filed and by certified mail if a formal hearing is required. The Division investigates; the superintendent appoints the hearing examiner and the Commission imposes penalties. Penalties include license suspension, revocation, additional education, a fine up to $2,500 per violation (no cap), and public reprimand. The superintendent can initiate an investigation on his/her own.

Chapter 3 Quiz

1. ***Post-licensing requirements include which of the following?***
   a. Complete a 10-hour post-licensing course within first year of being licensed
   b. Provide evidence to the Ohio Real Estate Commission that you've satisfied your post-licensing requirement
   c. Register your license with the Clerk of Courts
   d. Take no more than 10 hours of education per day

2. ***What is the license expiration and/or renewal procedure?***
   a. Licenses are automatically renewed at the end of each year
   b. Licenses expire December 31 unless you file a notice of continuation with the Division of Real Estate
   c. Licenses expire unless you can prove continued usage
   d. Licenses expire on licensee's birthday and are renewed by licensee filing a certificate of continuation (notice of renewal) with the Division of Real Estate

3. ***Which of the following is* not *a license status?***
   a. License inactive
   b. License active
   c. License on deposit
   d. License in escrow

4. ***A complaint procedure may result in any of the following,* except:**
   a. The investigation proceedings becoming a matter of public record
   b. A formal hearing
   c. An appeal to common pleas court
   d. A license suspension or revocation, and a fine of up to $2,500 per violation

5. ***The Real Estate Recovery Fund:***
   a. Is used to help licensees get unpaid commissions
   b. Is used to satisfy unpaid judgments against real estate licensees
   c. Can be used to fund grants for real estate research
   d. Can result in unlimited payment of judgments for fair housing violations

6. ***Suspension of a license means a license is temporarily withdrawn, and:***
   a. Is for an uncertain and unspecified period of time and may have conditions attached
   b. Is final and may not be appealed
   c. Can only happen after the third offense ("three strikes and you're out" rule)
   d. Is for a set period of time with reactivation after the suspension is lifted

7. ***Revocation of a license means a license is withdrawn, and:***
   a. Reapplication submitted may be denied by the Ohio Real Estate Commission
   b. Is final and may not be appealed
   c. Can only happen after the third offense ("three strikes and you're out" rule)
   d. Is for a set period of time with reactivation automatic on the day after the revocation is lifted

8. ***A license can be suspended or revoked for which of the following reasons?***
   a. Advertising in the newspaper where the paper was responsible for an error or omission
   b. Representing more than one party in a transaction, with the consent of only one of the parties
   c. Paying non-licensees salaries or wages as telemarketers
   d. Unknowingly making a misrepresentation, because your seller/client gave you the wrong information

Chapter 3 Quiz

4 THE REAL ESTATE INDUSTRY

CHAPTER OVERVIEW

As you pursue your real estate career, it's important to have some understanding of how the real estate industry works. The real estate industry is affected by a broad range of *economic, governmental, social,* and *physical factors*. The business of real estate is often pulled up and down in response to the health and activities of other businesses. We will explore this relationship, how it impacts real estate cycles, and why real estate cycles take longer to respond to these factors.

Our discussion examines the economic and governmental factors that affect the real estate market and real estate cycles and takes a brief look at some social factors. Our look at the economic factors at work in the real estate market includes the underlying causes for shifts in supply and demand and creating buyer's and seller's markets. Our look at the governmental factors that impact various aspects of the real estate industry includes discussion of land use controls by state and local governments and the importance of secondary mortgage markets in stabilizing real estate markets on a national level.

KEY TERMS

Cost of Money
The interest rate that people or businesses must pay to use another's money for their own purposes.

Economic Base
The main business or industry in an area that a community uses to support and sustain itself.

Eminent Domain
Government's constitutional power to take (appropriate/condemn) private property for public use as long as the owner is paid just compensation.

Escheat
When property reverts to the state after a person dies without a valid will and heirs (property also reverts to the state after abandonment).

Immobility
Physical characteristic of real estate referring to fact that it can't be moved from one place to another.

Inflation
An increase in the cost of goods or services or too much money chasing too few goods.

Land Use Controls
Public or private restrictions on how land may be used.

Police Power
Constitutional power of state (and local) governments to enact and enforce laws that protect the public's health, safety, morals, and general welfare.

Taxation
Process of a government levying a charge on people or things.
use another's money for their own purposes.

I. BUSINESS ASPECTS OF REAL ESTATE

To understand real estate as a profession and be competent as a salesperson (or in another related real estate career), it's important to know how it functions as a whole.

The factors that influence the real estate market can be broadly divided into **economic factors**, **governmental factors**, **social factors,** and **physical factors**.

II. ECONOMIC FACTORS

Economic factors cover a broad range of influences on the real estate market. First, we'll look at general **business cycles** and **real estate cycles**, then focus on more specific economic factors that influence real estate markets such as **supply and demand**, **inflation**, **cost of money**, **immobility**, **uniqueness and scarcity** of a particular piece of real estate, and the **economic base** of an area.

BUSINESS CYCLES

Business cycles are general swings in business activity resulting in expanding and contracting activity during different phases of the cycle. These cycles last for varying periods of time depending on a number of different economic factors.

Many of these activities and factors are so interrelated they carry up and pull down other businesses along with them. It's difficult to even out these cycles because it's hard to know when they start or what's causing them (although the government does try). Most of the time, a cycle must ride itself out—either to a point where interest rates or other costs become so high that no one can afford to buy things so prices begin falling, or to a point where interest rates or costs are so low that even people reluctant to spend can't pass up such low rates or prices and begin to spend again.

REAL ESTATE CYCLES

Real estate cycles are general swings in real estate activity resulting in increasing or decreasing activity and property values, during different phases of the cycle. Real estate cycles are dependent on business cycles. When business cycles are on an upswing, people feel secure in their jobs and have money to spend and invest. This results in increased real estate activity just as it results in increased activity in many other markets and industries. Conversely, when business cycles are in a downswing, people are worried about their future and are less likely to spend money on real estate or other large purchases. Real estate cycles trail behind business cycles because they depend on many elements of business cycles (e.g., steady jobs) to be in full swing before real estate cycles respond.

Real estate cycle swings are generally the result of the real estate market responding to supply and demand. These cycles last for varying periods of time depending on a number of factors. Many of these factors also affect business cycles.

Supply and Demand

The law of **supply and demand states** that when supply exceeds demand, prices will fall, and when demand exceeds supply, prices will rise. This plays an important role in real estate because of the inherent difficulties in adjusting supply and demand.

UNIQUENESS AND SCARCITY. The uniqueness and scarcity of real estate are important concepts. Uniqueness refers to the fact that each piece of land, each building, and each house is said to be a different piece of real estate. This is also called non-homogeneity ("not the same"). Even if two houses look the same, they are still held to be unique because of their particular locations. Scarcity refers to the fact that there's a limited supply of real estate. There is a lot of land in Montana and Alaska, but it all comes back to location; fewer people want to live there than other places, and most people don't want to live too far from their job and their family, so we're back to a limited supply of real estate.

Compare this view of real estate with the goods produced by other businesses in other industries. For most goods, businesses can simply make more, or consumers can choose a ready substitute in the marketplace. In real estate, there are no ready substitutes as each piece of land is said to be unique, and it's not possible to make more. Real estate derives much of its value from being in a specific location, and no other piece of real estate is just like it.

IMMOBILITY. Immobility is a physical characteristic of real estate referring to the fact that the real estate itself cannot move from one place to another. Customers are also somewhat immobile. It's impossible to move a house from Columbus to Dayton where there's a buyer, and usually a person in Cincinnati won't relocate to Cleveland to buy a certain house since his or her job cannot move. The immobility of land helps its value in a good market since other land can't be moved in to take away potential customers, but it hurts it in a bad market as it can't be relocated to a better position to attract buyers. The immobility of customers means they can't easily move to take advantage of real estate in other cities, and demographic patterns show that most people stay within a given region.

This imperfect ability to react skews the supply and demand model in the real estate market, making it more susceptible to a temporary shortage or oversupply of houses. What makes the problem worse is the time lag between the recognition of a shortage or oversupply situation in the housing market and the time it takes for the construction industry to react. Houses take time to build, and during that time there's an imbalance in the market. This leads to a **buyer's market** or a **seller's market**.

BUYER'S MARKET. A **buyer's market** is a housing market with a large selection of properties from which buyers can choose. This situation may be the result of population or demographic shifts away from an area, overbuilding by the construction industry, or bad economic conditions such as a plant closing or layoffs by a local employer. A buyer's market can be somewhat neutralized if some of the sellers take their houses off the market, but a glut is a glut, and usually there remains a downward pressure on prices. Generally in this situation, the buyer is in a position to negotiate for a lower price or more favorable terms.

SELLER'S MARKET. A **seller's market** is a housing market where sellers can choose from a large number of buyers who are looking for houses in a particular area. This situation may result from people moving into a particular area, little building by the construction industry in response to a previously perceived glut in the housing market, high construction costs for labor or materials, good economic conditions such as a new plant being opened, massive hiring by a local employer, or lower interest rates. Generally in this situation, the seller is in a position to stay closer to the original price or negotiate more favorable terms.

EXAMPLE

A: Widget Company opens a new plant employing 600 people on Big City's west side. Land is cheaper because there isn't much development. Widget's new hires begin looking for houses near their job, but there aren't enough homes available. Most residents like living there and don't plan to move. But some don't want to be near Widget; others see a good chance to sell.

For a while, there will be a seller's market on Big City's west side. There's a limited supply of housing and a large influx of people wanting to move there. Those who want to sell can probably get better prices and terms than before Widget came to town. Of course, there's a limit to how high prices can go. Above a certain level (which no one knows), the new workers of Widget will decide to live further away to save money or wait for new homes to be built.

New houses being built will alleviate the housing shortage and bring supply and demand for houses in the area more into balance. These new homes will cost more than other areas due to higher land costs and more demand in the area because of Widget.

The law of supply and demand says that all home prices will fall slightly from their high points as the supply of homes in the area rises, but the overall effect of Widget moving in is higher price levels for all area homes.

B: The laws of supply and demand work in reverse as well. Suppose that many years later, Widget closes its facility on the west side of Big City. Now there may not be a reason for many people to live there. Some may decide to stay, but others who moved there because of Widget are likely to move, and those transferred to another Widget location may also move.

EXAMPLE (continued)

Now there's a buyer's market. The supply of homes in the area outstrips demand. There may be a few people looking to move into the area for other reasons, but there are probably more looking to move out. Not only are people looking to sell their existing homes, but the construction company may have been caught off guard and have a few homes in various stages of completion.

The prices for most of these homes will have to drop to attract new buyers. No one knows what level is low enough, but at some price level, people will see the homes in this area as a good bargain even if they are now living or working somewhere else. At some level, some of the people who wanted to sell, but are not forced to sell, may decide they are better off staying in their current home than selling at such a low price.

The laws of supply and demand necessitate that all housing prices will start to rise again from their low points as some people sell their homes and other homes are pulled off of the market decreasing the supply of homes in the area. But unless another company moves in, the overall effect of Widget moving out of the area is that the price levels for all homes will start from new lower levels than before.

Although we talked about buyers' and sellers' markets in real estate that exist because of the lag time for market forces (e.g., construction companies) to respond to supply and demand situations for housing, these same forces can work other ways. Buyers' and sellers' markets can occur within a city, from one neighborhood to the next, and even within the same neighborhood from one street to the next or from style to style among houses. For example, if we are looking at a neighborhood of two-story homes, but there is one street with tri-level homes for sale that no one seems to want, then we could say that we have a buyer's market for tri-level homes.

It is also important to remember that the real estate market cannot react like other markets because of the immobility, uniqueness, and scarcity of real estate. Property can't be moved to satisfy demand changes, and there's a limited supply of real estate in any given area. Finally, real estate cycles follow business cycles, but real estate cycles take longer to recover because housing decisions are dependent on job security and the stability of other business cycle factors.

INFLATION

Inflation is an increase in the cost of goods or services. This is also called **cost inflation** because it's the result of manufacturers and others passing along increases in their costs to the consumer. With real estate, cost inflation mostly affects new home prices (builders pass along their higher costs for labor and materials).

Inflation is also defined as too much money chasing too few goods. This is called **demand inflation.** It's driven by demand because too many people want to buy the same thing. In real estate, demand inflation mostly affects existing home prices (many people want to live in a certain area where the home supply is limited).

High inflation hits a real estate cycle harder than a business cycle because the actual costs are larger. A person will think twice about buying a $100,000 house that has increased in price by $10,000 but is much more likely to shrug off a $5 rise in a $50 pair of shoes—even though both prices rose by the same percentage.

Low inflation has both good and bad effects on real estate. Low inflation is good since it keeps costs down on newly built homes and keeps interest rates low. Low inflation can hinder real estate because wages that aren't going up quickly or significantly may stop some people from committing to buy a home, and low inflation can flatten prices for existing homes making owners decide to stay where they are rather than selling. Generally, the benefits of low inflation—low interest rates and economic stability—outweigh the disadvantages.

COST OF MONEY (INTEREST RATES)

The **cost of money** is the interest rate people or businesses must pay to use another's money for their own purposes. When borrowing money to buy a house, you must find a bank or lender with an interest rate you are willing. Conversely, a bank or lender must pay a high enough interest rate to potential depositors, so the bank will have enough money to lend others and make money for itself and its shareholders.

Inflation can be one of the factors that pushes the cost of money higher or lower. The cost of money has a great influence on the decision to buy property. Higher interest rates affect most big-ticket items, but higher rates hinder real estate more than other goods since mortgages are long-term commitments. Lower interest rates that go with low inflation are generally good for real estate. When rates are low and stable, more people can afford mortgage payments and are willing to make a commitment; banks are more willing to lock in lower rates for the entire loan because there's little fear that their cost of money will rise suddenly.

ECONOMIC BASE

The **economic base** of an area is the main business or industry that a community uses to support and sustain itself. Essentially, it's the business or industry that's responsible for bringing money into the area from outside sources. A community could not sustain itself if it only recycled its own money internally. The money in a community must be expanded by selling something to the outside world.

While the presence of an economic base is important for all businesses in a region, it's critical for the real estate market. In the absence of an economic base, other businesses could advertise to try and draw people from other areas, find ways to "export" their products or services outside their area, or simply close up shop, take their labor and inventory, and open in a new location. These options are not available to the real estate market! Since land can't be moved from one place to another, every community needs a healthy economic base to maintain real estate market values.

III. GOVERNMENTAL FACTORS

Governmental factors also have a significant influence on real estate. State and local governments have two types of laws that influence real estate: **revenue generating laws** and **right to regulate laws**. **Revenue generating laws** deal with taxes and, although they're passed primarily to raise revenue, they can have other effects on real estate as well. **Right to regulate laws** deal with the **police power** that governments reserve for themselves. Federal government factors that influence real estate are **fiscal policy**, **monetary policy**, **secondary mortgage markets**, and **government programs**. Many federal government actions are a deliberate attempt to counteract the cycles we've discussed. Let's look at each of these.

TAXATION

Taxation is the process of a government levying a charge on people or things, like property taxes, that state and local governments impose on property owners to pay for schools, improvements, or other public needs. Taxes also directly impact the spending habits and abilities of all businesses and individuals. Higher taxes curtail economic activity on an individual level while lower taxes tend to encourage spending and investing. While some would argue that government spending is necessary in many areas and has the same net result in total economic activity, higher taxes result in people having less money to buy real estate.

SPECIFIC TAX POLICIES. Specific tax policies are tax laws enacted by government that can encourage or discourage a certain behavior or activity. Some tax policies have a direct and deliberate effect on real estate. On state and local levels, tax breaks can be given to businesses as an incentive to bring jobs or real estate development to an area. At the federal level, deductions for home mortgage interest and real estate taxes from taxable income encourages home ownership and stimulates housing activity. Another example is federal capital gains tax code changes in 1997, which added beneficial tax treatment for homeowners with a new tax exclusion on the sale of a principal residence. (The exclusion is now $500,000 for married couples filing jointly and $250,000 for singles. The exclusion can be used as often as every two years if you've owned the home for two of the past five years, used the property as a principal residence for at least two of the past five years, and not used the exclusion in the prior two years.)

Specific tax policies can also adversely affect real estate. On the local level, high real estate taxes that generate revenue for school districts may mean better schools, but they can also discourage new home construction. Another example is federal tax code changes in 1986 that made real estate investing less attractive. Be aware that tax laws can influence real estate, but *never* give tax advice to anyone. Send people to tax professionals because tax laws are complicated and change often.

POLICE POWER

Police power is the constitutional power of state (and local) governments to enact and enforce laws that protect the public's health, safety, morals, and general welfare. Many of the police powers fall under the state's authority, but they're often delegated to local governments. Police power can take the form of **land use controls**, **zoning laws**, **environmental protection laws**, **eminent domain,** and **escheat**.

LAND USE CONTROLS. Land use controls are any public or private restrictions on how land may be used and are usually government-enacted zoning laws.

ZONING. Zoning laws are local ordinances dividing a city, county, etc., into zones, allowing different types of land use in different zones. Zoning and other laws restricting land usage (e.g., building codes) are passed to protect the health, safety, and welfare of the community. Land use controls impact real estate since they may limit development and affect property values. Land may be more valuable with an office building instead of a house, but zoning laws may not permit that land usage. Land use controls can also be used to stimulate real estate or economic activity. Governments looking for more revenue or jobs may change, lift, or ease restrictions to encourage these activities.

ENVIRONMENTAL PROTECTION LAWS. Land use controls at state and federal levels are increasing as a means to protect the environment. Regulations can involve blocking or restricting use of land where there are environmental concerns. Sometimes this conflicts with landowners' usage of land. For example, land may not be used for a hazardous waste site (or some industrial uses) without government approval.

The federal government also controls land use in protecting wildlife, endangered species, and wetlands. Federal agencies may deem land a safe haven or a protected area that can't be developed. Of course, the rules may be revised to permit uses perceived as beneficial. These policies are often controversial as the benefits of preservation and conservation are weighed against the benefits of usage.

EMINENT DOMAIN. Eminent domain is the government's constitutional power to appropriate (condemn) private property for public use as long as the owner is paid just compensation. Eminent domain affects real estate because of government involvement in fair market pricing and by making adjacent land more or less valuable depending on the proposed use (e.g., freeway interchange versus a landfill).

ESCHEAT. Escheat means that property reverts to the state after a person dies without leaving a valid will and without heirs. (Property also reverts to the state after abandonment.) Since the rights of property ownership are derived from the government, those rights should revert to the state if they aren't assigned to someone else by the owner or if there are no heirs.

FISCAL POLICY

Fiscal policy is the government's plan for spending, taxation, and debt management. The legislative and executive branches of government enact fiscal policy by passing legislation that sets the government's priorities for how much money will be collected, how it will be collected, and how it will be spent. The ultimate goals are supposed to be economic growth and full employment. Unfortunately, there's much debate over which policies actually promote those results.

Fiscal policy influences real estate through the amount of taxes collected and by incentives in the tax code. Higher taxes result in less spending by people and businesses and more by government. This hinders real estate because the government doesn't typically buy or build houses. (Subsidized housing is a separate issue since it deals with only certain real estate in certain areas and is a small amount.)

MONETARY POLICY

Monetary policy is the means by which the government can exert control over the supply and cost of money. The Federal Reserve Board (also referred to as the Fed) is responsible for U.S. monetary policy and regulating commercial banks. The Fed's policies are implemented with the goals of high employment, economic growth, price stability, interest rate stability, and others.

We're most concerned with the effects of the Fed's monetary policy on interest rates. Although the Fed's actions have no direct effect on the prime rate or mortgage rates banks charge, these long-term rates usually follow the lead established by Fed policy. This affects real estate by making money easier to borrow or by making it harder to spend money on a home. Through monetary policy, the Fed can make more or less money available for banks to lend, which raises or lowers interest rates. The three main ways that the Fed controls interest rates are through **reserve requirements**, **federal discount rates,** and **open market operations**. The Fed can also use moral suasion to attempt to control interest rates. **Moral suasion** is essentially trying to use persuasive influences on the public and financial markets to perceive credit in a specific way.

RESERVE REQUIREMENTS. **Reserve requirements** are the percentage of customers' deposits that commercial banks are required to keep on deposit, either on hand at the bank or in the bank's own accounts—money the bank can't lend to other people. When the Fed raises reserve requirements, this effectively raises interest rates. Lowering reserve requirements lowers interest rates.

FEDERAL DISCOUNT RATES. **Federal discount rates** are the interest rates charged by Federal Reserve Banks on loans to member commercial banks. When the Fed increases the federal discount rate, this increase is passed along to customers in the form of higher interest rates. Lowering the federal discount rate lowers interest rates.

OPEN MARKET OPERATIONS AND MORAL SUASION. **Open market operations** are the Fed selling or buying government securities. The Fed does this to try to hit a target Fed funds rate established at its Federal Open Market Committee (FOMC) meeting. Although the Fed funds rate only affects the interest rate banks charge each other for overnight loans, this usually causes other longer-term rates (e.g., prime rate or mortgage rates) to eventually head in the same direction. As the Fed sells securities in exchange for a bank's (or person's) money, the Fed is increasing its stockpile of cash and taking money out of circulation, which raises interest rates. As the Fed buys securities, it puts more money into circulation, which lowers interest rates. **Moral suasion** is an application of pressure, not force, by an authority (such as the Federal Reserve Board) to get members to adhere to a policy.

SECONDARY MORTGAGE MARKETS

Secondary mortgage markets are the private investors and government agencies that buy and sell real estate mortgages. This is in contrast to the primary mortgage market, which consists of primary lenders such as neighborhood banks that make loans directly to homeowners. The difference is secondary mortgage markets buy real estate loans as investment vehicles adding to the supply of money available for more loans from all over the country. This tends to standardize the requirements, terms, rates, and other factors that make up a typical real estate loan.

Our discussion of the secondary mortgage market focuses on the three agencies responsible for the majority of its activity:

- The Federal National Mortgage Association (Fannie Mae)
- The Government National Mortgage Association (Ginnie Mae)
- The Federal Home Loan Mortgage Corporation (Freddie Mac)

History, purpose, and function of each of these agencies are discussed later in this book and in your Real Estate Finance course. The function of these agencies is to buy and sell mortgages of local banks, lending institutions, and other primary sources of home mortgage money around the country. This has important and profound influences on the real estate market in all areas of the country.

First, by buying up mortgages from local banks, those local banks now have more funds to lend again to other potential homeowners in their area.

Second, by selling mortgages to local banks that have surplus funds, the effects of local real estate cycles can be moderated by providing for stable investments from other regions of the country.

Third, is the standardization of loan criteria. Any new changes implemented by the secondary mortgage markets become requirements around the country for those who want to sell their mortgages in the secondary market. All of these functions serve to make local real estate markets more stable.

GOVERNMENT PROGRAMS

Government programs are assistance mechanisms enacted by legislation and administered by the executive branch of the federal government. In the case of housing, the two main government programs are the **Federal Housing Administration** (FHA) and the **Veteran's Administration** (VA). Both will be covered in depth later in this book and in your *Ohio Real Estate Finance* textbook, but we'll briefly mention them here.

FEDERAL HOUSING ADMINISTRATION (FHA). FHA is administered by the Department of Housing and Urban Development (HUD). FHA provides mortgage insurance to help people who have smaller down payments qualify for home mortgages by insuring lenders against losses on the mortgage loan.

VETERAN'S ADMINISTRATION (VA). VA is also administered by the federal government (but not through HUD). VA guarantees mortgage loans for eligible veterans, even allowing them to buy a home with no down payment, in some cases, by guaranteeing repayment to lenders (up to a certain amount) in the event of default.

IV. SOCIAL FACTORS

Social factors also have an important effect on business cycles and real estate cycles. These factors include demographic changes like population growth, population age, the size of families, and migrations of the population. As populations grow and change, so do housing needs.

When looking at the social trends in an area in relation to their overall impact on real estate, it's important to understand that land values can benefit from an influx of people or be devastated by a large exodus of people.

V. PHYSICAL FACTORS

Physical factors also affect real estate cycles because of land's immobility, indestructibility, uniqueness, and scarcity. Land availability and locational desirability are important factors in real estate cycles just as overall supply and demand of housing is.

VI. INTERACTION OF FACTORS IN THE REAL ESTATE MARKET

Let's recap the major economic, governmental, social, and physical factors that influence real estate. Remember, they're interrelated and interact with each other.

ECONOMIC FACTORS	GOVERNMENTAL FACTORS	SOCIAL FACTORS	PHYSICAL FACTORS
Supply and demand	Taxation	Demographics	Indestructibility
Inflation	Police power	Population growth	Immobility
Cost of money (interest rates)	Land use controls	Population age	Uniqueness
Immobility	Fiscal monetary policy	Size of families	Scarcity
Uniqueness/scarcity	Secondary markets	Migrations of populations	Land availability
Economic base of area	Government programs	Social trends	Location desirability

The single most important factor in determining *supply* in the real estate market is the economic base of an area. If the economic base is expanding, the real estate supply will also expand—at first because people want to sell at higher prices caused by increased demand and later because of new construction in response to increased demand and in anticipation of continued economic expansion. If the economic base is shrinking, the real estate supply will also shrink. At first, there's an oversupply as people sell to move to new jobs or areas, but overall the supply will stay low because new construction will cease, and more people will be forced to keep their property rather than sell at lower values due to falling demand.

Although demand is also greatly affected by the economic base of an area, **the single most important factor in determining *demand* in the real estate market is interest rates (cost of money)**. Low interest rates increase demand for property; high interest rates decrease demand. Interest rates outweigh the economic base factor in determining real estate demand because even when an economic base isn't growing, real estate activity can be spurred by a drop in interest rates.

All of the following can be found on the Division's Web site. **Bring a copy of each to the next class:**

1. Agency Disclosure Statement
2. Residential Property Disclosure Form
3. Consumer Guide to Agency Relationships
4. Waiver of Duties Form

Chapter 4 Summary

1. Economic factors that influence real estate markets include business cycles, real estate cycles, supply and demand, inflation, cost of money (interest rates), immobility, uniqueness, and scarcity of a piece of land, and economic base of an area. Real estate cycles are general swings of increasing or decreasing activity and property values. Real estate cycles depend on business cycles.

2. The law of supply and demand says that for all products, goods, and services when supply exceeds demand, prices will fall, and when demand exceeds supply, prices will rise. There's an inherent difficulty in adjusting supply and demand in the real estate market because an immobile, unique, and scarce product is being sold instead of a commodity and because there's a lag time before the construction industry can respond to a shortage or oversupply of houses in an area. This creates buyers' markets and sellers' markets.

3. Inflation is an increase in cost of goods or services; it is also called cost inflation because manufacturers pass along their increased costs. Inflation is also too much money chasing too few goods; it is also called demand inflation because too many people with money want to buy the same thing. Cost of money is the interest rate that people or businesses must pay to use another's money for their own purposes. Inflation can push interest rates higher or lower. Interest rates are a primary factor in determining demand for real estate.

4. The economic base of an area is the main business or industry a community uses to support itself. A healthy economic base is critical to maintain home values. This is primarily due to the immobility of real estate (and customers). Houses can't be moved to the buyers' locations and many times customers can't move their jobs to another city where a specific house is located. The economic base of an area is a primary factor in determining the supply of real estate.

5. Governmental factors that influence real estate markets on state and local levels include revenue generating laws (taxation and specific tax policies) and right to regulate laws (police power). Police power includes land use controls (zoning and building codes), environmental protection laws, eminent domain, and escheat. Federal government factors that influence real estate include fiscal policy (taxation), monetary policy (the Fed influencing interest rates), secondary mortgage markets (Fannie Mae, Ginnie Mae, and Freddie Mac, buying and selling mortgages), and government programs (FHA-insured loans and VA-guaranteed loans). The Fed uses reserve requirements, federal discount rates, open market operations, and moral suasion to influence interest rates.

6. Social factors that influence real estate include demographics, population growth, population age, the size of families, and migrations of the population. Land values can benefit from an influx of people (for jobs or other reasons) or be devastated by a large exodus of people. Physical factors that influence real estate markets include immobility (can't be moved), indestructibility (can't be destroyed), uniqueness (can't be duplicated), and scarcity (can't be created).

CHAPTER 4 QUIZ

1. ***The economic base of an area:***
   - a. Does not influence the local housing market
   - b. Is responsible for government money coming in to support an area
   - c. Gives stability to a region and supports real estate values
   - d. Creates buyer's markets but not seller's markets

2. ***The cost of money:***
   - a. Greatly influences a homebuyer's decision
   - b. Is not the same as interest rates
   - c. Does not affect demand for real estate
   - d. Has no influence on a homebuyer's decision

3. ***Immobility in the real estate market can be defined as:***
   - a. The inability to move a piece of real estate
   - b. The inability of customers to readily move from city to city
   - c. Both a and b
   - d. a but not b

4. *The law of supply and demand says that:*

a. For all products, goods, and services when demand exceeds supply, prices will fall and when supply exceeds demand, prices will rise
b. Real estate does not respond to the forces of supply and demand at all
c. There will always be a shortage of houses due to population growth
d. For all products, goods, and services when supply exceeds demand, prices will fall and when demand exceeds supply, prices will rise

5. *The Federal Reserve Board influences interest rates by all of the following* except:

a. Open market operations
b. Federal discount rates
c. Reserve requirements
d. Buying notes

6. *All of the following are benefits of the secondary mortgage market* except:

a. Moderates real estate cycles by providing local banks and others with stable investments from other regions of the country
b. Primary mortgage lenders can charge higher interest rates
c. Banks have funds they can lend again to other potential homebuyers
d. Standardization of loan criteria

7. *Governments (local, state, or federal) can control or restrict private land use, and have an influence on real estate markets through which of the following?*

a. Zoning restrictions and building codes
b. Guaranteeing loans to veterans
c. Adverse possession
d. Underwriting loans

5 OVERVIEW OF REAL ESTATE LAW

CHAPTER OVERVIEW

Now that you have an understanding of the real estate profession, licensing procedure, and the real estate market, we'll discuss the law as it affects real estate. *Five general areas of real estate law are:* 1. license law, 2. agency law, 3. contract law, 4. general property law, and 5. fair housing law. These are vital to the real estate business (and the licensing exam). As a licensee, you're responsible for knowing these laws, even though you can't offer anyone legal advice. Our focus in this chapter will be general property law.

KEY TERMS

Appurtenance
A right that goes with ownership of real property.

Easement
A right to use another person's real property for a particular purpose.

Encumbrance
A non-possessory interest that burdens a property owner's title.

Fixture
Man-made attachment. A major fixture (building) is called an **improvement**.

Freehold Estate
A possessory interest of uncertain (and often unlimited) duration. ownership

Leasehold Estate
An interest that gives the holder a temporary right to possession. lease

License
A revocable, non-assignable permission to enter another's land for a particular purpose.

Lien
A financial claim against real property that allows foreclosure if debt is not paid. encumbrance

Lis Pendens
A recorded notice of a pending lawsuit that may affect title to land.

Possessory Interest
Entitles holder to possession of property, now or in the future.

Restrictive Covenant
Restriction on real property use, imposed by a former owner.

Trade Fixture
Equipment installed by a tenant for business, and which can be removed before the lease ends.

I. GENERAL PROPERTY LAW

General property law includes several important topics including the nature of real property, real property interests, and land use restrictions. The **nature of real property** section looks at real property rights that are transferred with ownership and distinctions between real and personal property. The **real property interests** section discusses different ways property can be possessed or owned. Finally, the **land use restrictions** section details private and public restrictions that can be placed on land usage. These concepts form the basis for knowledge and understanding needed in real estate every day, even beyond the test.

II. THE NATURE OF REAL PROPERTY

The rights of ownership that go with real property and the distinction between real property and personal property are explained here. These real property rights and laws are important because they determine what is being sold.

REAL PROPERTY RIGHTS

Real property rights are defined in terms of a **bundle of rights,** which are conferred by ownership. These rights are the **right of use**, the **right of enjoyment,** and the **right of disposal**. If one secures the bundle of rights, he or she is the owner of real property. There are also air rights, water rights, mineral rights, etc., which a person owns and can sell separately.

RIGHT OF USE. The **right of use gives** the owner the right to make the land productive. The owner may make use of the land in any way seen fit, as long as that use is legal and does not interfere with the rights of others.

RIGHT OF ENJOYMENT. The **right of enjoyment** gives the owner freedom to use the land without undue interference from the outside. This includes the responsibility to ensure that neighbors' enjoyment of their land is not adversely affected.

RIGHT OF DISPOSAL. The **right of disposal allows** the owner to transfer all or some of the above rights to others. The landowner normally has the right to sell, lease, give away, divide, and retain part of the land, or dispose of it.

Certain activities interfere with a property owner's bundle of rights like **trespassing**, **encroachment,** and **nuisance**.

TRESPASS. **Trespass** is a *physical invasion of land by another person who has no lawful right to enter it*. Trespass interferes with the owner's possessory interest in the land, diminishing the owner's right of use and right of enjoyment, since during the trespass, the owner of the land has less than full possession of the land.

ENCROACHMENT. **Encroachment** is a *legal synonym for trespass*, but the term refers to *objects*, such as buildings; whereas, *trespass refers to people*. Thus, a neighbor's garage built over your property line encroaches on your land. Legal steps can be taken to force a landowner to remove the encroachment by tearing it down or forcing him or her to buy the land on which it sits. Furthermore, a tree growing over a property line may be trimmed to the line with full support of the law.

NUISANCE. **Nuisance** interferes with the quiet enjoyment of land from outside causes like loud noises, unsightliness, and obnoxious odors; thus, it doesn't involve possessory rights. To be actionable in court, a nuisance must be a continuing unreasonable use of land by the offending landowner, but a court usually won't support an action if a landowner moved there with knowledge of the nuisance.

REAL PROPERTY AND PERSONAL PROPERTY

The law classifies all property as either **real property** or **personal property**. By definition, **real property** is *land and all rights and things attached to it*; **personal property** is *any property that is moveable and not fixed to land*. The distinction becomes important when land ownership or possession is transferred. Unless otherwise agreed, all real property is included in the transfer, but personal property that happens to be on the land is not included. There can be disagreements about whether something is real property or personal property.

THE LAND ITSELF

People tend to think of the land itself when they hear the term "real property." However, land is legally considered to include the surface of the earth, the subsurface to the center of the earth, and the air above the land within reasonable limits to permit commercial air travel. When describing land in a legal description, only the surface is detailed. The law implies that subsurface and air rights are included as part of the land even though they're usually not written. The transfer of land also includes things that are attached to the land, whether natural or man-made, (**attachments**), and rights that go along with ownership of the land (**appurtenances**).

ATTACHMENTS

Two categories of attachments are **natural** and **man-made**.

NATURAL ATTACHMENTS. **Natural attachments** are plants growing on the land, whether naturally occurring or planted. They're considered part of real property while growing and personal property when removed.

> **EXAMPLE** A rose bush growing on the land is part of the real property. Once the flowers are picked, however, they become personal property.

The same rule applies to crops. Until they have been harvested, the crops are part of the real property. Thus, unharvested crops are treated as part of the real property in a sale of land. The buyer takes titles to the grains, fruits, or vegetables unless it's specifically agreed that the crops are to be excluded from the sale.

There's also a special rule for crops planted by tenant farmers. The **doctrine of emblements** allows a tenant farmer to re-enter land to harvest the first crop that matures after the tenancy ends.

MAN-MADE ATTACHMENTS. **Man-made attachments** are called **fixtures**. **Fixtures** are *personal property items that have been attached to, or closely associated with, real property*. They legally become part of the real property. Major fixtures that increase land value (e.g., buildings) are called **improvements**.

Annexation is the legal term for attaching personal property to real property. (**Severance** is the term for detaching a fixture and reverting it back to personal property.) Since fixtures and improvements are part of the land, they don't need to be stated in purchase contracts. They're included by implication in the description of real estate.

Trouble can arise, however, when one runs into items that could be classified as real or personal property depending on whom you ask. Real estate agents deal with this all the time. Is a built-in dishwasher a fixture? Is a shed an improvement? Is a chandelier personal property? Is a satellite dish a fixture? To avoid trouble, a real estate agent should write questionable items in the purchase offer or contract to make sure everyone knows what is and isn't part of the sale.

INTENTION AND PURPOSE. The Ohio Supreme Court ruled that the most important considerations in deciding whether an item is a fixture are the *intent* of the annexer and *purpose* of the annexation. The annexer is the owner of the personal property that was brought onto real property. Did he or she intend for it to become part of the real property, or to remain as personal property? Did he or she buy the item to improve the real property or simply for personal use?

In answering these questions, the court will look for objective evidence of the annexer's intent. It's not enough to claim that you always intended to remove the item. Other considerations, such as the nature of the item and manner of annexation, are viewed as objective evidence of intent. For example, setting a statue in concrete shows intent to make it a permanent feature; just setting one out on the lawn doesn't.

MANNER OF ANNEXATION. Physical attachment of an item is taken into account when the court decides if something is a fixture, but it's not decisive. The court still looks at other factors such as intent and purpose.

Actual annexation means a fixture is physically attached to real property. **Constructive annexation** occurs when personal property is associated with real property in such a way that the law treats it as a fixture because it is important to the use of the real property, even though it's not attached to the real property. A good example is the key to the house. Other things specially designed for the property (e.g., wall-to-wall carpet) are also likely to be treated as fixtures. Even items that have been temporarily removed from the real property for servicing (e.g., built-in dishwasher at the repair shop on the day of closing) can still be fixtures.

Relationship of the Parties

Another factor courts often take into consideration in fixture disputes is the relationship of the parties. Between a seller and a buyer of real property, the rules for determining whether an item is a fixture are usually interpreted in favor of the buyer.

Between a landlord and a tenant, however, the rules tend to be interpreted in favor of the tenant. A tenant who installs a chandelier (or some other ornamental item) usually has the right to remove it at the end of the lease. These rules tie to considering the annexer's intentions; the law presumes a homeowner intends to improve real property, but a tenant installs things only for personal use.

That doesn't mean a tenant is invariably allowed to remove everything he or she installed. If a tenant built a deck onto the back of a rented house, it would almost certainly be considered a fixture and part of the landlord's real property. As usual, the court would look at the nature of the item, the manner of annexation, how difficult it would be to remove, and so forth.

WRITTEN AGREEMENT. Regardless of the previously discussed considerations, if there's a written agreement between the parties stating how an item is to be treated, a court will enforce the agreement. So, when a seller wants to remove items that may be considered fixtures, he or she should inform a buyer by including a statement in the purchase contract naming items that are excluded from the sale. A buyer should also make sure the purchase contract lists personal property a seller is including in the sale. It's a good idea for the buyer to get a **bill of sale,** which transfers title to personal property (like a deed transfers title to real property).

In the practice of real estate, two problems face the real estate agent:

1. Fixtures the seller wishes to remove
2. Personal property items the buyer wishes to include in the sale

In the first case, an agent can suggest to the seller that the item(s) be removed or replaced prior to showing. This makes it impossible for a buyer to expect a particular item to be included in the sale and resolves all issues regarding whether the buyer saw the item and assumed it would transfer. This situation can even occur when "red tagging" items as to what is and is not included in the sale. The tag may be accidentally removed, or the buyer may misunderstand the meaning of the tag and assume that he or she is getting an item the seller never intended to be sold as part of the real property transaction.

In the second case, regarding personal property, resolve the issue by including a list of the items in the offer to purchase. This way, there are no assumptions regarding whether something will or will not be included in the sale. In either case, recommend that everything be put in writing, and you can be of genuine assistance to your client or customer should a dispute arise.

TRADE FIXTURES. **Trade fixtures** are any equipment or personal property a tenant installs for *business purposes*. They have their own rules. A tenant is allowed to remove trade fixtures before a lease ends (unless a written document forbids it). Thus, a tenant who opens a pizza shop can remove the ovens, even though they're attached to the floor, but the tenant must repair any damage caused by the removal.

Appurtenances

Appurtenances are rights that go with real property. When property is sold, appurtenant rights are usually sold with it. They can, however, be sold separately and may be limited by past transactions. You need to know what items are considered part of the real property, and you need to understand what rights are transferred along with it. An owner has rights to the surface of the land within the property's boundaries, plus everything under or above the surface. This includes certain air, water, mineral, and support rights.

AIR RIGHTS. A property owner's rights go to the upper limits of the sky. Because of air travel, though, Congress gave the federal government control over U.S. airspace. Property owners still have the right to use the lower reaches over their land, but they may not interfere with air traffic. Owners also have the right not to be harmed by use of the airspace above their property. The classic example is when an airport is built near a chicken farm, and the noise of the airplanes flying overhead causes the chickens to stop laying eggs. The farmer may be able to recover damages.

A property owner may also sell air rights over a property separate from the land. In cities where downtown land is at a premium, shopping centers or offices may be built spanning roadways or railways. A more common example is a condominium sale. Someone who buys a unit in a high-rise building purchases not just the physical condominium but also the airspace in which the unit is situated.

WATER RIGHTS. There are two main types of water rights that can be acquired: **riparian/littoral rights** and **appropriative rights**. Riparian/littoral rights are gained by land ownership; appropriative rights are obtained by government permit.

Riparian Rights and Littoral Rights. **Riparian rights** are water rights of a landowner whose land adjoins a river. **Littoral rights** are water rights of a landowner whose land adjoins a lake. The owner of riparian or littoral land has the right to make reasonable use of the water. (Keep in mind this isn't the same as owning the water.) All riparian or littoral landowners share the right to use the water for recreational purposes. They also have the right to take water for domestic uses (e.g., drinking or washing) and irrigation rights for use on their riparian or littoral land.

Appropriative Rights. **Appropriative rights** are water rights granted by government permit independent of land ownership. Government permits allow the holder to take water from a particular body of water for a specified use such as crop irrigation. Appropriated water doesn't have to be used on riparian or littoral land, but riparian and littoral landowner rights are considered when issuing appropriation permits. Appropriative rights usually can't interfere with riparian or littoral rights.

MINERAL RIGHTS. A landowner owns all the solid minerals in or under his or her land. Minerals are considered real property until they are extracted from the earth. A landowner may sell or lease mineral rights separate from the surface land, and most do since they don't have the necessary skill or equipment to mine or drill.

Oil and gas are governed by the **rule of capture**. The **rule of capture** says *whoever drills a well on his or her land owns all the oil or gas the well produces even though it may have migrated from under a neighbor's land*. A landowner can drain oil or gas from beneath his or her own land *and* from neighboring land because oil and gas flow toward the point of lowest pressure where the reservoir was pierced by the well. The rule of capture is designed to stimulate oil and gas production, since the only way to stop oil or gas from going to a neighbor's well is by drilling your own well.

SUPPORTING RIGHTS. A piece of land is supported by the land that surrounds it. A landowner has a right to the natural support provided by land beside and beneath it. **Lateral support** is support from adjacent land. A neighbor's excavations may make your land shift and settle. In some cases, the neighbor can be held liable for resulting damage if there was negligence. **Subjacent support** is support from the underlying earth. Generally, the mining party is liable for surface damage caused by underground mining even if excavations were performed carefully.

ACCESSION. When something is added to a parcel of real property by **annexation** or the **forces of nature**, the owner acquires title to the addition by **accession**.

ANNEXATION. **Annexation** changes personal property into real property with the real property owner also owning the annexed property. When a person builds a home, installs a pool, or plants a tree, personal property is annexed to real property.

FORCES OF NATURE. The land itself can move or change shape through the forces of nature, which can result in a transfer of title. **Erosion** is a gradual wearing away of land by wind, rain, or other natural forces. If eroded soil moves over property lines, X loses title to the soil, and Y gets title to it. **Accretion** is a gradual process of waterborne silt being deposited in a river or lakebed or on the shore. These deposits are called *alluvion* or *alluvium*. Riparian or littoral property is increased this way, and the landowner acquires title to the silt. **Avulsion** means the land is torn away by flowing water. Avulsion doesn't transfer title if the severed land is identified and reclaimed by the original owner. **Reliction** means water recedes exposing more of the bed. In Ohio, reliction doesn't add to land since owners already have title to the bed to the water's midpoint.

III. REAL PROPERTY INTERESTS

A person with a property right or a claim against property is said to have an *interest* in the property. An interest may be an ownership right (e.g., a life estate), right to use the land (e.g., an easement), or a financial claim against the title (e.g., a mortgage). This section explains various types of interests, how they're created and terminated, and how they affect property. We'll also look at forms of ownership.

POSSESSORY INTERESTS: ESTATES

An **estate** is a possessory interest in real property. A **possessory interest** entitles the holder to possession of the property now or in the future. A right to possession now is called a **present interest**. A right to future possession is called a **future interest**. In addition to being classified as to time of enjoyment (present or future), interests are also classified as a **freehold** or a **leasehold estate**.

FREEHOLD ESTATES. A freehold estate is a *possessory interest* of uncertain duration; it may end, but no one knows when. Freehold estates can be fee simple estates or life estates.

FEE SIMPLE ESTATES. A **fee simple absolute** estate is the fullest freehold estate interest that exists in real property. A person referred to as the "owner" of land usually holds a fee simple absolute interest. Since the fee simple estate is absolute, this implies there are no conditions on title. It's inheritable, transferable, and perpetual. The owner of a fee simple absolute has the right to possess the property for an unlimited period of time and may sell it, transfer all or part of it, or pass it to heirs.

When a fee simple absolute owner deeds an interest in property to someone else, it's presumed that the entire estate is transferred, unless the deed language specifies otherwise. So if A owns land in fee simple absolute and deeds it "to B," without any limiting language, then B owns the land in fee simple absolute.

FEE SIMPLE DEFEASIBLE. A **fee simple defeasible**, also called **conditional, determinable,** or **defeasible fee**, means a grantor puts a condition or requirement in the deed and limits the title. Since the fee simple estate is defeasible, this means the fee estate interest in real property can be defeated or undone if certain events occur or conditions aren't met. For example, deed language may transfer land "to B, as long as the land is used as a park." If B uses the land for another purpose, title may revert to A (or A's heirs).

Note that people commonly refer to "fee simple title," without specifying which kind of fee simple. If this is the case, they always mean fee simple absolute.

LIFE ESTATES. A **life estate** is a freehold estate that *lasts only as long as a specified person lives;* thus, a life estate cannot be willed. For example, if A owns property in fee simple, he or she could deed it "to B for life." B then has the right to occupy and use the property for life. But when B dies, the life estate ends. Life estates are created for a variety of reasons: to simplify the division of property in a will or so property won't have to be probated after death.

The holder of a life estate is called a **life tenant**. When A grants property "to B for life," the life estate's duration is measured by the lifetime of the life tenant—B. A life estate may also be based on another person's life. For example, a grantor could deed property "to B for the life of C." B's life estate would end when C died. This is called a life estate **pur autre vie** (for another's life). C is called the **measuring life**.

A life tenant owns an interest in land that can be sold, mortgaged, or leased. But a person can only transfer the interest that he or she owns. Someone who buys a life tenant's interest has only a life estate; the buyer's interest ends when the measuring life dies. Also, a mortgage signed by a life tenant becomes an invalid lien when the life estate ends, and a lease signed by a life tenant ends when the life estate ends.

FUTURE INTERESTS. As with defeasible fee estates, life estates also create a future interest. The life tenant holds a present possessory interest, and the one who will possess the land upon death of the measuring life holds a future possessory interest. This future interest is either **reversionary** or **remainder** depending on who holds the future interest.

If the grantor deeds the property "to B for life," title reverts to the grantor (*or the grantor's heirs*) upon death of the life tenant. The grantor's interest is always called **reversionary,** even if it passes to heirs. If the grantor deeds the property "to B for life, then to C," C has a **remainder** interest and is known as the **remainderman.** When a life estate ends, the remainderman (*or heirs*) takes title in fee simple.

A life tenant may not commit **waste** to the property, which means using the property in a way that damages it or reduces its market value. Thus, a life tenant has restricted rights of use that are transferred with the life estate.

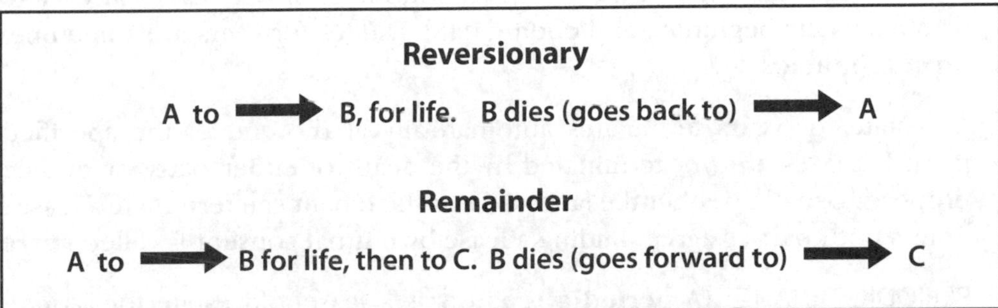

DOWER. **Dower** is a special real property interest the law gives as a statutory life estate to a spouse when a married person owns real property in Ohio. Dower rights attach with marriage for property brought into the marriage or when property is acquired during the marriage. As long as the married person owns the property or remains alive, the spouse's dower rights are **inchoate** (pronounced in-KOE-it), meaning contingent, inactive, or incomplete. These inchoate rights aren't possessory; they are only potentially possessory. Dower rights are terminated by divorce and can't be willed to heirs since dower is a life estate interest.

Dower rights become **choate** (active or complete) when the owner spouse sells the property without benefit of dower release, and/or the owner spouse dies before the other spouse. If and when these events happen, the surviving spouse acquires a life estate amounting to an undivided one-third interest in any property transferred.

Dower must be released in almost all real estate transactions involving married sellers. Real estate agents should always have spouses sign listing agreements because by signing a listing, they agree to provide marketable title to a buyer. *There's a serious issue of marketable title if there's no dower release.* Even if there's a pre-nuptial agreement, title companies often still require a spouse to release dower because there's always a chance the agreement could be declared void in the future.

LEASEHOLD ESTATES

A **leasehold estate** is an interest that gives the holder a temporary right to possession of the estate without title. A leasehold estate is more limited than a freehold estate. The holder of a leasehold estate is called the **lessee** or **tenant**. A tenant has the right to exclusive possession of the property but only for a limited time. An owner who leases property to a tenant is called the **lessor** or **landlord**.

Possession reverts to the landlord when the lease ends. Three types of leasehold estates are:

1. Estate for years
2. Periodic tenancy
3. Tenancy at will

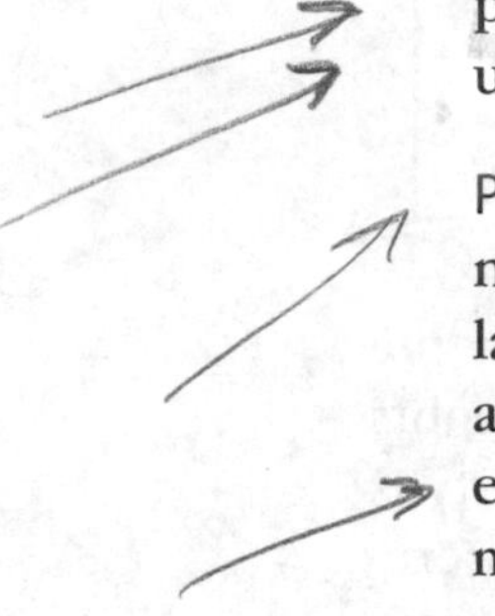

ESTATE FOR YEARS. An **estate for years** is any leasehold estate for a fixed time period. In spite of the name, the term doesn't have to be a period of years. The tenancy may last ten days, ten months, or ten years—any fixed period with a specific beginning and ending date. Estates for years are sometimes called **term tenancies**.

An estate for years terminates automatically at the end of the specified rental period. Leases are *not* terminated by the death of either party or by sale of the property. Usually, neither the landlord nor the tenant can terminate a lease sooner, unless both parties agree. Ending a lease by mutual consent is called **surrender**.

PERIODIC TENANCY. A **periodic tenancy** is a leasehold estate for a time period not limited to a specific term. It continues from period to period, until the landlord or tenant gives the other party notice of termination. The period may be any length of time agreed to, with the tenancy automatically renewing itself at the end of each period until one party terminates it. Month-to-month tenancies are most common.

TENANCY AT WILL. A **tenancy at will** is a leasehold estate with no specified termination date and with no regular rental period. Sometimes no rent is paid (e.g., apartment manager), or the rent owed has no reference to periods of time (e.g., "35% of gross profits"). Either party can end it at any time. A tenancy at will can arise after an estate for years ends if a lease expires and the tenant stays on with the landlord's permission, without signing a new lease. But if the tenant pays the landlord rent at regular intervals, that creates a periodic tenancy instead of a tenancy at will.

A tenancy at will can't be assigned and ends on the death of landlord or tenant (unlike the other two lease types, which can be assigned and don't end upon death.) Tenancy at will is not recognized in Ohio (but may appear on the state exam).

TENANCY AT SUFFERANCE. **Tenancy at sufferance** describes possession of property by a tenant who came into possession of the property under a valid lease, but stays on after the lease expires without the landlord's permission. A tenancy at sufferance isn't a leasehold estate. A tenant at sufferance isn't much different from a trespasser, except that the tenant at sufferance originally had a right to be there. A landlord isn't required to give a tenant at sufferance notice of termination, but the landlord can't use force to regain possession of the property.

EVICTION. The legal eviction process must be used to remove a residential tenant. The eviction process is comprised of three steps: **notice to vacate**, **forcible entry and detainer action**, and **writ of execution**.

Notice to Vacate. A **notice to vacate** is a notice to a tenant, demanding that he or she vacate the leased property. The notice must be served on the tenant at least **three days** before a lawsuit for eviction is filed. For residential tenants, the notice must read:

> "You are being asked to leave the premises. If you do not leave, an eviction action may be initiated against you. If you are in doubt regarding your legal rights and obligations as a tenant, it is recommended that you seek legal assistance."

For a residential eviction based on breach of an obligation affecting health and safety, the landlord must send a notice stating that the tenancy will terminate on a particular date—at least **30 days** after the notice is delivered to the tenant—unless the tenant takes care of the problem by the specified date. If the tenant doesn't comply by that date, the landlord may serve a three-day notice to vacate. Remember: good tenants (on a month-to-month tenancy) get 30-days' notice; bad tenants (not paying rent) get 3-days' notice.

Forcible Entry and Detainer. A **forcible entry and detainer** action is a lawsuit filed by a landlord to evict a defaulting tenant and regain possession of property. The landlord may begin legal proceedings to evict the tenant when a tenant doesn't move out within **three days** (or other time specified in the notice) after receiving a notice to vacate.

Writ of Execution. A **writ of execution** is a court order directing a public officer (often the sheriff or marshal) to seize and/or sell property to regain possession for the owner and/or satisfy a debt. If the court finds that the landlord is entitled to possession of the property, a writ of execution is issued to the sheriff. If the tenant doesn't move out within **ten days**, the sheriff can forcibly remove the tenant and his or her belongings from the property. If the tenant files an appeal, the court will issue a stay of execution directing the sheriff to wait for further orders from the court.

NON-POSSESSORY INTERESTS: ENCUMBRANCES

Non-possessory interests are also called **encumbrances,** since they encumber (burden) a real property owner's title. Someone who holds a non-possessory interest has a claim or right concerning the real property but does not have the right to possess the property. Two types of non-possessory interests detailed in this section are **easements** and **liens**. (Restrictive covenants also create non-possessory interests and are discussed later in this chapter under land use restrictions.)

EASEMENTS

An **easement** is a right to use another person's real property for a particular purpose. That right can be limited in a number of ways. An easement is classified as either an **appurtenant easement** or an **easement in gross**.

APPURTENANT EASEMENTS. An **appurtenant easement** *burdens one piece of land*, the servient tenement, for the benefit of another piece of land, the dominant tenement. As we learned, appurtenances are rights that go with real property (e.g., air rights), so an appurtenant easement is a right that goes with land ownership. If the title is transferred, the easement is also transferred. The new landowner owns the easement or takes title subject to the burden of the easement. Thus, an appurtenant easement runs with the land meaning it benefits and burdens the other piece of land.

EASEMENTS IN GROSS. An **easement in gross** *benefits a person*, dominant tenant, not a piece of land. There's a person benefiting from the easement but *no* land benefits from the easement. (Of course, there's still a piece of land burdened by the easement, servient tenement, and an owner burdened by the easement.) An easement in gross that belongs to a person can't be assigned and ends if the easement holder dies. Easements in gross that belong to companies can be assigned. For example, a utility company has easements so its employees may enter someone's land to install lines. If Big Power Company buys Tiny Power Company, it also buys the company's easements in gross.

CREATION OF EASEMENTS. Easements can be created in two different ways: ***voluntarily or involuntarily***. Easements created by agreement of the parties involved must be in writing to be valid. A document granting an easement should be drawn up and signed just like a deed and should be recorded to ensure that anyone who buys the land has notice of the easement. If the buyer doesn't have notice, the easement probably won't run with the land. Other ways to create easements are:

1. **Easement by Express Reservation/Easement by Express Grant.** Both of these easements are created by a deed or other document. An **easement by express reservation** means a landowner divides land and includes deed language, so the seller retains an easement across his or her former land. An **easement by express grant** can also be part of the deed transfer or be in a separate document conveying only the easement. Easements by express grant may benefit either party.
2. **Easement by Implication.** An **easement by implication** is created by law when land is divided, and there's a long-standing apparent use that's reasonably necessary for the enjoyment of the land. This is also called an **implied easement**. Generally, easement by implication arises when a tract of land was originally held by one owner, then divided into two or more parcels. The original owner would keep an **ingress** or **egress**—a means into or a way to exit a piece of land.
3. **Easement by Necessity.** This is a special easement that arises if a piece of land would be completely useless without the easement—even if there's no long-standing apparent use. An example is a landlocked piece of land with no access, in which case a court would declare an easement by necessity. A claimant must prove that an easement is strictly necessary (not just reasonably necessary) to use the land; if there's another way to your land, you can't get an easement by necessity.
4. **Easement by Prescription.** An **easement by prescription** is created by open and notorious, hostile and adverse use of another person's land for 21 years. **Open and notorious** use of the land means the use must be obvious and unconcealed, so if the landowner is kept reasonably well informed about the property, he or she would be aware of the use. **Hostile**

and adverse means use without the owner's permission and against his or her interests. If the owner gives permission, there's no easement by prescription. **Continuous use for 21 years** is required in Ohio. It doesn't have to be constant use, just regular use, normal for that type of property. **Tacking** allows two or more users in succession to add together their periods of use to equal the required 21 years.

TERMINATION OF EASEMENTS. An easement can be terminated several ways:

1. **Release:** is a document in which a legal right is given up. It can release an easement holder's interest in the property if he or she is willing to give up or be paid for the easement. Easement releases should always be recorded.
2. **Merger:** uniting two or more separate properties by transferring ownership of all to one person. If one person owns the property benefiting from the easement *and* the property burdened by the easement, the easement is terminated by merger. You can't have an easement on your own property. If the land is later divided again, the easement no longer exists and must be recreated if desired.
3. **Abandonment:** the failure to occupy and use property, which may result in a loss of rights. An easement ceases to exist if the owner abandons it. Non-use alone, however, isn't enough for abandonment. There must be an act or statement that clearly expresses the owner's intention to abandon the easement.
4. **Prescription:** loss of easement by **prescription** occurs after 21 years of non-use. If an easement owner doesn't use it for 21 years, it can be lost by prescription.
5. **Destruction:** the involuntary destruction of the building (e.g., by fire) ends the allowed easement by **destruction**. If the building is rebuilt, the easement doesn't automatically revive.
6. **Failure of Purpose:** an easement terminates when the purpose for which it was created no longer exists. So, an electric company's easement for power lines across a farmer's property ends from **failure of purpose** if the company removes the lines.

Easements versus Licenses

A **license** is a revocable, non-assignable permission to enter another's land for a particular purpose. A license is similar to an easement because it grants permission to use another's property. Unlike an easement, a license does *not* create an interest in property and isn't considered an encumbrance.

Some other differences are: easements are usually for an indefinite period of time, while licenses are often temporary; easements are created by written agreement or action of law, but licenses may be created by oral contract; easements run with the land, but licenses don't have to, and easements can't be revoked; whereas, licenses may be revoked at any time except where the licensee makes a substantial financial commitment in reliance on the license. Also, like a personal easement in gross, a license can't be assigned and becomes invalid if the licensee dies.

Easements versus Encroachments

An encroachment is a physical object intruding onto a neighbor's property (e.g., a shed that extends 2 feet over a property line). Although most encroachments are unintentional, they're a form of trespassing in the eyes of the law. If a neighbor sues, the court can order removal of the encroachment or payment of damages to the neighbor by the encroacher.

An encroachment isn't an encumbrance because it's not a right or interest that's held. The encroacher could get an easement from the neighbor, allowing the encroachment, or it could become an easement by prescription if ignored for 21 years.

LIENS (FINANCIAL ENCUMBRANCES)

A **lien** is a financial interest in property. It's security for a debt, giving the creditor (**lien holder**) the right to foreclose on the debtor's property if the debt isn't paid. In foreclosure, the property is sold and the lien holder collects the amount of the debt from the proceeds of the foreclosure sale.

Liens against property don't prevent its transfer, but the liens still exist. The buyer takes the property **subject to** the liens. This means that the buyer takes the property with the liens but without being personally liable. The buyer must keep paying the liens to keep the property but only loses his or her equity in the event of default. The creditor can't go after the new owner personally for these debts because the new owner did not assume the debts. In most real estate transactions, the seller must clear the title of liens at closing by paying off the debts.

CLASSIFICATION OF LIENS

	Voluntary	Involuntary	General	Specific
Property Tax Lien		X		X
Special Assessment		X		X
Mortgage	X			X
Vendor's Lien		X		X
Mechanic's Lien		X		X
Commercial Broker Lien		X		X
IRS Lien		X	X	
Judgment Lien		X	X	

Voluntary Liens

Voluntary liens are placed against property with consent of the owner. The most common form is a mortgage or, similarly, a home equity line of credit.

MORTGAGES. **Mortgages** are written instruments that use real property to secure payment of a debt. Without a debt, there can be no mortgage. The debt is created by a separate instrument called a **note** or **promissory note**. A **note** is a written, legally binding promise to repay a debt. The note creates the debt, and the mortgage secures payment. A mortgage is a powerful incentive for an owner to pay since it represents a potential transfer of title to the mortgagee in case of **default**. **Default** is the failure to fulfill an obligation, duty, or promise as when a borrower fails to make payments. The mortgage instrument itself defines what constitutes default. The most common reason for default is not making payments by the due date, but other factors (e.g., failing to pay property taxes) may also result in default.

The lender is a *secured creditor*. A **secured creditor** is a creditor with a lien on specific property, in this case holding the mortgage as security. If default occurs, the lender can pursue **judicial foreclosure** requiring a court-ordered **sheriff's sale** of the property to repay the debt. If the foreclosure sale doesn't yield enough to pay the debt, a **deficiency judgment** could result. A **deficiency judgment** is granted by the courts and allows the creditor to go after other property owned by the debtor. It is enforceable and collectable in the same manner as any other judgment at law.

REQUIREMENTS FOR A VALID MORTGAGE. The requirements for a valid mortgage in Ohio include the requirements for contract formation: *meeting of the minds, legal capacity, and legally sufficient consideration*. The mortgage must also be in writing and executed before a notary and two witnesses. Between the owner and mortagee, the mortgage is valid even if unrecorded, but the mortgage only takes effect as to third parties from the time it's recorded. An unrecorded mortgage has no effect as to third parties in Ohio, even if the third party actually knew about it.

TRANSFERS. A mortgage does not prevent the owner from selling a property. The owner of mortgaged real estate may sell it **subject to an existing mortgage**. This means the buyer takes the property along with the existing mortgage but without accepting personal legal responsibility for the debt. The buyer must make the payments to keep the property but only loses his or her equity in the event of default.

The buyer may be able to **assume** the seller's mortgage, making him or her personally liable for the debt. The bank must approve the transfer of responsibility and may prevent this by enforcing an **acceleration clause** or **due-on-sale clause** in the original mortgage. Both of these clauses have the effect of making the entire loan balance due immediately and payable upon transfer of the property.

Involuntary Liens

Involuntary liens, also referred to as **statutory liens**, arise by operation of law without consent of the property owner. These liens are created to protect creditors of the landowner. These liens can be **general** or **specific**. A **general lien** attaches to all property owned in the county by the debtor. A **specific lien** attaches to specific property. *Involuntary liens can be general or specific*.

VENDOR'S LIENS. **Vendor's liens** are liens to secure payment of the purchase price balance of real estate if a buyer doesn't pay the seller in full at closing. In such a case, the seller automatically has a lien against the property for the balance of the purchase price. It's called a vendor's lien since "vendor" is another term for seller. A vendor's lien doesn't attach if the seller accepts a mortgage from the buyer for the amount owed. *A vendors' lien is an involuntary, specific lien.*

MECHANIC'S LIENS. **Mechanic's liens** are liens claimed by someone who performed work on real property and has not been paid. The property serves as security for payment of the labor and material costs. Each person who works on a project or supplies materials for it can obtain a mechanic's lien. If the owner doesn't pay the bills, the holder of a mechanic's lien can force the sale of the property and collect the debt from the proceeds. *A mechanic's lien is an involuntary, specific lien.*

TAX LIENS. **Property tax liens** are liens on real property to secure the payment of real estate taxes used by counties, cities, school districts, etc., to raise revenue. In Ohio, real property tax liens automatically attach to property on January 1 each year. *Real property taxes create an involuntary, specific lien against real estate.*

Special assessments are taxes that pay for public improvements in a neighborhood (e.g., new sewers). Property owners who benefit from an improvement must pay their share of its cost. *Special assessments create involuntary, specific liens.*

Unpaid federal income taxes create tax liens that attach to all real and personal property of a taxpayer. *Income tax liens are involuntary, general liens.*

JUDGMENT LIENS. **Judgment liens** are liens against a person's property through court action. At the end of a lawsuit, if it's determined that one party owes the other money, a judgment is entered. The winner (the **judgment creditor**) may claim a lien against the loser's (the **judgment debtor's**) real property.

To claim a lien, the judgment creditor obtains a **certificate of judgment** from the court issuing the judgment and files it in the county where the judgment debtor owns real property. A judgment lien attaches to all of a debtor's real property in each county where the certificate is recorded. It's valid for five years from the judgment date, renewable for five more years. *Judgment liens are involuntary, general liens.*

COMMERCIAL BROKER LIEN LAW. A broker in a commercial transaction has an automatic lien against a property that is the subject of a contract, for the contracted commission amount, when the contract is fulfilled and the broker files a lien affidavit in the recorder's office in the county where the property is located. Residential real estate brokers must sue in court to enforce a commission payment.

ATTACHMENT LIENS. **Attachment liens** are liens intended to prevent transfer of property pending the outcome of litigation. When a plaintiff files a lawsuit, there's a danger that before a judgment is entered, the defendant may sell all property, making a judgment worthless. To prevent this, at the outset of a lawsuit, a plaintiff can ask the court to issue an **order of attachment**. The order directs the sheriff to seize personal property or to create an involuntary lien against real property. A notice of a pending suit, called a **lis pendens**, may also be recorded. Although this is not a lien, it can serve notice to potential buyers that there's a lawsuit pending, and the outcome may affect title to the subject property.

LIEN PRIORITY. It's not unusual for real estate to have several liens against it at the same time (e.g., mortgage, mechanic's lien, and property tax lien). Sometimes, the total owed for the liens is more than the land will bring at a forced sale, so there's an order of priority for paying off liens after foreclosure. Generally, liens are paid in the order they attached to the land. An important exception is a *property tax lien, which is superior to all other liens* on the property.

HOMESTEAD LAWS. Homestead laws give owner-occupied residences some protection from lien foreclosure by exempting some of a homeowner's equity in real estate. In Ohio, homestead protection is limited to $5,000 ($10,000 for land co-owned by a married couple). The exemption only applies to attachment or judgment liens. A special homestead exemption may also result in a lower assessed property value for tax purposes for homeowners age 65 or older with limited incomes.

Adverse Possession

Adverse possession is acquiring title to someone else's real property by possession of it. Possession and use of property can mature into title. This law is designed to encourage productive use of land with the rationale that it's better to give title to someone who actively uses the land instead of someone who ignores it.

Acquiring title to land by adverse possession requires **open and notorious**, **hostile and adverse**, **exclusive** and **continuous use** of another's land for 21 years. These requirements are similar to those for easement by prescription, but the adverse possessor's use must be exclusive (not so for an easement). An adverse possessor actually acquires title to the property not just an easement. Most property can be adversely possessed except land owned by federal or state governments, municipal streets, and Torrens system registered land (explained later).

IV. LAND USE RESTRICTIONS

Land ownership in Ohio can be absolute, but the absolute right to own land is not equal to the absolute right to use and enjoy it. There can be restrictions placed on the land by the public sector (government) or private sector (individuals or companies).

PUBLIC RESTRICTIONS

Public restrictions take the form of **zoning ordinances**, **building codes**, **subdivision regulations**, and **environmental laws**.

ZONING ORDINANCES

Zoning ordinances are local laws that divide a city or county into zones allowing different land uses in different zones. The kinds of activity in different zones are regulated to protect the public. *Four typical land use categories are* residential, commercial, industrial, and agricultural/rural with numerous subcategories.

Each zone generally sets minimum lot size, building height limit, setback and side yard rules governing building position, and may even limit how much of a lot a building can cover. Zoning laws are also likely to set rules for off-street parking, landscaping, outdoor lighting, and other items local governments feel are necessary.

EXCEPTIONS TO ZONING LAWS. Zoning laws are often controversial because they can have a big impact on the use and value of property. A zoning law is constitutional only if it applies in the same manner to all similarly situated property owners. To prevent undue hardships, zoning laws usually provide for limited exceptions to their rules: **nonconforming uses**, **variances**, and **conditional uses**.

Know

Nonconforming Uses. **Nonconforming uses** occur when land use doesn't conform to current zoning laws but is legally allowed because the land use was established before the new laws were enacted. These landowners are permitted to continue using their land the same way they always have under a nonconforming use. Permission to continue nonconforming uses aren't tied to a particular owner. If the property is sold, the new owner can continue with the nonconforming use.

Variances. **Variances** are granted by the zoning authority to allow some deviation from strict compliance with zoning laws. Variances permit a building or property usage that's not otherwise allowed. **Area variances** bend the rules regarding building size, height limits, setbacks, side yards, and so on. **Use variances** permit property owners to use land in a way that's not allowed in that zone—such as a commercial use in a residential zone. When a zoning board denies or grants a variance, the applicant or neighbors can appeal to common pleas court.

Conditional Uses. **Conditional uses** mean that land usage doesn't comply with the general zoning rules regarding location, but the use is permitted there because it benefits the public good (also called **special exceptions**). Most zoning laws permit uses that are inconsistent with a neighborhood's zoning designation, but are necessary or beneficial to the community, such as schools, hospitals, and churches.

REZONING. **Rezoning** is a revision in zoning law, usually changing from one zone type to another. A rezone is actually a change in zoning law, not just an exception. A landowner in an R-1 zone (single-family homes) might ask to have part of the zone changed to R-3 (multi-family). A rezone usually must be consistent with a community's comprehensive plan, so drastic changes (e.g., from residential to industrial) are rare.

Spot Zoning. **Spot zoning** is an illegal rezoning that favors or restricts one landowner without justification. In this way, the rezoning process can be abused. Isolated zoning changes can be illegal because the law isn't applied the same way to all landowners. If there is a sound reason for a rezone that can be demonstrated, then it is probably constitutional.

ENFORCEMENT OF ZONING LAWS. To enforce zoning laws, a board of county commissioners, township trustees, or city or village officials may establish a **zoning certificate** system. Before constructing or altering any building, a property owner must first obtain a zoning certificate that is only issued if the building plans conform to the zoning laws. Zoning laws may also be enforced through the courts.

BUILDING CODES

Building codes set construction standards requiring builders to use particular methods and materials. A local government usually has many building codes: a fire code, plumbing code, electrical code, etc., In Ohio, minimum building standards are set by state law, but a local government can require more.

Building codes are mainly enforced through a **permit system**. An owner who wants to build or remodel a building must submit plans to a local building department for approval. A building permit is issued only if the plans comply with the codes. The project may be inspected during construction, and an inspector can stop work if problems arise. The finished building is also inspected to check for compliance.

Every structure must comply with building codes, not just new or remodeled ones. There are routine fire and health inspections for most buildings except homes. When new, stricter standards are imposed, property owners may have to bring old buildings "up to code." Fines and injunctions are used to enforce building codes.

SUBDIVISION REGULATIONS

Subdivision regulations are state and local laws that must be followed before land can be subdivided. In this way, local authorities can also control land use. These regulations may govern the size of the lots in a subdivision and the location of streets, sidewalks, and sewer and water lines. These regulations may also require the developer to provide open spaces and recreational areas within the subdivision.

A local government enforces subdivision regulations by requiring subdividers to submit a *plat* for approval. A **plat** is a detailed survey map of the subdivision showing lot boundaries, streets, etc. If the plat is approved, it's recorded with the county recorder. It's illegal to sell subdivision lots before a plat is approved and recorded. Under state law, a local government can require an owner to submit and record a plat if land is subdivided into two or more lots, and if any lot is five acres or less.

PLANNED UNIT DEVELOPMENTS (PUDS). A planned unit development (PUD) is a special type of subdivision that doesn't have to comply with all standard zoning and subdivision regulations. For example, non-residential and residential buildings may be combined in the overall plan. Since PUD developers don't have to follow setback and lot size rules, buildings may also be closer together, creating large open spaces for public use and enjoyment. Detailed plans must be submitted to a planning or zoning commission to get permission to build a PUD.

ENVIRONMENTAL LAWS

Environmental laws are laws enacted by federal and state governments to protect the country's land, air, and water. These laws are designed to keep the land, air, and water clean and to promote conservation of land, air, water, and natural resources.

FEDERAL ENVIRONMENTAL LAWS. National Environmental Policy Act (NEPA) requires federal agencies to prepare an **environmental impact statement** (EIS) for any project that would have a significant effect on the environment. An EIS details a project's impact on energy use, sewage systems, drainage, water facilities, schools, and other environmental, economic, and social areas. NEPA applies to all federal development projects such as dams or highways and to private projects that require a license or permit from a federal agency or a federal loan.

Clean Air Act. The Clean Air Act requires the federal Environmental Protection Agency (EPA) to regulate air pollutant emissions. States are required to prepare a **state implementation plan** (SIP) for meeting national air quality standards of the EPA. States are authorized to stop projects that interfere with clean air objectives.

Clean Water Act. Under the Clean Water Act, the EPA sets national water quality standards. A land use that discharges an unacceptable amount of pollutants into a waterway is prohibited. The Clean Water Act dictates that the adequacy of treatment facilities be considered before allowing new construction and encourages localities to look at new technology and alternatives to wastewater plants.

Residential Lead-Based Paint Hazard Reduction Act. This Act requires sellers to disclose known lead paint hazards for homes built prior to 1978. EPA and HUD regulations issued to implement these disclosures are summarized as follows:

1. Sellers and landlords must disclose any known lead-based paint hazard in homes and must give buyers and tenants any reports available from prior lead tests.
2. Sellers and landlords must give buyers and renters a pamphlet about how to protect families from lead in homes.
3. Home buyers have a 10-day period (or other mutually agreed on time) to conduct a lead paint inspection or risk assessment at their own expense if desired.
4. Sellers, landlords, and real estate agents must include certain language in sales contracts and/or leasing agreements to ensure that disclosure and notification actually take place. This is included in most board real estate contracts.

Sellers, landlords, and real estate agents share responsibility for ensuring compliance with lead paint disclosure rules. According to HUD, real estate agents must comply with the law if the seller or landlord fails to do so, but the agent is not responsible if the owner conceals information or fails to disclose it. As long as the agent has informed the sellers or lessors of their obligations to disclose, the agent can't be held liable. Thus, in addition to the lead paint notification language included in many standard board real estate contracts, many brokers and licensees also use Lead-Based Paint Disclosure forms as a way to prove compliance with the lead paint disclosure requirements of HUD and the EPA since the penalty for failure to disclose lead hazards is a fine of up to $10,000 and up to one year in jail plus treble damages. The written disclosure and pamphlet must be given *prior to* a seller accepting a buyer's written offer to purchase or *prior to* a landlord accepting a tenant's offer to rent. (Remodelers must also give the pamphlet but not the form.)

Sellers aren't required to remove lead paint, correct hazards, or do any testing. The contingency language in a purchase contract should explain what happens if lead paint or lead paint hazards are found. For example, the contract may allow a buyer (tenant) to rescind the contract if unacceptable levels of lead are found, or a seller (landlord) may have the right to remove the lead. Other times, lead hazards are negotiated (as a price reduction) like any other property defect or contingency.

Properties exempt from lead paint disclosure rules include: zero-bedroom units such as lofts or dormitories, leases for less than 100 days, housing exclusively for the elderly, housing for the handicapped (unless children live there), rental units that have been inspected and found to be lead-free, and houses sold by foreclosure.

Disclosure of Information on Lead-Based Paint and/or Lead-Based Paint Hazards

Lead Warning Statement

Every purchaser of any interest in residential real property on which a residential dwelling was built prior to 1978 is notified that such property may present exposure to lead from lead-based paint that may place young children at risk of developing lead poisoning. Lead poisoning in young children may produce permanent neurological damage, including learning disabilities, reduced intelligence quotient, behavioral problems, and impaired memory. Lead poisoning also poses a particular risk to pregnant women. The seller of any interest in residential real property is required to provide the buyer with any information on lead-based paint hazards from risk assessments or inspections in the seller's possession and notify the buyer of any known lead-based paint hazards. A risk assessment or inspection for possible lead-based paint hazards is recommended prior to purchase.

Seller's Disclosure

(a) Presence of lead-based paint and/or lead-based paint hazards (check (i) or (ii) below):

(i) ______ Known lead-based paint and/or lead-based paint hazards are present in the housing (explain).

____

(ii) _____ Seller has no knowledge of lead-based paint and/or lead-based paint hazards in the housing.

(b) Records and reports available to the seller (check (i) or (ii) below):

(i) ______ Seller has provided the purchaser with all available records and reports pertaining to lead-based paint and/or lead-based paint hazards in the housing (list documents below).

____

(ii) _____ Seller has no reports or records pertaining to lead-based paint and/or lead-based paint hazards in the housing.

Purchaser's Acknowledgment (initial)

(c) ________ Purchaser has received copies of all information listed above.

(d) ________ Purchaser has received the pamphlet *Protect Your Family from Lead in Your Home.*

(e) Purchaser has (check (i) or (ii) below):

(i) _____ received a 10-day opportunity (or mutually agreed upon period) to conduct a risk assessment or inspection for the presence of lead-based paint and/or lead-based paint hazards; or

(ii) _____ waived the opportunity to conduct a risk assessment or inspection for the presence of lead-based paint and/or lead-based paint hazards.

Agent's Acknowledgment (initial)

(f) ________ Agent has informed the seller of the seller's obligations under 42 U.S.C. 4852(d) and is aware of his/her responsibility to ensure compliance.

Certification of Accuracy

The following parties have reviewed the information above and certify, to the best of their knowledge, that the information they have provided is true and accurate.

Seller	Date	Seller	Date
Purchaser	Date	Purchaser	Date
Agent	Date	Agent	Date

OHIO'S ENVIRONMENTAL LAWS

To comply with federal laws, Ohio passed air and water pollution control laws and set up the Ohio EPA to administer those laws. OEPA permits are required for any large discharge of pollutants into the water or air. OEPA's grant or denial of a permit can be appealed to the state Environmental Board of Review.

Private Restrictions

Private restrictions on land can also be imposed by a former owner or developer. Often they prohibit uses that zoning laws would permit (e.g., only single-family homes in a zone for any residential use). Two types are **conditions** and **covenants**.

CONDITIONS. **Conditions** are provisions in a deed, or other document, that make the parties' rights and obligations depend on the occurrence (or non-occurrence) of some event. When an owner transfers a defeasible fee, the grantee's title is contingent on the deed condition. For example, a deed may grant land "To X, on condition the barn never be torn down." If the condition is broken (the barn is razed), a court may rule the grantee forfeited the land, so title reverts to the grantor. Deed conditions are rare.

COVENANTS. **Covenants** are promises or guarantees, express or implied, in a deed or other document. Deed covenants are more common. **Restrictive covenants** are binding promises about land use and can cover the same items as conditions. For example, a deed may state, "The grantee covenants never to tear down the barn." But a covenant doesn't make title conditional. If the grantee razes the barn, a court may order him or her to rebuild it or pay damages to the grantor, but he or she will not lose title to the land.

CREATING RESTRICTIVE COVENANTS. Restrictive covenants can be imposed in a deed. To prevent objectionable land uses by new owners, a grantor puts restrictions on a grantee's title. This is common when land is subdivided. Restrictive covenants can also be created by express agreement between two parties, but to make a restriction enforceable against third parties, it must be recorded. Once a covenant is in the recorded chain of title, future buyers take title **subject to** the restriction even if it's not stated in their deed. Restrictive covenants **run with the land**.

Related to the Property. Restrictive covenants can only run with the land if they **"touch and concern the land"**; they must relate to the use, maintenance, or improvement of the real property. A covenant that says a grantee may never smoke can't run with the land, but a covenant prohibiting smoking *on* the land might.

TERMINATING RESTRICTIVE COVENANTS. A restrictive covenant is extinguished if it was created before the current owner's root of title (document going back 40 years from the current title), unless it's preserved by recording a deed or notice at any time after the root of title. An attorney will make sure the deed or notice states that the property is subject to the restriction and specifically mentions the recorded document where the restriction was created. Other ways to terminate restrictive covenants include termination date, release, merger, abandonment, and changed circumstances. A restrictive covenant that becomes illegal will automatically terminate. Example: A deed restriction may state that people of certain religious beliefs or nationality may not purchase a home. After 1968, creed, national origin, and ancestry (Ohio) became protected classes and made these deed restrictions illegal.

Subdivision Restrictions

Today most private restrictions are imposed by subdivision developers by recording a **declaration of covenants, conditions, and restrictions** known as **CC&Rs**. (Note that although CC&Rs stands for covenants, *conditions*, and restrictions, they virtually never make a grantee's title subject to forfeiture.) The purpose of CC&Rs is to keep the subdivision attractive and protect the market value of homes. It is important, though, to check these thoroughly as they can restrict a buyer's enjoyment of the property. For example, they may forbid installation of a satellite dish.

Developers use CC&Rs to establish a **general plan** of restrictions for the whole subdivision by clearly stating in the subdivision's recorded plat, or in the deed to the first buyer of each lot, that CC&Rs are binding on all homeowners. Although any homeowner can enforce CC&Rs, usually a homeowners' association enforces them. Subdivision CC&Rs are terminated the same ways as other restrictive covenants.

Chapter 5 Summary

1. Real property is land and everything attached or appurtenant to it. Real property rights are a bundle of rights: *right of use, right of enjoyment, and right of disposal*. Trespass, encroachment, and nuisance interfere with these rights. *Appurtenances* are rights that go with land: air, water, mineral, and support rights. These rights usually transfer with land but may be sold separately. *Water rights*: riparian/littoral (adjoin water) or appropriative (government permit).

2. *Natural attachments* (plants) are real property in the ground but personal property when picked. *Doctrine of emblements* lets tenant farmer return and pick first crop after tenancy ends. Man-made attachments are fixtures; major fixtures are improvements. Attachments go with land; personal property doesn't. Fixtures are personal property attached to real property—legally part of real property due to annexation. Courts decide if item is a fixture mostly by looking at annexer's intent and purpose of annexation. Written agreements take precedence. Bill of sale transfers title to personal property. Trade fixtures, installed by tenant for business, may be removed before lease ends.

3. Estates are *possessory interests* in real property, either now or in the future. Freehold estates are of uncertain duration; leasehold estates are temporary. Freehold estates can be fee simple—inheritable, transferable, and perpetual ownership,or life estates—possession as long as specified person lives (grantor's interest is reversionary; third party is a remainderman). Fee simple absolute is fullest interest in property. Defeasible fee estate can be undone. If conditions aren't met, title reverts to grantor. Can sell, lease, mortgage life estate; can't will or waste. *Eviction process*: notice to vacate (3 days—30 days if health/safety), forcible entry, and detainer (3 days), writ of execution (10 days). Spouses have inchoate dower rights in other spouse's land (till land sold/spouse dies).

4. Easements are a non-possessory right to use another's land for acertain purpose. They're appurtenant or in gross and created by express grant, reservation, implication, necessity, or prescription. Liens are also non-possessory interests (financial encumbrances). A lien holder can foreclose on land to have debts paid by sheriff's sale. Can sell land subject to existing mortgage (buyer takes land with mortgage but not personally liable—if pays, can keep; if doesn't pay, loses equity). Common liens are mortgages, mechanics' liens, judgment liens, or tax liens. Land tax liens always have priority. Lis pendens is a recorded notice stating there's a lawsuit pending, which may affect title to property.

5. *Public land use restrictions*: zoning, building codes, subdivision rules, environmental laws. Zoning laws separate land use in different areas—can dictate lot size, building height, setbacks, etc., Rezoning is zoning law change. Spot zoning is illegal. Exceptions to zoning laws are nonconforming uses, variances, and conditional uses. Building codes set minimum standards for construction and materials. Owner may also have to bring an existing building up to code. Subdivision regulations must be complied with (e.g., plat must be approved and recorded) before land can be subdivided. Environmental laws include: Clean Air Act, Clean Water Act, Lead Paint Disclosure Rules.

6. Private restrictions are conditions or covenants. Deed conditions are rare. Restrictive covenants relate to use of property, and may run with the land. Developers can impose restrictions on a subdivision by recording CC&Rs.

Chapter 5 Quiz

1. ***Which of the following rights are* not *transferred with real property?***
   a. Support rights
   (b.) Encroachments
   c. Disposal rights
   d. Easements

2. ***Chris owns a piece of land next to a lake and near a mountain, but needs to raise some money for a hot stock tip. Which of the following is* not *an option?***
   (a.) Sell appropriative rights only
   b. Sell mineral rights only
   c. Sell an easement
   d. Sell air rights only

3. ***A buyer and seller cannot agree on whether a particular item should be included in the sale of the house. What considerations will the court weigh most heavily?***
   a. The opinion of the real estate agent
   b. That the annexer said she always intended to remove the item
   (c.) The intention of the annexer and the purpose of the annexation
   d. How complete the house will look without the item

4. ***Which of the following is* not *considered a fixture to real property?***
   a. The keys to the house
   b. The built-in washer that's at the repair shop on the day of closing
   c. The white picket fence around the house
   (d.) The curio cabinet in the living room that the buyer thought looked perfect with the room decor

5. ***A candy maker has a five-year lease. The candy maker installs a marble counter to roll candy on. When the lease is up, the candy maker:***
   a. May not remove the counter because of a verbal agreement
   (b.) May remove the marble counter because it's a trade fixture
   c. May remove the counter because it isn't a fixture
   d. May not remove the counter because he didn't ask the owner if he could install it

6. ***All of the following describe a real property interest for a limited period of time* except:**
   a. Life estate
   b. Life estate pur autre vie
   c. Leasehold estate
   (d.) Defeasible fee estate

7. ***Which of the following does not apply to fee simple absolute?***
   a. It's inheritable
   b. It's transferable
   c. It's perpetual
   (d.) It's conditional

8. ***Which of the following is not a valid time period for an estate for years?***

a. Two weeks
b. Two months
c. Two years
d. Until all inventory is sold

9. ***Which of the following is not an encumbrance on real property?***

a. Restrictive covenant
b. Personal license
c. Judgment lien
d. Appurtenant easement

10. ***In deciding who will be paid from a foreclosure sale, which is first in lien priority?***

a. The mortgagee or original lender
b. The mechanic who file a mechanic's lien
c. The first lien recorded
d. The state's lien for delinquent property taxes

11. ***JJ gets a personal easement in gross to hunt on CC's land. Later CC changes her mind. How can CC get out of the situation?***

a. Post a "No Trespassing" sign on her property
b. Buy JJ's property
c. Record a release from JJ that he won't hunt on her land anymore
d. Prove in court that there isn't any more wildlife to hunt on CC's land

12. ***Jerry operates a farm in a suburb of Urbana, Ohio. Later, the city expands and Jerry's farm is now in the middle of an R-1 residential zoned neighborhood. Jerry:***

a. Must sell his farm and move
b. Can keep his house, but needs to tear down his silos and barn within the next five years
c. Can continue to operate the farm as a nonconforming use
d. Could not consider subdividing his farm because of the zoning change

13. ***Pat is buying a house from Terry subject to an existing mortgage. Later, Pat can't make the payments. What will happen?***

a. Nothing, since Pat bought the house subject to the existing mortgage, the old mortgage is of no concern and Pat can continue to live there
b. Pat will be sued by the lender to try and collect the debt because buying the house subject to the existing mortgage was the same as an assumption
c. Everything; Pat will lose the house and have to pay the entire debt
d. Pat will lose the equity paid into the home, but is not liable to repay any other money for the debt

14. ***Which of the following is not a possessory interest in real estate?***

a. Fee simple absolute
b. Fee simple defeasible
c. Fee simple indeterminable
d. Life estate

6 BROKERS, SALESPEOPLE, AND THE AGENCY RELATIONSHIP

CHAPTER OVERVIEW

This chapter focuses on duties and responsibilities to the broker, the clients, the customers, and the public. The law of agency defines the special agency relationships that are involved with being a real estate agent. One must be loyal to those who ask to be represented. The law dictates strict rules of conduct that must be followed when representing other parties in a real estate transaction. Use your knowledge to help the public and put the best interests of clients above your own. We'll discuss how agency relationships are created and terminated, agents' duties, responsibilities, and liabilities.

KEY TERMS

Agent
A licensed person who represents another in a real estate transaction or a person authorized to represent the principal in dealings with third parties.

Customer
Party in a transaction with whom an agent does not have a fiduciary duty or relationship but with whom an agent must still be fair and honest.

Dual Agent
Licensee who enters into any of the dual agency relationships set forth in Ohio license law. A licensee who represents both the buyer and seller in the same transaction; all management-level licensees at that brokerage and the broker are dual agents. A management-level licensee is **not** a dual agent if there is more than one management-level licensee in the brokerage and that manager either personally represents the buyer or the seller or is the buyer or the seller.

Fiduciary
A person in a position of trust held by law to high standards of good faith and loyalty.

Fraud
Intentional or negligent misrepresentation or concealment of material facts.

Management-Level Licensee
A licensee employed by or affiliated with a real estate broker and who has supervisory responsibility over other licensees employed by or affiliated with that real estate broker.

Negligence
An unintentional breach of a legal duty, resulting from carelessness, recklessness, or incompetence.

Principal
Person who grants another person (an agent) authority to represent him or her in dealings with third parties. ~~There are actually two principals in every transaction: one is your client, the other is the customer.~~

KEY TERMS *cont.*

Seller
A party in a real estate transaction who is the potential transferor of property. Seller includes a property owner seeking to sell property and a landlord who is seeking to rent or lease property to another person.

Split Agency
When one licensee in the same brokerage represents the seller and another licensee represents the buyer in the same transaction. Each agent is a single agent while the broker is a dual agent.

Subagent
The agent of an agent; a person to whom an agent has lawfully delegated authority so the delegate can assist in representing the delegating agent's client.

I. THE BROKER-SALESPERSON RELATIONSHIP

A salesperson is an agent of his or her broker, acting as an independent contractor. A real estate salesperson may not work independently of his or her licensed broker and, in fact, can function only through the broker with whom he or she is associated. Everything must be done with consent of the broker. The salesperson cannot independently enter into listing agreements or other contracts to represent people. Furthermore, a salesperson cannot independently conclude a sale, receive a commission, or advertise. All of these actions must be done in the name of the broker.

As we discuss agency, remember that the broker-salesperson relationship is also an agency relationship. All duties of good faith and loyalty that you must adhere to with respect to principals and clients, must also be observed with your broker. As a salesperson, you must put the best interests of your broker above your own.

A **management-level licensee** is a licensee who is employed by or affiliated with a real estate broker and who has supervisory responsibility over other licenses employed by or affiliated with that real estate broker.

DUTIES OF THE BROKERAGE AND MANAGEMENT-LEVEL LICENSEES. The brokerage and management-level licensees in a dual agency situation must objectively supervise the affiliated licensees in the fulfillment of their duties and obligations to their respective clients, refrain from advocating or negotiating on behalf of either the buyer or seller, and refrain from disclosing confidential information to other agents, clients, or parties. This includes a duty to see that confidential information is not used by anyone to benefit one party or client over the other. *Remember*, a management-level licensee is **not** a dual agent if the brokerage has more than one management-level licensee and the management-level licensee either personally represents the seller or buyer, or is the seller or buyer.

II. CREATING AN AGENCY RELATIONSHIP

Agency is a relationship of trust created when one person (a principal) gives another person (an agent) the right to represent the principal in dealings with third parties. *An agent's authority always comes from the principal.* When an agent acts within the scope of his or her authority, the principal is legally liable for the agent's acts. So, a third party can sue the principal instead of, or in addition to, an agent. But if an agent exceeds his or her authority, the principal may not be liable.

AUTHORITY

Depending on the scope of authority, an agent may be classified as **universal**, **general**, or **special**. A **universal agent** is authorized to do everything that can be lawfully delegated to a representative. A court-appointed guardian is an example of a universal agent. A **general agent** is authorized to handle all of the principal's affairs in one area or in specified areas. A property manager is an example of a general agent. A **special agent** has limited authority to do a specific thing or conduct a specific transaction. A real estate broker is an example of a special agent.

ACTUAL VERSUS IMPLIED AUTHORITY. **Actual authority** is power or permission given intentionally to an agent by the principal, expressly or by implication. Express authority is power or permission for a specific act or outcome communicated by the principal to the agent.

Implied authority is power or permission to do everything reasonably necessary to carry out the principal's express orders. For example, a seller gives a broker express authority to find a buyer for the property. The broker has implied authority to market the property. ***You can't have implied authority without express authority.***

Actual authority in an agency relationship for real estate transactions is created with a written document called a **listing agreement**. A **listing agreement** is a written agency contract between seller and broker stating that the broker will be paid a commission for finding a ready, willing, and able buyer on the seller's terms for the seller's property. **A listing agreement is considered an employment agreement, so the statute of frauds does not require it to be in writing, but Ohio real estate licensing law does require listing agreements lasting for one year or more to be in writing. All listing agreements (even those for less than one year) must be in writing to be enforceable in a court of law**. Having listing agreements in writing and signed also helps avoid misunderstandings. Check your broker's policies in this area. **Buyer broker** agreements also confer actual authority in an agency relationship.

III. REAL ESTATE AGENCY

The basic real estate agency relationship is between a broker and a seller or a broker and a buyer. The one with whom the broker (licensee) has **entered into a contract** to represent and owes a fiduciary responsibility to is the **client. The other principal in the transaction is referred to as the customer**. All **third parties** are referred to as **customers**. This distinction will become important later as we define the different fiduciary responsibilities a licensee has to clients and customers.

The agency relationship is usually established by written agreement. It can take the form of a listing agreement for sellers or a buyer broker agreement with buyers. The **Consumer Guide to Agency Relationships** will help clients and customers understand who represents them and what loyalties and responsibilities are owed to them. Documents disclosing agency relationships must be signed to comply with Ohio's license law. It's important to understand that the promise of payment to a broker or the source of compensation doesn't establish or determine an agency relationship.

The broker's salespersons are **subagents** of the broker's client. A **subagent** is an agent of an agent: a person to whom authority has been delegated, so the subagent can assist in carrying out the principal's orders. Salespeople are subagents of the broker's client since the broker is the one who actually has entered into a contract with the client. Subagents represent the broker's client through their broker or a cooperating broker. It's illegal for a salesperson to represent a client directly without a broker. Depending on the circumstances, both the principal and agent can be held liable for a subagent's acts.

OHIO'S AGENCY LAW

In traditional real estate transactions, ***a real estate broker is presumed to be representing the seller*** unless there is a specific agreement stating that the broker is representing the buyer. The wide acceptance of buyer brokerage has made brokers representing buyers more common. Buyers like this arrangement because they have an advocate, and sellers and listing agents like this arrangement because they don't need to worry about liability for representations made by the buyer's agent or broker since that person is no longer their subagent. The law finally reflects real estate practice and Ohio Agency Law no longer has a presumption of representation.

Agency Relationships

Under Ohio's Agency Law, there are five types of agency relationships:

1. Agency relationship between a broker and a seller
2. Agency relationship between a broker and a buyer
3. Dual agency relationship between a broker and both seller and buyer
4. In-company or "split" agency relationship between two licensees in the same brokerage: one licensee representing the seller and the other licensee representing the buyer. The broker being a dual agent
5. Subagency relationships where a co-broker represents another broker's client

Note: This form of agency relationship can be done *only* with the seller's written consent (many brokers in Ohio will not allow subagency).

When an agency relationship is formed between a licensee and a client under any of these arrangements, the brokerage with whom the licensee is affiliated and the management-level licensees in that brokerage are also considered agents of that client.

A management-level licensee is not a dual agent if there is more than one management-level licensee in the brokerage and:

- The management-level licensee personally represents the seller or the buyer, ***or***
- The management-level licensee is the seller or the buyer

Furthermore, any licensee affiliated with the brokerage who receives confidential information from an agent of the client is also considered an agent of that client. This has always been true for agency relationships formed under Ohio law.

Know!!

Except for these two provisions, Ohio law recognizes other licensees from the same brokerage as **not** being agents of that client unless a licensee assisted in establishing the agency relationship or is specifically appointed, with the client's consent, to represent that client. Thus, two salesperson-level licensees in the same brokerage can represent two different parties in the same transaction with only their broker (and/or other management-level licensees) being considered a dual agent. This agency relationship is known as **split agency**.

EXAMPLE Dick and Jane are salespersons at Spot Realty under Sally, their affiliated broker. Dick has a listing for a house. Dick and Sally are both agents for the seller who's considered a client to both of them. Dick and Sally have a fiduciary responsibility to act in the best interests of the homeowner.

Jane has been working with a buyer who likes the house that Dick has listed. Jane has a buyer who is being treated as a client. Jane and Sally are both agents for the buyer. The buyer is considered to be a client to both of them, so both Jane and Sally have a fiduciary responsibility to act in the best interests of the buyer. Thus, Sally (the broker) is the only dual agent in this situation.

CONFIDENTIAL INFORMATION. In this example, Sally is the only one who's in a potentially compromising position since she has access to confidential information about both the buyer and seller. The integrity of the process can be destroyed if Dick accidentally learns confidential information about Jane's buyer or if Jane inadvertently stumbles across confidential information about Dick's seller.

To avoid possible problems, Ohio's Agency Law provides that each brokerage must develop and maintain a written policy that states the types of agency relationships that its licensees may establish, whether dual agency relationships are allowed, and specific procedures to safeguard confidential information including how the brokerage intends to cover affiliated licensees with respect to confidential information. Each brokerage ***must*** create a flyer or statement on the company's agency and confidentiality policies that must be given to clients and customers on request. The agency and confidentiality policies must comply with minimum standards established by the Superintendent of Real Estate and Ohio Real Estate Commission. It's important to note the implementation of such a policy doesn't relieve the brokerage from liability for failure of the brokerage, or any affiliated licensee or employee, to keep a client's information confidential.

Consumer Guide to Agency Relationships

The Consumer Guide to Agency Relationships is Ohio's new consumer-friendly method of providing clients and prospective clients information regarding the type(s) of agency relationships a brokerage practices. The broker has *five models of business under which a brokerage may operate*:

1. Split and dual agency
2. Dual agency on all in-house transactions
3. Exclusive buyer agency only
4. Exclusive seller agency only
5. Split agency but no dual agency

Prior to performing any duties in an agency relationship, this disclosure document must be provided to and acknowledged by the client or customer. The following disclosures must be included in a brokerage's Consumer Guide:

1. All permissible types of agency relationships allowed in Ohio
2. The brokerage's policy regarding representation of buyers and sellers, dual agency, and split agency
3. Whether the broker offers compensation to or seeks compensation from cooperating brokerages;
4. That a brokerage that has a buyer as a client represents the buyer's interests even though the seller's brokerage or seller may compensate the buyer's agent
5. The brokerage policy on customers, whether buyers or sellers, who are not represented
6. That Ohio law requires the Consumer Guide to Agency Relationships be presented to and acknowledged by the consumer
7. The brokerage's name, Fair Housing language, and logo

The client or *customer signs the form indicating receipt* and must be given a copy of the signed form. *Note*: **the Consumer Guide is required whether the licensee is an agent for the seller or the buyer and must be presented at the first substantive contact a licensee has with a consumer. The first substantive contact is defined as being no later than the occurrence of certain events, depending on whether a licensee is working with sellers, buyers, or both, in a particular transaction.**

LICENSEES WORKING WITH SELLERS. A licensee working as a seller's agent must give the seller a Consumer Guide to Agency Relationships **prior to marketing or showing the seller's property.** As a practical matter, it's wise to take care of this disclosure requirement at the time you enter into a listing agreement. Check with the broker for the specific procedures that have been established as office policy.

LICENSEES WORKING WITH BUYERS. A licensee working with a buyer, regardless of what agency relationship may develop, must provide the buyer with a Consumer Guide to Agency Relationships at the first substantive contact but **no later than prior to the earliest of the following**:

1. Initiating a pre-qualification evaluation to determine whether the buyer has the financial ability to buy or lease a particular property

2. Requesting specific financial information from the buyer to determine the buyer's ability to buy or finance real estate in a certain price range
3. Showing a property **other than an open house**
4. Discussing making an offer to buy real property with the buyer
5. Submitting an offer to buy or lease real property on behalf of the buyer

If the agent's earliest contact with a buyer is by telephone and covers any of these events, the licensee must make a verbal disclosure of the agency relationship, which the licensee may have with both the buyer and the seller. The licensee is then required to get the buyer to acknowledge receipt of a Consumer Guide to Agency Relationships at the first meeting with the buyer following the verbal disclosure of the possible agency relationships.

Agency Disclosure Statement

While the Consumer Guide to Agency Relationships provides information to clients and customers on the possible types of agency relationships they may enter into with a brokerage, the *Agency Disclosure Statement* discloses the actual agency relationship that will result in a property specific transaction.

The Agency Disclosure form is initiated by the agent writing the offer when the buyer indicates a desire to write an offer on a property, thus becoming transaction specific.

BUYER'S AGENTS DEALING WITH SELLERS. The seller must receive a copy of a buyer's signed Agency Disclosure form before an offer is presented. If the agent preparing the offer doesn't represent the seller, the form should be given to the seller's agent with the offer. The seller's agent must present and explain the Agency Disclosure form to the seller, obtaining the seller's signature consenting to the agency relationship indicated, *prior* to presenting the offer to purchase.

SELLER'S AGENTS DEALING WITH BUYERS. **If the licensee is a seller's agent, the licensee is not required to give an Agency Disclosure statement to a buyer unless the licensee engages in any of the activities listed previously with the buyer.** The form has three sections:

1. Transactions involving two agents from different brokerages
2. A transaction involving two agents from the same brokerage
3. A transaction involving only one agent.

Within each of these sections, the appropriate agency relationship resulting from an offer on one specific property can be determined. The buyer and the seller must both consent to the indicated agency relationship by signing and dating the form.

The reverse side of the form explains dual agency in detail. This information includes:

1. What the agent and the brokerage shall and shall not do in a dual agency relationship
2. How management-level licensees will function in this relationship

3. Responsibilities of the buyer and seller in the transaction
4. That compensation, unless otherwise agreed upon, will be pursuant to the agency agreement, (listing or buyer's brokerage agreement)
5. That by signing the form the parties consent to dual agency
6. How to contact the Division of Real Estate

Failure to comply with The Consumer Guide to Agency Relationships or the agency disclosure requirements will be deemed *prima facie* evidence of misconduct on the part of the licensee in violation of Ohio Agency Law. Failure to comply could also subject the licensee to a citation issued by the Superintendent of the Ohio Division of Real Estate.

EXEMPTIONS. These disclosure form requirements aren't required for referrals from one licensee to another, open houses (unless an offer is written), rental or leasing of residential property for a term of 18 months or less, and transactions dealing with foreign real estate or cemetery lots.

IV. THE AGENT'S DUTIES TO THE PRINCIPAL

The relationship between an agent and a principal is described as a **fiduciary relationship**. A **fiduciary relationship** is a relationship of trust and confidence in which one party owes the other (or both parties owe each other) loyalty and a higher standard of good faith than they owe to third parties. A **fiduciary** is someone in a position of trust held by law to high standards of good faith and loyalty. The fiduciary must act for the benefit of the principal and not exploit that trust.

A broker is an agent of the client, so the broker is the fiduciary, and the client is the principal. Although a client is often the seller, the client can also be a buyer. The client is the one with whom a contract has been entered into or whomever the broker represents, as indicated in the Consumer Guide to Agency Relationships. Salespeople are subagents of their broker's client. (Also, a salesperson is an agent of his or her broker; the salesperson is the fiduciary, and the broker is the principal/client.)

FIDUCIARY RESPONSIBILITIES

The basic fiduciary duties are: **obedience, loyalty, disclosure, confidentiality, accountability**, and **reasonable care (OLD CAR)**. These common law duties define the agency relationship.

OBEDIENCE. **Obedience** means the agent must follow the (legal) directions of the principal, obey the restrictions of the agency relationship, and not stray beyond the scope of his or her authority. If agents don't follow this duty, they could be held liable to the principal for losses sustained together with other damages. Of course, if the principal gives an illegal instruction, such as telling you to discriminate against a potential buyer, you must not follow this instruction.

LOYALTY. The duty of **loyalty** holds that the agent must put the principal's interests above all others including the agent's own.

DISCLOSURE. An agent must make a complete **disclosure of all material information** and be sure not to conceal anything from the principal. Any fact that could influence the principal's judgment in a transaction must be brought to his or her attention. An agent representing a seller should be sure to inform the principal of:

- True property value
- All offers to purchase

    ➢ *Note:* If there is more than one offer on a property at the same time, all offers must be presented. The order of presentation is unimportant.

- Identity of the prospective buyer
- Buyer's financial condition, if known
- Any commission-splitting arrangements with other brokers
- Any relationship between the buyer and the broker

Property Value

When trying to obtain a listing, an agent may be tempted to inflate the value of property. A high value may make sellers more willing to sign an exclusive listing, but that's a breach of an agent's duty to act in good faith. An agent must tell sellers a property's true value and should point out things that he or she may know about the title or property that may affect its worth or suggest inexpensive repairs that may increase the selling price. If during the listing period an agent finds information (e.g., new comparable sales) affecting valuation, the seller must be told.

ALL OFFERS TO PURCHASE. Even if an offer seems unacceptable, the agent must present it to the principal. The principal, not the agent, decides if an offer is acceptable. The agent must present an offer to the principal even if its acceptance would mean a smaller commission, because the agent's first loyalty is to the principal.

IDENTITY OF BUYER AND BUYER'S FINANCIAL INFORMATION. A seller's agent must tell the seller all facts known about a buyer's financial position—assets, income, or credit rating, as well as the source of down payment (e.g., a loan from friends rather than savings), or the form of earnest money deposit. This is especially important if a contract is contingent on the buyer's ability to obtain financing.

COMMISSION-SPLITTING ARRANGEMENTS WITH OTHER BROKERS. This requirement is part of the disclosures that must be made under Ohio's agency law.

RELATIONSHIP BETWEEN THE BUYER AND THE BROKER. This prevents self-dealing and secret profits.

SELF-DEALING AND SECRET PROFITS

A **secret profit** is a financial benefit that an agent takes from a transaction without authorization from the principal and without informing the principal of the benefit retained. The most common examples involve **self-dealing**. **Self-dealing** means an agent buys the principal's property (or sells it to a relative, friend, etc.,) without disclosing that fact to the principal and then sells it again for a profit.

An agent may buy property from the principal, but the agent must inform the seller that he or she (or a relative, friend, etc.,) is the buyer. This alerts the seller to a possible conflict of interest, so he or she may choose to find another agent.

An agent must tell the principal things that can be done to increase the selling price of property (e.g., repairs, cleanup, minor changes). If an agent buys the property and does these improvements, the agent used a superior knowledge of real estate for personal gain, not for the principal's gain, in breach of loyalty and good faith.

Confidentiality

To keep from destroying the integrity of the agency process, all information given by the client to the agent or gained by the agent from other sources must be kept confidential **forever.** The principal often discloses confidential information to the agent. The agent must not reveal this information to others or take advantage of it for personal benefit.

Accountability

The duty of **accountability** recognizes that money received in an agency relationship belongs to the principal, not the agent. Often the relationship calls for money to be paid to the broker to aid in the purchase or sale of property. Since an agent acts on behalf of the principal, the agent has the duty to account strictly to the principal for any amount received. The broker must put this money into a separate, non-interest bearing trust account so as not to **commingle** the principal's funds with those of the brokerage. Failure to do so breaches the agency relationship, which could result in legal liability and loss of license.

Reasonable Care

Reasonable care and skill must always be used by an agent when acting on behalf of a client. The agent is viewed as a professional and an expert. A form filled out incorrectly or a misunderstood law could cause problems for a client. If a client loses money due to an agent's incompetence or carelessness, the agent can be held liable for **negligence**. **Negligence** is an unintentional breach of a legal duty.

All real estate agents are held to a minimum standard of competence. An agent claiming expertise in a special area (e.g., appraisal) is held to an even higher standard. Never take on tasks beyond your ability or claim expertise where you have no special training or skills. If you're not qualified in an area, tell a client to seek advice from a lawyer, accountant, appraiser, or other expert to protect yourself from liability.

UNAUTHORIZED PRACTICE OF LAW. Many aspects of real estate transactions raise legal questions or have legal consequences. Real estate agents need to remember and to remind their clients that they aren't licensed to practice law. Agents should never give legal advice or perform any acts that require a lawyer's expertise.

In Ohio, a real estate agent is permitted to complete standard listing forms, purchase agreement forms, and promissory note forms. An agent should **never** draft an original agreement or add complicated clauses to forms. That may be considered an unauthorized practice of law. Courts have held that due to licensees' unauthorized practice of law, they weren't entitled to commission or were subject to Ohio Real Estate Commission disciplinary action—license suspension or revocation.

Other Fiduciary Responsibilities to a Client

In addition to the basic fiduciary duties detailed previously, Ohio Agency Law states that a licensee should use his or her best efforts to further the client's interests by:

1. Performing the terms of any written agency agreement
2. Following the lawful instructions of the client
3. Disclosing any material facts of the transaction that the licensee becomes aware of and which are not considered confidential information
4. Advising the client to obtain expert advice related to material matters when necessary or appropriate
5. Keeping all confidential information confidential

Waiver of Duties

The duties required of a licensee under section 4735.62 of the Revised Code **may not be waived** by a client.

(B) A licensee shall perform the duties required under section 4735.63 or 4735.65 of the Revised Code unless the client agrees to waive these duties, and signs a waiver of duties statement pursuant to division (C) of this section.

(C) The superintendent of real estate, with the approval of the Ohio Real Estate Commission, shall establish by rule a waiver of duties statement that shall contain the following:

1. The fiduciary duties required of all licensees under section 4735.62 of the Revised Code;

2. A list of those duties contained in section 4735.63 or 4735.65 of the Revised Code, which shall be set forth in a manner that allows for the parties to indicate which of those duties are being waived;

3. A statement that no other licensee is required to perform the waived duty on behalf of the client;

4. A statement that legal counsel or other professionals may be hired by the client;

5. A place for the client and licensee to sign and date the statement.

Negotiating with Another Broker's Client

A broker who has the exclusive authority to represent a client under a written exclusive agency agreement, exclusive right to sell agreement, or exclusive purchaser agency agreement (discussed in the next chapter) may authorize other licensees to negotiate directly with that client. The authorization shall be in writing and the broker shall comply with the requirements of section 4735.621 of the Revised Code.

> **(B)** A licensee who negotiates directly with a seller, purchaser, lessor, or tenant pursuant to a written authorization as described in division (A) of this section does not violate division (A)(19) of section 4735.18 of the Revised Code and negotiations conducted by a licensee pursuant to the authorization shall not create or imply an agency relationship between that licensee and the client of that exclusive broker.
>
> **(C)** As used in this section and division (A)(19) of section 4735.18 of the Revised Code, "negotiate" means any the following:
>
> 1. Delivering or communicating an offer, counteroffer, or proposal
> 2. Discussing or reviewing the terms of any offer, counteroffer, or proposal
> 3. Facilitating communication regarding an offer, counteroffer, or proposal and preparing any response as directed

V. SPECIFIC DUTIES OF A LICENSEE REPRESENTING A BUYER

In representing a purchaser in an agency relationship, a licensee shall:

1. Seek a property at a price and with purchase or lease terms acceptable to the purchaser. Unless the client so directs, the licensee is not obligated to seek additional purchase or lease possibilities if the purchaser is a party to a contract to purchase property, or has entered into a lease or has extended a letter of intent to lease.
2. Within the scope of knowledge required for licensure, answer the purchaser's questions and provide information to the purchaser regarding any offers or counteroffers.
3. Assist the purchaser in developing, communicating, and presenting offers or counteroffers.
4. Present any offer to purchase or lease to the seller or the seller's agent in a timely manner, even if the property is subject to a contract of sale, lease, or letter of intent to lease, and accept delivery of and present any counteroffers to the purchaser in a timely manner.
5. Within the scope of knowledge required for licensure, answer the purchaser's questions regarding the steps the purchaser must take to fulfill the terms of any contract.

A licensee does not breach any duty or obligation to the purchaser by showing the same properties to other purchasers or by acting as an agent or subagent for other purchasers, or as an agent or subagent for sellers, except that any dual agency relationship must be disclosed to a client pursuant to section 4735.71 of the

Revised Code. *Nothing in this section shall be construed as permitting a licensee to perform any act or service that constitutes the practice of law.*

VI. SPECIFIC DUTIES OF A LICENSEE REPRESENTING A SELLER

In addition to the basic fiduciary duties and disclosure requirements discussed previously, Ohio's Agency Law requires that a licensee representing a seller in an agency relationship shall:

1. Seek a purchase offer at a price and with terms acceptable to the seller. Unless the seller so directs, the licensee is not obligated to seek additional offers if the property is subject to a contract of sale, lease, or letter of intent to lease.
2. Accept delivery of and present any purchase offer to the seller in a timely manner, even if the property is subject to a contract of sale, lease, or letter of intent to lease.
3. Within the scope of knowledge required for licensure, answer the seller's questions and provide information to the seller regarding any offers or counteroffers.
4. Assist the seller in developing, communicating, and presenting offers or counteroffers.
5. Within the scope of knowledge required for licensure, answer the seller's questions regarding the steps the seller must take to fulfill the terms of any contract.

A licensee does not breach any duty or obligation to a seller with whom the licensee has an agency relationship by showing alternative properties to a prospective purchaser or by acting as an agent or subagent for other seller. *Nothing in this section shall be construed as permitting a licensee to perform any act or service that constitutes the practice of law.*

VII. ACTS THAT REQUIRE A CLIENT'S CONSENT

Ohio's Agency Law does **not** permit licensees representing buyers or sellers to do either of the following without the knowledge and consent of their clients:

1. Extend an offer of subagency to other licensees *or*
2. Offer compensation to, or accept compensation from, a broker representing another party in a transaction

VIII. DUAL AGENCY

Traditionally, **dual agency** means a licensee represents both buyer and seller in a transaction. Ohio's Agency Law has expanded this traditional definition. *Dual agency requires consent of all parties before it is active.*

A dual agent owes fiduciary duties to both buyer and seller. An agent must be careful not to disclose confidential information to the other party, especially with regard to price. When an agent has an ongoing relationship with one party (friend, relative, or established client) in a dual agency relationship, that ongoing relationship must be disclosed in writing, and both the buyer and seller must consent to it.

Critics of dual agency point out that there is an inherent conflict of interest in the arrangement. A seller is looking for the highest price while the buyer is looking for the lowest price. It is difficult, if not impossible, to adequately represent these two opposing interests. Ohio's Agency Law has addressed some of these issues.

DUAL AGENCY UNDER OHIO'S AGENCY LAW

A dual agency relationship may be entered into *only* by a brokerage firm in Ohio after the brokerage has established a procedure to safeguard confidential information during the transaction and provided that the licensee for each client in the dual agency relationship fulfills the licensee's duties exclusively to that client. Ohio's Agency Law has expanded the definition of dual agency to allow these three forms:

1. One licensee may represent both the buyer and seller (or lessor and lessee) as clients in the same real estate transaction
2. Two licensees affiliated with the same brokerage, one representing the buyer or lessee while the other represents the seller or lessor, where the broker and management-level licensees are dual agents (unless a management-level licensee falls under the exemption discussed below)
3. Two licensees affiliated with the same brokerage, one with the buyer or lessee as a client and the other with the seller or lessor as a client, where every licensee in the brokerage represents every client, therefore both agents are dual agents

Depending on the brokerage's policy on agency relationships, two different dual agency relationships can exist in an in-company transaction. Two salesperson-level licensees in the same brokerage can represent two different parties in the same transaction, and their broker, and other management-level licensees, depending on the situation, are considered dual agents. A licensee assigned by a broker to represent a buyer or seller in the same in-company transaction is referred to as a *split agent*, or brokerage policy states that every licensee in the brokerage will function as a dual agent.

A dual agency situation can be entered into only if both the seller and the buyer have full knowledge of the dual representation and consent to it in writing. If the buyer and seller are represented in a transaction by two different agents who are non-management-level licensees affiliated with the same brokerage (split agency), the appropriate statement in Section II of the Agency Disclosure Form must be completed after it's determined that a dual agency situation exists. However, if both buyer and seller are represented by the *same* agent in a transaction, the first statement in Section III of the Agency Disclosure Form must be completed.

Dual Agency Disclosures

In addition to providing the dual agency disclosure information found on the reverse side of the Agency Disclosure Form, which details the exact implications of the dual agency relationship and options available to the client, the licensee must first disclose to both the buyer and seller all relevant information to enable each party to make an informed decision regarding consent to the dual agency relationship. Furthermore, if after consent is obtained there is a material change in the information disclosed to the buyer and seller, the licensee must disclose the change of information and give each party a chance to revoke his or her consent.

The brokerage (agent) must make the dual agency disclosure to both buyer and seller as soon as practical after it's determined that a dual agency exists. Usually, this will occur when the buyer asks the licensee to write an offer on a property listed by the licensee. The seller must be informed of, and consent to, the dual agency prior to receipt of the offer. The parties must sign and date the Agency Disclosure Statement indicating dual agency in a timely manner, but the form must be signed and dated prior to the signing of any offers.

Duties of the Brokerage and Management-Level Licensees

The brokerage and management-level licensees in a dual agency situation must objectively supervise the affiliated licensees in the fulfillment of their duties and obligations to their respective clients, refrain from advocating or negotiating on behalf of either the buyer or seller, and refrain from disclosing confidential information to other agents, clients, or parties. This includes seeing that confidential information is not used by anyone to benefit one party or client over the other. Remember, a management-level licensee is **not** a dual agent if the brokerage has more than one management-level licensee and the management-level licensee either personally represents the seller or buyer or is the buyer or seller.

Duties of Two Non-Management-Level Licensees

When two non-management-level licensees affiliated with the same brokerage represent clients in the same transaction, each licensee may serve as the agent of only the party in the transaction whom the licensee agreed to represent, and must fulfill duties owed to the respective client (split agency), or both agents may represent both clients as stated in their broker's Consumer Guide to Agency Relationships and agreed to in the Agency Disclosure Statement/Dual Agency agreement and set forth in the Agency Law.

A licensee who obtains confidential information concerning another client of the brokerage in a dual agency relationship must not, under any circumstances, disclose that information to, or use that information for the benefit of, the licensee's client. If a brokerage determines that confidential information of one client in a dual agency relationship has become known to any licensee representing the other client in a dual agency, the brokerage must notify both clients of the situation. Such notification must include an offer of resignation of the agency relationship. If a client chooses to accept the resignation, the brokerage may not receive compensation from or on behalf of that client.

IX. THE AGENT'S DUTIES TO THIRD PARTIES

In addition to having a duty to the principal, an agent owes third parties a duty of good faith and fair dealing. An agent is not a fiduciary in relation to a third party. The agent isn't required to advance the third party's interests. The agent's duty of loyalty to the principal will often prohibit that.

In a real estate transaction, *fair dealing basically means two things*:

1. The seller's agent must disclose certain information to prospective buyers
2. The seller's agent must avoid misrepresentation

DISCLOSURE TO THE BUYER

In Latin, *caveat emptor* means, "Let the buyer beware." This rule says a buyer is expected to examine property carefully instead of relying on the seller to point out problems. That warning applies to real estate transactions in Ohio. This is another reason buyer-brokers are becoming more popular as buyers desire an agent to look after their interests during the real estate transaction.

In Ohio, a buyer is always supposed to inspect the property before agreeing to buy it. Although the seller and the seller's agent must tell the buyer about any known **latent defects** (defects that are not visible or apparent), the seller and the seller's agent generally aren't required to tell the buyer about **patent defects** (defects that are visible and would be discovered in a reasonably thorough inspection). This is true even if the buyer never actually inspected the property as long as he or she was given the opportunity. The rule also applies if the buyer inspects the property and sees the defect but doesn't recognize that it's a problem.

Remember, a seller and seller's agent *are* required to tell a buyer about any **known** latent defects. Ohio law says a licensee must disclose any material facts pertaining to the physical condition of the property that the buyer would not discover by a reasonably thorough and diligent inspection including material defects in the property, environmental contamination, and information that any statute or rule requires be disclosed. Also, knowledge of facts is inferred if a licensee acts with reckless disregard for the truth.

DISCLOSURE BY THE SELLER

For residential real estate purchase contracts for one- to four-dwelling units, Ohio law has created a "**Residential Property Disclosure Form**" to be delivered to the buyer prior to an offer to purchase the property.

The form allows for a detailed description of the property's condition (water, sewer, roof, etc.,), whether the property has been inspected for mold, if there has been any smoke damage to the property, whether the property is located in a flood plain, as well as more meaningful disclosure of problems and defects with mechanical systems, water quality and intrusion, and nonconforming uses of the property. It also includes notification to the purchaser of how to obtain information on Ohio's Sex Offender Registration and Notification Law, know as "Megan's Law." The form is signed by both the seller and buyer. While the owner's statements are to be based on "actual knowledge" of the property's condition, the form also has a catchall space for "known material defects" (non-observable physical conditions or problems). The agent should *not* assist in completing this form since it could result in liability if misstatements are made.

The form can be delivered by any method, including fax, and applies to every prospective transfer. The form is to be delivered prior to entering into a purchase contract. If the disclosure form is not delivered before this deadline, the purchaser may rescind the purchase contract by delivering a signed and dated recession letter to the seller prior to the following:

1. The date of closing
2. Thirty (30) days after the seller accepted the purchase contract
3. Within three (3) business days following the purchaser's (or his or her agent's) delivery of the disclosure form, or an amendment to it

If the disclosure statement is delivered on time, no additional right to cancel the contract (other than the conditions of the contract) is created.

Also, as the disclosure form states, it is *not* a warranty statement, nor does it create any additional liability on the real estate agent or broker for the property's condition, and it is not intended as a substitute for a professional inspection.

FRAUD

Fraud is an intentional or negligent misrepresentation or concealment of a material fact. Failing to disclose required information can be a form of fraud. It also includes actively concealing information and making false or misleading statements. Fraud can be **actual fraud** or **constructive fraud**.

Actual Fraud

Actual fraud is an intentional misrepresentation or concealment of a material fact or information or making statements known to be false or misleading. When any of these are done with intent to deceive, they constitute actual fraud. (Also called **deceit** or **intentional misrepresentation**).

Know

Constructive Fraud

Constructive fraud is a negligent misrepresentation or concealment of a material fact. When information is not disclosed or a person makes false statements unintentionally, it may be considered constructive fraud. In this case, the false statements or failure to disclose results from carelessness or negligence. (Also called **negligent misrepresentation**.)

Opinions, Predictions, and Puffing

As a general rule, a seller or agent can't be sued for misrepresentation if the statements were merely opinions, predictions, or puffing. These are usually statements that build up the property's benefits, like:

- (Opinion) "Compared to the sales prices for other homes in the neighborhood, this one appears to be an excellent buy."
- (Prediction) "Historically, property values have gone up 4 percent a year, and there, currently, is no reason to believe this will change for this area."
- (Puffing) "Look at this back yard!" (Even though you know the house really backs up to a park, but you don't mention this.)

To prove fraud based on a false statement, it's necessary to show the person relied on the statement. Because of their non-factual or exaggerated nature, opinions, predictions, and puffing aren't considered the type of statements a reasonable person would rely on in making a decision to buy property, so they do not generally fall under the fraud category.

A real estate agent should be very cautious about stating unsubstantiated opinions. In special circumstances, opinions may be actionable. A court may allow recovery based on opinions stated by an expert hired to give advice or a person who has superior knowledge and is acting in a fiduciary relationship. Someone who states an opinion that he or she doesn't actually believe may also be held liable.

"As is" Clause

An **"as is" clause** is a provision in a purchase agreement stating the buyer accepts the property in its present condition. The implication is that the buyer has inspected the item and agrees to accept it *as is*. While an "as is" clause can apply to most personal property purchases, it usually cannot apply to real property purchases of residential real estate.

In summary, Ohio law states that an "as is" clause does not protect the seller from liability for nondisclosure of a latent defect. Also, an "as is" clause cannot protect the seller or agent if he or she deliberately conceals a defect from the buyer. An "as is" clause is not a defense to fraud.

EXCEPTIONS TO FRAUD RULES. A licensee is not liable to any party for false information the licensee's client provided to the licensee and the licensee, in turn, provided to another party in the transaction unless the licensee had actual knowledge that the information was false or acted with reckless disregard for the truth.

From the client's standpoint, no cause of action may be brought against a client for any misrepresentation a licensee made while representing the client unless the client had actual knowledge of the licensee's misrepresentation.

X. PENALTIES FOR BREACH OF DUTY

When a real estate agent breaches a duty to a principal or third party, there are consequences. There can be disciplinary action by professional associations, action by the Ohio Division of Real Estate, civil lawsuits filed by the injured parties, and, in serious cases, the filing of criminal charges against the agent. (Errors and omissions insurance can help protect you from some of the financial penalties for mistakes but not fraud.)

ACTION BY PROFESSIONAL ASSOCIATIONS

A *code of ethics* is a system of moral standards and rules of conduct adopted by many real estate professional organizations to set standards for members' conduct toward the public, clients, and other members. (This should not be confused with the Canons of Ethics: standards of conduct put forth by Ohio Real Estate Commission.)

The most widely recognized code is the National Association of REALTORS'® Code of Ethics. Although not legally binding, all the NAR members voluntarily agree to follow it. A member who violates the code may be expelled from the organization. If this happens, the relationship with your NAR broker may end as you must be a member of the NAR to use the REALTOR® name.

ACTION BY THE DIVISION OF REAL ESTATE

A real estate agent's breach of duty is often a violation under the license law. The superintendent can investigate the conduct of an agent even without a complaint. These remedies are cumulative and may be imposed in addition to civil and/or criminal penalties. The Commission may also suspend or revoke the broker's license when a salesperson has engaged in disreputable conduct if the broker was aware and did not intervene.

CIVIL LAWSUITS

A real estate agent may be sued by a client or customer for breach of duty. If the plaintiff is able to prove that he or she suffered harm as the result of the breach of duty, the agent will be liable. An agent found liable for breach of duty may have to pay **compensatory damages** compensating the injured party for any monetary loss resulting from the breach. If the injured party was a client, the agent may be required to re-pay the commission. In a case involving secret profits, the court may order the agent to release the profits earned unjustly.

In addition to compensatory damages, a court may award **punitive damages** punishing the wrongdoer and attempting to deter others from similar acts. Generally, punitive damages are awarded only when the act was intentional or malicious.

CRIMINAL CHARGES

Sometimes a serious breach of duty is a crime (e.g., acting as a real estate agent without a license). Under certain circumstances, fraud or misappropriation of trust funds may result in felony prosecution. Remember that criminal penalties, fines, and jail sentences may be imposed in addition to, not instead of, civil liability.

XI. TERMINATING AGENCY

An agent's powers end when the agency ends. *Agency may be terminated by*:

- **Accomplishment of Purpose**: Perhaps the most common reason for termination of an agency relationship is that the purpose of the agency has been accomplished. The agency relationship between a client and a real estate broker ends when the reason for the agency relationship ends. However, even when the relationship has ended, it is necessary to maintain confidentiality of all information received during the relationship.
- **Expiration:** If an agency agreement specifies that the agency is for a limited term, either a certain period of time or with a set expiration date, the agency ends automatically when the term expires. **All real estate agency agreements are required by Ohio Licensing Law to have an expiration date.**
- **Operation of Law**: An agency relationship ends automatically, as a matter of law, if certain events occur. An agency is terminated by operation of law if:
  - ➢ Either party dies or becomes incapacitated
  - ➢ Either party goes bankrupt
  - ➢ The property that's the subject of the agency is destroyed or condemned
  - ➢ The agent (broker) loses his or her license
- **Mutual Agreement**: Agency is a consensual relationship, meaning it's based on the consent of both parties. If both the principal and agent want to end the agency, they can agree to terminate it at any point. When an agency is terminated by mutual consent, neither party is liable to the other for breach of contract. **This is considered the best and most correct way for early termination of an agency.**
- **Renunciation:** Renunciation means something that has been granted is later given up or rejected. If an agreement is left open ended, without a specific termination date, a party may renounce the contract at any time with no obligation. But if there is an end date (e.g., in a listing agreement), the renunciation may be a breach of contract, making the agent liable to the principal for damages.
- **Revocation:** Revocation means the withdrawal of something granted or offered. Principals may revoke agency power any time (but may incur liability). The principal is firing the agent. For open-ended agreements, a principal has only to reimburse an agent for expenses incurred. For agreements with ending dates, a principal may be liable to an agent for damages for breach of contract.

EXAMPLE Chris is planning to sell his warehouse and signs a 90-day exclusive listing agreement with Brenda, a real estate broker. Two weeks later, Chris starts dating a broker and decides to change the listing to her firm. Chris tells Brenda that her agency is revoked because he's changing to a different broker.

Now, Brenda is no longer authorized to represent Chris and Chris can't be held liable for Brenda's acts. The revocation was a breach of contract, so Chris may have to pay Brenda damages. That might mean paying Brenda the full commission she would have earned under the original listing contract.

An exception to the rule allowing a principal to revoke an agency agreement is a principal doesn't have a right to revoke an agreement if the agency is **coupled with an interest**. That means the agent has a financial or security interest in the property that is the subject of the agency. For example, if a listing agreement provides that the real estate broker will invest money to improve the property, the seller can't revoke the broker's agency. Also, an agency coupled with an interest isn't terminated by the death, incompetency, or bankruptcy of the principal.

Chapter 6 Summary

1. Agency is a relationship of trust created when one person (the principal) gives another person (the agent) the right to represent the principal in dealings with third parties. Agency creates a fiduciary relationship. Principal may be liable for agents' acts. An agent is universal, general, or special depending on authority given. Authority is given to an agent by a listing agreement; this gives express authority to find a buyer and implied authority to market the property. There is no implied authority without express authority.

2. Basic real estate agency is between a broker and seller/lessor, or broker and buyer/lessee. The party with whom a broker enters into a contract to represent (and owes a fiduciary responsibility to) is the client; all other parties are customers. Salespersons are broker's agents and subagents to their broker's client. Dual agency means a licensee represents both buyer and seller in the same transaction or represents different parties in the same transaction with the broker and all management-level licensees in that brokerage being dual agents, unless the management level licensee meets the exemption under agency law. Principals must acknowledge receipt of a Consumer Guide to Agency Relationships at the first substantive contact. The consumer must be given a copy of a broker's agency and confidentiality policies on request. A seller must receive a copy of the buyer's signed agency disclosure statement before an offer is presented.

3. An agent owes fiduciary duties to the principal. These basic fiduciary duties are obedience, loyalty, disclosure, confidentiality, accountability, and reasonable care and skill. Disclosure is a key responsibility. An agent must be careful to inform the principal of the true property value, all offers to purchase, identity of the buyer, buyer's financial condition, any commission splitting with other brokers, and relationship between the buyer and broker. A real estate agent must not conceal material information from the principal or take any secret profits from a transaction.
4. Agents have duties of good faith and fair dealing to third parties. Sellers and sellers' agents must tell buyers about latent (hidden) defects, but because of the caveat emptor rule, they usually don't have to tell buyers about patent defects that could be found by a reasonably thorough inspection. Intentional misrepresentation or concealment of material facts is actual fraud. Negligent misrepresentation or concealment of material facts is constructive fraud. Opinions, predictions, and puffing aren't fraud since they're non-factual and exaggerated. A reasonable person wouldn't rely on them to buy property. Agents must never guarantee anything and make only statements they believe.
5. Penalties for breach of duty to principals or third parties include disciplinary action by professional associations, action by the Ohio Division of Real Estate, civil lawsuits filed by the injured parties, and, in particularly serious cases, the filing of criminal charges against the agent.
6. Agency can be terminated by accomplishment of purpose, expiration of agency agreement, operation of law, mutual agreement, renunciation by agent, or revocation by principal. All of these should be terminated with written documentation releasing broker and client from responsibility to fulfill the contract. Agency ends by operation of law if a party dies, becomes incapacitated or goes bankrupt, property is destroyed or condemned, or the agent loses license. Agency coupled with an interest should be terminated by mutual consent.

Chapter 6 Quiz

1. ***Which of the following is true about the broker-salesperson relationship?***
   a. It's not a fiduciary relationship since a salesperson works for the client
   b. It's usually a subcontractor relationship
   c. Salespeople are agents of their broker
   d. All of the above statements are true
2. ***Which of the following statements is true with regard to listing agreements and Ohio law?***
   a. Listing agreements for less than one year need to be in writing
   b. Listing agreements for one year or more do not need to be in writing
   c. Any listing agreement must be in writing to be enforceable in a court of law
   d. Listing agreements are not agency contracts because there's an agency disclosure form

3. ***All of the following are true about an agency relationship,* except:**
   a. The seller has a fiduciary responsibility toward the buyer
   b. It may be created between a licensee and a buyer
   c. Subagency is when a licensee is an agent of an agent
   d. It's illegal for a salesperson to represent a client directly, without a broker

4. ***Under Ohio's Agency Law, two licensees from the same brokerage are considered dual agents if which of the following conditions are met?***
   a. The two agents are non-management-level licensees at the same brokerage
   b. Company policy says that all agents represent all clients of the brokerage
   c. The two licensees acted independently in establishing an agency relation ship with their respective clients and did not assist one another
   d. Both licensees co-listed a property

5. ***When must a seller's agent give a Consumer Guide to Agency Relationships to a seller?***
   a. Before the buyer's offer is presented
   b. Prior to showing a buyer the property
   c. At the same time a listing agreement is entered into
   d. On initiating a pre-qualification evaluation

6. ***When must a buyer's agent give a Consumer Guide to Agency Relationship to the buyer?***
   a. After the buyer's offer is presented
   b. Immediately after marketing or showing the property
   c. At the same time a listing agreement is entered into
   d. At the open house, if the buyer wants to write an offer on the home

7. ***When must a buyer's agent give an Agency Disclosure Statement to a buyer?***
   a. Before the buyer's offer is written
   b. Prior to marketing or showing the property
   c. At the same time a listing agreement is entered into
   d. On initiating a pre-qualification evaluation

8. ***When must a buyer's agent give an Agency Disclosure Statement to a seller?***
   a. Before the buyer's offer is presented
   b. Immediately after marketing or showing the property
   c. At the same time a listing agreement is entered into
   d. It's not required unless the agent requests confidential information from the buyer

9. ***Trisha wants to sell her house quickly because her new job in another city begins the first of next month. She tells Ed to do whatever it takes to sell her house. Which of the following represents Ed's fiduciary duty?***
   a. Tell prospective buyers that Trisha wants her house sold as quickly as possible because he must follow all instructions of the client
   b. Have his friend buy the house at a lower price because he feels that Trisha's primary interest is in selling the house quickly, not the price
   c. Weed out offers that seem unreasonable or for which Ed knows the buyers can't obtain financing to keep Trisha from wasting her time
   d. Find a suitable buyer as quickly as possible, even if this means Ed must make less of a commission on the deal than he had anticipated

10. ***Marsha is a broker at Johnson Realty. She has a property listed that is a little run-down. The owner hasn't made any effort to fix it up over the years and has ignored Marsha's suggestions. Ron, one of Marsha's non-management-level licensees at Johnson, wants to buy the property. Which of the following is true?***

a. Since Ron is a non-management-level licensee, Marsha does not need to make any further disclosures to the seller

b. Marsha should again suggest some improvements to the seller, and then make all necessary disclosures and have forms signed with regard to Ron as a potential buyer of the property

c. Suggest additional improvements again to the seller, but nothing else

d. Marsha doesn't need to do anything as long as she keeps any confidential information that she received from the seller confidential

11. ***Which of the following is not dual agency?***

a. A licensee represents both the buyer/customer and seller/client in the same real estate transaction

b. A brokerage represents both the buyer and seller as clients in the same real estate transaction

c. The only manager in the company represents a client in an in-company real estate transaction

d. Two licensees in the same company represent their own individual clients in the same transaction

12. ***A salesperson who is not an agent of the buyer is responsible for telling the buyer:***

a. Nothing, since a fiduciary relationship does not exist

b. Everything, since the agent has the duties of good faith and fair dealing

c. All known latent defects in the property, whether or not the buyer asks about them

d. All known patent defects in the property, whether or not the buyer asks about them

13. ***Eve is the real estate agent with whom Shane has listed his house for sale. Shane tells Eve about the leaks in the roof because he thinks a new buyer might see them anyway. What he doesn't tell Eve is that the house will also need a new well because the old one isn't deep enough and mud gets into the pipes every time there's a heavy rain. As a rule, Eve usually has an inspection done on homes that she represents and discovers that Shane's house also has termites. Some months later, Eve has shown the house to 13 buyers and none has been interested, so Eve decides on a different strategy to sell the house. She decides not to tell her new prospect about the leaky roof because she thinks that's easy to spot, but also decides not to mention the termites because the inspection report was not required and the new prospect never asked her about it. Are any of these items considered to be actual fraud or constructive fraud?***

Item #1: roof; Item #2: well; Item #3: termites

a. All three items represent actual fraud for both Shane and Eve

b. All three items represent constructive fraud

c. The roof is a non-issue; the well is actual fraud by Eve, and the termites is constructive fraud by Shane

d. The roof may be an issue depending on how visible it was; the well is actual fraud by Shane, and the termites are actual fraud by Eve.

14. *An "as is" clause in a purchase agreement:*

a. Protects the seller from liability for nondisclosure of a latent defect
b. Applies to patent defects in the purchases of residential real estate
c. Gives a buyer no recourse for problems with the property
d. Is a defense against a fraud lawsuit

15. *Agency may not be terminated in which of the following ways?*

a. Action by the National Association of REALTORS®, but only if either party is a member
b. Accomplishment of purpose
c. Renunciation by the agent
d. Revocation by the principal

16. *Agency coupled with an interest should be terminated in which of the following ways?*

a. Revocation by the principal
b. Death of the principal
c. Bankruptcy of the principal
d. Mutual agreement

7 REAL ESTATE CONTRACTS, AGREEMENTS, AND DOCUMENTS

CHAPTER OVERVIEW

Now that you have an understanding of agency, it's time to examine the contracts, agreements, and documents that are used in real estate. This is important because most lawsuits result from problems in this area. Listing agreements are the primary instruments that give agents the authority to represent clients. These follow basic rules of contract law. Purchase contracts are another important type of contract. Finally, we'll review options, leases, and other real estate documents.

KEY TERMS

Assignment
When one party (the assignor) transfers his or her rights or interests under a contract to another person (the assignee). When a contract is assigned, assignor remains secondarily liable and can be sued if assignee doesn't perform.

Consideration
Anything of value such as money, services, goods, or promises, given to induce another to enter into a contract.

Counteroffer
A counteroffer represents a change; it's a response to an offer, changing some terms of the original offer, thus rejecting the original offer and creating a new offer.

Material Breach
An unexcused failure to perform according to the terms of a contract, important enough so that the other party isn't required to perform.

Novation
When one party to a contract withdraws and a new party is substituted, relieving the withdrawing party of liability. Also refers to substitution of a new obligation in place of the original one with the consent of both parties.

Offer and Acceptance
The two elements that demonstrate the parties' mutual consent to the terms of a contract. Also referred to as a **meeting of the minds**.

Specific Performance
A legal remedy in which a court orders the breaching party of a contract to perform as agreed instead of simply paying damages.

Statute of Frauds
A law that requires certain types of contracts to be in writing and signed to be enforceable.

Tendering Performance
Offering to fulfill your side of a contract.

I. CONTRACT LAW

Contract law is important to understand because it touches many aspects of real estate. The basic concepts and requirements of contract law are the same whether we're talking about a listing agreement, a purchase contract, or any other type of agreement. In fact, agreement is another word for contract.

A contract doesn't need to be a lengthy document, but to be enforceable in a court of law there are some rules for contract formation.

II. CONTRACT CLASSIFICATIONS

A **contract** is an agreement between two or more parties to do, or not do, something. Contracts are legally enforceable promises, with the law providing remedies for breach. Contracts can be classified several ways. Every contract is either **express** or **implied**, **unilateral** or **bilateral**, and **executory** or **executed**.

EXPRESS VERSUS IMPLIED

An **express contract** is an agreement that's been *expressed in words*, either spoken or written. Signing a work order at the garage to fix you car is an express contract. An **implied contract** is an agreement that hasn't been put into words but is *implied by actions* of the parties. Eating at a restaurant is an implied contract. It's understood that you agree to pay the bill, even if you don't actually discuss it before you sit down or finish eating.

UNILATERAL VERSUS BILATERAL

A **unilateral contract** means only one party makes a binding promise to the other. An option is an example of a unilateral contract. A **bilateral contract** is when each party makes a binding promise to the other. A listing agreement is an example of a bilateral contract. The seller agrees to pay a commission if the broker finds a buyer, and the broker agrees to advertise and market the property and carry out other responsibilities to the seller. A purchase offer submitted by a buyer for a particular piece of real estate is a unilateral contract. But when the seller signs the offer, agreeing to the price and terms, it becomes a purchase contract, which is a bilateral contract; the buyer is obligated to pay the sum of money stated, and the seller is obligated to deliver good title to the property.

EXECUTORY VERSUS EXECUTED

An **executory contract** is one in which one or both parties have not yet completed performance of their contractual obligations. They may be in the process of carrying out their duties. An **executed contract** is a contract in which both parties have fully performed their contractual obligations (not to be confused with *executing* a contract, which is merely the act of signing it. People do say that a signed contract is "executed," but in a true legal sense a contract is only "executed" after all promises have been fulfilled). Contracts start out executory and end up executed.

Status of Contracts

In addition to being express or implied, unilateral or bilateral, executory or executed, a contract is *valid, void, voidable, or unenforceable*.

VALID. A **valid** contract is a binding, legally enforceable contract. It meets all of the legal requirements for contract formation. If one party doesn't fulfill his or her side of the bargain, the other party can sue to have the contract enforced.

VOID. A **void** contract is a contract that isn't enforceable because it lacks one or more of the requirements for contract formation, or is defective in some other respect. In the eyes of the law, it isn't a contract. If one party doesn't perform, and the other party sues, a judge will rule that there was no contract.

VOIDABLE. A **voidable** contract is a contract that one of the parties can end without liability because of a lack of legal capacity or other factor such as fraud or duress. This generally happens when one of the parties is a minor or was taken advantage of in some way. The injured party can choose whether or not to go through with the contract. If he or she decides against it, the injured party can **disaffirm** the contract by taking action that notifies the other party the contract is terminated.

UNENFORCEABLE. An **unenforceable** contract is a contract that a court would refuse to enforce. For example, a contract may be unenforceable because its contents can't be proven (a problem with an oral contract), because it's not in writing (such as a real estate contract), or because the statute of limitations has run out (even though the contract was valid before). Vaguely worded contracts may also be unenforceable.

III. CONTRACT FORMATION

There are five essential elements for a valid contract:

1. Contractual capacity
2. Offer
3. Acceptance
4. Consideration
5. Lawful and possible objective

These requirements apply to *all* contacts. Also, certain contracts (such as those for the sale of real property) must be in writing and signed to be enforceable.

CONTRACTUAL CAPACITY

Contractual capacity is the legal ability to enter a contract. This is also called **contractual ability**. To make a valid contract in Ohio, a person must be at least 18 years old and mentally competent. This requirement protects minors and the mentally ill who otherwise might enter into contracts without understanding the consequences. When an adult enters into a contract with a minor, the contract is voidable by the minor only. Even if the minor pretended to be over 18, he or she can disaffirm the contract at any time before turning 18 or within a reasonable time thereafter. The minor may choose to enforce the contract and require the adult to perform. The adult does not have the power to disaffirm the contract.

EXAMPLE Marc was only 17 when he signed a contract to buy a house from Sherry who didn't realize Marc was underage. A few weeks later, when the sale is ready to close, Marc changes his mind and tells Sherry the deal is off. Sherry can't sue to enforce the contract. But, if the tables were turned and Sherry wanted to back out, Marc could sue Sherry to enforce the contract.)

An adult who is incapable of understanding the nature and consequences of a contract also doesn't have capacity to contract. After a person has been declared incompetent by a court (because of mental illness, retardation, or senility), any contract he or she enters into is considered void. Neither the incompetent person nor the other party can have it enforced.

Even if a person hasn't been declared legally incompetent, in some cases it can be proven that he or she was not of sound mind when the contract was signed. So, a court may rule in different ways, depending on the circumstances in each case. The contract may be voidable by the incompetent person, but if the other party acted in good faith without notice of the incompetency, a court might decide to enforce the contract.

OFFER

An **offer** occurs when one party proposes a contract to another party. If the other party accepts the offer, a contract is formed. For a contract to be binding, all parties must consent to its terms. This mutual consent is sometimes referred to as a **"meeting of the minds"** and is achieved through offer *and* acceptance. Here we will discuss the first half of this requirement.

REQUIREMENTS FOR AN OFFER. The process of forming a contract begins when one party (the **offeror**) makes an offer to another party (the **offeree**). For this to serve as the basis for a contract, there are two basic requirements for an offer. an intent to contract and definite terms.

Intent to Contract. The intent requirement is concerned with **objective intent** (what the offeror says and does) rather than **subjective intent** (what the offeror is actually thinking). If you say or do something a reasonable person could interpret as a serious expression of the intention to make a contract, that may be a legally binding offer—even if you were just kidding.

Definite Terms. The offer must also have definite terms. An offer isn't binding if it's vague. The offer should state at least such basic items as the subject matter, the time for performance, and the price. In some cases, a court will fill in the blanks with a reasonable time or price, but if too many terms are left unspecified, no contract is formed.

OFFERS REGARDING REAL ESTATE. Note that a real estate listing is *not* considered a property owner's offer to sell. By listing the property, the seller is merely soliciting

offers from potential buyers. A buyer doesn't create a contract by accepting the seller's listing. Instead, a buyer makes an offer to purchase and the seller accepts or rejects the offer. The listing is considered an independent contract between the seller and a real estate broker, not part of the contract between the seller and buyer.

TERMINATION OF AN OFFER. To create a binding contract, an offer must be accepted before it terminates. An offer can be terminated by **lapse of time**, **death or incapacity** of one of the parties, **revocation**, or **rejection**.

Lapse of Time. Many offers state they will expire at a certain time—"after five days" or "on March 31." When an offer doesn't specify an expiration date, it expires after a reasonable time. Even when an offer has an expiration date, however, it may be terminated sooner by death or incapacity, revocation, or rejection.

Death or Incapacity. The death or incapacity of one of the parties makes it impossible to form a contract. This would also terminate an offer before a stated expiration date. For instance, suppose an offer made on March 1 states that it will expire on March 31. If the offeror dies on March 23, before the offer has been accepted, the offer terminates on that date; it doesn't continue until March 31. The offeree cannot create a contract by accepting the contract on March 24.

Revocation. An offer is terminated if the offeror revokes or withdraws it before the offeree accepts it. At the point that the offer has been revoked, the offeree has lost the chance to accept it. This is true even if the offer stated that it was irrevocable or that it wouldn't expire until a particular date.

EXAMPLE On April 15, Heidi submits a written offer to buy Steve's house for $90,000. The offer states that it will remain open until April 23. While Steve is making up his mind, Heidi finds a different house she wants instead of Steve's. She calls Steve on April 18 and revokes her offer. Now, even if Steve sends Heidi an acceptance before April 23, it won't create a binding contract.

It's a different matter if an offeree pays the offeror a sum of money to keep the offer open. Then the offer can't be revoked during the specified period. The offer has been turned into an **option** (discussed at the end of this chapter).

Rejection. An offer is also terminated when it's rejected by the offeree. If I reject your offer on Monday, I can't change my mind and call back on Tuesday to accept it. If you're still interested in the deal, we can start the process of offer and acceptance over again, but your original offer was terminated by my rejection. If you've lost interest, I can no longer hold you to your offer.

ACCEPTANCE

Acceptance occurs when a party agrees to the terms of an offer to enter into a contract. When an offer is accepted, a contract is formed. At that point, the parties are legally bound. Neither can back out unless the other is willing to end the contract. Acceptance is part of the mutual consent needed to reach a

"meeting of the minds." The licensee tries to get offers accepted by the other parties. The licensee often is the one who delivers the signed offer or contract or communicates acceptance of the offer or contract to a client or on behalf of a client.

Requirements for Acceptance

To complete the formation of a contract, the offer must be accepted. There are four basic requirements for acceptance:

1. Acceptance of an offer **can be made only by the offeree**
2. Acceptance must be **communicated to the offeror**
3. Acceptance must be **made in the manner specified**
4. Acceptance must **not vary the terms of the offer**

ACCEPTANCE OF AN OFFER CAN ONLY BE MADE BY THE OFFEREE. This may sound obvious, but there is an important distinction. It means that if A makes an offer to B, and B decides not to accept it, C can't accept the offer and force A to deal with him. Of course, A may be willing to work with C, but in legal terms, any contract between A and C is based on a new offer, not on the offer A made to B.

ACCEPTANCE MUST BE COMMUNICATED TO THE OFFEROR. You may have decided to accept my offer, but until you let me know you've accepted it, I can still revoke it. Even giving you an earnest money deposit check that you cash is not enough for me to know you've accepted my offer. You must tell me directly.

"The mailbox rule" says that an acceptance not communicated directly, in person, or over the phone is effective as soon as it's *sent in the mail* to the offeror, even though the other party hasn't yet received it. If B puts a letter accepting A's offer into the mailbox at 1:00, and at 1:30 A calls B to revoke the offer, A's revocation was too late. A contract was formed when B mailed an acceptance even before A received it.

Note that the *mailbox rule only applies to acceptances* and not revocations. If an offeror mails a revocation to the offeree, it's not effective until the offeree actually receives it. Until the offeree has received notice of revocation, a binding contract can still be created by accepting the offer.

ACCEPTANCE MUST BE MADE IN THE MANNER SPECIFIED. Many offers specify a certain manner of acceptance (e.g., "in writing," "via fax," or "by delivering a cashier's check"). This avoids the mailbox rule problem. The offeree's acceptance won't be effective unless the instructions in the offer are followed. Suppose the offer states that the acceptance must be in writing, and the offeree calls and accepts over the phone. That doesn't create a binding contract; the offeror can still revoke the offer.

When an offer doesn't specify how it is to be accepted, any reasonable method of acceptance will be effective to bind the offeror and prevent revocation. This rule applies to all contracts—even those that are required by law to be in writing and signed, such as real estate purchase agreements. Remember, the *offeror* can be bound by an oral acceptance even if the contract is required to be in writing, but only a written, signed acceptance is binding on the *offeree*.

EXAMPLE B submits a written, signed offer to buy S's home. S accepts over the phone. If B tries to back out of the deal, S can sue to enforce the contract. But if S decides not to sell, B is out of luck since S didn't sign the contract.

ACCEPTANCE MUST NOT VARY THE TERMS OF THE OFFER. To create a contract, the offeree must accept exactly those terms offered. The offeree can't modify them or add new terms. If an offeree makes changes, that response to the offer isn't an acceptance, it's a *counteroffer*. A **counteroffer** represents a change. It's essentially a rejection and a new offer. The person who originally was the offeror has become the counterofferee, and the original offeree is now the counterofferor. A binding contract isn't created unless the counterofferee accepts the counteroffer.

Since a counteroffer is a rejection, it terminates the original offer. If your counteroffer is rejected, it's too late to go back and accept the original offer. You can start again with a new offer identical to the original one, but if the original offeror has had a change of heart, you can no longer hold him or her to the original offer.

Sometimes an offeree rewords the offer slightly or adds a phrase to clarify or emphasize a certain clause. As long as these revisions or additions don't materially change the terms of the offer, the response is still an acceptance not a counteroffer.

Genuine Assent

A **genuine assent** means consent must be freely given to create a binding contract. Offer and acceptance aren't freely given as mutual consent when either is the result of **fraud**, **undue influence**, **duress**, or **mistake**. If any of these factors is present, they make a contract voidable by the victimized party.

FRAUD. **Fraud** is intentional or negligent misrepresentation of material facts and occurs when a person relied on another to be truthful. The fraud results in a contract that would not have been completed had the truth been known. Fraud compromises assent allowing the defrauded to escape the contract.

UNDUE INFLUENCE. **Undue influence** is putting excessive pressure on someone, thus, preventing him or her from making a rational or prudent decision. A contract is voidable if you persuade someone to sign by taking advantage of another's trust in you or weakness of mind (exhaustion, senility, etc.). This may involve telling someone there's no time to consult a lawyer because papers must be signed right away.

DURESS. **Duress** is threatening violence against or unlawfully confining a person, or any member of that person's family, to force him or her to sign a document. Duress can also be a threat of injury to reputation, i.e., blackmail. **Economic duress** (also called **business compulsion**) is a threat of taking action that will be financially disastrous to the victim (e.g., non-payment). These actions make a contract voidable.

MISTAKE. **Mistake** occurs when one or more parties to a contract were mistaken about a fact or law. Usually this doesn't involve bad faith or intentions. If both parties are mistaken about something important to their contract (**mutual mistake**), either may disaffirm it. If only one party is mistaken (**unilateral mistake**), the contract isn't voidable unless the other party knew of the mistake and did nothing.

CONSIDERATION

Consideration is anything of value such as money, services, goods, or promises given to induce another to enter into a contract. It is also called **valuable consideration**. A contract can't be one-way; each party must give something to the other. Consideration for most contracts is a *promise* to give something of value. Thus, the parties to a contract are sometimes referred to as the **promisor** (one making a promise) and the **promisee** (one who gets the benefit of a promise).

An earnest money deposit given with an offer is *not* consideration. In fact, earnest money is not required for an offer. Instead, earnest money is an inducement to have the buyer's offer accepted and a means of showing the seller that the buyer is serious and able to follow through with the financing necessary to buy the property. Typically, the earnest money is held in the selling broker's trust account. It could, however, be held in the listing broker's trust account if both the buyer and seller agree. In either case, the money will not earn interest. If the buyer wants his or her earnest money to earn interest, it will have to be held by the seller in an interesting-bearing account, or the buyer and seller could open an interest bearing account. Once a contract is entered into and earnest money has been deposited into the broker's trust account, it can be released only if one of the following occurs:

- Completion of the sale
- Mutual release signed by all parties to the contract
- Court order

Exchanging consideration distinguishes a contractual promise from the promise of a gift. A promise isn't enforceable in court unless it's a contractual obligation for which both parties exchanged consideration. In a typical real estate contract, the buyer promises to pay the seller money and the seller promises to transfer title to the buyer. These promises create an executory contract; when they're fulfilled (buyer pays seller; seller gives buyer a deed), the contract is executed.

Promising something you're already legally obligated to do (or promising not to do something the law doesn't allow you to do) isn't consideration. If A and B already have a contract for A to clean B's gutters, A can't stop in the middle and demand more money with a threat of not finishing the job. Even if B agrees, this isn't an enforceable contract—A can't sue B if she won't pay extra money—because A was already obligated to finish the job.

Something you've already done can't be consideration either. If A says to B, "Because you graduated, I'm going to buy you a car," that's not a contract. B already graduated, so he didn't do anything (or give up anything) in exchange for A's promise.

Adequacy

It's important to understand that the value of the consideration one party gives doesn't have to be equal to the value of what the other gives. In other words, even if one party struck a bad bargain, both still have an enforceable contract.

> **EXAMPLE** A house was appraised at $97,000, but the seller accepts an offer for $29,000 since the seller expects to leave the country next week for a new job. Later, the seller doesn't have to leave and wants to back out of the sale, but the buyer won't allow it. Their contract is binding since each gave consideration.

Of course, grossly unequal consideration may mean there was fraud, undue influence, duress, or mistake involved. But the contract is enforceable unless this is proven. In the previous example, a judge may rule that $29,000 is not legally **adequate** consideration. If so, the seller may have to pay damages for breach of contract but can't be forced to sell the home (see **specific performance** later in this chapter).

LAWFUL AND POSSIBLE OBJECTIVE

Lawful and possible objective means the purpose or objective of a contract must be lawful at the time the contract is made. When one person promises to pay someone for committing an illegal act, the contract is void. A court may also refuse to enforce a contract that's not strictly illegal, if its objective violates public policy.

Many contracts have more than one purpose and they are often *severable*. **Severable** means that one part or provision of a contract can be held unenforceable without making the entire contract unenforceable. The unenforceable part is severed, or cut, from the rest of the agreement, but the rest can be enforced.

In addition to being lawful, a contract objective must be possible. That doesn't necessarily mean possible for the one who promised it; it means possible for anyone.

> **EXAMPLE** S contracts to sell a house, which he doesn't own, to B. This contract is not void because of impossibility. It's impossible for S to perform as promised without owning the house, but it's not impossible for anyone to perform. S may be required to buy the house and sell it to B, or pay B damages.

IV. THE STATUTE OF FRAUDS

The **statute of frauds** is a law requiring certain types of contracts to be in writing and signed to be enforceable. As the name implies, they're required to be in writing to prevent fraudulent claims and false testimony. Parties to unwritten contracts are likely to later disagree about exactly what each agreed to do.

Contracts that Must be in Writing

In Ohio, the statute of frauds applies to contracts that can't be performed within one year from the time they're made, contracts for the sale of goods for $500 or more, contracts for the sale of personal property for $5,000 or more, contracts made in exchange for marriage proposal, promises to guarantee another's debt, leases for more than one year, options for more than six months, and purchase contracts for real property. All of these types of contracts must be in writing and signed.

REAL ESTATE. Ohio's statute of frauds applies to contracts conveying an interest in real estate. These can be purchase contracts, options, mortgages, or deeds. A written contract is needed to enforce these agreements.

In addition, the statute of frauds applies to any **power of attorney** authorizing someone to sell another's real estate. A **power of attorney** is an instrument authorizing one person (called an attorney in fact) to act as another's agent to the extent stated in the instrument. Unlike an attorney at law, an attorney in fact can be anyone. This person's authority is usually severely limited and always restricted to those things specifically stated in the agreement. A power of attorney conferring the right to sell another's real property must be in writing, signed, witnessed by two competent witnesses, acknowledged before a notary, and recorded with the county recorder in the county where the land is situated to become effective.

LISTING AGREEMENTS. A listing agreement is considered an employment agreement, ***so the statute of frauds does not*** require it to be in writing, but Ohio real estate ***licensing law does require*** listing agreements that last for one year or more to be in writing. And all listing agreements (even those for less than one year) must be in writing to be enforceable in a court of law. Ohio's licensing law also requires that expiration dates be stated as a date certain in listing agreements and that true copies must be left with all parties. Having listing agreements in writing and signed also helps avoid misunderstandings. Check with your broker regarding policies in this area.

Type of Writing Required

To satisfy the statute of frauds, the writing doesn't have to be a formal legal document. A note or memo is enough if it indicates there's an agreement between the parties, and it's signed. Keep in mind that contracts need to be signed only by "the party to be charged"—that is, the party who may want to back out. A full signature is not necessary; initials are enough. In fact, anything the signer intends as a signature will do, but keep in mind that a wavy line or an "X" could be denied later.

Part Performance

The **doctrine of part performance** allows an Ohio court to enforce an oral agreement that should have been in writing if the promisee has taken irrevocable steps to perform his or her side of the bargain, and failure to enforce the contract would result in an unjust benefit for the promisor. Some cases involving the statute of frauds seem unfair, since one party gets away with breaching a contract because the other party didn't know the law requires that type of contract to be in writing.

Part performance tries to stop unfairness in some cases because one party began to perform his or her side of the contract, relying on the other party's promises.

Interpretation of Written Contracts

In a breach of contract lawsuit, the court must interpret the parties' agreement to decide if it's been breached. The court tries to decipher and put into effect what the parties intended when they entered the contract. As a general rule with written contracts, the court is supposed to determine the parties' intention from the written document alone if possible.

Parole Evidence Rule

Parole evidence is evidence concerning negotiations or oral agreements that wasn't included in a contract. This may directly contradict what's actually written in the contract. Courts generally refuse to admit this kind of evidence, but if a document is unclear or ambiguous, a judge may allow testimony about contract negotiations to determine what the parties intended.

V. ASSIGNMENT

In an **assignment**, one of the parties (the **assignor**) transfers his or her rights or interests under a contract to another person (the **assignee**). In Ohio, all contracts are assignable unless the contract states otherwise. Also, either party can assign the contract without the other's consent, unless the contract says consent is required.

One exception concerns contracts for personal services. A party to a personal service contract can only assign the contract with consent of the other party. If you hire me to sing at your wedding, you can't make me sing at someone else's wedding, and I can't send my friend instead of me. (Listing agreements are considered personal service contracts.) Another exception is that a contract can't be assigned without consent if assignment would change the party's duties or increase his or her risks.

LIABILITY

When a contract is assigned, the assignor is *not* relieved of liability under the contract. The assignor remains secondarily liable to the other party and can be sued if the assignee doesn't perform. This rule applies even when the other party consents to the assignment.

NOVATION

Novation means one party to a contract withdraws and a new party is substituted, relieving the withdrawing party of liability. This is better than an assignment because the withdrawing party avoids secondary liability. A novation can be arranged only with the other original party's consent.

The term **novation** also refers to the substitution of a new obligation in place of the original. If the original parties tear up a two-year lease and execute a five-year lease, that's a novation. Both parties must give their consent.

ACCORD AND SATISFACTION

Accord and satisfaction is an agreement to accept something different (and usually less) than what the original contract requested. To extinguish the original obligation, the promisee must execute a document stating that the promisor's performance has been accepted in satisfaction of the obligation.

VI. PERFORMANCE AND BREACH OF CONTRACT

If one party to a contract performs his or her side of the bargain, the other party is required to perform, too. If one party fails to perform and the failure is not excused, he or she has breached the contract. When one party breaches, the other party is not required to perform. If I contract to paint your garage for $5,000, and I don't paint the garage, you don't have to pay me $5,000.

Unfortunately, it isn't always so easy to determine whether there has been a breach. Suppose one party (A) does all of the things promised, but the other party (B) feels they were not done well, or A does nearly everything promised, but some details aren't finished, or A does everything promised but takes longer to do it than agreed. In these cases, there's room for argument about whether the contract was breached and whether B is required to perform his or her side of the bargain. B's obligation to perform depends on whether there has been **substantial performance** or a **material breach**.

Substantial Performance versus Material Breach

Substantial performance means a promisor doesn't perform all of his or her contractual obligations but does enough so that the promisee is required to fulfill his or her part of the deal. If A hasn't fulfilled every detail of a contract but has carried out its main objectives, that may be treated as substantial performance. Although B may be able to sue for damages because of the unfulfilled details, B still must perform as agreed.

Material breach is a breach of contract important enough to excuse the non-breaching party from performing his or her contractual obligations. If A fails to perform some important part of the contract or performs very badly, that will be treated as a material breach. If A commits a material breach, B may be able to sue for damages and is excused from fulfilling his promises.

Which provisions of a contract are so important that failure to fulfill them amounts to a material breach? That depends on the circumstances of the case. If the promisee emphasized that a particular detail of the contract was especially important, failure to comply with that detail may be held to be a material breach.

TIME IS OF THE ESSENCE. Many contracts state "time is of the essence." The purpose of this phrase is to emphasize that timely performance is an essential part of the contract, and failure to perform on time will be a material breach. When a contract does not provide a "time is of the essence" clause, usually performance within a reasonable time after a stated deadline is not a material breach.

Thus, if "time is of the essence" **is not** in the contract and the buyer was late in performing, then the seller could give the buyer a reasonable time to perform even though the deadline in the contract had passed. The contract would be voidable at that point by the seller and the seller could terminate the contract at anytime.

Whereas, if "time is of the essence" **is in** the contract, then, the contract is void as soon as the deadline has passed, as the buyer would be in material breach. The only way to save the contract would be for the buyer and seller to agree to extend the contract before the deadline passes.

EXAMPLE S agreed to sell B her house with closing set for August 15. That date arrives, but S hasn't cleared the title or completed the repairs yet. B doesn't complain. Finally, three weeks later, S is ready to go. But now B has decided he doesn't want that house, so he refuses to pay S and accept the deed. When S sues, B objects that S breached the contract by missing the deadline. The court rules that B's actions waived the right to treat S's delay as a material breach. Thus, B is required to perform his side of the bargain.

Conditions

Conditions are contract provisions (or a deed) that make the parties' rights or obligations depend on the occurrence (or non-occurrence) of certain events. These are also called **contingency clauses**. Contracts often include one or more conditions. If the event doesn't occur, the promisor can withdraw without liability for breach of contract. For example, a purchase agreement may be contingent on the sale of the buyer's current home, the buyer qualifying for financing, satisfactory results of a home inspection, pest inspection, or soil test.

When a contract is conditional, the promisor must make a good faith effort to fulfill the condition. He or she can't deliberately prevent its fulfillment to get out of the contract. A condition can be waived by the party it was intended to benefit or protect. When a condition is included for the benefit of both parties, neither can waive it without the other's consent.

Tendering Performance

Tendering performance is offering to perform your side of a contract. A **tender offer** or simply a **tender** is an unconditional offer by one party to perform his or her part of a contract. If A believes that B isn't going to fulfill the contract because B hasn't taken any steps to carry it out, A must *offer* to perform his side of the deal (which B isn't likely to accept) before A can sue B for breach of contract.

ANTICIPATORY REPUDIATION. **Anticipatory repudiation** means one party to a contract informs the other before the set time of performance that he or she doesn't intend to perform as agreed. When a party to a contract clearly and unequivocally states that he or she doesn't intend to perform, that party is said to have repudiated the contract. Once one party has repudiated a contract, the other party may immediately file a lawsuit for breach of contract without making a tender offer.

EXAMPLE B tells A that she isn't going to go through with the purchase of A's property. A does not have to wait until the scheduled closing date or tender his performance before suing B for breach of contract.

Remedies for Breach of Contract

If a promisee performed badly or refused to perform (either by anticipatory repudiation or by rejecting a tender offer), the promisor can turn to the courts for help. If a court finds there's been a breach, remedies available include **compensatory damages**, **liquidated damages**, **specific performance,** and **rescission**.

COMPENSATORY DAMAGES. **Compensatory damages** are a damage award, usually money, intended to compensate the plaintiff for harm caused by the defendant's act or failure to act. This is the most common remedy for breach of contract. The award is usually the amount that will put the non-breaching party in the same position he or she would have been in if the other party had fulfilled the contract.

EXAMPLE Calvin had a contract with Liz to build her a house for $100,000, but later gets a more lucrative contract and doesn't build Liz's house. Liz gets Oscar to do the work instead, but he charges her $125,000. If Liz sues Calvin for breach of contract, Calvin will likely have to pay her only $25,000 in compensatory damages—the extra amount Liz had to pay.

Note that if Oscar's price was only $90,000, Liz would have actually been better off and probably not entitled to a judgment against Calvin since she wasn't damaged by the breach. A contract lawsuit is to compensate a party for actual damages not to punish a party for breach. (Punitive damages are for cases involving torts or fraud.)

MITIGATION OF DAMAGES. **Mitigation** means the non-breaching party takes action to minimize the losses resulting from a breach of contract. The non-breaching party in a contract dispute is required to do whatever is possible to reduce the losses or mitigate the damage resulting from the other party's breach.

EXAMPLE Bob contracts to buy Sue's home for $100,000, then refuses to go through with the deal. Sue must make an effort to find a new buyer; she can't just sue Bob for $100,000, and she can't sell it to a friend at a bargain either.

LIQUIDATED DAMAGES. **Liquidated damages** are a sum of money that the parties to a contract agree to in advance (before entering the contract) and that will serve as compensation in the event of breach. A liquidated damages clause is included in some contracts to lessen the chance of expensive litigation. Since the parties have agreed in advance to damages as a specified sum or figured using a specified formula, a non-breaching party must accept liquidated damages instead of suing for actual damages. If the breaching party refuses to pay, the case ends up in court.

For a liquidated damages clause to be enforceable, it must have seemed likely when the contract was made that calculating actual damages for a breach would be difficult. If the parties should have realized that actual damages would be easy to calculate, a court may refuse to enforce a liquidated damages clause and simply award actual damages. In addition, if the amount specified as liquidated damages is unreasonably large (much more than actual damages would be), a court may regard it as a penalty and refuse to enforce it awarding only actual damages instead.

In purchase offers and purchase contracts, there's often a clause calling for forfeiture of the earnest money deposit to the seller if the buyer does not complete the purchase of the property. This is an example of a liquidated damages provision.

SPECIFIC PERFORMANCE. **Specific Performance** is a legal remedy in which a court orders someone who has breached a contract to perform as agreed, rather than simply paying money damages. This occurs most often when the non-breaching party to a contract cannot be compensated for harm that resulted from the other's breach. In such a case, the non-breaching party has the right to compel the other party to do what was promised in the contract.

Courts usually won't grant specific performance when a damages award will be as effective. For example, a car dealer won't be ordered to sell you a particular car when you could get an identical one from another dealer. If you have to pay more at the second dealer, the first dealer will be ordered to pay you the difference as a damages award. But when the object of a contract is one of a kind, like real estate, then specific performance is an appropriate remedy since a damages award won't enable you to buy another identical item. A court can't grant specific performance in some instances. For example, a court can never grant specific performance as a remedy for breach of a personal service contract, since no one can be forced to work for someone or to employ someone. You can't be ordered to perform a contract if you didn't receive legally adequate consideration. For example, if you agreed to sell your $300,000 house for $175,000, the contract is enforceable even though the consideration is inadequate. You may have to pay the buyer damages, but you can't be forced to complete the sale.

RESCISSION. **Rescission** means a contract is terminated, and each party gives anything acquired under it back to the other party. This occurs when one party doesn't want to enforce the other party's promise; one party didn't provide the promised consideration, or a voidable contract is disaffirmed. Each party agrees to undo the contract and go back to the beginning. When a contract is rescinded, each party returns any consideration the other has given. This is called **restitution**. When a contract is rescinded, all contractual obligations are terminated.

CANCELLATION. **Cancellation** is the termination of a contract without undoing acts that have been performed under it and can be done without going to court. Both parties must agree that they prefer to cancel the contract instead of rescinding it. When a contract is cancelled, all further obligations are terminated.

VII. REAL ESTATE CONTRACTS AND AGREEMENTS

A real estate agent needs to be familiar with several kinds of contracts. Each applies the basic rules of contract law outlined in the first part of this chapter. Here we'll take a brief look at **listing agreements**, **buyer agency agreements, purchase contracts**, **options,** and **leases**.

LISTING AGREEMENTS

Listing agreements are written agency contracts between a seller and a real estate broker stipulating the conditions under which the broker will be paid a commission with regard to the seller's property. They are employment contracts between a seller and a real estate broker. The seller hires the broker to find a buyer and, in exchange for the broker's services, the seller will pay a commission.

The commission rate or amount must be negotiated between seller and broker. **It's a violation of federal and state Sherman antitrust laws for brokers to set uniform commission rates.** Any discussion of rates among members of competing firms could give rise to a charge of price fixing.

PAYMENT OF COMMISSION. Payment of a broker's commission may be dependent on any lawful condition. The listing agreement may specify the commission is due when the seller signs a binding contract with a buyer or only if a sale actually closes.

Unless otherwise agreed, the broker is entitled to a commission when a **ready, willing, and able** buyer is found. A buyer is considered **ready and willing** if he or she makes an offer that meets the terms established by the seller in the listing agreement. A buyer is considered **able** if he or she has the financial ability to complete the purchase. Under the terms of most listing agreements, once a ready, willing, and able buyer has submitted an offer, the broker has earned a commission—even if the sale never closes.

If a buyer's offer doesn't exactly match the terms the seller specified in the listing, the seller can refuse to contract with that buyer, without owing the broker a commission. This makes it very important to have the seller's terms clearly defined in the listing agreement.

LISTING AGREEMENT REQUIREMENTS. Ohio's real estate licensing law requires any type of listing agreement to include a **definite expiration date**. Most exclusive listing agreements contain an **extension clause** that covers a certain period after the listing expires. (Also called a **broker protection clause**.) An extension clause provides that the broker is still entitled to a commission if the property is sold during the extension period, and the buyer is someone with whom the broker negotiated during the listing term. The broker should provide the seller with a list of prospects he or she introduced to the property. If the seller isn't aware that the buyer is someone with whom the broker dealt, the seller may not have to pay the commission.

Types of Listing Agreements

A broker's right to a commission also depends on the type of listing agreement. The four main types of listing agreements are **exclusive right to sell**, **exclusive agency**, **open listing**, and **net listing**.

EXCLUSIVE RIGHT TO SELL OR LEASE LISTING AGREEMENT. Exclusive right to sell or lease means an agency agreement between a seller or landlord and broker that meets the requirements of section 4735.55 of the Revised Code and does both of the following:

1. Grants the broker the exclusive right to represent the seller or landlord in the sale or lease of the seller's property
2. Provides that the broker will be compensated if the broker, the seller, or any other person or entity produces a purchaser or tenant in accordance with the terms specified in the listing agreement, or if the property is sold or leased during the term of the listing agreement to anyone other than to specifically exempted persons or entities

EXCLUSIVE AGENCY AGREEMENT. Exclusive agency means an agency agreement between a seller and broker that meets the requirements of section 4735.55 of the Revised Code and does both of the following:

1. Grants the broker the exclusive right to represent the seller in the sale or lease of the seller's property
2. Provides that the broker will be compensated if the broker or any other person or entity produces a purchaser or tenant in accordance with the terms specified in the listing agreement or if the property is sold or leased during the term of the listing agreement, unless the property is sold or leased solely through the efforts of the seller or to a specifically exempted persons or entity

OPEN LISTING. An **open listing** agreement is a non-exclusive listing given by a seller to as many brokers as he or she chooses. If the property is sold, a broker is entitled to a commission only if he or she is the **procuring cause** of the sale.

To be the **procuring cause** of a sale, the agent must be primarily responsible for bringing about a sale (e.g., introducing the buyer to a property or negotiating the contract between buyer and seller). The agent's actions must start a chain of events that result in the sale. Only the licensee who finds a buyer will be paid. Note that open listings are unilateral contracts: seller promises to pay a commission if the broker is procuring cause of the sale, but the broker doesn't actually promise to do anything.

NET LISTING. A **net listing** agreement is one in which the seller sets a net amount he or she is willing to accept for the property, with the broker being entitled to keep the excess as commission if the actual selling price exceeds that amount. Although not expressly forbidden by Ohio law, net listings are strongly discouraged by the

Division of Real Estate because they can lead to charges of fraud by a seller who may not have understood the listing terms and feels misled.

Exclusive listing agreements result in better service for sellers than open listing agreements because the broker's claim to a commission is more secure, so he or she is likely to work harder to bring about the sale.

RESIDENTIAL WORK SHEET. The Residential Work Sheet is a form that supplies all required information for the Multiple Listing Service (MLS) entry for that property. (Required information is highlighted in red on the actual form. Commercial forms are similar to these.) Facts about a property are taken from this form and published, often with a picture, in an MLS book or online computer service regularly updated by the local real estate board.

Most items in the work sheet are self-explanatory. **Always give clients copies of all documents they sign!** Failure to do so can cause loss of license.

Rules of Advertising

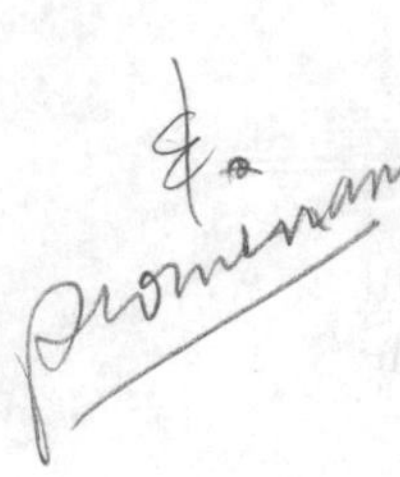

Advertising law mandates that the broker's name must be of equal or greater size than the salesperson's name in any real estate advertising. This law applies to internet advertising as well. The broker's name must be on every viewable page of the salesperson's Web page. The salesperson must update his or her Web page every 14 days, and the latest date must also show on the Web page. *Remember*: The superintendent of the Ohio Division of Real Estate may impose a citation of up to $200 for every advertising law violation.

A real estate broker who is representing a seller under an exclusive right to sell or lease listing agreement shall not advertise such property to the public as "for sale by owner" or otherwise mislead the public to believe that the seller is not represented by a real estate broker.

BUYER AGENCY AGREEMENTS

EXCLUSIVE PURCHASER AGENCY AGREEMENT. Exclusive purchaser agency or a buyer's broker agreement means an agency agreement between a purchaser and broker that meets the requirements of section 4735.55 of the Revised Code and does both of the following:

1. Grants the broker the exclusive right to represent the purchaser in the purchase or lease of property
2. Provides that the broker will be compensated in accordance with the terms specified in the exclusive agency agreement or if a property is purchased or leased by the purchaser during the term of the agency agreement unless the property is specifically exempted in the agency agreement

PURCHASE CONTRACTS. Purchase contracts are contracts in which a seller promises to convey title to real property to a buyer in exchange for the purchase price. These are also called purchase agreements, sale contracts, sale agreements, purchase and sale agreements, or earnest money agreements. In Ohio, the purchase contract form usually serves three purposes:

1. It's the buyer's offer

2. It's the receipt for the earnest money deposit
3. It's the contract between the buyer and seller (in some parts of the state where escrow closings are common, the contract may also serve as the escrow agent's instructions

Purchase Contract Requirements. First, the buyer makes an offer by filling out a purchase contract form or, more commonly, by having a real estate agent fill it out. At the same time, the buyer often gives the agent an earnest money deposit, and the agent signs the section of the form acknowledging receipt of the deposit. The agent then submits the offer to the seller or to the seller's agent. If the seller decides to accept it, he or she signs the same form creating a binding contract between buyer and seller.

At the very least, the purchase contract should identify the parties, the property, and the interest to be sold. Ideally, it will state all terms of the sale as clearly as possible: what is and isn't included in the sale, total price, and method of payment. Any conditions must be spelled out in the contract. Purchase contracts are often contingent on buyers being able to obtain financing or sell their current home.

Many purchase contracts provide that if the buyer defaults, the earnest money deposit is forfeited to the seller. This is a type of liquidated damages provision. The seller keeps the deposit instead of suing for breach of contract.

OPTIONS

Options are contracts giving one party the right to do something without obligation to do so. The most common type of real estate option is an option to purchase. An option to purchase gives one party (the **optionee**) the right to buy the property of another (the **optionor**) at a specified price within a limited time. Within that period, the optionee may choose to exercise the option, but the optionee is under no obligation to exercise the option.

An option is supported by consideration. The optionee pays the optionor for the option right. For example, if an owner tells a prospective buyer she's willing to sell her house for $100,000, the buyer might pay her $1,000 to keep that offer open for a month. The payment of consideration makes the option irrevocable until it expires. If the optionor dies before the option expires, it's still binding on the optionor's heirs.

An option to purchase real property must be in writing and signed. It must also be exercised in writing if the optionee decides to go through with the purchase of the real property under the option. The option agreement should be as specific as possible stating all the terms of the potential sale. Usually, it is not necessary to draw up a separate purchase contract when an option is exercised since the option document also serves as the purchase contract.

An option can be recorded (to protect the optionee) only if it states a definite expiration date. The optionee's claim automatically ends on that date, and the recorded option is no longer a cloud on the title.

Right of Preemption

A **right of preemption** is a right to have the first chance to buy or lease property if the owner decides to put it up for sale or lease and is also called a **right of first refusal**. It is not the same as an option. An optionee can purchase the property at any time during the option period on the stated terms. With a preemption right, a person only has the right to purchase the property before anyone else does if the owner decides to sell it and must match the terms of any offer.

LEASES

Leases are contracts in which one party pays the other rent in exchange for possession of real estate; thus, a lease is the conveyance of a leasehold estate from the fee owner to a tenant. Leases must contain all of the elements necessary for a valid contract to be legal and enforceable. Furthermore, a lease must be in writing if the term will last for more than one year, and attested and acknowledged if the term is for more than three years. Leases must also be recorded to ensure that a third party who buys a building has notice of the leases and will honor the terms.

Types of Leases

While residential leases are usually straightforward exchanges of rent for occupancy, commercial leases are usually more complex and varied in their terms. Four main types of commercial leases are **gross lease**, **net lease**, **percentage lease,** and **land lease** (or **ground lease**).

GROSS LEASE. A **gross lease** means the owner or landlord pays all property taxes, mortgage payments, insurance, etc., and the tenant pays all utilities. This is similar to a residential lease except that the commercial version can provide for future rent increases tied to inflation or taxes. A gross lease is usually used for professional tenants like lawyers, doctors, and executives.

NET LEASE. In a **net lease**, the tenant pays all property taxes, mortgage payments, insurance, etc., as well as all utilities, in addition to a monthly rent payment. This is a variation of the gross lease, but the owner or landlord has shifted much of the risk for increased costs to the tenants who pay a proportional amount of the property taxes, insurance, and sometimes maintenance costs.

PERCENTAGE LEASE. A **percentage lease** means the tenant pays a percentage of his or her gross sales to the landlord, often in addition to a fixed monthly rental payment. Utilities may or may not be included in this type of arrangement, which is used most commonly for retail tenants.

LAND LEASE. A **land lease** (or **ground lease**) means a tenant leases only the land from the landlord, but the tenant actually owns the building. This is usually first done when the land is vacant, but the owner of the building is free to sell the building at will and have the buyer assume the land lease. Likewise, the landlord can sell the land subject to the lease of the building owner. This type of lease usually has a term equal to the life expectancy of the building or as long as 99 years.

OTHER REAL ESTATE DOCUMENTS

There are many other types of real estate documents. Among these are the Agency Disclosure Form, Residential Property Disclosure Form (both discussed in Chapter 6), and deeds (discussed in Chapter 8). You'll also be exposed to additional forms and contracts depending on your specialized area of real estate. These are often provided by brokers or real estate boards to members. A broker can help familiarize you with the specific forms you'll need.

Chapter 7 Summary

1. Contracts are express or implied, unilateral or bilateral, executory or executed; also valid, void, voidable, or unenforceable. A listing agreement is a bilateral contract; purchase offer is a unilateral contract; purchase contract is bilateral. *Contract requirements*: capacity, offer, acceptance, consideration, and lawful and possible objective. Capacity is age 18 and mentally competent. Offer and acceptance are mutual consent to contract—meeting of minds. If offeree changes terms, it's a counteroffer not acceptance. A counteroffer represents a change. Licensee's role in acceptance is facilitator. Consent due to fraud, undue influence, duress, or mistake makes contract voidable by victim.

2. Contracts are invalid without consideration, but enforceable even if unequal. Earnest money deposit given with an offer is *not* consideration. Earnest money is not required for an offer. Earnest money is an inducement. Unlawful or impossible objective voids contract. Contract provisions are often severable where unenforceable part is cut from contract but rest is enforced.

3. Statute of frauds requires many contracts to be written and signed, including real estate contracts, purchase contracts, options, and powers of attorney. Lease must be written if for more than one year, plus attested and acknowledged if longer than 3 years. *Four lease types* are gross, net, percentage, and land. Listing agreement is an employment contract—must be written if for one year or more.

4. In Ohio, all contracts are assignable unless the contract states otherwise. In an assignment, one of the parties (the assignor) transfers his or her rights or interests under a contract to another person (the assignee). An exception is personal services contracts, which aren't assignable. When a contract is assigned, the assignor remains secondarily liable and can be sued if the assignee doesn't perform. Novation is when one party to a contract withdraws, and a new party is substituted relieving the withdrawing party of liability.

5. A party isn't required to perform if the other commits a material breach, but if there's substantial performance by one party, the other must perform. A promisor can't defeat a conditional contract by preventing the condition from being fulfilled, but the party it's intended to benefit can waive the condition. Compensatory damages are remedy for breach of contract; punitive damages are usually only awarded for tort or fraud. Non-breaching party must mitigate damages. Liquidated damages clause says how much a party collects if there's a breach. Specific performance is only available when damages can't compensate.

6. Listing agreements, buyer agency agreements, purchase contracts, options, and leases must comply with rules of contract law. *Most common types of listings* are exclusive right to sell, exclusive agency, and open listings. Net listings are not illegal but strongly discouraged by the Division of Real Estate due to possible charges of fraud. Listing agreements must have an expiration date. Unless listing contract says otherwise, commission is earned when a ready, willing, and able buyer is found on seller's terms. Setting uniform commission rates is a violation of federal and state antitrust laws.

Chapter 7 Quiz

1. ***Mike signed a listing agreement with Wendy to sell her home. The listing agreement specifically stated in paragraph 4 that Mike could put a "For Sale" sign in the yard and show the home. Can Mike market the home in other ways?***
   a. No, unless he wants his license suspended
   b. Yes, because the listing agreement gave him express authority to do so
   c. No, since the listing agreement did not specifically mention that he could
   d. Yes, because the listing agreement gave him implied authority to do so

2. ***Mike later learns that Wendy was only 17 years old when she signed the listing agreement, but had a birthday last week and is now 18. The listing agreement is:***
   a. Valid
   b. Void
   c. Voidable by Wendy
   d. Voidable by Mike

3. ***Given the circumstances in question #2, what should Mike do?***
   a. Have Wendy's parents join her on the listing agreement
   b. Have Wendy execute a new listing agreement now that she is 18
   c. Resign the listing for Wendy now that she's 18
   d. Turn himself in to the Superintendent of Real Estate for disciplinary action

4. ***After Mike gets Wendy's listing straightened out, he gets Tyler to put an offer on the property. What's the first thing Mike should give Wendy?***
   a. Tyler's offer
   b. Tyler's earnest money deposit
   c. Tyler's signed Agency Disclosure Form
   d. All three (a, b and c above) should be given to Wendy simultaneously

5. ***Wendy decides to accept Tyler's offer, so she signs the offer and gives it to her agent. At this point:***
   a. Wendy has made a counteroffer
   b. Because of the mailbox rule, Wendy and Tyler are in contract
   c. Wendy can still withdraw her acceptance until Tyler is notified of the acceptance
   d. Wendy and Tyler have a binding contract

6. ***When a seller makes a counteroffer, what is the buyer's responsibility?***
   a. The buyer doesn't have any responsibility
   b. The buyer has a three day right of rescission before there is a binding contract
   c. The buyer may not make another offer or counteroffer
   d. The buyer must agree to his or her original offer if the seller later decides to accept the terms of the original offer

7. ***Which of the following will terminate an offer?***
   a. The broker's license is suspended for 15 days and 10 of those days are waived
   b. Death of the agent
   c. Counteroffer
   d. No earnest money

8. ***Stacy contracted with Biff (a big, burly guy) to "coerce" her neighbor into signing an easement release she's been after for the past five years. Which is (are) true?***
   a. Stacy and Biff's contract is void due to unlawful purpose
   b. Stacy and her neighbor's contract is voidable due to duress
   c. Both a and b are true
   d. Neither a nor b are true

9. ***Which is the best type of listing agreement for the real estate agent and why?***
   a. The exclusive right to sell, because the broker is guaranteed a commission no matter who sells the property
   b. The exclusive agency, because then only the agent's brokerage may collect a commission on the sale of the property
   c. The open listing, because increased competition will cause the agent to work harder to make sure he or she is the one who gets paid
   d. The net listing, because he or she can make an unlimited amount of money over and above what the seller wants to get from the property

10. ***Listing agreements are not required to:***
   a. Comply with the rules of contract law
   b. Be in writing to satisfy the license law
   c. Have an expiration date
   d. Have the Ohio Division of Real Estate address and phone number

11. ***A counteroffer represents:***
   a. A new offer while keeping the first offer in primary position
   b. A change
   c. A new purchase contract
   d. An acceptance

12. ***A novation:***
   a. Is an assignment of a contract
   b. Is an assumption of a contract
   c. Is a new contract
   d. Is an amendment to a contract

13. ***Under a novation:***
   a. The original party remains primarily liable
   b. The original party remains secondarily liable
   c. The original party shares liability equally with the new party
   d. The original party is relieved of liability

14. *Under an assignment:*

a. The original party remains primarily liable
(b.) The original party remains secondarily liable
c. The original party shares liability equally with the new party
d. The original party is relieved of liability

8 DEEDS AND OWNERSHIP

CHAPTER OVERVIEW

Now that you have an understanding of real estate law and contracts, let's look at one of the most important real estate documents: ***deeds***. Deeds are evidence of title in the transference of real property. We'll look at requirements for a valid deed, different kinds of deeds, and the process of recording a deed. Finally, we'll look at how ownership in real property can be held: in severalty (one person) or co-ownership.

Purchaser land contract Vendor Vendee

KEY TERMS

Acknowledgment
When a party signs a document before a notary stating that it was signed voluntarily.

Attestation
The act of witnessing the execution of a legal document, such as a deed or will, to affirm that the parties' signatures are real; ***Note:* Attestation of a deed is not required in Ohio, but it may be required in other states.**

Chain of Title
Record of ownership (deeds) passing title for a piece of land from owner to owner.

Clouds on the Title
Encumbrances or outstanding claims that could affect the owner's title; problems or uncertainties with a title to real property.

Deed
An instrument that conveys a grantor's interest, if any, in the real property.

Donative Intent
Intent by the grantor of real property to transfer title immediately and unconditionally.

Equitable Title
An interest in property created on the execution of a valid sales contract, whereby actual title will be transferred by deed at future date.

Government Survey System
A type of legal description for land referencing principal meridians and base lines designated throughout much of the country. Also called **government rectangular survey** or **rectangular survey system**.

Lot and Block System
A type of legal description used for platted property. The description states only the property's lot number and block number in a particular subdivision. To find the exact location, a plat map must be consulted.

Marketable Record Title
Unbroken chain of recorded titles going back 40 years.

KEY TERMS *cont.*

Metes and Bounds System
A type of legal description that starts at an easily identifiable point of beginning (POB), then describes the property's boundaries in terms of courses (compass directions) and distances, returning to point of beginning.

Severalty
Ownership of real property by one person.

Title
The actual lawful ownership of real property. Referring to the legal bundle of rights that are the rights of ownership. Title is a theory ***not*** a document.

I. DEEDS

Deeds are important real estate documents with which you must be familiar. Deeds are the means by which property ownership is transferred. A deed to property does not necessarily prove ownership of the property.

Much of the discussion about deeds involves the practice of law, so it's not an area where you can advise clients or customers. It's necessary for your professional development and overall knowledge to know about deeds, since a real estate transaction culminates in delivery and acceptance of a properly drafted deed.

DEED VERSUS TITLE

A **deed** is an instrument that conveys a grantor's interest, if any, in real property. The deed is the *document* used by the owner of real property to transfer all or part of his or her interest in the property to another. The deed is mere evidence of title.

Title is the actual lawful ownership of real property and refers to holding the bundle of rights conveyed. Title is *not* a document but rather a theory dealing with ownership. The deed is written proof of the rights conveyed to the owner, but having title to the land is what must be held to actually "own" it.

This distinction is important because it's possible to have a deed to land yet not have title to that property. It's rare, but it can happen. If the seller (**grantor**) doesn't own the land, but thinks that he or she owns a piece of land as part of a larger tract, or already conveyed part of the land to someone else in a prior transaction and forgot, this grantor can't pass good title by merely giving the buyer (**grantee**) a deed to the land. We'll also see other ways that a deed might be invalid.

EQUITABLE TITLE. **Equitable title** is an interest in property created on the execution of a valid sales contract, whereby actual title will be transferred by deed at a future date (closing). This isn't the same as having title, but the person who holds equitable title still enjoys certain rights and privileges (e.g., the benefit of minerals found on land after a valid sales contract is signed and completed, but before the closing and passage of actual title to the new owner).

Also note that **land contracts** pass equitable title even though actual title is not transferred until all, or a specified portion of, payments have been made.

II. REQUIREMENTS FOR A DEED

For a deed to be valid in Ohio, it must be in writing and contain necessary information on its face. Note that deeds don't need to be recorded to be valid, but recording a deed ensures that it's valid as to third parties. Requirements for a valid deed are:

1. **Competent grantor's signature**
2. **Identifiable grantee** to whom title will pass, named in such a way so as to reasonably separate this person from all others
3. **Words of conveyance** stating the grantor's intent to convey the land
4. **Description** of the property being conveyed adequately enough to distinguish it from all other parcels of land
5. **Consideration** recited to prove that a sale of land took place
6. **Acknowledgment** signature of the grantor before a notary public, stating the sale of land is a free and voluntary act

Once the deed is valid, **delivery and acceptance** of the deed, during the grantor's life, will transfer the title from the grantor to the grantee.

COMPETENT GRANTOR'S SIGNATURE

A **competent grantor** is a person wishing to grant or convey land and who is of sound mind for the purposes of entering a contract and who has reached the age of majority (18 years of age in Ohio). A competent grantor's signature (and the grantor's spouse, if married) is vital for a valid deed to transfer title. A valid deed must have a grantor who can be bound by it. Five possible problems are:

1. Mental capacity
2. Minors
3. Married persons
4. Corporations
5. Partnerships

MENTAL CAPACITY. The term "competent grantor" presumes a sound mind. The test for mental capacity in Ohio is whether the grantor can formulate an intention to convey his or her property. This capacity is measured when the deed is signed. Capacity is presumed to exist, and the burden of proof falls on the one trying to invalidate a deed on this basis. If a mentally incapable grantor signs a deed, the incompetent person, or his or her representatives, has the option of voiding the deed.

The term "competent grantor" also refers to the legal ability of a person to enter into a valid contract. In Ohio, a person must be at least 18 years old, **the age of majority**, to enter a legally binding contract. A person younger than 18 is referred to as a **minor**, and a deed executed by a minor results in a voidable transaction at the option of the minor, within a reasonable time after reaching the age of majority.

MARRIED PERSONS. A married grantor must be joined by his or her spouse in signing the deed to release the dower interest that the law allows the spouse. Without this release, marketable title is severely compromised.

CORPORATIONS. A corporation is a competent grantor, and the deed must recite the grantor's corporate status on its face. It's imperative that a person representing the corporation has the power and authority to do the transaction. Before listing corporate property, a listing broker must get a copy of the **corporate resolution** allowing the corporation to list and sell the asset. The resolution should appoint the broker as agent and grant authority to an officer or director to sign the purchase agreement and deed.

PARTNERSHIPS. A partnership is also a competent grantor, and the deed must recite the status of partnership on its face. Make sure that you deal with the correct person with the power and authority to complete the transaction. The issue of dower interest in partnership property is unclear, so the safe course is to obtain dower releases from the spouses of the partners.

IDENTIFIABLE GRANTEE. An identifiable grantee is the person to whom the interest in real property is to be conveyed and identified in such a way so as to reasonably separate this person from all others in the world. This would include getting proper and complete full names of the grantee(s), as well as designations, such as Jr., Sr., etc. Furthermore, a deed must name a grantee in existence at the time of conveyance. Thus, a conveyance to an unincorporated business reciting corporate status would fail for lack of a grantee in existence at the time of conveyance. Grantee identification often falls to the agent on the buying side of the transaction, so it's important to get the correct information to the person preparing the deed. Any unclear situations should be investigated first.

WORDS OF CONVEYANCE. Words of conveyance are a clause in the deed that states that the grantor intends to convey title to the land. Also called the granting clause, these words identify the document as one which involves the transfer of interest from one person to another. The wording of the deed must communicate a definite and clear intent by the grantor to part with the subject land. The words "give, grant, bargain, sell, and convey" leave no doubt as to the intent of the grantor. Following this is the habendum clause. This clause, included after the granting clause in many deeds, begins "to have and to hold" and describes the type of estate granted.

DESCRIPTION. Description of the property being conveyed should be thorough and complete and based upon either the government survey system, lot and block system, or metes and bounds system. The test of a valid description of property is the ability to identify and distinguish that property from any and all other parcels of land.

Government Survey System

The **government survey system/rectangular survey system** is a type of legal description for land referencing **principal meridians and base lines** designated throughout much of the country. A particular piece of land is identified by directions and coordinates, which count from these lines as reference points.

Additional north-south lines, *called ranges or range lines,* run parallel to principal meridians at 6-mile intervals, and additional east-west lines, *called township lines,* run parallel to base lines at 6-mile intervals. This divides land into 6-mile-by-6-mile squares called **townships**.

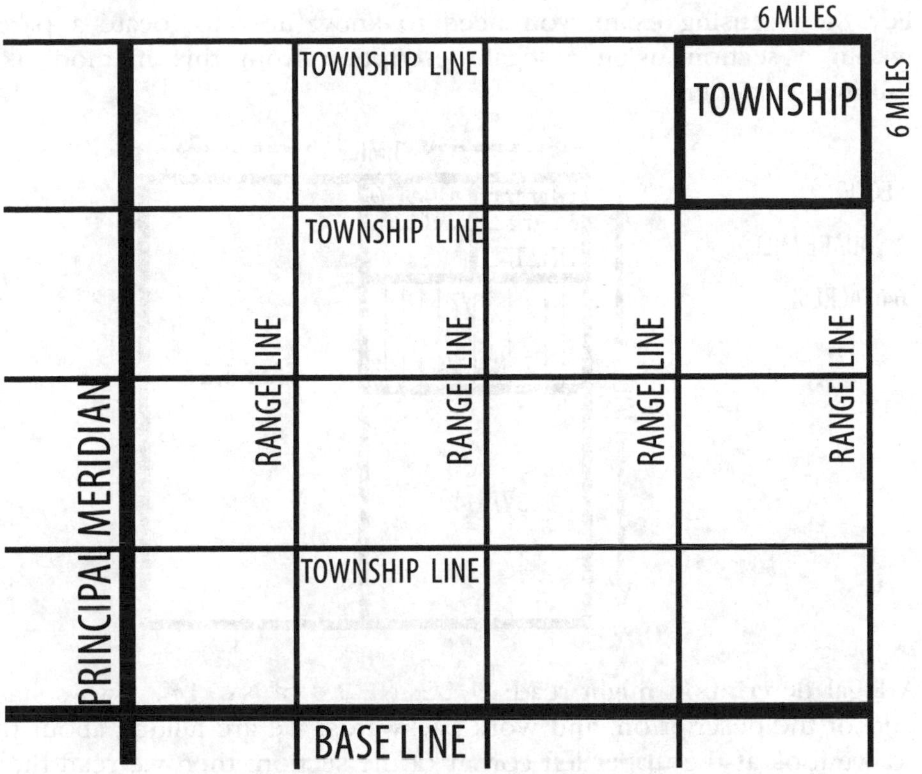

TOWNSHIP IDENTIFICATION: Using principal meridians and base lines (each principal meridian and base line has a unique name or number.)

The 36 square miles of a township are subdivided into 36 **sections** of 1-square-mile (640 acres) each. Each section in a township is numbered sequentially, so a person can locate land by referring to the section number and subsequent references to half and quarter sections with compass points. Any portion of land that cannot be divided into equal fractional lots is designated as a government lot.

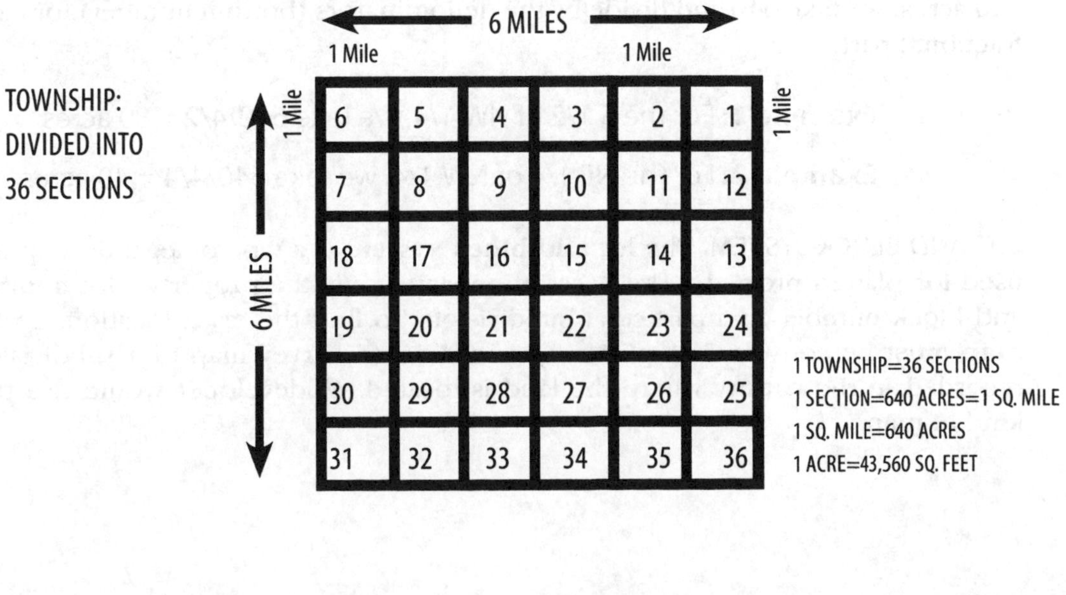

6	5	4	3	2	1
7	8	9	10	11	12
18	17	16	15	14	13
19	20	21	22	23	24
30	29	28	27	26	25
31	32	33	34	35	36

1 TOWNSHIP=36 SECTIONS
1 SECTION=640 ACRES=1 SQ. MILE
1 SQ. MILE=640 ACRES
1 ACRE=43,560 SQ. FEET

For the licensing exam, you need to know how to locate a parcel of land within a section using a legal description from this method. Look at the following diagram.

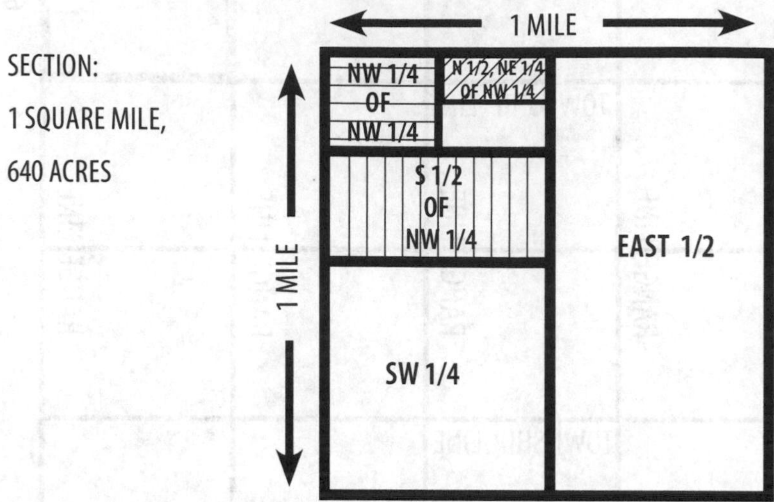

A legal description might read: N 1/2, NE 1/4 of NW 1/4. Always start from the end of the description, and work backwards. We are talking about the NW 1/4, so we look at the upper left corner of the section; then we read the rest of the description to determine which part of the NW 1/4 we are talking about. Here are some examples.

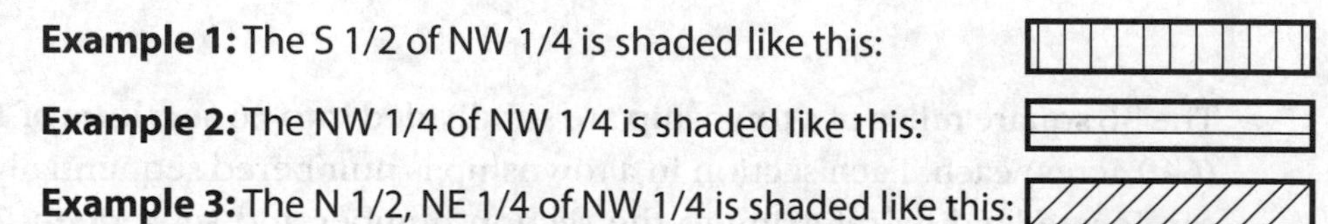

For the licensing exam, you will also need to know how to calculate the land acreage for a given parcel of land in the government survey system. Again, start from the end and work backwards. Since we know that the entire section equals 640 acres, we take 640 and divide by the denominators (bottom number) for each fractional part.

Example 1: For the S 1/2 of NW 1/4, we take 640/4/2 = 80 acres

Example 2: For the NE 1/4 of NW 1/4, we take 640/4/4 = 40 acres

LOT AND BLOCK SYSTEM. The **lot and block system** is a type of legal description used for platted property. The description states only the property's lot number and block number in a particular subdivision. To find the exact location, a **plat map** must be consulted. A **plat map** is a detailed survey map of a subdivision recorded in the county where the land is located. (A developer would use this kind of map.)

SAMPLE SUBDIVISION PLAT MAT: Golden Valley Estate, Block 17, Lots 1-22.

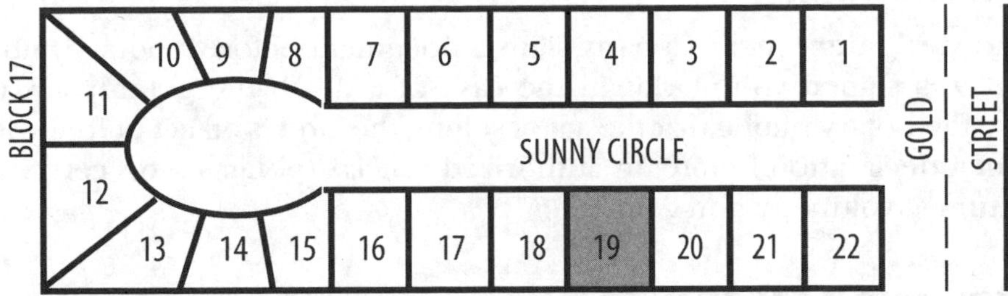

GOLDEN VALLEY ESTATE.

METES AND BOUND SYSTEM. The **metes and bounds** system is a type of legal description that starts at an easily identifiable **point of beginning (POB)** or point of origin and describes a property's boundaries in terms of courses (compass directions) and distances, ultimately returning to the point of beginning. The legal description may also refer to **monuments or markers**, which are fixed physical objects used as reference points, or **pins**, which are rods driven into the ground.

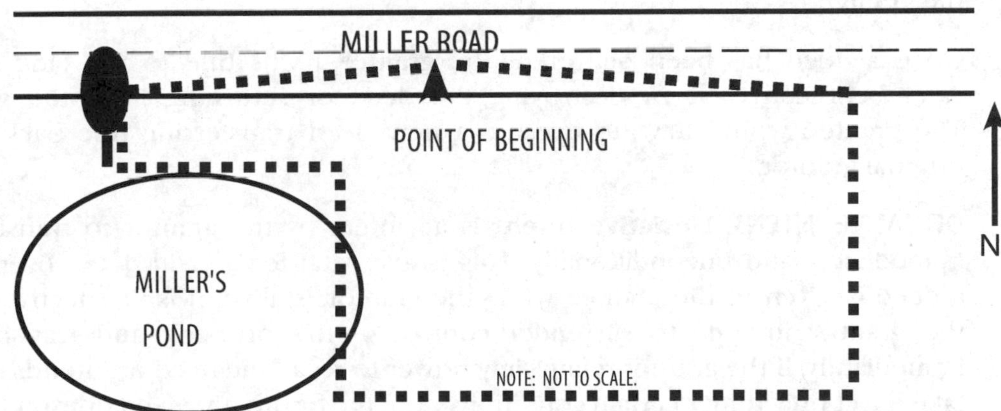

Sample Metes and Bounds Survey. *Beginning at the pin in the center of Miller Road, go SE 300 feet at an angle until the edge of the road meets another pin, then due south 250 feet until you hit a pin at the adjoining property's fence; then, go due west 350 feet until you hit a pin at the edge of Miller's Pond; then, north 200 feet to another pin; due west 100 feet to a pin near the base of an old oak tree; then due north to a pin at the edge of the road, then NE at an angel to the point of beginning at the pin in the center of Miller Road.*

CONSIDERATION

Consideration is anything of value such as money, goods, services, or promises, which is given to induce another person to enter into a contract. Consideration recited on the deed is necessary to prove that a sale of land took place, not a gift, since a gift may be attacked by creditors. The actual price paid need not be recited, but the full consideration must be stated in cases involving public sale, such as at foreclosure.

ACKNOWLEDGMENT

Acknowledgment means a party signs a document before a notary public stating that it was signed voluntarily. In the case of a deed, the grantor acknowledges before the notary public that the act of selling the land is an act of free will. There's a formal declaration before an authorized official (notary) who certifies that the signature is voluntary and genuine.

DELIVERY AND ACCEPTANCE

Even when a deed has been properly executed, it has no legal effect until there has been delivery of the deed by the grantor with the intention of transferring title and acceptance by the grantee receiving the land. This delivery and acceptance must take place while the grantor is alive, or it has no legal effect.

Delivery of a deed means the grantor actually places the deed in the grantee's possession or gives it to a third party with instructions to give it to the grantee.

Acceptance of a deed by a grantee is also necessary for title to be transferred. The law presumes the deed has been accepted if the grant is beneficial to the grantee.

Once a deed has been delivered, the grantee holds title to the land, and it can't be reconveyed by destroying the deed or returning it to the grantor. The grantee would have to execute a new deed transferring title back to the original grantor.

DONATIVE INTENT. **Donative intent** is an intent by the grantor to transfer title immediately and unconditionally. This is also vital for a valid deed. Even when a deed is given to the grantee while the grantor is alive, it isn't effective unless the grantor intends to surrender control of the property and transfer title immediately. If the grantor retains any power to recall the deed or intends for it to take effect only under certain conditions or in the future, the deed doesn't transfer title to grantee.

III. TYPES OF DEEDS

There are two general classifications of deeds in Ohio: **warranty deeds** and **deeds without warranties**. We'll discuss both kinds.

WARRANTY DEEDS

Warranty deeds are deeds that carry warranties of clear title and the grantor's right to convey title. They transfer title in real property with the grantor making certain guarantees (also called warranties or covenants) to the grantee regarding status of the title. For example, if the grantor is married and fails to obtain a dower release from his or her spouse, that's a breach of warranty under a warranty deed.

The guarantees that go with a deed differ depending on whether a **general warranty deed** or a **limited warranty deed** is used. The Ohio legislature has created a statutory form for both types of warranty deeds. If the statutory form

Example of a General Waranty Deed: Note that in addition to being a written document, this sample contains 6 of the 7 requirements for a valid deed—delivery and acceptance cannot be illustrated here.

WARRANTY DEED 2922 PAGE 561 FUTURE TAX BILLS TO THE CALHREA ... MORTGAGE CO. COLUMBUS BLANK BOOK CO., COL., O. FORM NO. L12-9

Know all Men by these Presents

That Ralph B. S. Mowery, Widower 19096

of the City of Columbus, County of Franklin and State of Ohio Grantor, in consideration of the sum of One Dollar ($1.00) and other good and valuable considerations to him paid by William A. Thompson and Helen Thompson. **5. Consideration**

of the City of Columbus, County of Franklin and State of Ohio Grantees, the receipt whereof is hereby acknowledged, does hereby **grant, bargain, sell and convey** to the said Grantees William A. Thompson and Helen Thompson **2. Grantee** **3. Words of Conveyance**

their heirs and assigns forever, the following **Real Estate** situated in the County of Franklin in the State of Ohio, and in the City of Columbus and bounded and described as follows:

Being Lot Number Eighty-five (85) of CHARLES R. CORNELL'S SUBDIVISION in the said City of Columbus, Ohio, as the same is numbered and delineated upon the recorded plat thereof, of record in Plat Book No. 5, page 48, Recorder's Office, Franklin County, Ohio. **4. Description**

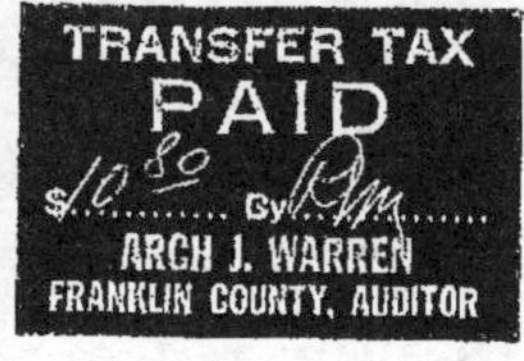

Last Transfer: Deed Record Volume 734, Page 67

To have and to hold said premises, with all the privileges and appurtenances thereunto belonging, to the said Grantees their heirs and assigns forever.

And the said Grantor for himself and his heirs, does hereby covenant with the said Grantees their heirs and assigns, that he is lawfully seized of the premises aforesaid; that the said premises are **Free and Clear from all Incumbrances whatsoever** Except taxes and assessments due and payable hereafter and all conditions, easements and restrictions of record.

VOL PAGE

and that he *will forever* **Warrant and Defend** *the same, with the appurtenances, unto the said Grantee*s their *heirs and assigns against the lawful claims of all persons whomsoever*

In Witness Whereof *the said Grantor*

Ralph B. S. Mowery, Widower

has hereunto set his *hand, this* 27th *day of* August *in the year of our Lord one thousand nine hundred and* sixty-eight *(1968)*

Signed and acknowledged in presence of

Ralph B. S. Mowery

1. Grantors' Signatures

The State of OHIO FRANKLIN **County** ss.

Be it Remembered *That on this* 27th *day of* August *, A.D. 19*68 *, before me, the subscriber, a* Notary Public *in and for said county, personally came the above named* Ralph B. S. Mowery

6. Acknowledgment

the Grantor in the foregoing Deed, and acknowledged the signing of the same to be his *voluntary act and deed, for the uses and purposes therein mentioned.*

In Testimony Whereof, *I have hereunto subscribed my name and affixed my official seal on the day and year last aforesaid.*

C. RICHARD O'NEIL
ATTORNEY-AT-LAW
NOTARY PUBLIC, STATE OF OHIO

This instrument was prepared by C. RICHARD O'NEIL
ATTORNEY-AT-LAW
2346 N. HIGH ST.
COLUMBUS 2, OHIO

Warranty Deed

MAIL TO

Transferred ____ 19__
COUNTY AUDITOR

STATE OF OHIO
COUNTY OF FRANKLIN ss
RECEIVED FOR RECORD ON THE AUG 28 1968 day 19__
at ____ o'clock __ M
and RECORDED AUG 30 1968 19__ in
DEED BOOK ____ PAGE ____
COUNTY RECORDER
RECORDERS FEE $ 2.50

COLUMBUS BLANK BOOK CO.

is followed, it isn't necessary to actually state the warranties on the face of the deed. Instead, the warranties are incorporated into the deed by reference to the statute.

When a warranty is breached, the grantee has the right to sue the grantor for compensation. But the grantor may have left the jurisdiction or may be judgment-proof, so the grantee can't collect. Title insurance protects the grantee much more reliably than deed warranties.

GENERAL WARRANTY DEEDS. **General warranty deeds** are deeds in which a grantor warrants title against defects that may have arisen before or during his or her ownership (also called **standard warranty deeds** or simply **warranty deeds**.) A general warranty deed gives the grantee the greatest possible protection. Most real estate transfers in Ohio use general warranty deeds. Grantor guarantees:

1. **Covenant of seizen:** the grantor owns the estate and has the right to convey
2. **Covenant against encumbrances:** the property is free of encumbrances not recited as exceptions in the deed
3. **Covenant of quiet enjoyment:** the grantee can possess the land without claims of title from others
4. **Covenant of warranty forever:** the grantor will defend the grantee's interest against all lawful claims of title

LIMITED WARRANTY DEEDS. **Limited warranty deeds** are deeds in which the grantor warrants title only against defects arising from the time he or she owned the land but not before that time (also called **special warranty deeds**). Grantor only:

1. Guarantees there aren't any encumbrances he or she created
2. Promises to defend title against anyone claiming under him or her

DEEDS WITHOUT WARRANTIES

Deeds without warranties can also transfer title to real property, but with them the grantor makes no warranties regarding title, nor does the grantor guarantee that he or she has the right to convey title. There are four kinds of deeds without warranties:

1. Quitclaim deeds
2. Bargain and sale deeds
3. Fiduciary deeds
4. Transfer on death deeds

QUITCLAIM DEEDS. **Quitclaim deeds** are deeds that convey any interest in a piece of real property the grantor has at the time the deed is executed. A quitclaim deed makes no warranties regarding the title, if any, held by the grantor. It conveys whatever right, title, or interest the grantor holds in the property without representation that there is any interest at all. Often, quitclaims are used to clear up title problems known as **clouds on the title** (e.g., a spouse may use a quitclaim deed to release dower interest not conveyed). It may also be used in the case of a life estate to deed the remainder interest to a life tenant, creating marketable title by **merger**.

BARGAIN AND SALE DEEDS. **Bargain and sale deeds** are deeds that imply that the grantor owns the property and has a right to convey it, but there are no warranties that go with them. This type of deed is rarely used in Ohio.

FIDUCIARY DEEDS. **Fiduciary deeds** are deeds executed by a trustee, executor, or other fiduciary conveying property the fiduciary doesn't own but is authorized to manage. A fiduciary is one in an appointed position of trust acting on another's behalf. The fiduciary can't give general warranty provisions since the fiduciary is acting on behalf of someone else. The only warranties fiduciaries can give, by law, involve their role as fiduciaries not the condition of title to land. Fiduciaries warrant that they've been duly appointed by a court of competent jurisdiction as fiduciaries, and the act of selling the land falls within their duties as a fiduciary.

TRANSFER ON DEATH DEED. A transfer on death deed, established in Ohio law in 2000, can be a deed with or without a warranty and works like a payable on death bank account (avoids probate). One present owner of the real property may designate one or more death beneficiaries and may also name contingent beneficiaries.

The beneficiary may be a person, trust, charity, business, or other entity, but must be specifically named. For example, to list a beneficiary on a transfer on death deed as "my grandson" is not sufficient; it must read: "my grandson, Kevin Smith."

The named beneficiary or contingent beneficiary has a future interest in the property not a present interest. Therefore, the property owner may change the transfer on death deed at any time, and the sale or other conveyance of the property terminates the transfer on death provision.

The original transfer on death and any subsequent deeds must be recorded to establish transfer of the property on death. Additionally, a lien or foreclosure action may be taken against the present property owner not against the beneficiary's interest.

IV. RECORDING

The recording system makes it possible to determine who holds an interest in any piece of property. The purpose of recording is to provide **notice** to others protecting property buyers and lenders against secret conveyances and encumbrances.

Any legal document that affects title to real estate can be recorded, and most should be: *deeds, easements, restrictive covenants, court orders, long-term leases*, etc. Certain documents have no legal effect unless they're recorded (e.g., mortgages and mechanics' liens). Other documents are binding on the parties even if they're not recorded. Deeds don't have to be recorded to transfer title from grantor to grantee. The purpose of notice with regard to deeds is to let everyone know you now own the property. There are different kinds of notice and different rights and responsibilities that go along with each, but let's look at the mechanics of recording first.

THE RECORDER'S OFFICE

Recording a document involves filing it at the county recorder's office and paying a fee. The document is scanned into the recorder's computer allowing public access on the Internet. If the document is not online, it can be found on microfilm at the recorder's office. Anyone can look at a document online or with microfilm and obtain a copy.

The documents are scanned in the order they were filed for record. This is very important since deed priority or lien priority often depends on when the documents were filed. Each document is numbered, so it can be located easily.

The recorder keeps an index of all recorded documents. The index is divided into two parts: **direct index** (also called **grantor/grantee index** because it lists all documents alphabetically by grantor's last name) and **reverse index** (also called **grantee/grantor index** because it lists all documents by grantee's last name). The index provides the volume and page where a document is located in the public record.

The recorder may also maintain a **sectional index**, which lists documents under the tax parcel number of the property, thus grouping together all recorded documents affecting that piece of property (also called a **tract index**).

NOTICE

When two people have conflicting claims, their rights and liabilities sometimes depend on whether one had *should* know.

The law holds that everyone has constructive notice of recorded documents. Even if someone didn't know about a particular recorded document, he or she could have found it by searching the public record. The law expects a buyer or lender to take that step for his or her own protection. The law won't look after a buyer or lender who doesn't bother to check.

EXAMPLE Tom grants an easement across his land to Deb, so Deb records the easement document. Tom then sells his land to Jasmine. Jasmine claims she doesn't have to honor the easement since she couldn't tell it existed by looking at the land, and Tom never told her about it. The easement, however, is still valid because Jasmine is deemed to have constructive notice of it. Although she didn't have actual notice, she could have found out about the easement granted to Deb by checking the public records.

It's possible for a recorded document to fall outside the **chain of title**. The **chain of title** is the chain of deeds passing title for a piece of land from one owner to the next, as disclosed in the public records. A deed outside the chain of title is said to be a **wild deed**. Buyers and lenders aren't held to have constructive notice of it.

EXAMPLE Lisa buys a house and records her deed. Later she sells the house to Scott, but Scott doesn't record his deed. Scott sells the land to Cecil, and Cecil records his deed promptly. Now there's a break in the chain of title; the record shows only Lisa's deed and Cecil's deed, but the link between them (Scott's deed) is missing, so Cecil's deed is a wild deed. Lisa is aware that Scott never recorded his deed, and she decides to sell the same property a second time to Matt. Matt doesn't know about Scott or Cecil, so he has no reason to look up those names in the grantee/grantor index. He looks up Lisa's name in the index and, as far as he can tell from the record, she still owns the property. So Matt buys the house. Matt doesn't have constructive notice of Cecil's interest in the property because Cecil's deed was outside the chain of title.

In addition to actual notice and constructive notice, there's **inquiry notice**. A person has inquiry notice when there's an indication of a claim or other situation that would alert a reasonable person to a possible problem, causing further inquiry about the title. If you don't find a claim because you fail to look further, you may still be held to have inquiry notice of a claim. When someone's in possession of land, a buyer is held to have inquiry notice of the possessor's claim even if the buyer never visited the land. That's why you shouldn't buy land sight unseen.

RACE/NOTICE RULE. If an owner sells land to two different people, Ohio follows the **race/notice rule**. Figuratively speaking, the two grantees race each other to the recorder's office, and whoever records a deed first wins. The first to record has title to the property unless he or she had notice of an earlier conveyance.

If a couple buys land and doesn't have notice of another buyer before them (like Matt in our previous example), they're *not* deemed to have constructive notice of the unrecorded deed. The later grantees are **subsequent good faith purchasers without notice**, and they have valid title to the land even if someone else bought it first. They may have to pay damages but can't be forced to give up possession.

The race/notice rule only protects subsequent good faith *purchasers*. If gift recipients don't record their deeds, they lose their interest in the land.

Note that Ohio does *not* apply the race/notice rule to mortgages. A recorded mortgage has priority over all unrecorded or subsequently recorded interests, even if the mortgagee had actual notice of those interests. With mortgages, Ohio follows a pure race rule: notice doesn't matter; winning the race is all that counts.

THE MARKETABLE TITLE ACT

The Marketable Title Act is intended to improve the marketability of title and simplify the title search process by extinguishing certain old claims against a title. The Marketable Title Act makes it necessary to search back only 40 years.

Under the Act, an owner with an unbroken chain of recorded titles going back at least 40 years has a **marketable record title.** The **root of title** is the deed (or other document of transfer) that, 40 years ago, was the most recently recorded. When an owner establishes a marketable record title, any claims that arose before the root of title are extinguished unless they've been preserved.

An easement, use restriction, or other interest is preserved if it's specifically mentioned (by volume and page number) in a deed (or other document) recorded after the root of title. Even if no deed mentions an easement, it's preserved if an easement holder records a notice preserving it within 40 years after the root of title. The notice must be an affidavit (sworn statement), including a description of all land affected by the interest and names of the current landowners.

The easement would be extinguished if no transfer document recorded since the root of title specifically mentioned the easement and no affidavit was filed. A general reference in a deed isn't enough. The reference must be specific. Once an interest is gone, it can't be revived by affidavit after the 40-year deadline has passed. Exceptions to the Marketable Title Act are: ***easements with observable physical evidence of use, easements for pipes, cables, etc., lessors' rights at the end of a lease, railroad, utility easements, interests in coal, mortgages, and government interests***.

THE TORRENS SYSTEM

The Torrens system of title registration is an alternative to the recording system. An owner registers land with the state Torrens registrar. A careful title search and survey of the land are performed, and a Torrens certificate is issued. The original certificate is kept in the registrar's office, and the property owner receives a duplicate certificate. When the owner sells the property, he or she must surrender the duplicate certificate to the registrar.

Once land has been "Torrenized," no deed, mortgage, lien, easement, or other encumbrance has any legal effect unless it's registered with a Torrens registrar. If a lien is recorded and not registered, the lien has no effect. A buyer or lender can check title status with the Torrens register with no need to search public records. Despite its convenience, the Torrens system is rarely used because it's expensive.

V. OWNERSHIP

Since deeds transfer ownership, the next logical step is to look at how ownership can be held. Two types of real property ownership are **ownership in severalty** owned by one person or entity, and **co-ownership** owned by more than one person with each person having an **undivided interest** in the property. **Undivided interest** gives each co-owner right to possession of the whole property, not just part of it.

With co-ownership, any number of people may join in the ownership of real property. The relationship these people share depends on deed language, which is evidence of their right to title to the land. Legal title to land can be held by more than one person as:

- Tenancy in common
- Joint tenancy
- Statutory survivorship tenancy
- Tenancy by the entireties

TENANCY IN COMMON

In Ohio, when two or more persons have an undivided interest (unity of possession) in the entire land but no right of survivorship, **tenancy in common** exists. ***This is the most common form of co-ownership.*** A court will set up a tenancy in common if the deed language isn't specific. No special words are needed to create a tenancy in common.

Each co-owner in common may own equal shares or shares of different proportions; it doesn't matter. The deed must show the fractional interests of the parties. If the deed is silent as to the interests of the parties, the shares will be equal. ***Remember***:

1. **Tenancy in common** is the only co-ownership that **does not have** the right of **survivorship**
2. **Tenancy in common** is the only co-ownership that **can be owned in unequal portions**
3. **Tenancy in common** is the form of co-ownership that **Ohio law presumes (defaults to)**
4. In **tenancy in common**, each owner **owns their share in severalty** (solely)

STATUTORY SURVIVORSHIP TENANCY

JOINT TENANCY WITH THE RIGHT OF SURVIVORSHIP. **In statutory survivorship tenancy,** each co-owner has an **equal** undivided **interest** in real property and the **right of survivorship**. This is the other form of coownership in Ohio.

Statutory survivorship tenancy creates different legal relationships than tenancy in common. The main feature of statutory survivorship tenancy allows co-owners to take ownership shares of a deceased co-owner without going through probate. Since survivors take equally and simultaneously, a person can't will or inherit a survivorship estate.

JOINT TENANCY. Joint tenancy is not used in Ohio, but it could be on the exam. Each joint tenant has an equal undivided interest in the land and the right of survivorship, like statutory survivorship tenancy, but when a joint tenant conveys his interest, only the survivorship right in that interest ends. The new co-owner is a tenant in common in relation to other co-owners.

EXAMPLE A, B, and C co-own a property as joint tenants. C conveys his interest to D. D will be a tenant in common while A and B will still be joint tenants. D's interest will go to his heirs upon his death while A and B's interest will go to the survivor of the two of them upon one of their deaths. For joint tenancy, all four unities, sometimes referred to as the equalities, must be present: unity of possession, unity of interest, unity of time, and unity of title (**4 unities = PITT: possession, interest, time, title**).

TENANCY BY THE ENTIRETIES

Tenancy by the entireties was **abolished** by the Ohio General Assembly in 1985 because some of the court decisions interpreting the statute were controversial. Tenancy by the entireties only involved husband and wife owners and did have survivorship. Tenancy by the entireties created before 1985 may still exist, but any co-ownership created after 1985 will have to be either tenancy in common or joint tenancy with the right of survivorship.

OWNERSHIP BY ASSOCIATIONS

Ownership in severalty and co-ownership can be further categorized into ownership by associations. These include businesses, non-profit groups, and other organizations. Depending on its form, an association may be a legal entity separate from its members or owners. Title to property can be held in the name of an association, a trust, or LLC.

CORPORATIONS. A **corporation** is a legal entity in which individuals hold shares of stock and is regarded by the law as an artificial person separate from the individual stockholders. When a corporation owns property, it owns it in severalty as a real person. Shareholders don't own the corporation's property and aren't personally liable for the corporation's debts. A shareholder's spouse has no dower rights in corporately owned property.

GENERAL PARTNERSHIPS. A **general partnership** is an association of two or more individuals as co-owners of a business run for profit. It doesn't have to be formally organized. For most purposes, the law doesn't recognize a general partnership as an entity independent from the individual partners, so the general partners would own the partnership as tenants in partnership. This is a form of co-ownership giving each partner an equal, undivided interest in the land. A married partner's spouse doesn't have dower rights in partnership property.

LIMITED PARTNERSHIPS. A limited partnership, like a general partnership, is an association of two or more persons as co-owners of a business. A limited partnership differs from a general partnership in that a limited partnership has one or more general partners plus one or more limited (silent) partners. The rights and duties of general partners in a limited partnership are the same as in a general partnership, but limited partners have no say in partnership matters. The partners' liability is limited to their original investment.

REAL ESTATE INVESTMENT TRUST (REIT). A real estate investment trust **(REIT)** is a real estate investment business, with at least 100 investors, organized as a trust. In a trust, one or more trustees manage property for the benefit of the beneficiaries. A trust document vests title to the property in the trustees. The trustees have only those powers expressly granted to them in the trust document. The beneficiaries have no legal interest in the property; they do have power to enforce performance of the trust.

REITs can transact real estate business only in Ohio if a copy of the trust document and a special report is filed with the secretary of state listing names and addresses of all trustees. Title to land can be in a REIT's name or one of the trustees.

SYNDICATES. A **syndicate** is not a recognized legal entity. Like "company," the term "syndicate" can refer to almost any form of business. The XYZ Syndicate might be a corporation, partnership, or REIT and would hold title to real estate accordingly.

CONDOMINIUMS AND COOPERATIVES

As cities become more crowded, single-family homes get harder to find and more expensive to buy. Condominiums and other housing alternatives are gaining popularity. They combine (physically and legally) individual ownership with co-ownership.

CONDOMINIUMS. **Condominiums** are property developed for co-ownership, with each co-owner having a separate interest in an individual unit and an undivided interest in the **common areas** (grounds, lobby, hallways, etc.,) of the property. Common areas are owned and used by all. **Limited common areas** are owned by all but used by only one owner. An example of a limited common area would be a balcony that extends out into the air owned by all but used by the unit owner. Designated parking spaces are another example of limited common area. The word **designated** or **assigned** will inform the client that he or she has this space exclusively for his or her use even though all the owners own the land. Condominium residents must follow the **Declarations and By-Laws** set forth by the founder of the condominium and maintained and enforced by the owners association. Most condominiums are designed for residential use. Condos can look like apartments, homes separated by a common wall and under one roof, or freestanding homes. Residents usually have exclusive ownership of their units in severalty or co-ownership and co-owner interest in the common areas with all of the other condo owners as tenants in common.

ENCUMBRANCE AND TRANSFER. Each owner may give a lender a mortgage on his or her unit and undivided interest in common areas. Each owner's creditors can claim a lien and undivided interest against that unit. If a lien holder forecloses, only that unit and its undivided interest are affected, without jeopardizing the entire condominium. Property taxes are also levied against each unit separately and don't affect the whole property. Owners association levies, maintenance fees to pay for common area expenses, and upkeep are divided among unit owners and can also result in a lien if unpaid.

When a condominium unit is sold, an undivided interest in common areas and membership in the owners association are automatically transferred, too. A person can't sell his or her unit without transferring his or her interest in the common areas or vice versa.

COOPERATIVES. **Cooperatives** are buildings owned by corporations with the residents as shareholders who each receive a proprietary lease on an individual unit and the right to use common areas. Title to the cooperative building is held by a corporation formed for that purpose (owned in severalty). A person who wants to live in the building buys shares in the corporation, instead of renting or buying a unit, and is given a proprietary lease for a unit in the building. **Proprietary leases** have longer terms than ordinary leases and offer more rights than an ordinary tenant.

A cooperative shareholder pays a prorated share of the building's expenses and property taxes. If a resident doesn't pay his or her share of expenses, the entire cooperative may be threatened with foreclosure, so an agreement may provide that a shareholder can't transfer an interest without the other shareholders' consent. To transfer a cooperative interest, a shareholder conveys his or her stock and assigns the proprietary lease to the new shareholder.

Chapter 8 Summary

1. Deed is the instrument that conveys ownership of land. Deed is evidence of title; title is actual ownership of rights. Title is *not* a document but rather a concept or theory dealing with ownership. Seller is the grantor; buyer is the grantee. Equitable title is an interest in property created upon execution of a valid sales contract when actual title will be transferred by deed at a future date (closing). This is not the same as having title—only deeds can transfer title. Land contracts also pass equitable title.

2. Valid deeds must be written and contain a *competent grantor's signature, identifiable grantee, words of conveyance, description of property, consideration,* and *acknowledgment*. Delivery and acceptance are required to transfer title. Competent grantor means age 18 and of sound mind; identifiable grantee must be alive at the time of conveyance and separate that person from all others; words of conveyance should say *give, grant, sell, convey* to leave no doubt; property description must distinguish property from all others—should be government survey system, lot and block system, or metes and bounds system; consideration recited to prove not a gift; delivery and acceptance during grantor's lifetime. Donative intent by grantor to transfer title immediately and unconditionally.

3. General warranty and limited warranty deeds give some guarantees. Quitclaim, bargain and sale, and fiduciary deeds have no warranties. General warranty deeds give the best protection. Quitclaim deeds convey only interest grantor *may* have in land without warranting that there is any interest (used to clear up clouds on title, e.g., dower release).

4. Recording documents give notice of ownership or rights. Actual notice is knowing a fact. Constructive notice is all information in the public record. Inquiry notice is when land is being used by people. Ohio uses race/notice rule—first to record gets title, except subsequent good faith buyers (if no knowledge of unrecorded deeds) and mortgages (pure race rule—always priority).

5. Marketable Title Act says unbroken chain of title deeds back 40 years to root of title establishes proper title. Easements and other rights must be recorded or mentioned specifically in deed to preserve. *Marketable Title Act exceptions*: easements with observable evidence of use, easements for pipes, cables, etc., lessors' lease rights, railroad/utility easements, coal interests, mortgages, and government interests. *Wild deed:* unrecorded deed outside chain of title. *Torrens system*: must record things with Torrens registrar to be valid.

6. **Ownership can be in severalty (one person) or co-ownership (many people). Co-ownership: tenancy in common, statutory survivorship tenancy, joint tenancy, or tenancy by the entireties. Tenancy in common: undivided interest in land, no survivorship rights. Statutory survivorship tenancy: undivided equal interest in land, survivorship rights; joint tenancy: undivided equal interest, survivorship rights until conveyance—four unities; tenancy by the entireties: abolished in Ohio. Ownership by associations can be held by corporation, general or limited partnership, REITs, or syndicates. Corporate resolution must authorize purchase or sale of corporate land. Condos have ownership of individual units and undivided interest in common areas; mortgages, taxes, etc., only affect individual units. Cooperatives owned by corporations with residents as shareholders get a proprietary lease on a unit.**

Chapter 8 Quiz

1. ***A deed:***

a. Is the actual ownership of rights to real estate
b. Is better than title
c. Is evidence of title
d. Is a document that must be recorded

2. ***A grantor acknowledges a deed before a:***

a. Federal official
b. Lender representative
c. Notary public
d. Witness

3. ***In Ohio, a deed is required to have which of the following?***

a. Acknowledgement by the grantee
b. Consideration
c. Identifiable grantor
d. The property address

4. ***Equitable title is:***

a. An interest in real property created by the execution of a valid sales contract
b. Actual lawful ownership of real property
c. Evidence of title
d. An instrument that conveys ownership of real property

5. ***Alice and Conrad bought a house and received a general warranty deed. Later, they discover that the previous owner's wife didn't release dower. What's the easiest way to take care of this?***

a. Have the owner and his wife execute another general warranty deed
b. Have the owner execute a quitclaim deed
c. Have the wife execute a quitclaim deed
d. Have the owner and his wife issue a wild deed

6. *Why are documents recorded?*

a. To give actual notice
(b) To give constructive notice
c. To give inquiry notice
d. To give legal notice

7. *The Marketable Title Act says that proper title is established by:*

(a) An unbroken chain of title deeds back 40 years to the root of title
b. Searching the public records for forty years
c. Making sure that no wild deeds exist
d. Buying adequate title insurance

8. *ABC corporation wants to sell some of its land. What does the broker need to do?*

a. Get an employee of the company to sign the listing agreement
b. Find out how many stockholders there are to determine if land is being held in severalty or in co-ownership
(c) Get a corporate resolution authorizing the land to be sold and appointing him or her as broker to sell the land
d. All of the above

9. *Bill, Bob, and Ben bought a home for $90,000 with each putting in $30,000. How did they take title?*

(a) In tenancy in common
b. In joint tenancy with right of survivorship
c. In tenancy by the entireties
d. In severalty

10. *Jim, Jack, and Joe bought real property together. Jim died and his 1/3 share went to his daughter, Susan. How did Jim, Jack, and Joe own their real property?*

(a) Tenancy in common
b. Statutory survivorship tenancy
c. Joint tenancy
d. Tenancy by the entireties

11. *Betty left real property to her daughters, Bonnie and Beatrice. When Bonnie died suddenly, her husband did not get the property even though her will said that all her worldly possessions would go to him. Instead, it went to her sister, Beatrice. How did Bonnie and Beatrice own the property?*

a. Tenancy in common
(b) Joint tenancy with the right of survivorship
c. Co-owners of common area
d. Undivided interest tenancy

9 REAL ESTATE CLOSINGS

CHAPTER OVERVIEW

Now that you have the tools to help your broker's real estate clients list, sell, buy, value, and finance their property, we'll discuss real estate closings. This is how money and title change hands. We'll discuss the different types of closings (escrow and roundtable) as well as the role of escrow agents, lenders, attorneys, and title companies. We'll also look at requirements a lender may have, types of evidence of title, and kinds of title insurance. Finally, we'll look at settlement statements and the important skill (at least for the exam) of prorating costs and expenses.

KEY TERMS

Abstract of Title
A brief summary of the history of title to a piece of property listing all recorded documents that affect the title.

Closing
Transfer of real property ownership from a seller to a buyer according to the terms and conditions stated in the sales contract or escrow agreement.

Location Survey
Survey to determine if a property's buildings encroach on adjoining property or any adjoining property's buildings encroach on subject property.

Marketable Title
Title that is free from defects and that gives a person holding it the right to transfer ownership of the property.

Proration
The allocation of expenses between buyer and seller in proportion to their actual usage of the item represented by that expense.

RESPA
(**R**eal **E**state **S**ettlement **P**rocedures **A**ct) Federal law dealing with real estate closings, which sets forth specific procedures and guidelines for disclosure of settlement costs. RESPA lets buyers compare cost of services, requires specific statements/disclosures, prevents kickbacks, and limits escrows lender can hold. RESPA requires HUD booklet be given to buyers, requires good faith estimate of settlement costs, requires use of HUD settlement statement, and gives buyer the right to inspect HUD settlement statement one business day prior to closing.

Settlement Statement
Document prepared by the closing agent that itemizes all expenses and costs paid by buyer and seller to close the real estate transaction.

Survey
Process of physically determining size and/or boundaries of property.

Title Insurance
An insurance policy guaranteeing that title to the property is good and insuring the policyholder against loss or damages from defects in title.

I. REAL ESTATE CLOSINGS

"Closing" is a word with several meanings in the real estate field. When getting a listing or making a sale, closing means the ability to convince or persuade people that listing their property or buying a particular piece of property with you is in their best interests. After the sale is made, closing is the date of ownership. Closing can also refer to the act of transferring ownership.

The ability to sell and advise people to list property with you or make a sale is important, but knowing the mechanics of the closing process is also critical. As a real estate agent, your broker may give you the task of closing the deal. Buyers and sellers may have questions and concerns, especially if it's their first time through the process. At first, the broker may need to help, but your knowledge of the closing process will grow from experience.

II. KINDS OF REAL ESTATE CLOSINGS

Closing is the transfer of real property ownership from a seller to a buyer according to the terms and conditions stated in the sales contract or escrow agreement. There are two kinds of closings used in Ohio: the **escrow closing** and the **roundtable closing**. Escrow closings are common in northeastern Ohio, while roundtable closings are common in the rest of the state.

ESCROW CLOSING

An **escrow closing** is conducted by a disinterested third party referred to as an **escrow agent**. This person can be an attorney or a representative of a title agency, title company, or the lender. The escrow agent is responsible for performing the closing procedures as detailed in the purchase contract, or in a separate set of escrow instructions, signed by both the buyer and seller. The same agent usually performs duties for both buyer and seller since there's no conflict of interest when procedures are followed as prescribed.

The escrow agent's duties begin when the buyer's earnest money deposit is received and placed in the escrow company's trust account. If there's no earnest money or if the money remains in the broker's trust account, the escrow agent's duties begin upon receipt of a copy of the sales contract or escrow instructions. The seller gives an executed deed for the property to the escrow agent along with any inspections or required documentation. The buyer gives the escrow agent all funds needed for closing. If there's financing involved, the buyer's lender gives a loan commitment prior to closing and pays the loan amount at closing.

The escrow agent completes the closing after all conditions of the closing have been met, as spelled out in the sales contract or other instructions including receipt of the executed deed and all required money. The escrow agent prepares the settlement statement and disburses all funds as instructed. The closing must take place within the closing date stated in the sales contract or within a reasonable amount of time if no date is specified. The buyer and seller do not usually attend this type of closing.

ROUNDTABLE CLOSING

A **roundtable closing** is a closing conducted with all parties present. This would include the seller, listing broker (or subagent of the broker), buyer, and possibly a buyer/broker (or subagent of the buyer/broker). If the property is financed, the lender will also be represented at the closing. In addition, the seller and/or buyer may choose to be represented by legal counsel. A roundtable closing may be conducted by any of these parties, but is usually done by the lender's agent, an attorney, or a title company.

At a roundtable closing, the same documents are exchanged as at an escrow closing. The seller is responsible for bringing the executed deed to the closing as well as any inspections or other documents required. The buyer must bring the funds necessary to buy the house or sign a mortgage with the lender, so the lender will release funds to the seller with the buyer supplying the balance.

Like the escrow closing, a settlement statement is prepared, but it can be done by the brokerage that listed the property, title company representative, escrow company, or other third party. After everyone is satisfied that the terms of the sales contract have been fulfilled, all funds are disbursed, and deed and title to the property change hands. The closing must take place by the stated closing date or within a reasonable amount of time if no date is specified.

III. THIRD PARTY INVOLVEMENT IN CLOSINGS

There may be many other parties involved in a closing, besides the buyer and seller. Typically, a buyer and seller will have their representatives involved in the closing. These may include their real estate agent, an attorney, and an escrow agent.

Other parties that have an important function in a real estate closing are the **lender** and a **real estate attorney,** or **title company**.

LENDER

A **lender** plays an important role in the closing procedure for property that's financed. By the time the closing takes place, the lender should have already performed a large amount of work in approving the loan. This includes verifying information about the buyer through a credit report, employment records, etc., as well as verifying information about the property through an appraisal, survey, check of the public records, inspections, etc. Once the lender follows its procedure and is comfortable with the property and the buyer, a loan commitment is made.

The loan commitment is submitted to the escrow agent, and funds are disbursed after other conditions have been met. These other conditions *always* include that proper paperwork be signed by the buyer, including the note and mortgage to secure the loan.

HOMEOWNER'S INSURANCE. Homeowner's insurance is a policy that will cover loss or damage to the home or property in the event of fire or other disaster. The lender will require that this policy be sufficient to replace the home or reimburse the mortgage amount with the lender being named on the actual policy.

INSPECTIONS. There are a number of inspections that a lender may require, above and beyond what the purchase contract requires. These include inspections for termites, structural integrity, septic systems, and radon gas, among others. If a desired bank inspection is in the purchase contract, the bank will review the report. If an inspection isn't part of the contract, the bank will have it done. Either way, the loan will likely be conditioned upon satisfactory results.

ESCROW/ACCOUNT RESERVE ACCOUNT. An escrow account (also called a reserve account) is not related to an escrow closing. It is an account that the buyer and lender set up as a way of making sure that property taxes, insurance premiums, and other items are covered. The buyer's monthly principal and interest payment for the mortgage is increased by an amount equal to 1/12 of these other payments. This extra money is deposited into a separate account, with money from this account used to pay semi-annual real estate taxes, annual insurance premium, etc., when each comes due.

SURVEY. A **survey** is the process of physically determining the size and/or boundaries of a piece of property. A bank may require this type of survey, but it's expensive. A bank is more likely to request a **location survey**, which determines whether the property's buildings encroach onto adjoining property, or any adjoining property's buildings encroach on the subject property. The exact boundaries of the property aren't certified by a location survey, but it is often required for the secondary mortgage market.

EVIDENCE OF MARKETABLE TITLE. **Marketable title** means that a title is free from defects, and a person has the right to transfer ownership of the property. There are generally four ways to show evidence of marketable title:

1. Abstract of title
2. Certificate of title
3. Title report
4. Title insurance

Lenders usually require title insurance because of the protection it offers.

REAL ESTATE ATTORNEY

A real estate attorney can perform several functions in a closing. Attorneys can represent either a buyer or seller, so the attorney is responsible for protecting his or her client's interests by explaining contract details and other important points of law that may affect the transaction or the property.

A real estate attorney may also be a neutral party who works for the title company or may be retained to do title examination work. The two main types of attorney-related title evidence are **abstract of title** and **certificate of title**.

ABSTRACT OF TITLE. An **abstract of title** is a brief summary of the history of title to a piece of property, listing all recorded documents that affect the title. The bank may accept this instead of a title insurance policy, provided that a satisfactory **letter of opinion** from an attorney is issued regarding the title. In this letter, the attorney examines the chain of title, also called an **abstract**, which follows the history of the title and updates any new liens, encumbrances, or other recorded documents that were filed affecting the property since the previous owner bought it. There's no guarantee associated with this type of title evidence, so the homeowner or lender does *not* have any recourse if title defects are discovered later.

CERTIFICATE OF TITLE. A **certificate of title** is a document prepared by an attorney stating the attorney's opinion of the status of the title to a piece of property after performing a title search and reviewing the public records. There's no guarantee associated with this type of title evidence, so the homeowner or lender does *not* have any recourse if title defects are discovered.

TITLE COMPANY

A **title company** is responsible for examining and researching titles. Evidence of title is provided through a **title report** or the issuance of **title insurance**.

TITLE REPORT. A **title report** is a document stating the current title status of a piece of property. This report is also called a **title guaranty**. This type of report lists all encumbrances, covenants, and defects associated with the title and shown in the public record. A title report, however, does not detail the chain of title to a piece of property like an abstract of title does. Guarantees are limited to mistakes made in reading or interpreting items in the public record.

TITLE INSURANCE. **Title insurance** is an insurance policy guaranteeing that title to property is good title and insuring the policyholder against loss or damages from defects in the title. The defects could be liens or claims against title, and these may be recorded or unrecorded claims. Title insurance offers the most protection to the homeowner or mortgagee.

IV. TYPES OF TITLE INSURANCE POLICIES

There are two broad categories of title insurance policies: **standard coverage** or **extended coverage**, and they can be further divided into four classes: **owner's policies**, **mortgagee's policies**, **leasehold policies**, and **easement policies**. The typical procedure is the same for each type of policy. The title searcher prepares a report; the title company's attorney reviews the report and then draws up a letter of opinion. The title insurance policy is written based on the report and opinion letter.

STANDARD COVERAGE

With standard title insurance coverage, the title insurance policy states all possible clouds or problems with the title, like liens or unpaid taxes. These, along with any other defects discovered in the public records (or by other means), are listed in the actual title insurance policy. Listed problems become exceptions to the title insurance policy coverage. In other words, the title insurance company writes the policy to exclude these known items from the coverage.

If there's a claim against the title by a lienholder who was disclosed to the new buyer in the title search results and stated in the title insurance policy, the title insurance company might not have to pay compensation for this claim. It would be the new homeowner's responsibility, since he or she was made aware of this possible claimant. Title insurance protects the homeowner from claimants *not* stated in the insurance policy, including defects in the public records such as forged documents, improper deeds, and other mistakes in the public records.

EXTENDED COVERAGE

Extended coverage title insurance policies, coverages, and restrictions are similar to a standard coverage policy with additional protections. The extended coverage policy, for example, covers additional defects in title that may be discovered only through actual inspection of a survey. Extended coverage protects the property owner from unrecorded liens (provided the new property owner did not have actual notice of the liens).

American Land Title Association (ALTA) is a national association of title companies, abstractors, and attorneys. Members agree to promote uniformity, quality, and professional standards in title insurance policies. Policies issued by ALTA members follow specific guidelines.

OWNER'S POLICIES

Owner's fee title insurance policies are issued in the name of the property owner. Coverage runs from the time of purchase for as long as the policyholder owns the property. When a new party purchases the property, he or she will need to buy a new policy and be named as beneficiary to collect on a claim from a title defect.

To purchase title insurance, a one-time payment is made when buying property. The maximum exposure for the company issuing the policy is the full value of the property at the time the policy is purchased, unless the policy provides for inflation adjustment. Claims are paid based on the actual decrease in value caused to the property. The full-face amount of the policy (full value of the property) is rarely paid out unless a serious defect causes the owner to lose title to the property (except, of course, foreclosure). A company issuing title insurance usually reserves the right to pursue third parties to regain any claim money paid (also called subrogation).

MORTGAGEE'S POLICIES

Like other types of insurance, the mortgagee (the lender) may have a policy drawn in its own name to protect its interests in the property. The mortgagee's policy is for the loan amount that's outstanding at the time a claim would be paid. The owner's policies and the mortgagee's policies typically coincide, so the title insurance issuer is not paying twice on the same claim to the mortgagee and owner.

LEASEHOLD POLICIES

A less common type of title insurance is the *leasehold policy*. Lessees typically obtain this type of insurance when a substantial amount of money has been invested in a property, such as for a building owned on leased land.

EASEMENT POLICIES

Another type of uncommon title insurance is the *easement policy,* which is used to protect easement owner's interests across another's property.

V. SETTLEMENT STATEMENTS

Another important aspect of a closing is the **settlement statement,** also called a **closing statement**. A **settlement statement** is a document prepared by the closing agent, which itemizes all expenses and costs paid by the buyer and seller to close the real estate transaction. A separate statement is prepared for each party.

ITEMS LISTED ON SETTLEMENT STATEMENTS

Any cost to a buyer or seller can be listed on a settlement statement. Items on settlement statements can vary from closing to closing because the payment of any item is always negotiable between the buyer and seller. To understand the final amount of money that a buyer will have to pay or a seller will receive from a closing, it's important to understand the concept of **debits** and **credits**.

DEBITS. **Debits** (like debts) are any sum of money that is owed. A debit is charged to a particular party on a balance sheet to represent money that ***must be paid to the other party***. Whatever amount is expected from the transaction is reduced by the debit amount. So, if you were supposed to receive $100,000 from the sale of your house, but you agreed to pay for a termite inspection that cost $500, you are debited $500 and receive only $99,500. The total is reduced by the agreed payment.

CREDITS. **Credits** are any sum of money that is to be received. A credit is given to a particular party on a balance sheet to represent money that ***should be paid by the other party***. Whatever amount is expected from the transaction is increased by the credit amount, or the amount of money you were supposed to pay is reduced by the credit amount. So, if you were supposed to pay $100,000 to buy a house, but the seller agreed to reimburse you the $500 you spent for a termite inspection, you are credited $500 and need to pay only $99,500.

DEBITS VERSUS CREDITS. Debits and credits work together when figuring the total money owed to each party. When the credits are added on one side, they must equal the total debits on the other side.

PRORATION

Proration is the allocation of an expense between buyer and seller in proportion to the actual usage of the item represented by that expense. For example, if a house is sold July 1 of a given year, but the seller already paid the insurance on January 1 for the entire year, the insurance premium would be prorated so that the seller paid for the first half of the year only. An amount would be calculated that the buyer would owe, representing the amount of insurance due for the second half of the year when the buyer actually had use of the property.

Proration is an important concept to understand for real estate practice, as well as for the real estate licensing exam. Debits and credits may be whole numbers, but there are many **accrued items** (e.g., taxes) and many **prepaid items** (e.g., insurance) that must be prorated to determine who pays what amount.

ACCRUED ITEMS. **Accrued items** are expense items on a settlement statement for which the cost has been incurred, but the expense has not yet been paid. Real estate taxes are an example. Mortgage interest can be another. Accrued items start from the position that nothing has been paid, so the seller's portion must be calculated so he or she can be debited and the buyer credited for this amount. The seller owes the money—even though the bill may not have arrived. If the buyer gets credited for that amount, the buyer is responsible for paying the entire amount when the bill comes due because the seller has already taken care of his or her obligation by giving credit to the buyer.

PREPAID ITEMS. **Prepaid items** are expense items on a settlement statement that the seller has already paid in advance, usually at the beginning of the year for the rest of the year or longer. Homeowner's insurance policies are an example. Special assessments may be considered another. Since the seller has already paid for these items, he or she wants to get credit for the portion that has been paid but will not be used, since he or she no longer owns the home.

OTHER ITEMS. Other expense items such as surveys, inspections, or fees can be shared between buyer and seller. These items are easy to prorate because they are calculated as a percentage of the item used and are not based on days of usage. Payments of all items are usually open to negotiation between buyer and seller.

RULES OF PRORATION. There are a few important rules of proration to know to understand the math correctly. ***The two most important rules are:***

1. The seller always pays for the day of closing
2. Always use a calendar year (365 days) when computing prorations (unless you are specifically told to use a 360-day year—where each month equals 30 days)

There are additional proration rules that deal with rents and deposits when buying or selling rental properties, but these are not relevant to the state exam. These should be discussed with your broker if you choose to go into commercial real estate.

DO THE MATH!

Prorations: Accrued or Prepaid, Buyer or Seller

There are two simple tricks to help you calculate the problem more easily:

1. Whether a problem asks for accrued or prepaid, buyer or seller, the math is the same! Calculate the seller's portion and the buyer's potion is what's left.
2. Always divide annual dollar amounts by 365 to get a daily rate.

EXAMPLE #1: Semi-annual property taxes are $728. If the closing is July 10, how much of the taxes must the seller pay?

Solution #1: We know several things:

1. We must use a 365-day year because the problem didn't say otherwise
2. The seller pays for the first part of the year, *up to and including* July 10
3. This is an accrued item, but that's not important because we calculate the same way

Step #1: TAXES PER DAY = ($728 X 2) ÷ 365 = 3.9890 [use four decimal places]

Step #2: Total days seller owes for = 191 days

[Jan. = 31 days + Feb. = 28 days + Mar. = 31 days + Apr. = 30 days + May = 31 days + Jun. = 30 days + Jul. = 10 days]

Step #3: Total amount seller owes = Taxes per day x Total days owed for, or

? = 3.9890 x 191

$761.899 rounded to $761.90 = Seller owes for property taxes.

EXAMPLE #2: Based on Example #1, how much of the tax is the buyer responsible for?

Solution #2: Still calculate seller's portion first; buyer's portion is what's left.

Step #1: Buyer's portion = Total tax – Seller's portion

? = ($728 x 2) – $761.90

$694.10 = Buyer's portion of property taxes

EXAMPLE #3: Seller bought a three-year insurance policy for $2,150 on March 1, 2004. If closing is July 10, 2006, what is the seller's refund?

Solution #3: We know several things:

1. We must use a 365-day year because the problem didn't say otherwise
2. The seller pays for first part of the policy, up to AND INCLUDING July 10
3. It's a prepaid item—math is the same but seller's refund is calculated like buyer's part

Step #1: Insurance cost per day = ($2,150 ÷ 3) ÷ 365 = 1.9635

Step #2: Total days seller owes for = (365 + 365 + 31 + 30 + 31 + 30 + 10) = 862 days

365	365	31	30	31	30	10
3/04-3/05	3/05-3/06	3/06	4/06	5/06	6/06	7/06

Step #3: Seller refund = Total premium – (Insurance cost/day x Days used)

? = $2,150 – (1.9635 x 862)

$457.46 = Seller refund for unused insurance premium.

TYPES OF SETTLEMENT STATEMENTS

There are several types of settlement statements with different purposes. The form shown provides a good faith estimate of total settlement costs that a buyer (and/or seller) can expect to pay to close the real estate transaction. This form details the type and cost (or price range) of each function the escrow company or other closing agent performs or contracts with another party to perform.

This page is located on the U.S. Department of Housing and Urban Development's Homes and Communities Web site at **http://www.hud.gov/offices/hsg/sfh/res/resappc.cfm**.

Sample Good Faith Estimate

As of May 1, 1996

PART 3500 -- APPENDIX C

Appendix C to Part 3500 -- Sample Form of Good Faith Estimate

[Name of Lender]\1\

The information provided below reflects estimates of the charges which you are likely to incur at the settlement of your loan. The fees listed are estimates -- the actual charges may be more or less. Your transaction may not involve a fee for every item listed.

The numbers listed beside the estimates generally correspond to the numbered lines contained in the HUD - 1 or HUD - 1A settlement statement that you will be receiving at settlement. The HUD - 1 or HUD - 1A settlement statement will show you the actual cost for items paid at settlement.

Item\2\	HUD - 1 or HUD - 1A	Amount or range
Loan origination fee	801	$XXXX
Loan discount fee	802	$XXXX
Appraisal fee	803	$XXXX
Credit report	804	$XXXX
Inspection fee	805	$XXXX
Mortgage broker fee	[Use blank line in 800 Section]	$XXXX
CLO access fee	[Use blank line in 800 Section]	$XXXX
Tax related service fee	[Use blank line in 800 Section]	$XXXX
Interest for [X] days at $XXXX per day	901	$XXXX

Mortgage insurance premium	902	$XXXX
Hazard insurance premiums	903	$XXXX
Reserves	1000 - 1005	$XXXX
Settlement fee	1101	$XXXX
Abstract or title search	1102	$XXXX
Title examination	1103	$XXXX
Document preparation fee	1105	$XXXX
Attorney's fee	1107	$XXXX
Title insurance	1108	$XXXX
Recording fees	1201	$XXXX
City/County tax stamps	1202	$XXXX
State tax	1203	$XXXX
Survey	1301	$XXXX
Pest inspection	1302	$XXXX
[Other fees -- list here]		$XXXX

Applicant

Date

Authorized Official

These estimates are provided pursuant to the Real Estate Settlement Procedures Act of 1974, as amended (RESPA). Additional information can be found in the HUD Special Information Booklet, which is to be provided to you by your mortgage broker or lender, if your application is to purchase residential real property and the Lender will take a first lien on the property.

Footnotes

\1\The name of the lender shall be placed at the top of the form. Additional information identifying the loan application and property may appear at the bottom of the form or on a separate page. Exception: If the disclosure is being made by a mortgage broker who is not an exclusive agent of the lender, the lender's name will not appear at the top of the form, but the following legend must appear:

This Good Faith Estimate is being provided by XXXXXXXX, a mortgage broker, and no lender has yet been obtained.

\2\Items for which there is estimated to be no charge to the borrower are not required to be listed. Any additional items for which there is estimated to be a charge to the borrower shall be listed if required on the HUD - 1.

[58 FR 17165, Apr. 1, 1993, as amended at 59 FR 6521, Feb. 10, 1994]

A different form is used to determine the total amount owed by and owed to each party in a transaction. This statement lists the property's price, and details, deposits, adjustments, prorations, and other costs paid as part of a closing. The closing agent uses this to ensure accuracy.

The final type of closing statement is the HUD-1 Settlement Statement. This is similar to the previous form, but more detailed as required under the Real Estate Settlement and Procedures Act (RESPA). A sample HUD-1 Settlement Statement follows on pages 166 and 167.

REAL ESTATE SETTLEMENT AND PROCEDURES ACT (RESPA)

RESPA rules and compliance are administered by HUD. Their purpose is to regulate settlement and closing procedures and practices. RESPA laws call for the disclosure of all settlement costs using a standardized settlement statement, which is given to the buyer. The HUD settlement statement used for RESPA compliance shows how much was paid, to what companies or parties, and for what purpose. RESPA laws apply to all one- to four-family residences or condominiums that utilize federally related loans and loans made by lenders that invest more than $1 million in residential mortgages.

RESPA laws were designed to let buyers compare the cost of services from different lenders or closing agents and give buyers several advantages. *RESPA*:

1. Prohibits kickbacks and fees for services not performed during the closing
2. Limits the amount of escrow money reserve lenders require for taxes or insurance
3. Requires a HUD information booklet be given to buyers explaining RESPA
4. Requires a good faith estimate of closing costs be given to the buyer
5. Requires use of the HUD settlement statement
6. Gives buyer the right to inspect HUD settlement statement one day before closing
7. Requires brokers and lenders to disclose multiple relationships without obligating parties to use suggested referrals

RESPA laws also set limits on the amount of escrow reserves a lender can hold or require a buyer to deposit in advance to cover real estate taxes, real estate insurance premiums, and other similar costs.

ITEMS NOT LISTED ON SETTLEMENT STATEMENTS

Although most costs appear on settlement statements, some don't. If an item is paid outside of closing, the party paid the cost personally. Examples of items that don't appear on the statement are the fee for a professional home inspection or an attorney representing one of the parties to the transaction. In these cases, the party paid the professionals directly. The escrow deposits lenders require a buyer to pay to cover future property taxes or homeowner's insurance *are* required to appear on the settlement statement.

A. **Settlement Statement**

U.S. Department of Housing and Urban Development

OMB Approval No. 2502-0265 (expires 9/30/2006)

B. Type of Loan			
1. ☐ FHA 2. ☐ FmHA 3. ☐ Conv. Unins. 4. ☐ VA 5. ☐ Conv. Ins.	6. File Number:	7. Loan Number:	8. Mortgage Insurance Case Number:

C. Note: This form is furnished to give you a statement of actual settlement costs. Amounts paid to and by the settlement agent are shown. Items marked "(p.o.c.)" were paid outside the closing; they are shown here for informational purposes and are not included in the totals.

D. Name & Address of Borrower:	E. Name & Address of Seller:	F. Name & Address of Lender:

G. Property Location:	H. Settlement Agent:	
	Place of Settlement:	I. Settlement Date:

J. Summary of Borrower's Transaction		K. Summary of Seller's Transaction	
100. Gross Amount Due From Borrower		**400. Gross Amount Due To Seller**	
101. Contract sales price		401. Contract sales price	
102. Personal property		402. Personal property	
103. Settlement charges to borrower (line 1400)		403.	
104.		404.	
105.		405.	
Adjustments for items paid by seller in advance		**Adjustments for items paid by seller in advance**	
106. City/town taxes to		406. City/town taxes to	
107. County taxes to		407. County taxes to	
108. Assessments to		408. Assessments to	
109.		409.	
110.		410.	
111.		411.	
112.		412.	
120. Gross Amount Due From Borrower		**420. Gross Amount Due To Seller**	
200. Amounts Paid By Or In Behalf Of Borrower		**500. Reductions In Amount Due To Seller**	
201. Deposit or earnest money		501. Excess deposit (see instructions)	
202. Principal amount of new loan(s)		502. Settlement charges to seller (line 1400)	
203. Existing loan(s) taken subject to		503. Existing loan(s) taken subject to	
204.		504. Payoff of first mortgage loan	
205.		505. Payoff of second mortgage loan	
206.		506.	
207.		507.	
208.		508.	
209.		509.	
Adjustments for items unpaid by seller		**Adjustments for items unpaid by seller**	
210. City/town taxes to		510. City/town taxes to	
211. County taxes to		511. County taxes to	
212. Assessments to		512. Assessments to	
213.		513.	
214.		514.	
215.		515.	
216.		516.	
217.		517.	
218.		518.	
219.		519.	
220. Total Paid By/For Borrower		**520. Total Reduction Amount Due Seller**	
300. Cash At Settlement From/To Borrower		**600. Cash At Settlement To/From Seller**	
301. Gross Amount due from borrower (line 120)		601. Gross amount due to seller (line 420)	
302. Less amounts paid by/for borrower (line 220)	( )	602. Less reductions in amt. due seller (line 520)	( )
303. Cash ☐ From ☐ To Borrower		**603. Cash ☐ To ☐ From Seller**	

Section 5 of the Real Estate Settlement Procedures Act (RESPA) requires the following: • HUD must develop a Special Information Booklet to help persons borrowing money to finance the purchase of residential real estate to better understand the nature and costs of real estate settlement services; • Each lender must provide the booklet to all applicants from whom it receives or for whom it prepares a written application to borrow money to finance the purchase of residential real estate; • Lenders must prepare and distribute with the Booklet a Good Faith Estimate of the settlement costs that the borrower is likely to incur in connection with the settlement. These disclosures are manadatory.

Section 4(a) of RESPA mandates that HUD develop and prescribe this standard form to be used at the time of loan settlement to provide full disclosure of all charges imposed upon the borrower and seller. These are third party disclosures that are designed to provide the borrower with pertinent information during the settlement process in order to be a better shopper.

The Public Reporting Burden for this collection of information is estimated to average one hour per response, including the time for reviewing instructions, searching existing data sources, gathering and maintaining the data needed, and completing and reviewing the collection of information.

This agency may not collect this information, and you are not required to complete this form, unless it displays a currently valid OMB control number.

The information requested does not lend itself to confidentiality.

Previous editions are obsolete

Page 1 of 2

form **HUD-1** (3/86)
ref Handbook 4305.2

L. Settlement Charges

	Paid From Borrowers Funds at Settlement	Paid From Seller's Funds at Settlement
700. Total Sales/Broker's Commission based on price $ @ % =		
Division of Commission (line 700) as follows:		
701. $ to		
702. $ to		
703. Commission paid at Settlement		
704.		
800. Items Payable In Connection With Loan		
801. Loan Origination Fee %		
802. Loan Discount %		
803. Appraisal Fee to		
804. Credit Report to		
805. Lender's Inspection Fee		
806. Mortgage Insurance Application Fee to		
807. Assumption Fee		
808.		
809.		
810.		
811.		
900. Items Required By Lender To Be Paid In Advance		
901. Interest from to @$ /day		
902. Mortgage Insurance Premium for months to		
903. Hazard Insurance Premium for years to		
904. years to		
905.		
1000. Reserves Deposited With Lender		
1001. Hazard insurance months@$ per month		
1002. Mortgage insurance months@$ per month		
1003. City property taxes months@$ per month		
1004. County property taxes months@$ per month		
1005. Annual assessments months@$ per month		
1006. months@$ per month		
1007. months@$ per month		
1008. months@$ per month		
1100. Title Charges		
1101. Settlement or closing fee to		
1102. Abstract or title search to		
1103. Title examination to		
1104. Title insurance binder to		
1105. Document preparation to		
1106. Notary fees to		
1107. Attorney's fees to		
(includes above items numbers:)		
1108. Title insurance to		
(includes above items numbers:)		
1109. Lender's coverage $		
1110. Owner's coverage $		
1111.		
1112.		
1113.		
1200. Government Recording and Transfer Charges		
1201. Recording fees: Deed $; Mortgage $; Releases $		
1202. City/county tax/stamps: Deed $; Mortgage $		
1203. State tax/stamps: Deed $; Mortgage $		
1204.		
1205.		
1300. Additional Settlement Charges		
1301. Survey to		
1302. Pest inspection to		
1303.		
1304.		
1305.		
1400. Total Settlement Charges (enter on lines 103, Section J and 502, Section K)		

Previous editions are obsolete — Page 2 of 2 — form **HUD-1** (3/86) ref Handbook 4305.2

Chapter 9 Summary

1. Closing is the transfer of real property ownership from a seller to a buyer according to terms and conditions in a sales contract or escrow agreement. Closings can be escrow closings (conducted by a neutral third party—escrow agent) or roundtable closings (with all parties present). Escrow agent's duties begin on receipt of buyer's earnest money deposit or receipt of the sales contract or other escrow instructions. All documents—deed, note, mortgage, etc.,—and funds are given to escrow agent and disbursed after a final check.

2. Third parties often involved in closings include lenders, attorneys, and title companies. A lender always requires a buyer to sign the note and mortgage. May also require homeowner's insurance, inspections, escrow accounts, surveys, and evidence of marketable title. Escrow account/reserve account has buyer make monthly deposits for annual property taxes and insurance to ensure they're paid when due. Bank-required surveys are usually location surveys (check for encroachments) since they're less expensive. Evidence of marketable title includes abstract of title, certificate of title, title report, or title insurance. Real estate attorneys create abstract of title or certificate of title, but these don't give recourse for future title defects; title companies create title report or issue title insurance.

3. Title insurance can be standard or extended coverage and can be an owner's policy, mortgagee's policy, leasehold policy, or easement policy. Standard coverage insurance policy lists all possible clouds or problems with title like liens or unpaid taxes excluding those items from coverage. Title insurance protects against claimants not listed in a policy, including defects in public records such as forged documents, improper deeds, or other mistakes. Extended coverage adds protection for defects that can only be known by survey or visual inspection and unrecorded liens unknown to the buyer.

4. Settlement statements are prepared by closing agents to itemize all expenses and costs paid by buyer and seller to close a real estate transaction. One type of settlement statement is used to determine the total amount of money owed by, and to, each party. It lists price and details deposits, adjustments, prorations, and other costs paid as part of closing. Another kind of settlement statement gives a buyer a good faith estimate of settlement costs needed to close the transaction. The third kind is the HUD settlement statement required by RESPA. Some items don't appear on settlement statements and costs paid outside of closing (e.g., attorneys) may not also.

5. RESPA is the Real Estate Settlement Procedures Act. It prohibits kickbacks, limits escrow reserves, requires HUD booklet be given to buyers, requires good faith estimate of settlement costs, requires use of HUD settlement statement, and lets buyers inspect HUD statement one day prior to closing. RESPA also limits escrow reserves a lender can require a buyer to make.

6. Proration allocates expenses between buyer and seller in proportion to their actual use of items. Items are prepaid or accrued (due, but not paid)—math is the same for both. *Proration rules:* seller pays for day of closing and use calendar year of 365 days (unless told to use 360 days). Calculate seller's part first, then buyer's part is left. Divide annual dollar amount by 365 for daily rate.

Chapter 9 Quiz

1. ***What dictates the procedures that an escrow agent follows to conduct escrow closings?***
   a. Real Estate Settlement Procedures Act (RESPA)
   b. Procedures outlined by the escrow company or title company
   c. Procedures detailed in the sales contract or escrow agreement
   d. Real estate licensing laws

2. ***Lenders always require which condition before funds can be disbursed?***
   a. The seller must obtain a homeowner's insurance policy
   b. The buyer and seller must obtain a title insurance policy
   c. The buyer must have a termite inspection performed
   d. The buyer must acknowledge the note and mortgage

3. ***All of the following can show evidence of marketable title* except:**
   a. Location survey
   b. Abstract of title
   c. Certificate of title
   d. Title report

4. ***Which type of evidence of title gives a homeowner or lender recourse if title defects are later discovered?***
   a. Abstract of title
   b. Certificate of title
   c. Title insurance
   d. Attorney's opinion

5. ***Title insurance protects policyholders from all of the following defects* except:**
   a. A forged deed
   b. An unrecorded lien that the buyer knew about
   c. Mistakes in the public records
   d. Improper deeds

6. ***Which type of title insurance policy will the lender hold?***
   a. Mortgagor's policy
   b. Mortgagee's policy
   c. Owner's policy
   d. The lender can't hold title insurance

7. ***When determining the portion of a prorated item that a party pays:***
   a. Find out who agreed to pay for the day of closing
   b. Always charge the day of closing to the buyer
   c. Always charge the day of closing to the seller
   d. Split charges for the day of closing equally by buyer and seller

8. ***Annual property taxes are $1,776. If closing is on May 1, what is the seller portion?***
   a. $623.40
   b. $628.60
   c. $1,484.07
   d. $588.76

9. *RESPA does all of the following* except:

a. Prohibits kickbacks and limits the amount of escrow reserves
b. Requires HUD booklet and estimate of settlement costs be given to buyer
c. Requires use of HUD settlement statement and gives buyer the right to inspect the settlement statement at least one day prior to closing
d. Applies to one- to six-family residences and condos 1-4 families

10. *Which of the following costs might not appear on a settlement statement?*

a. Professional home inspection fee
b. Escrow company fees
c. Lender fees
d. Title insurance fees

10 REAL ESTATE PRACTICE

CHAPTER OVERVIEW

Now that you have an understanding of the laws that govern real estate transactions and you know how property is financed, appraised, and transferred, we'll take a look at the actual practice of real estate. We'll discuss making a sale, getting clients, qualifying clients, showing properties, answering objections, and closing sales. Then, we'll look at how the things we've learned fit into the process—like writing contracts, looking at financing options, and computing a net to seller. Finally, we'll look at some issues you must understand in your practice of real estate including Multiple Listing Services changeover to online computers, changing government regulations, and the need for errors and omissions insurance.

KEY TERMS

Errors and Omissions (E & O) Insurance
Professional liability insurance that protects real estate licensees from mistakes or negligence. A typical policy pays legal fees and judgments resulting from real estate activities. It doesn't cover fraud, transactions of buying or selling your own real estate, and, depending on the policy, may not cover civil rights violations (because punitive damages are usually exempt).

Farming an Area
A phrase used to create an image of working on a specific area over a period of time for prospects. Like farming, you plant seeds and wait for them to grow. Farming encompasses a number of techniques—from calling all the houses on each street to passing out brochures in an area.

Multiple Listing Service (MLS)
A listing service whereby local member brokers agree to share listings and commissions on properties sold jointly. The MLS generally consists of a book published regularly and updated to include new listings. Many localities have added access to listings via online computer services. (The MLS is a benefit of joining state and local affiliated boards of the National Association of REALTORS®.)

Net to Seller
An estimate of the money a seller should receive from a real estate transaction based on a certain selling price after all costs and expenses have been paid. Note that this is *not* a guarantee, but rather an approximation of what the seller should receive in the end.

Sphere of Influence
People you know (and whom you can ask for referrals).

I. MAKING A SALE

Real estate salespeople do a lot of selling. You'll need to sell real estate as well as yourself, your brokerage, and your services. In fact, getting listings requires almost as much sales ability as selling houses. We'll look at a few areas where sales ability is important to your success as a real estate salesperson.

GETTING CLIENTS

As you begin a real estate career, getting buyers or sellers will be one of the biggest challenges. Many people are reluctant to work with salespeople without much experience, but you can't get experience if people are reluctant to work with you. Here are some tips that can help you gain clients.

First, remember that when you're selling yourself, you are also selling the services offered by your brokerage. Take advantage of the fact that your broker has vast experience. Mention that you work closely with your broker, who has vast experience closing real estate deals. Your broker can help you answer the "experience" questions you'll get from prospective clients. Never lie or exaggerate about your experience. Clients won't trust you (or recommend you) when they learn the truth—and they will because it only takes a phone call to the Division of Real Estate to find out when your license was issued.

A second way to get new clients is through people you know. This is often referred to as your **sphere of influence**. The experience factor may not play such an important role because they know you or the person who has recommended you. Of course, family and friends come to mind, but think beyond this circle. Everyone knows influential individuals like lawyers, bankers, accountants, doctors, people from your religious organization, and other business or professional people. Each of these people interacts with lots of people every day, and a referral from them could get you started.

Once you get your first listing and successfully sell your first house, each following sale will be easier if you continue to market yourself and your brokerage. If the seller or buyer was especially happy with your professional and courteous service, he or she may recommend you to others. You could also ask them for names of people they know who might be in the market to buy or sell real estate; neighbors who see your sign in a yard are another source of prospects, as are any people who come through an open house. Then, of course, there's phone calling, advertising, and word of mouth.

FARMING AN AREA. **Farming an area** is a phrase used to create an image of working on a specific area over a period of time for prospects. Like farming, you plant seeds, and wait for them to grow. Do not expect overnight results. It will take time and effort on your part. Like food farming, prospect farming in an area is a patient endeavor needing constant attention. You want to keep your name in people's minds, so they think of you when they're ready to buy or sell a house.

Farming encompasses a number of techniques from calling all the residents on each street to passing out brochures in an area. You must find what works best in your area. Ask your broker for suggestions. You can't work a whole city, so pick an area where you feel comfortable and keep working it for results.

Qualifying Clients

Later, we will talk about qualifying buyers by looking at their income and determining their housing expense ratio and total debt service ratio. Buyer qualifications are also important when people want to apply for a VA loan or other special program. Make sure buyers meet the eligibility requirements. If you're unsure about the requirements, talk to your broker, a lender, or other person who knows. Be sure you're talking with the people who have the authority to make a decision, including buyers or sellers. One spouse may defer to the other; parents giving money for a down payment may have final say, and an officer may have to approve corporate sales. Never assume the person you're dealing with has the ultimate power to make the decision. Always ask to make sure you don't waste time making presentations only to find that someone else must be consulted before a decision can be made.

While determining price range, down payment and monthly payment are important concepts that you should review. Remember, selling real estate is about working with people. The financial part means nothing if clients don't feel you're taking care of their personal needs as well. Always take time to listen to what your clients are looking for, whether they're buying or selling.

1. What services or features are important to them?
2. What do they expect from you?
3. What do they want or need in a house?
4. How many bedrooms do they want?
5. Do they need a garage?
6. What style of house or building material do they prefer?
7. Is a certain school district important?
8. Is public transportation a concern?

You can impress clients with what your brokerage has to offer or by demonstrating a thorough understanding of real estate finance knowledge as you qualify them for a particular type of loan, but you'll impress clients even more by demonstrating a thorough understanding of people by uncovering and addressing their needs and wants. Ask what they're looking for; listen attentively, and follow through with customized service based on that knowledge.

AVOIDING TROUBLE. When trying to qualify prospects based on their financial situation, needs and desires, or other criteria, be sure *not* to interject your own opinions or biases into what the prospect desires in a particular house. Of course, with the financial qualifications, it's a little easier; a particular house costs a certain price, and the buyers can afford a certain price. But, be careful. If a house is listed at $140,000 and the prospective buyer wants to offer $100,000, you must present the offer to the seller or the seller's agent. You may feel uncomfortable doing this, and you may mention to your clients that such a drastic price cut is unusual, but you must honor the wishes of the client you're representing as long as it's a legal request.

You must be especially careful when qualifying buyers' needs and wants. As stated previously, you must not interject your own opinion into the situation. For example, in the discussion of the client's needs and wants, the issue of school districts may arise. It's natural for people to ask what you think as a real estate professional because they're unfamiliar with the area or they want a second opinion. A positive or negative assessment of the school district can set you up for a lawsuit. The best approach to this to direct people to sources for objective answers to their questions. This might be the public library, superintendent of the school district, or other similar authoritative source, but it should **never** be your personal opinion.

Showing Properties

When showing properties, there are three areas in which you need to prepare: *buyer, seller,* and *property*. Of course, responsibilities differ depending on whom you represent as your client.

THE BUYER. If you're representing the buyer, you must become familiar with the property or properties that you plan to show. When the buyer has a question, you'll appear professional and put the client at ease if you're able to answer it. If you don't have the answer, tell the buyer you'll find out. Never guess or make up an answer. If you've done your homework, there should be only a few questions you can't answer.

You may want to go through the home by yourself before showing it to a potential buyer if you're not the listing agent. Being familiar with the home is a big advantage. At the very least, you should talk with the listing agent to get as much information before you show a home to a client or customer. Any problems with the home that are discussed with a prospective buyer ahead of time seem less ominous than those discovered later.

THE SELLER. If you're representing the seller, you should be familiar with the property before showing it. You may or may not be around when the property is shown, depending on the wishes of the seller and the buyer's agent, but you should always make sure that the seller is not around when you're showing the house. The seller can meet the buyers but then should make an excuse to leave. The seller needs to understand that he or she has hired you as the professional to deal with prospective buyers. You need to get an honest assessment of the buyer's feelings about the house, so you can respond to objections and move toward the sale. It's difficult for a buyer to be honest and open when a seller is around, as the buyer may not want to criticize the home in front of the seller.

THE PROPERTY. The property should always be shown in its best light. That means well-lit and bright rooms and showing off the features that make the property more desirable. This might include a nice fireplace, large kitchen with built-in cupboards and dishwasher, walk-in closets, etc. Try to find a positive feature to point out in each room as prospective buyers walk through. This makes the house more memorable and highlights things they might have missed. You can also help the buyers visualize themselves in the house by pointing out how their furniture, workbench, etc., would look in a particular location.

You should also make sure that the seller has removed as much clutter as possible from the rooms. It's okay for the house to look lived in, but all rooms, including garages and basements, shouldn't look cramped or messy. Furniture should be moved closer to the walls. Rooms look smaller with furniture in them, so this gives buyers a better perspective on how big the rooms really are. It's not necessary for the seller to paint something just to change the color to something more saleable (unless the wall needs paint anyway) because you never know what buyers will like.

Finally, when bringing buyers to a home, you may want to take the scenic route if they aren't familiar with an area. Point out parks, schools, shopping, etc., on the way.

Handling Objections

Objections occur during a sale. This is true when you're selling yourself and your real estate brokerage firm's services to a prospective seller, and it's true when you're selling a house to a prospective buyer. Being prepared to respond to these objections skillfully demonstrates professionalism. With more experience, objections can be overcome, and anticipating objections makes your client feel more comfortable.

Welcome objections because they're an opportunity to sell. Theoretically, if you overcome the objections, you should make the sale. Objections don't mean that you've done a bad job or that the house isn't right for someone. Perhaps the person just needs more information.

TYPES OF OBJECTIONS. There are three types of objections in sales:

1. Invalid objections
2. Valid objections that are answerable
3. Valid objections that are not answerable

Invalid objections are really excuses or stalls and often have nothing to do with the property. There's not much you can do if prospects are too busy or decide they aren't ready to buy now. *Valid* objections need to be addressed. If it's an *answerable objection*, such as the house needs a new roof, you should be prepared. Explain that the price has been discounted to reflect this fact. If the buyer doesn't think there's enough shopping nearby, list stores in the area and their distances from the property. If you don't have an answer or don't know, be honest about that and find the answer. If the objection is ***not answerable,*** for example the house being in the wrong school district, there's not much you can do except admit that this is a valid objection. Find out if this is the only objection; then try to find out if there's room to compromise on this point and how high of a priority it is to the buyer. Don't ignore these concerns; just see if there's any chance to negotiate. You need to understand the objection and understand the prospect's reason for this objection.

METHODS FOR HANDLING OBJECTIONS. There are many ways you can answer objections, but here are a few general rules:

1. Restate an objection before trying to answer it. This ensures that you truly understand the objection, avoids misunderstandings on both sides, and gives you a little more time to think.

2. Never make a big deal out of an objection. Make your answer short and direct to the question at hand. If prospects need to hear more, they'll ask, but if you dwell on something too much, the objection may seem bigger than it really is.
3. Respond to objections by asking questions. This helps you understand the objection, the prospect's thinking, and the real reason for the objection. In addition, it can help a prospect answer his or her own objection.
4. No property is perfect. Every pro and con about the property must be weighed to find the best fit for a prospect. Sit down with the prospect, and write out this list, helping to focus on the positive things.
5. Use third parties to support answers to objections, if possible. If a prospect is concerned about the basement leaking, having an expert's opinion is stronger than your opinion, and legal trouble may be avoided.

Closing Sales

Closing sales is the logical conclusion to the hard work of getting clients, qualifying clients, showing properties, and answering objections. If you've done these things well, closing sales will go smoothly. Knowing when to close the sale is something that comes with experience.

Closing a sale is getting a client or customer to sign the contract and commit to a listing or a purchase. There really is no right or wrong time to close a sale, but you must take the initiative and **ask for the sale**. A good time to go for the close would be right after you've answered an important question or overcome a key objection. Many experienced salespeople ask for the close early and often. Watch for verbal or physical clues. If the prospect likes what he or she sees or hears, there is an opportunity to turn that enthusiasm into a sale. Remember, a prospect will rarely ask you for the offer or contract, but if you ask a prospect to sign at the right time, the sale has a good chance of succeeding.

Don't be pushy. However, there's nothing wrong with a confident suggestion that if they like what they see, they should sign now before someone else does. You're the professional who's seen other houses slip away from people who hesitated or people who waited to list a house and missed buyers who couldn't wait to purchase. Feel confident that you're providing a genuine service to clients and customers, and realize that you're the one they're going to blame if they miss an opportunity. When in tune with the physical and verbal clues of people, you'll know how and when to close a sale.

CLOSING TECHNIQUES. Salespeople try different techniques with different people. Here are few to consider:

- First, put the buyers into the home by pointing out the shorter commute to work once they've moved into their new home.
- Second, ask buyers questions about what they'll do with the new home, like whether they'll paint the family room beige or blue.
- Third, ask buyers a no-lose question: Do you want to take possession in 30 or 60 days?

- Fourth, have some extra information for buyers if they act now, like locking in a mortgage rate at X percent if they sign a contract today instead of waiting, when rates may go up.

Of course, there are many other techniques. Find ones that work best for you in each situation. With more experience, you'll know when to use one of these suggestions, when to tell your prospects the story about the one that got away, and when to sit down and go through a list of the pros and cons of the property.

CLOSINGS AND CONTRACTS. Help make people feel at ease with making an offer or signing a contract to buy a house by sitting down with them and going through each part of the offer they are about to sign. This helps them understand what they're signing. Second, you'll show them that most of the contract has clauses to protect the buyer. And third, you'll impress people with your knowledge of the contract and real estate.

Another thing that many real estate salespeople do is actually write the offer in the part of the house that impressed or interested your clients or customers the most. If they liked the big family room, write the contract there. Try to avoid any interruptions that can derail everyone's train of thought. Let your prospects focus on signing the offer or contract. Finally, encourage their attorney to look over the documents. This often makes people feel more secure.

THE FINAL STEPS. Now that you have a signed offer, convince the seller to agree to the price and terms written in the buyer's offer. If you're not the listing agent, you can't talk directly to the seller, but your message should be the same to the seller or the listing agent. Many of the same techniques you used on the buyers can be used with sellers. Listen to what the seller wants in the transaction. Discover the seller's objectives. Determine how long the property has been for sale. Be prepared to say why this is a good offer for the seller to accept.

You can get some help from the buyers in convincing the seller to accept their offer. Even though a contract offer is legal with just a single dollar bill, the more earnest money deposit the buyers put down, the better response you will get from the seller. Earnest money demonstrates that the buyers are serious.

Finally, once both sides have agreed and signed the contract, remember it's up to you to make sure that your clients understand the process and length of time it takes from the time the contract is signed to the actual closing and transfer of possession of the house or other property. Your broker can be of assistance with this. Having worked with a large number of title companies, escrow agents, and lenders he or she can provide the necessary information.

II. REAL ESTATE PROCEDURES

There are a number of things that we've learned that will be an important part of your real estate career, and the more you practice these suggestions, the more successful you can become. Writing contracts (filling out listing agreements, purchase contracts, or purchase offers), looking at financing alternatives, and computing net to seller forms are necessary skills to master.

WRITING CONTRACTS AND OFFERS

Previously, we took an extensive look at contracts and contract law. There are two important concepts that you should review. They won't necessarily show up on your licensing examination, but they will be a part of your everyday real estate practice and an important part of your success.

The two most important contracts you will deal with on a regular basis are:

- Exclusive Right to Sell Listing contract
- Real Estate Purchase contract

You'll also need to be familiar with the Residential Work Sheet for the Multiple Listing Service. Be familiar with these forms, and get guidance from your broker to avoid mistakes when completing them.

Financing Options

In Chapters 12 and 13, we will take an extensive look at lenders, financing, and mortgages. There are several important parts of those chapters that you should read and review for the licensing exam and your everyday real estate practice.

First, be familiar with the different loans that buyers can obtain and their requirements. Understand alternative financing that can help buyers qualify for larger loans. These include buydowns, adjustable rate mortgages, and FHA and VA loans. Finally, be familiar with the qualifying standards for Fannie Mae, Freddie Mac, FHA, and VA loans. Although there aren't many questions on the licensing exam about the loan process, you will be of great service to clients and customers if you can help them through this process.

Net To Seller

Although we have not discussed the concept of the **net to seller** form directly, we have discussed a number of its components. A **net to seller** is an estimate of the money a seller should receive from a real estate transaction based on a certain selling price after all costs and expenses have been paid. This is **not** a guarantee but rather an approximation of what the seller should receive.

This is an important factor for a seller in determining the listing price of his or her home and what price to accept in a final offer from a buyer. If you're working with sellers, this is a vital skill; if you're working with buyers, you should still have an idea of what this figure is so you can talk intelligently with the listing agent. Your broker will have a form for you to use or, if you belong to the MLS, a Net to Seller sheet can be printed from your computer. Talk with your broker about the specific form and procedure that he or she recommends, but the basic concept is always the same.

RUNNING THE NUMBERS. Essentially, you start with the sales price and deduct all known factors and costs to calculate how much money the seller will actually receive when the transaction is complete. Of course, the seller must pay off all mortgages. You need to find the pay off amount from the lender and whether any penalties will need to be paid. Remember, FHA and VA loans don't have penalties.

Looking at the list, determine other costs the seller will pay. Most of these are open to negotiation between buyer and seller, so make sure you read the purchase contract carefully to see who's paying what. In the case of taxes and insurance, the seller will typically pay for the portion he or she used until the house is actually sold. This is where proration, covered in a previous chapter, will come in handy. Don't forget to subtract the brokerage fee (commission). Even if you're splitting the commission with another agent as a co-op or buyer broker, the total commission amount usually comes out of the seller's portion (provided the seller agreed to this in the listing contract).

PURPOSE OF NET TO SELLER. There are two main reasons to compute a net to seller. First, the seller needs to know how much money he or she can expect to make from a transaction after everything has been paid. This is often an important piece of information a seller wants before deciding whether to accept an offer. Second, the seller needs to know what to expect from the closing. One of the most frustrating situations a seller faces is getting less money than anticipated. This can reflect on you as the seller's agent and could hurt the chance for future referrals. Furthermore, it's your job to explain to the seller that there are many parties involved who must be paid in the transaction including lenders, title companies, escrow companies, etc., in addition to taxes. Invite the seller to compare costs if there's any question about the fees.

III. OTHER REAL ESTATE PRACTICE ISSUES

There are many other aspects of real estate practice. The laws and procedures often change in response to consumer demands and the changing needs of the profession, so continuing education is important. Some issues will depend on the specific practices and procedures established by your broker; other universal issues will be covered. These include Multiple Listing Services, changing government regulations, and errors and omissions insurance.

MULTIPLE LISTING SERVICE

The **Multiple Listing Service (MLS)** is a listing service whereby local member brokers agree to share listings and commissions on properties sold jointly. This is a benefit of joining state and local affiliated boards of the National Association of REALTORS®. Membership is not mandatory, unless your sponsoring broker is a member. The MLS generally consists of a book published regularly and updated to include new listings. This is a rapidly changing area of real estate practice; however, many localities have added access to listings via an online computer service or are planning to do so in the future. As these systems become more sophisticated, access to more information means clients will expect more. Be open to these changes because they will occur.

CHANGING GOVERNMENT REGULATIONS

It's important to keep abreast of changes in regulations at all levels of government. Local governments change zoning ordinances. States change license and continuing education requirements. The federal government changes FHA and VA loan rules and environmental regulations.

The latest changes in Ohio laws deal primarily with agency issues, the treatment of dual agency, and mortgage lending. On the federal level, most recent changes in laws deal with lead paint disclosure for houses built before 1978. Now, a lead paint brochure must be given to buyers; known lead paint hazards must be disclosed, and buyers must be given a 10-day period to have their own lead paint tests conducted. The penalty for failure to disclose lead hazards is a fine of up to $10,000 and up to one year in jail plus treble damages. These constant changes in the law are covered in the journals and publications you'll receive when you become a member of various real estate professional associations. Stay current!

ERRORS AND OMISSIONS INSURANCE

Errors and omissions (E&O) insurance is professional liability insurance that protects licensees from mistakes or negligence. A typical policy pays legal fees and judgments resulting from real estate activities. It doesn't cover fraud, transactions involving buying or selling your own real estate, and, depending on the policy, may not cover civil rights violations (because punitive damages are usually exempt). Normally, you'll be covered under your broker's policy for an additional fee. Brokers are not required to carry E&O insurance, so it's up to you to check. In a constantly changing profession with large and complex transactions, E&O insurance is critical.

Chapter 10 Summary

1. Selling involves selling yourself, your brokerage's services, and real estate. At first, sell the services and experience of your broker. People you know are a good source of clients: family, friends, and professionals. Once you get listings, ask for referrals from satisfied customers, neighbors of your listings, and people at your open houses. Phone calls, advertising, and word of mouth are other methods of finding clients. Farming an area involves working a specific area over a period of time for contacts. Farming can be done many ways—from calling houses to passing out brochures in an area.

2. Qualify clients financially and by identifying their needs and desires. Ask questions, and listen. Do not offer personal opinions. Refer clients to third parties for information on schools, area, etc. To show property, you must prepare buyers, sellers, and property. Tell buyers about problems early, so they don't seem big later. If you don't know an answer, find out. Politely tell sellers they shouldn't be around during showing because buyers often won't give honest opinions if seller is there. Move furniture closer to walls and point out key features in each room on house tour.

3. Objections are an opportunity to sell. Objections can be invalid, invalid and answerable, or unanswerable. Answer objections by restating them. Ask questions and help clients prioritize their needs and wants. Use third parties if possible to help answer objections. After you've answered an important question or overcome a key objection, try to close a sale. Ask for the sale by putting clients in the home, asking a question or no-lose question, or give them extra information as incentive. List pros and cons of property, if needed. Go over sales contract with clients, preferably in a room they like; try for no interruptions and welcome attorney involvement.

4. Writing Exclusive Right to Sell Listing contracts and Real Estate Purchase contracts are important skills to master. Know financing options, including qualifications for various loans and alternatives like buydowns and ARMs. Be able to compute a net to seller form, which is an estimate of the money a seller should receive from a real estate transaction after all costs and expenses have been paid. A net to seller is done so a seller can make a decision whether to accept an offer, and so a seller knows what he or she will receive at closing.

5. Real estate professionals must keep on top of change, such as computerization of MLS now or in future, and changes in government regulations. Ohio revised its agency law. The federal government introduced new lead paint rules for houses built before 1978. Now a lead paint brochure must be given to buyers; known lead paint hazards must be disclosed, and buyers must be given a 10-day period to have their own lead paint tests conducted. Real estate professionals must keep up with all publications to stay current with frequent law changes.

6. Errors and omissions insurance is professional liability insurance to protect real estate licensees from mistakes or negligence. Typical policies pay legal fees and judgments from real estate activities. They do not cover fraud, transactions involving your own real estate, and, depending on the policy, may not cover civil rights violations (because punitive damages are usually exempt).

Chapter 10 Quiz

1. ***You're showing a house to the Joneses and they ask about the schools. You should:***
   a. Tell them you think the school system is great
   b. Tell them you think the school system is lousy
   c. Tell them you have no opinion
   d. Tell them they should talk to the school superintendent

2. ***When you're showing a house to a customer and notice a crack in the wall, you should:***
   a. Run over and stand in front of it so the buyers can't see it
   b. Take the buyers a different way so they don't go past it
   c. Say nothing unless they ask because the crack is visible
   d. Make sure you point out the crack as you go past it

3. *If a buyer brings up an objection to buying a house, you should:*

a. Forget about this house and move to another one because he or she is not interested
b. Ask questions to understand the objection, so you can answer it
c. Tell the buyer that he's an idiot because this is a perfect house for him
d. Let the buyer talk to the seller

4. *If buyers are ready to sign an offer but want to ask their lawyer first, you should:*

a. Tell them time is of the essence and if they don't sign now they'll lose the house
b. Tell them normal procedure is for them to talk with a lawyer after signing
c. Tell them they should feel free to talk with their lawyer first
d. Tell them your broker can make them feel more at ease with the contract

5. *A net to seller is:*

a. A guarantee of the amount of money a seller will get from a transaction
b. An estimate of the amount of money a seller will get from a transaction
c. A declaration of how much you'll make in commission from a transaction
d. A safety feature for the seller in case she doesn't get as much money as she wants

6. *Which of the following does not represent a purpose for the net to seller form?*

a. Give the seller an estimate of money he or she will get from the transaction
b. Let the seller make an informed decision about accepting a specific offer
c. Prepare the seller as to what amount to expect from the closing proceeds
d. A declaration that assures that the seller will accept the offer

7. *Houses built before 1978 require all of the following* except:

a. A lead paint brochure be given to buyers
b. Known lead paint hazards be disclosed to buyers
c. Buyers be given a 10-day period to conduct their own lead paint test
d. The seller mitigates all lead paint

8. *Errors and omissions insurance covers all of the following,* except:

a. Negligence
b. Fraud
c. Mistakes
d. Buying and selling someone else's real estate

11 FAIR HOUSING

CHAPTER OVERVIEW

Fair housing is one of the most important issues you will face in your real estate practice and for the real estate licensing exam. We'll take an extensive look at the important topic of fair housing and discuss federal and state anti-discrimination laws that affect real estate transactions. Real estate agents need to know what conduct violates anti-discrimination laws to avoid potential liability. Agents also have a responsibility to make sure their clients understand these laws, so agents play an important role in combating discrimination.

KEY TERMS

Blockbusting
Trying to induce owners to sell their homes by suggesting that the ethnic or racial composition of a neighborhood is changing with the implication that property values will decline. Also called **panic selling** or **panic peddling**.

Disparate Impact
When a law that isn't discriminatory on its face has a greater impact on a minority group than it has on other groups.

Exclusionary Zoning
A zoning law that has the effect of preventing certain groups (such as minorities or low-income people) from living in a community.

Latent Defects
Defects that are not visible or apparent.

Negligence
An unintentional breach of a legal duty.

Patent Defects
Defects that are visible and would be discovered in a reasonably thorough inspection.

Redlining
Refusal to make loans on property located in a particular neighborhood for discriminatory reasons.

Steering
Channeling prospective buyers or tenants to particular neighborhoods based on their race, religion, or ethnic background.

Title VIII
Another name for the Federal Fair Housing Act, which is Title VIII of the Civil Rights Act of 1968.

I. FAIR HOUSING IN REAL ESTATE

In addition to ethical issues, there are mandatory fair housing issues that real estate licensees must understand. Although your Real Estate Law course examines fair housing in detail with case examples, we'll take another look at fair housing here because it's important to your real estate practice and to the real estate licensing exam. We'll look at federal and state law.

II. FEDERAL LEGISLATION

The two federal anti-discrimination statutes that have the greatest effect on real estate transactions are the Civil Rights Act of 1866 and Title VIII of the Civil Rights Act of 1968 commonly referred to as the Federal Fair Housing Act.

The Civil Rights Act of 1866

The Civil Rights Act of 1866 prohibits racial discrimination in *all* property transactions in the United States: real or personal, residential or commercial, improved or unimproved. The constitutionality of this Act was challenged, but in the 1968 landmark Supreme Court decision of *Jones v. Alfred H. Mayer Co.*, the court ruled that private individuals, in addition to the government, may not discriminate against people based on race when it comes to buying, selling, or owning property.

The ruling in favor of the Joneses established that the 1866 Act prohibited racial discrimination by private parties even without state action. The Court reasoned that the right to buy or lease property could be impaired just as effectively by those individuals who place property on the market as by government actions.

Originally, the 1866 Act was interpreted to prohibit only racial discrimination. However, the Supreme Court recently held that the act applies to discrimination based on ancestry as well as race. Thus Jews, Arabs, Greeks, and other ethnic groups are protected by the 1866 Act even though they're considered Caucasian.

ENFORCEMENT. A person who has been unlawfully discriminated against under the 1866 Act can sue only in federal district court. For incidents that occur in Ohio, action must be filed within one year after the discriminatory incident occurred.

Since the statute doesn't specifically prescribe remedies, the court fashions the remedies it finds necessary. Case law shows a claimant who proves discrimination that violates the 1866 Act may be entitled to several different remedies.

INJUNCTIONS. **Injunctions** are court orders requiring the defendant to do or refrain from doing a particular act. For example, a court might order the defendant to sell his or her house to the plaintiff in a discrimination case.

COMPENSATORY DAMAGES. **Compensatory damages** are damages awarded to an injured party to compensate the party for injuries suffered. In a discrimination suit, compensatory damages may include reimbursement for expenses caused by the discrimination (e.g., extra rent and moving costs), and compensation for emotional distress (humiliation, stress, and anger) resulting from being discriminated against. Damages can total thousands of dollars with awards over $100,000 in some cases.

PUNITIVE DAMAGES. **Punitive damages** are damages awarded to an injured party to punish the wrongdoer and discourage future similar acts. Punitive damages may be awarded if the acts of the defendant are deliberate or particularly egregious. There's no limit on punitive damages with awards exceeding $100,000 in some cases.

The Federal Fair Housing Act

Title VIII of the Civil Rights Act of 1968 is commonly called the Federal Fair Housing Act. The act prohibits discrimination based on **race, color, religion, sex, national origin, disability, or familial status** in the sale or lease of residential property, and it also prohibits discrimination in advertising, real estate brokerage, lending, and other services associated with residential transactions.

The law applies to most sales, rentals, and exchanges of residential property. This includes vacant land if it's offered for the construction of residential buildings.

EXEMPTIONS. Although the Federal Fair Housing Act covers the majority of residential transactions in the U.S., there are several specific exemptions:

1. The law doesn't apply to a single-family home sold or rented by a private individual owner provided that:

    - The owner owns no more than three such homes
    - No discriminatory advertising is used
    - No real estate broker (or any real estate professional) is used

    If the owner isn't the occupant or most recent occupant, he or she may use this exemption only once every 24 months.

2. The law doesn't apply to the rental of a room or unit in a dwelling with no more than four units provided that:

    - The owner occupies one unit as his or her residence
    - No discriminatory advertising is used
    - No real estate broker or agent is used

    This exemption is referred to as "the Mrs. Murphy exemption."

Ohio does not recognize these two exemptions.

3. In dealing with their own property in noncommercial transactions, religious organizations or affiliated nonprofit organizations may limit occupancy to or give preference to their own members provided that membership isn't restricted on the basis of race, color, or national origin.
4. Private clubs with lodgings that aren't open to the public and that aren't operated for a commercial purpose may limit occupancy to or give preference to their own members.

Even the limited exemptions listed previously are not often available. Remember that under the 1866 Civil Rights Act, discrimination based on race, color, or ancestry is prohibited in any property transaction regardless of any exemptions available under the Fair Housing Act. **No transaction involving a real estate licensee is exempt.**

Note also that the transactions listed in #1 and #2 are not exempt from Ohio's fair housing laws (see below). So even though the Federal Fair Housing Act doesn't prevent discrimination in those transactions, the Ohio Civil Rights Act does.

FAMILIAL STATUS. A condominium, apartment building, subdivision, or other development that qualifies as housing for older persons **can** have a "no kids" rule. Other housing developments can't. As mentioned earlier, the Fair Housing Act prohibits discrimination on the basis of familial status making it illegal to discriminate against a person because he or she is a parent or guardian who has custody of a child under 18 years old, but that rule doesn't apply to "housing for older persons." The act defines housing for older persons as any housing that is:

1. Provided under a state or federal program designed to assist the elderly
2. Intended for and solely occupied by persons 62 or older
3. Designed to meet the physical or social needs of older persons, if:
   - Management publishes and follows policies and procedures demonstrating an intent to provide housing for persons 55 or older, *and*
   - At least 80 percent of the units are occupied by at least one person 55 or older

DISABILITY. While most disabilities are covered under the Federal Fair Housing Act, there are minor exceptions, such as addiction to a controlled substance, which are not part of the protected class.

Under the Fair Housing Act, a disability is defined as a physical or mental impairment that substantially limits or curtails one or more major life activities. Discrimination would include the refusal by a landlord or rental agent to permit, at the expense of the disabled person, reasonable modification of the premises. Furthermore, under the Federal Fair Housing Act, discrimination also encompasses the building of new multifamily dwellings for first occupancy on or after April 1, 1991 that do not include certain accommodations for the disabled such as wheelchair-width doorways, accessible common areas, modified light switches, electrical outlets, thermostats, kitchen fixtures, and bathroom facilities.

The Americans with Disabilities Act (ADA) expanded the accommodations that must be made for people with disabilities as a means of prohibiting discrimination. One focus of the ADA is buildings that are designed to serve the public. All new construction as of 1/26/93 and all building renovations must be in compliance. Any employer with 15 or more employees must comply with the ADA by making provisions of accessibility in the workplace for individuals with disabilities.

REQUIREMENTS. The Federal Fair Housing Act requires all real estate brokers, salespeople, banking personnel, and all other people associated with housing to treat all persons equally with regard to housing choice, services provided, and all other facets of their real estate activities.

enforced by commission

The Federal Fair Housing Act further requires all real estate brokers and lenders to display fair housing posters in their offices. All brokers and lenders are also required to use the fair housing logo in their advertising. If a broker or lender is investigated for alleged discriminatory acts, failure to display the poster and use of the logo may be considered prima facie evidence of discrimination.

A copy of the fair housing poster provided by the Ohio Real Estate Commission for use in Ohio follows.

FEDERAL FAIR HOUSING ACT

Prohibits discrimination based on:

Race Color Religion Sex

Disability/Handicap National Origin Familial Status

Applies only to residential transactions.

Exemptions:

1. Certain single-family home sales and rentals

2. Rental of a unit in an owner-occupied residence

3. Nonprofit religious organizations

4. Private clubs

5. Housing for older persons (familial status only)

PROHIBITED ACTS. The following practices and activities violate the Federal Fair Housing Act if they are based on a person's race, color, religion, sex, national origin, disability/handicap, or familial status:

1. Refusing to rent or sell residential property after receiving a good faith offer
2. Refusing to negotiate for the sale or rental of residential property
3. Taking any action that would otherwise make residential property unavailable or deny it to any person (this general clause prohibits **steering** and **redlining** along with many other discriminatory practices and marketing methods)
4. Discriminating in the terms or conditions of any sale or rental of residential property or in providing any services or facilities in connection with such property

U.S. Department of Housing and Urban Development

We Do Business in Accordance With the Federal Fair Housing Law

(The Fair Housing Amendments Act of 1988)

It is Illegal to Discriminate Against Any Person Because of Race, Color, Religion, Sex, Handicap, Familial Status, or National Origin

- In the sale or rental of housing or residential lots
- In advertising the sale or rental of housing
- In the financing of housing
- In the provision of real estate brokerage services
- In the appraisal of housing
- Blockbusting is also illegal

Anyone who feels he or she has been discriminated against may file a complaint of housing discrimination:
1-800-669-9777 (Toll Free)
1-800-927-9275 (TDD)

U.S. Department of Housing and Urban Development
Assistant Secretary for Fair Housing and Equal Opportunity
Washington, D.C. 20410

Previous editions are obsolete

form HUD-928.1A(8-93)

5. Using discriminatory advertising or any other notice that indicates a limitation or preference or intent to make any limitation, preference, or discrimination
6. Making any representation that property is not available for inspection, sale, or rent when it is in fact available
7. Inducing or attempting to induce, for profit, any person to sell or rent property based on representations made regarding entry into the neighborhood of persons of a particular race, color, religion, sex, or national origin (**blockbusting**, also called **panic selling** or **panic peddling**)
8. Discriminating against anyone by a commercial lender in making a loan for buying, building, repairing, improving, or maintaining a dwelling or in the terms of such financing (includes **redlining**)
9. Denying access to a multiple listing service or any similar real estate brokers' organization or discriminating in terms or conditions for access to the organization
10. Coercing, intimidating, threatening, or interfering with anyone because of his or her enjoyment, attempt to enjoy, or encouragement and assistance to others in their enjoyment of the rights granted by the Federal Fair Housing Act.

As you can see, most discriminatory behavior in connection with residential transactions would violate federal law. Three terms mentioned above frequently come up in discussions of fair housing laws: **steering**, **blockbusting**, and **redlining**.

STEERING. **Steering** relates to buyers or renters. **Steering** is channeling prospective buyers or renters to specific neighborhoods based on their race (or religion, national origin, or other protected class) in order to maintain or change the character of a neighborhood. For instance, Caucasian customers might be shown homes only in Caucasian neighborhoods and African American customers shown homes only in African American neighborhoods. A real estate agent's good faith answer to a question from a prospective buyer about the racial or ethnic composition of a neighborhood probably wouldn't violate the law if the agent didn't intend to discriminate or encourage discrimination. Anything past a simple, factual answer could be considered steering, however. It's safest to avoid any discussion of race or ethnic background and direct clients to third parties for answers to these types of questions.

BLOCKBUSTING. **Blockbusting** relates to selling. **Blockbusting** is trying to induce owners to sell their homes by suggesting that the ethnic or racial composition of a neighborhood is changing with the implication that property values will decline. It is also called **panic selling** or **panic peddling**. The idea is to induce property owners to list their property for sale or sell at a reduced price, so the person making the predictions (usually a real estate agent) can profit. A wide variety of blockbusting "techniques" appear in the case law. Here are some examples of illegal activities:

- Passing out pamphlets stating that a member of a minority group has purchased a home nearby

- "Wrong number" phone calls where the callers indicate that they thought they were calling "the black family who just moved in"
- Purchasing a home in the area and selling it on contract to a minority buyer then suggesting to white owners that it's time to move

REDLINING. **Redlining** relates to lenders. **Redlining** is a refusal to make loans on property located in a particular neighborhood for discriminatory reasons. In the past, many lenders assumed that an integrated or predominantly black neighborhood was automatically a place where property values were declining. Based on that assumption, they refused to make loans there. Since it was almost impossible to get purchase or renovation loans, it was extremely difficult to market, maintain, or improve homes in those neighborhoods causing values to decline.

Lenders may still deny loans in neighborhoods where property values are declining, but this must be based on objective criteria regarding the condition and value of the property or area. A lender may not simply equate integrated or minority neighborhoods with declining property values.

ENFORCEMENT. A complaint under the Federal Fair Housing Act must be filed with the Office of Equal Opportunity (OEO) of HUD within one year after the incident occurred. HUD may file a complaint on its own initiative and can refer complaints to a similar state or local agency (e.g., Ohio Civil Rights Commission), or HUD can investigate on its own. If there's evidence of a violation, HUD's first step is negotiation to obtain voluntary compliance with the Federal Fair Housing Act. The second step is to have the dispute decided by one of HUD's administrative law judges, or either party may choose a civil lawsuit instead, which can be filed within two years after the discriminatory incident or the end of the HUD hearing. In addition, the U.S. Attorney General may bring a civil suit in federal district court against anyone engaged in an ongoing pattern or practice of discriminatory activities.

III. THE OHIO CIVIL RIGHTS LAW

The Ohio Civil Rights Law prohibits housing discrimination on the basis of **race, color, religion, sex, ancestry, national origin, disability, or familial status.** This applies to the sale or lease of any building used or intended to be used as a residence and any vacant land (*not just land for residential use*).

PROHIBITED ACTS. Ohio's statute covers most of the same ground as the Federal Fair Housing Law. The state law makes it illegal to discriminate by refusing to sell or rent, refusing to negotiate for sale or rental, or otherwise make housing unavailable. The law also makes it illegal to discriminate in the terms or conditions of a sale or lease or in furnishing facilities and services in connection with housing. The Ohio Civil Rights Law outlaws all of the following with regard to housing:

- Blockbusting
- Steering
- Discriminatory advertising
- Discriminatory restrictive covenants
- Interference with a person's enjoyment of his or her civil rights

- Discrimination by multiple listing services
- Discrimination by insurance companies (concerning homeowner's insurance and fire insurance)
- Redlining and other lending discrimination

The state law also generally prohibits asking questions (either in person or on an application form) about race, color, religion, sex, ancestry, disability/handicap, or national origin in connection with the sale or lease of housing. It **is** permissible to ask questions and keep records about race, religion, and so forth to monitor compliance with Ohio Civil Rights Law.

EXEMPTIONS. Like the Federal Fair Housing Act, the fair housing provisions of Ohio Civil Rights Law allow a religious organization to limit use of its noncommercial housing accommodations to its own members unless membership in the religious organization is restricted on the basis of race, color, or national origin. Similarly, a private or fraternal organization may limit use of its noncommercial lodgings to its members if operating the lodgings is only incidental to the organization's primary purpose. Remember, Ohio doesn't recognize the "Mrs. Murphy exemption" or allow the seller or lessor of a single-family home to discriminate.

Ohio Civil Rights Law

- Prohibits discrimination based on race, color, religion, sex, ancestry, national origin, disability, and familial status
- Applies only to transactions involving residential property or any vacant land
- Exemptions: accommodations operated by nonprofit religious, fraternal, or charitable organizations

ENFORCEMENT. The procedures for enforcing the fair housing provisions of the Ohio Civil Rights Law are very similar to those for enforcing the Federal Fair Housing Act. Complaints under the Ohio Civil Rights Law must be filed with the Ohio Civil Rights Commission within one year after the incident occurred. If there's evidence of a violation, the commission's first step is negotiation to obtain voluntarily compliance with Ohio Civil Rights Law. The second step is for the commission to hold a formal hearing. A victim of housing discrimination may also choose to file a civil lawsuit in common pleas court within one year after the discriminatory incident. If the commission finds a pattern or practice of housing discrimination, it may ask the Ohio Attorney General to file a lawsuit in the court of common pleas.

IV. FAIR HOUSING AND OHIO'S LICENSE LAW

When an Ohio real estate broker or salesperson has violated a local, state, or federal civil rights law pertaining to real estate transactions, the Ohio Real Estate Commission may suspend or revoke that person's real estate license. If it's the licensee's first offense, he or she must have been found guilty of a violation by a court. That isn't a requirement, however, in the case of later offenses. For a second offense, the commission must suspend the license for a minimum of two months or revoke it. If there are any subsequent offenses, the license must be revoked.

These rules about suspension or revocation of an agent's license apply only if the violation occurred in "a situation wherein parties were engaged in bona fide efforts to purchase, sell, or lease real estate." In other words, the rules don't apply if the case involves **checkers** from a fair housing organization instead of real buyers, sellers, or renters. **Checkers** are people from fair housing organizations who pretend to be interested in property as a test of discriminatory practices. (Also called **testers**.)

V. EXAMPLES OF DISCRIMINATION

The overall effect of federal and state legislation is to outlaw discrimination based on race or ancestry in all property transactions with no exceptions. Of course, this is not always the case, and sometimes discrimination is blatant.

Discrimination in Renting

In rejecting a prospective tenant, a landlord may make very little effort to conceal the fact that racism (or some other form of prejudice) is the reason for not accepting the person. Even if the landlord actually has legitimate financial reasons for rejecting people as tenants, when race, color, religion, sex, national origin, or disability/handicap is a factor in a refusal to sell or rent, it's a violation of fair housing laws.

Blatant discrimination has become less common over the past few decades. Today discrimination tends to be veiled. The landlord finds other ways to avoid minority applicants or pretends that all applicants are being treated equally. In one case, it was the property management company's policy to process only those rental applications that were accompanied by a deposit. The rental agents told white applicants about that policy, and accordingly, the white applicants all made a deposit. Black applicants weren't informed that a deposit was required, so they didn't make one, and their applications were never processed.

Discrimination in Selling

Discrimination in selling property may be relatively simple. For example, salespeople in a model home may go out the back door when a prospective buyer drives up. Or a developer might discourage minority buyers by making them pay higher closing costs. Sometimes, however, discrimination entails an elaborate scheme. In one case, when a black couple attempted to buy a home in an exclusive community, the residents voted to enforce a restrictive covenant giving the homeowner's association a 30-day assignable option to buy the property on the same terms that had been offered. Another buyer, (a white woman) who had viewed the home earlier, agreed to buy the association's option. The white buyer claimed she wasn't aware of the race of the other prospective buyers, but the court didn't believe her and awarded damages to the plaintiffs.

In another case, when a real estate agent went along with a client's discrimination, the agent and the client were forced to pay damages. This ruling and damages award came even after the plaintiffs ultimately bought the property in question before the court case was decided.

Discrimination in Advertising

Both federal law and Ohio law prohibit any advertising that indicates a limitation, preference, or intent to discriminate based on race or other protected class. Discriminatory advertising may be subtle. Seemingly innocent statements are sometimes intended or interpreted as discriminatory. In some areas, an advertisement describing a home as "near schools and churches" may be taken to mean that it's in a gentile neighborhood, and Jews (who attend temples or synagogues, not churches) are not welcome.

Under certain circumstances, even the newspapers a broker chooses for advertising may be held to have the effect of racial steering. In one case, discrimination was found in advertising because whenever the brokerage took a listing in one of the "changing areas" of the city (a neighborhood that was becoming more integrated or was becoming predominantly black), its standard practice was to advertise that home in the black newspaper and not in the newspapers of general circulation.

Discrimination in Municipal Actions

Exclusionary zoning laws are defined as any laws that have the effect of denying housing to minorities or other protected classes. The clause "make otherwise unavailable or deny" in anti-discrimination legislation has been interpreted to prohibit such exclusionary zoning.

Since it's currently unlikely that a municipality would enact an openly racist ordinance, these cases usually involve arguments based on the concept of **disparate impact**. A law with **disparate impact** may be neutral on its face, but it has a discriminatory effect since it has a greater impact on one group than it has on others.

Exclusionary zoning cases usually involve ordinances that prohibit or unreasonably restrict multifamily or low-income housing. In comparison to the white population, members of minority groups are much more likely to be low-income. As a result, it has been successfully argued in a number of cases that ordinances limiting low-cost housing have a disparate impact on minority groups, in effect excluding them from certain communities. In one case, the court found discrimination because the city of Arlington Heights near Chicago refused to rezone to permit the construction of multifamily dwellings within its boundaries. The population of the Chicago metro area was about 18 percent black, but Arlington Heights had only 27 black residents out of a population of about 65,000 (.04 percent). Since a greater percentage of the occupants of multifamily dwellings were black rather than white, the court ruled that the city's zoning ordinance had the effect of excluding black people from living there.

In another exclusionary zoning case, the U.S. Attorney General successfully sued Parma (a suburb of Cleveland) for violations of the Fair Housing Act because, according to the 1970 census, Parma's population was 100,216, but only 50 of its residents were black. Cleveland's population, by contrast, was 16 percent black at the time.

The court ruled that certain actions by city officials had the purpose and the effect of maintaining Parma as a segregated community. These actions included the refusal by city officials to enact a fair housing resolution welcoming "all persons of good will," refusal to participate in public low-income housing programs, denial of building permits for a privately sponsored low-income housing development, and the adoption of an ordinance requiring voter approval for subsidized housing projects. To correct the problem, the court issued a wide variety of injunctions and invalidated the community's ordinance requiring voter approval for subsidized housing projects.

VI. LIABILITY FOR DISCRIMINATION

For the purposes of the Fair Housing Act, the U.S. Supreme Court has held that it's not only actual buyers and renters who can sue for violation of the Act. In some cases, a fair housing organization also has standing to sue, as do the individual checkers from a fair housing organization, since it is said to be the whole community that is injured by housing discrimination.

In one case, the Supreme Court held that the actual rental applicant, a black checker, a white checker, and the fair housing organization were all entitled to sue because, in effect, they all had been injured by the defendants' discriminatory practices. The actual rental applicant's claim was based on straightforward allegations of denial of housing and racial steering. The black checker's claim was based on a provision of the Fair Housing Act making it unlawful for anyone to misrepresent that housing isn't available when in fact it is. The white checker's claim was based on a general right to enjoy the benefits of an integrated society. Finally, the fair housing organization had a right to sue on the theory that the defendants' practices interfered with the organization's housing counseling and referral services with a resulting drain on its financial resources.

So almost everyone affected by unlawful discrimination can sue under the Fair Housing Act. And almost everyone connected with the violation can be held liable either because of his or her own actions or because he or she is legally responsible for the actions of his or her agents: property managers, real estate brokers, real estate salespeople, and property owners. If a seller refuses to go through with a transaction because of the buyer's race, religion, ethnic background, etc., the broker may sue the seller for the commission.

VII. PROTECT YOURSELF AGAINST FAIR HOUSING VIOLATIONS

To protect yourself against fair housing violations, treat everyone equally and fairly. Let your clients direct what areas they want to see and don't want to see. Direct clients to third parties for answers to questions of quality, etc. Don't get trapped into rating one area over another. Keep good records of all meetings, phone calls, appointments, and missed appointments. If you find yourself being questioned or end up in court, at least you can demonstrate a conscious effort to be fair, open, and honest with *all* people.

FAIR HOUSING LAWS SUMMARIZED

	Civil Rights Act of 1866	Federal Fair Housing Act	Ohio Civil Rights Act
Race	X	X	X
Color	X	X	X
Religion		X	X
Sex		X	X
National Origin		X	X
Ancestry	X		X
Disability		X	X
Familial status		X	X
Age			
Marital status			
All property (Real+Personal)	X		
Only housing+land for housing		X	
Housing and any vacant land			X
Exceptions (FSBO= For Sale By Owner)	none	1. FSBO 2. FSBO, 4-Plex 3. Religious Groups 4. Private Clubs	1. No 2. No 3. Religious Groups 4. Private Clubs
Statute of Limitations	Same as State (1 Year in Ohio)	1 Yr—HUD Hearing 2 Yrs—Lawsuit	1 Yr—Hearing 1 Yr—Lawsuit

WHO CAN SUE FOR VIOLATION OF ANTI-DISCRIMINATION LAWS

Prospective Buyer/Tenant	Checker	Fair Housing Organization
State Attorney General	H.U.D.	U.S. Attorney General
	Ohio Civil Rights Commission	

WHO CAN BE HELD LIABLE FOR UNLAWFUL DISCRIMINATION

Seller/Landlord	Real Estate Broker	Lender
Property Manager	Real Estate Salesperson	Loan Officer
Resident Manager	Multiple Listing Service	Homeowners Association
	Rental Agent	

Chapter 11 Summary

1. Civil Rights Act of 1866 prohibits discrimination based on race or ancestry in any personal or real property transaction in U.S. Federal Fair Housing Act (Title VIII of Civil Rights Act of 1968) prohibits discrimination based on race, color, religion, sex, national origin, disability/handicap, or familial status in sale or lease of residential property. It also prohibits discrimination in advertising, lending, and brokerage in residential transactions. Steering, blockbusting, and redlining are outlawed by the Act. Steering is channeling buyers or tenants to particular areas based on their race, religion, or ethnicity. Blockbusting is inducing owners to sell their homes by suggesting that the ethnic or racial composition of an area is changing implying property values will decline. (Also called panic selling.) Redlining is refusing to make loans on property located in a particular neighborhood for discriminatory reasons. Federal Fair Housing Laws can be enforced by HUD or civil lawsuit.

2. Ohio Civil Rights Law prohibits discrimination based on race, color, religion, sex, ancestry, national origin, disability/handicap, or familial status. Ohio's fair housing provisions apply to sale or lease of housing and any vacant land. Also covers residential advertising, lending, and brokerage. Exemptions to Ohio fair housing laws allow religious groups, charitable organizations, and private clubs to limit use of their own accommodations to their own members. The law can be enforced by the Ohio Civil Rights Commission or civil lawsuit.

3. Seller or landlords who reject buyers or tenants violate anti-discrimination laws if a person's race (or religion, sex, etc.,) is a factor in a rejection even if there's also some legitimate reason. Exclusionary zoning violates fair housing laws if it has a disparate impact on minorities and other protected groups. Exclusionary zoning/ disparate impact cases involve laws prohibiting or restricting low-income housing, thus keeping minorities from an area.

4. Almost anyone involved in a real estate transaction can be held liable for fair housing violations. Supreme Court held that checkers and fair housing groups can sue for fair housing violations. Treat all equally; let clients direct you, and keep good documentation to protect yourself from fair housing violations.

Chapter 11 Quiz

1. ***The Civil Rights Act of 1866 prohibits:***
   a. Racial discrimination in all property transactions
   b. Ethnic discrimination in all property transactions
   c. Both a and b
   d. Neither a nor b

2. ***The Federal Fair Housing Act prohibits discrimination based on:***
   a. Race, color, religion, sex, age, national origin, disability, or familial status
   b. Race, color, religion, sex, ancestry, national origin, disability, familial status, or handicap
   c. Race, color, religion, sex, national origin, disability, or familial status
   d. Race, color, religion, sex, marital status, national origin, disability, or familial status

3. ***Which of the following exemptions to the Federal Fair Housing Act are recognized in Ohio?***
   a. Lodging offered by nonprofit religious, fraternal, or charitable organizations
   b. Sale or rental of a single-family home by a private individual
   c. Mrs. Murphy exemption
   d. Refusing to sell to someone whose family came from Italy

4. ***Which of the following statements appears on the Equal Opportunity Housing Poster?***
   a. Steering is also illegal
   b. Blockbusting is also illegal
   c. Redlining is also illegal
   d. Puffing is also illegal

5. ***Steering is:***
   a. Channeling prospective buyers or tenants to particular neighborhoods based on their race, religion, or ethnic background
   b. Trying to induce owners to sell their homes by saying that the ethnic or racial make up of an area is changing implying property values will drop
   c. Refusal to make loans on property located in a particular neighborhood for discriminatory reasons
   d. None of the above

6. ***Blockbusting is:***
   a. Channeling prospective buyers or tenants to particular neighborhoods based on their race, religion, or ethnic background
   b. Trying to induce owners to sell their homes by saying that the ethnic or racial make up of an area is changing implying property values will drop
   c. Refusal to make loans on property located in a particular neighborhood for discriminatory reasons
   d. None of the above

7. ***Redlining is:***
   a. Channeling prospective buyers or tenants to particular neighborhoods based on their race, religion, or ethnic background
   b. Trying to induce owners to sell their homes by saying the ethnic or racial make up of an area is changing implying property values will drop
   c. Refusal to make loans on property located in a particular neighborhood for discriminatory reasons
   d. None of the above

8. *Jim owns a store in Cambridge, which he put up for sale but refuses to sell to Abu because he's a Muslim. Jim has violated:*

a. The Civil Rights Act of 1866
b. The Federal Fair Housing Act
c. The Ohio Civil Rights Law
d. None of the above

9. *David owns a store in Cambridge, which he put up for sale but refuses to sell to Lisa because she's Buddhist, Chinese, and has bad credit. David has violated:*

a. The Civil Rights Act of 1866
b. The Federal Fair Housing Act
c. The Ohio Civil Rights Law
d. The equal credit opportunity act

10. *Some checkers attempt to buy a home and find evidence of discrimination. What will happen to the salesperson's license?*

a. It will be revoked
b. It will be suspended
c. It will be put in inactive status
d. Information is insufficient to determine what will happen

11. *Down Town's new zoning law contains no discriminatory language but has the effect of keeping minorities out of the city by restricting subsidized housing. So:*

a. The law is okay because it doesn't state any discriminatory intent
b. The law is okay because people in subsidized housing aren't a protected class
c. The law is not okay because it has a disparate impact on minorities
d. The law is not okay because it doesn't state its intent of exclusionary zoning

12. *All of the following can be held liable for housing discrimination,* except:

a. A landlord who will not rent to alcoholics
b. Real estate licensee
c. Multiple listing service
d. Sellers who will not sell to Catholics

12 OVERVIEW OF REAL ESTATE FINANCE

CHAPTER OVERVIEW

Now that you have an understanding of real estate law, we'll discuss the important topic of real estate finance. Salespeople must know the financing options available to clients. We'll begin by discussing various government influences on finance: secondary mortgage markets, government programs, and regulations. We'll also look at various types of lenders and different types of financing.

KEY TERMS

Alienation Clause
Gives lender the right to declare entire loan balance immediately due and payable, or exercise other rights when property ownership is transferred.

Amortized Loans
Loans with payments applied to principal and interest.

APR
Annual **P**ercentage **R**ate. Total cost of financing a loan in percentage terms as a relationship of the total finance charges to the total amount financed.

ARM
Adjustable **R**ate **M**ortgage. Permits a lender to periodically adjust the interest rate, so the rate reflects fluctuations in the cost of money.

Assumption
When one party takes over responsibility for the loan of another party.

Buydown
When additional funds in the form of points are paid to a lender at the beginning of a loan to lower interest rate and monthly payments on the loan.

Conforming Loans
Loans that meet Fannie Mae and Freddie Mac standards and can be sold on the secondary market. (**Nonconforming loans** don't meet the standards.)

Conventional Loan
Loan that is not insured or guaranteed by a government entity.

FHA
Federal **H**ousing **A**dministration. Government agency under the Department of Housing and Urban Development (HUD) that **insures** mortgage loans.

Loan Origination Fee
Points charged to a borrower to cover costs of issuing a loan.

Negative Amortization
When a loan balance grows because of deferred interest.

KEY TERMS cont.

Points
One percent of the loan amount. Points can be charged for any reason but are often used for buydowns (where they may also be called **discount points**).

Truth-in-Lending Act
Requires lenders to disclose consumer credit costs to promote informed use of consumer credit.

VA
Veteran's **A**dministration. Government agency that **guarantees** mortgage loans for eligible veterans.

upper 25% of the loan

I. REAL ESTATE FINANCE

The real estate market is influenced by a number of economic, governmental, and social factors. The real estate market and real estate finance are very interdependent: interest rates depend on supply and demand of money; loan activity depends on availability of money, and property values depend on the health of the economy.

We'll look at government influences on real estate finance through secondary mortgage markets. Then, we'll focus on a thorough examination of different types of financing. We'll compare conventional and alternative programs with government programs, look at seller financing, and finish the chapter by looking at federal regulations that influence real estate finance.

II. SECONDARY MORTGAGE MARKETS

key words → investors blocks

An important way that government influences real estate markets and finance is through the activities of the national secondary mortgage markets. **Secondary mortgage markets** are private investors and government agencies that buy and sell real estate mortgage loans. This is in contrast to **primary mortgage markets** that consist of lenders who make mortgage loans directly to borrowers such as neighborhood banks. The difference is secondary mortgage markets buy real estate loans as investment vehicles from all over the country; whereas, the primary mortgage market is typically local in nature.

FUNCTION OF SECONDARY MARKETS

To understand the function of secondary markets, let's review how the primary market works. The primary market is made up of the various lending institutions in local communities. If people want to buy a house, they typically go to a local bank or savings and loan to borrow the money they need. The source of funds for the primary market is largely made up of the savings deposits of individuals and businesses in the local area. The lending institution will use those savings to make real estate loans to members of the same community.

The function of secondary markets is to buy and sell the mortgages of primary market lenders. Loans are bought and sold for several reasons. The primary and secondary markets are both trying to maximize the returns on their investment dollars, and both are trying to make more funds available to be loaned again in local real estate markets. This has important stabilizing influences on real estate.

First, when the secondary market players buy mortgages from local banks, the banks then have more money that they can lend again to other potential homeowners in their area. *Second,* when local banks invest surplus funds in real estate investments from other regions of the country, the effects of local real estate cycles can be moderated by the banks having stable investments from other areas that may be going through different phases of a real estate cycle. *Third*, an important by-product of secondary mortgage markets is the standardization of loan criteria. Any changes implemented by secondary mortgage markets become requirements around the country for those who want to sell their mortgages in the secondary market. All of these functions serve to make local real estate markets more stable.

EXAMPLE

A: First Bank is located in a booming area. Businesses are coming to the area, and lots of people are moving there. Many of these people are looking to purchase a home and have come to First Bank to borrow money. The problem is that most of First Bank's deposits are already tied up in real estate loans. By selling its current home mortgage loans in the secondary market, First Bank can get more money to make new loans. First Bank and its customers are happy, and the effects of a potential credit crunch in the local real estate market are moderated because First Bank can get additional funds from the national secondary mortgage markets.

B: Later, First Bank finds itself in a different situation. The local community is still doing well, so First Bank has lots of people putting deposits in the bank, but there's little activity in the real estate market. With a surplus of deposits, First Bank may have trouble finding enough local investments to buy with a high enough return. In this case, First Bank could buy real estate mortgage loans on the secondary market. Since First Bank would then hold real estate investments from all over the country, First Bank would not need to worry as much about a downturn in its local real estate market because it's holding loans from other areas as well.

C: First Bank is considering some new home mortgage requests. The loans seem to be risky for reasons having to do with the borrowers and the property. First Bank is not so quick to approve these loans because, if they don't meet the criteria of the secondary markets, First Bank must hold the loans itself and can't sell them to the secondary market. This helps stabilize the local real estate market because it discourages banks from making too many risky loans. Furthermore, the standardized criteria helps First Bank feel fairly secure in the mortgage investments that it buys on the secondary market from other areas of the country, even though it may never see the actual borrowers and properties it's helping to finance.

HOW SECONDARY MARKETS WORK. The secondary market is able to function as it does because of the standardized underwriting criteria that are used to qualify borrowers and property. A mortgage will be purchased by the secondary market only if the lender conformed to the secondary markets' underwriting standards. Let's take a look at the make up of the secondary markets.

Although we define secondary markets as private investors and government agencies that buy and sell real estate mortgages, private investors are actually a very small percentage of the secondary mortgage markets. Thus, our discussion will focus on the three agencies responsible for most of the secondary mortgage market activity. They are:

- The Federal National Mortgage Association ("Fannie Mae")
- The Government National Mortgage Association ("Ginnie Mae")
- The Federal Home Loan Mortgage Corporation ("Freddie Mac")

FEDERAL NATIONAL MORTGAGE ASSOCIATION (FANNIE MAE)

Fannie Mae is the nation's **largest** investor in residential mortgages. Fannie Mae was created in 1938 as the first government-sponsored secondary market institution. It was originally formed as a government-owned corporation, but Fannie Mae has undergone several reorganizations and is now **privately owned** and managed (although it's still supervised by the Department of Housing and Urban Development). Fannie Mae is able to purchase conventional mortgages as well as FHA and VA mortgages.

Fannie Mae funds its operation by selling securities backed by its pool of mortgages. Conventional mortgage-backed securities may be guaranteed by Fannie Mae as to full and timely payments of both principal and interest. Fannie Mae buys mortgages or interests in a pool of mortgages from lenders. Lenders who wish to sell loans to Fannie Mae must own some stock in Fannie Mae. Hence, both the lender and Fannie Mae have an interest in the loans. Loans sold to Fannie Mae may be serviced by Fannie Mae or by the originating lender with Fannie Mae paying a service fee.

GOVERNMENT NATIONAL MORTGAGE ASSOCIATION (GINNIE MAE)

Ginnie Mae was created in 1968 as a government-owned corporation to replace Fannie Mae when it became privately owned. Ginnie Mae operates under the Department of Housing and Urban Development. A primary function of Ginnie Mae is to promote investment by guaranteeing the payment of principal and interest on FHA and VA mortgages through its mortgage-backed securities program. This program, supported by the federal government's borrowing power, guarantees timely interest and principal mortgage payments to the mortgage holders.

Mortgage-backed securities fall into two general types: **bond-type securities** and **pass-through securities. Bond-type securities** are long-term, pay interest semi-annually and provide for repayment at a specified date. **Pass-through securities**, which are more common, pay interest and principal payments on a monthly basis. Some types pay even if payments aren't collected from the mortgagor.

Ginnie Mae has special assistance financing (below-market rates to low-income families) for urban renewal or housing projects, but activity here has decreased.

FEDERAL HOME LOAN MORTGAGE CORPORATION (FREDDIE MAC)

Freddie Mac was created in 1970 as a nonprofit, federally chartered institution controlled by the Federal Home Loan Bank System and is now also privately owned (but still under government supervision). Freddie Mac does **not** guarantee payment of its mortgages. The primary function of Freddie Mac was to help savings and loans acquire additional funds for lending in the mortgage market by purchasing the mortgages they already held. Freddie Mac may deal in FHA, VA, and conventional mortgages, while Fannie Mae emphasizes the purchase of mortgage loans. Freddie Mac also actively sells the mortgage loans from its portfolio.

Freddie Mac issues its own mortgage-backed securities and purchases mortgages through its **immediate delivery program** or its **forward commitment purchase program.** In the **immediate delivery program**, sellers have up to 60 days to deliver mortgages that Freddie Mac agreed to buy. Failure to deliver may ban a seller from Freddie Mac sales for two years. In the **forward commitment purchase program**, commitments are made for six or eight months, with delivery of mortgages at the option of the seller. There's a non-refundable fee payable to Freddie Mac.

QUALITY CONTROL

The secondary market agencies have been actively involved in developing underwriting standards for mortgage loans. These standards assure uniform quality control, inspiring confidence in the buyers of the mortgage-backed securities. The buyers know that the mortgages backing the securities must be of a minimum quality, which lowers their risk in investing in properties they can't assess for themselves. Without the assurance of these underwriting standards, someone in Utah would be unlikely to invest in property in Ohio he or she has never seen.

Furthermore, since lenders want to sell their loans to the secondary agencies, they must follow the underwriting guidelines of those agencies. In their efforts to increase the quality of loans they purchase, the agencies force the lenders to upgrade the quality of loans they make. Not only can the agencies refuse to purchase loans that don't follow their guidelines, but they can also request lenders to repurchase loans already sold if it's later discovered the lender violated underwriting guidelines. So, the secondary market encourages lenders to implement their own quality control programs and review buyer and property qualifications more carefully.

Finally, because the secondary market performs such an important function in providing liquidity of mortgage funds, the standards set by the secondary market have a large influence on lending activities in the primary market. For example, once secondary agencies began accepting adjustable rate mortgages (ARMs), 15-year fixed-rate mortgages, and convertible ARMs, these types of financing became more readily available in the primary market. Lenders were more willing to make these kinds of loans when they knew the loans could be sold to the secondary market.

III. TYPES OF REAL ESTATE LENDERS

Our discussion of real estate lenders will focus on the major sources of financing in Ohio's primary market. The primary or local market consists of lenders (and individuals) who make loans directly to borrowers. We'll discuss **commercial banks**, **savings and loans**, **mortgage companies**, and a few others.

COMMERCIAL BANKS

Commercial banks are financial institutions that provide a variety of financial services including loans. Although banks remain the largest source of investment funds in the country today, their activities had been focused on relatively short-term loans. Until recently, residential mortgages were not a major part of their business, primarily because of government limitations on the amount of long-term investments they can make. Now commercial banks have increased their participation in home mortgage lending to take advantage of existing customer relationships built through checking accounts and other traditional services.

Changes in state and federal regulations have spurred additional mortgage activity by banks. The regulations require banks to hold back on reserve different percentages of funds for different types of loans based on the loans' perceived risks. First lien home mortgages are in the lowest risk category. Thus, banks need to maintain fewer funds on reserve to cover losses for home mortgage loans than for other types of loans, leaving more funds available for additional loans or investments.

SAVINGS AND LOAN ASSOCIATIONS

Savings and loan associations (S and Ls) are institutions that specialize in taking savings deposits and making mortgage loans. Traditionally, the major real estate lending institutions were the S and Ls investing roughly 75 percent of their assets in single-family mortgages. They were able to dominate local mortgage markets even though commercial banks had more assets to invest because deposits placed with S and Ls were savings deposits that were less subject to immediate withdrawal than demand (checking) deposits held by banks.

As interest rates rose sharply, S and Ls were left with long-term loans at low rates. In an effort to average these low-rate loans and get higher returns to attract more depositors who were demanding higher rates, S and Ls began to make riskier investments. Deregulation made matters worse as S and Ls now had to compete against additional investment vehicles to attract investment dollars.

Management mistakes, economic slumps, and even fraud led many institutions toward insolvency. Many S and Ls tried new, riskier investments regulators didn't always have the ability to evaluate. When insolvency loomed, some S and L officers decided to gamble even more. Since their deposits were insured by the federal government, the officers felt there was little to lose. The result of these risky investments was a dramatic increase in the failure rate of S and Ls, which cost the federal government and taxpayers billions of dollars and has caused a massive restructuring of the industry.

Despite this S and L crisis, they still remain a leading home mortgage lender. With the decreasing number of S and Ls and the increasing number of mortgage banking companies, it's likely that the mortgage banking industry will soon replace the S and L industry as the leading provider of residential mortgage loans.

MORTGAGE COMPANIES

Mortgage companies are institutions that function as the originators and servicers of loans on behalf of large investors such as insurance companies, pension plans, or the Federal National Mortgage Association. Since these large investors often operate on a national scale, they have neither the time nor the resources to understand the particular risks of local markets or to deal with the day-to-day management of their loans. Mortgage companies fill the gap functioning more as intermediaries than as sources of lending capital. The loans mortgage companies choose are resold to secondary market investors with the mortgage company acting as an agent to service the loans for a fee. Because they invest little of their own money, their activities are largely controlled by the availability of investment capital in the secondary market. Of course, their loan qualification criteria must reflect the standards of the national market to facilitate resale of the loans.

OTHER REAL ESTATE LENDERS

Other types of real estate lenders that make loans for residential mortgages include **mutual savings banks**, **real estate investment trusts**, **life insurance companies**, **pension plans,** and **private individuals**. **Credit unions** are also a source of home equity and home improvement loans.

IV. TYPES OF FINANCING

For the sake of simplicity and organization, we've divided the various types of financing programs used in Ohio into four general categories:

1. Conventional financing
2. Alternative financing tools (creative financing)
3. Government financing
4. Seller financing

V. CONVENTIONAL FINANCING

Conventional financing means that real estate is paid for or financed with a **conventional loan,** which is any loan not insured or guaranteed by a government agency. We'll look at traditional conventional loans and at variations in conventional financing today.

TRADITIONAL CONVENTIONAL LOANS

Traditional conventional loans are typically **long term**, **fully amortized**, **fixed rate** real estate loans. This is the type of loan most borrowers recognize.

LONG TERM. Long-term loans in real estate generally have total payments spread out over 25-30 years. Loans for 15 years or less with **balloon payments** are becoming common again but aren't considered traditional conventional loans. (**A balloon payment** is a single payment at the end of a loan to pay off the remaining balance.)

FULLY AMORTIZED. **Amortized loans** apply payments to the principal **and** interest (as opposed to interest-only loans). A loan that's *fully* amortized means the total payments over the life of the loan will pay off the entire balance of principal and interest due at the end of the term. Even though the payment stays the same for the life of the loan, the amount applied to principal and amount applied to interest are adjusted each month. If all payments are made on time, the loan will be paid off with the last scheduled payment.

FIXED RATE. Fixed rate loans have an interest rate that remains constant for the duration of the loan. This is both good and bad for the borrower and the lender. The biggest advantage is that a borrower doesn't need to worry about rates going up, and if rates go down enough, the borrower can refinance. Adjustable rate mortgages (explained later in this chapter) are becoming more popular because borrowers can usually start with a lower rate and fears of large rate increases have eased in recent years. These aren't considered traditional conventional loans.

80 PERCENT CONVENTIONAL LOAN

For years, the 80 percent conventional loan has been the standard conventional loan. An 80 percent conventional loan means that the **loan-to-value ratio (LTV)** is 80 percent of the appraised value or sale price of a property based on whichever is *less*. **LTV** is the amount of money borrowed compared to the value (or price) of the property. With this type of loan, the buyer makes a 20 percent down payment and obtains a 30-year, fixed-rate conventional loan for the balance of the purchase price.

For example, if you wanted to buy a house that cost $100,000, you would need to pay a 20 percent down payment or $20,000. An 80 percent conventional loan means that you can borrow 80 percent, or $80,000 of the sales price of the home, assuming that the property was actually appraised at $100,000 or higher. If the house were appraised for less than $100,000—say $95,000—you could only borrow 80 percent of that appraised value. If you still wanted to buy the home, you would need to pay the extra money as part of the down payment.

90 PERCENT CONVENTIONAL LOAN

If a buyer does not have enough money for a 20 percent down payment but still wants a conventional loan, he or she can try to get a 90 percent conventional loan with a 10 percent down payment. The 90 percent conventional loan became possible with the advent of private mortgage insurance. The qualifying standards for 90 percent conventional loans tend to be more stringent, and lenders adhere to those standards more strictly even though the loan is insured.

DOWN PAYMENT. For a 90 percent loan, the buyer must make a **10 percent down payment** with at least half of the down payment **(5 percent) from his or her own**

cash reserves. The rest of the down payment may be a gift from a family member, equity in other property traded to the seller, or credit for rent already paid under a lease/purchase.

HIGHER LOAN FEES AND INTEREST RATE. A 90 percent loan usually calls for higher loan origination fees (or service fees), which are charged as a percentage of the loan amount. A 90 percent loan also usually has a higher interest rate than an 80 percent loan. There are exceptions, but think of 90 percent financing as a more expensive loan.

95 PERCENT CONVENTIONAL LOAN

If a buyer does not have enough money for a 10 percent down payment but still wants a conventional loan, he or she can try to qualify for a 95 percent conventional loan with a 5 percent down payment. This higher loan-to-value ratio of 95 percent requires owner-occupancy.

DOWN PAYMENT. For a 95 percent loan, a buyer must make the **5 percent down payment from his or her own cash reserves**, without using secondary (owner) financing or gifts.

EVEN HIGHER LOAN FEES AND INTEREST RATE. A 95 percent loan usually has higher loan origination fees (or service fees) and a higher interest rate than an 80 percent or 90 percent loan. The typical lender's view is "the smaller the down payment, the greater the risk of default," so it's easy to understand why a 95 percent loan is usually more costly.

PRIVATE MORTGAGE INSURANCE (PMI)

Private mortgage insurance (PMI) is offered by private companies to insure a lender against default on a loan by a borrower with less than a 20 percent down payment. PMI is what made 90 percent and 95 percent loans possible. Up to that time, lenders would only lend 80 percent of the value of a property because it was thought that a 20 percent down payment was the incentive needed for the borrower to keep mortgage payments current, and the lender felt comfortable that in the event of default, a foreclosure sale would yield 80 percent of the original sale price (or appraised value) to cover the loan.

PMI evolved to compensate the lender for the reduced borrower equity making loans easier for borrowers and safer for lenders. Both Fannie Mae and Freddie Mac also require third-party insurance on home loans with less than 20 percent down payments.

HOW MORTGAGE INSURANCE WORKS. When insuring a loan, the mortgage insurance company shares part of the lender's risk. The insurer does *not* insure the entire loan amount but the upper portion of the loan—the loan amount that exceeds the standard 80 percent LTV. The amount of coverage can vary but is typically 20 percent to 25 percent of the loan amount.

Example: 20% coverage on a 90% loan

$100,000	total sale price
x .90	LTV
$ 90,000	90% loan
x .20	amount of coverage
$ 18,000	amount of policy

TOTAL SALE PRICE

10%	**Down payment**
18%	**Coverage** (20% of loan amount)
72%	**Exposure** (80% of loan amount)

In the event of default and foreclosure, the insurer will take over the property or allow the lender to sell the property. Either way, the lender can make a claim for reimbursement of actual losses (if any) up to the face amount of the policy. Losses incurred by the lender take the form of unpaid interest, property taxes, hazard insurance, attorney's fees, and costs of preserving the property during the period of foreclosure and resale as well as the expense of selling the property itself.

PMI PREMIUMS. The private mortgage insurance company charges a **one-time fee at closing** when the loan is made and a recurring fee, called a **renewal premium**, that's added to the borrower's mortgage payment. These charges are also referred to as simply **PMI** (private mortgage insurance) or MIP (mortgage insurance premium).

Some private mortgage insurance companies offer a one-time mortgage insurance premium with no renewal fee. Combining the initial premium and renewal premiums into one single payment allows the buyer to finance the PMI premium.

PMI CANCELLATION. Since lenders require mortgage insurance on high LTV, low down payment loans as protection against borrower default, once the increased risk of borrower default is eliminated, the mortgage insurance has fulfilled its purpose. In the past, many lenders did not cancel PMI when the risk was reduced. But now federal law says that for all loans made after July 1999, lenders must cancel PMI when a home has been paid down to 78 percent of its original value. Freddie Mac requires lenders to drop PMI coverage when a borrower-paid appraisal shows that a loan has been paid down to 80 percent of the property's current value.

SECONDARY FINANCING

Secondary financing means a buyer borrows money from any source to pay part of the down payment or closing costs. This is another way that a buyer can get a conventional loan without having a 20 percent down payment (but **not** for 95 percent loans).

With secondary financing, it's often the seller who "carries" the extra financing. The primary lender insists on certain conditions with secondary financing from any source. Among these are that 5 percent of the down payment must come from the borrower's own funds; the buyer must be able to afford the payments on both the first mortgage and second mortgage, and the secondary financing must have regularly scheduled payments that equal interest on the loan.

ASSUMPTION OF CONVENTIONAL LOANS

Assumption means one party (buyer) takes over primary liability for the loan of another party (seller) usually implying no change in loan terms. (The seller remains secondarily liable unless he or she gets a release from the lender.)

Often loan assumption is *not* possible with loans written today. Lenders try to protect their interests by approving a new buyer and often want to change interest rates, charge fees, or change loan terms for a new party. Options are:

1. The lender will accept the assumption and leave the loan terms intact.
2. The lender will accept the assumption but will charge an assumption fee and/or increase the loan's interest rate.
3. The lender will **not** allow the assumption and **call the note**, i.e., demand full payment of the loan now. (This right must be stated in the note or mortgage.)

Always consult the lender, an attorney, or other individual who's qualified to advise. Do not give buyers and sellers advice on the assumption of a loan unless it's a certainty! Do not take chances when writing offers that call for assumptions of existing mortgages! It's too late after a sale to find out what a lender can or will do.

PREPAYMENT PENALTIES. Conventional lenders used to penalize early loan repayment to discourage it, but most lenders today would rather reinvest the money. Standard Fannie Mae and Freddie Mac notes and mortgages don't have prepayment penalties.

CONFORMING VERSUS NONCONFORMING LOANS

Conforming loans are loans that follow the criteria set by secondary markets, primarily Fannie Mae and Freddie Mac. Loans conforming to these criteria may be sold to the secondary market. The conventional loan programs discussed in this chapter represent conforming loans. Lenders try to make as many of their loans as possible conforming loans because lenders like the option of being able to liquidate real estate loans on the secondary market if they need more funds.

Nonconforming loans are loans that don't follow Fannie Mae/Freddie Mac criteria and can't be sold to Fannie Mae or Freddie Mac. (There are other secondary markets where nonconforming loans can be sold.) Lenders who have the option of keeping loans in their own portfolio (mostly banks and S and Ls) can, within the limits of the law, deviate from the standards set by secondary markets. For example, "jumbo" loans exceed the maximum loan amount Fannie Mae or Freddie Mac will buy (currently $275,000 for a single-family home), so they're nonconforming loans that can't be sold to them.

The distinctions between conforming and nonconforming loans are becoming blurred. Fannie Mae and Freddie Mac are constantly implementing new loan program standards to meet consumers' needs. The conforming market eagerly follows into areas once only nonconforming. For example, we'll discuss only the traditional conventional loan programs accepted by Fannie Mae/Freddie Mac, but now Fannie Mae offers 97 percent LTV loans and even 103 percent LTV loans for those with "golden credit."

VI. ALTERNATIVE FINANCING TOOLS

Alternative financing tools are terms or financing concessions other than those that are typical for conventional loans. When interest rates are high or buyers can't qualify for conventional financing, alternative financing tools can be used to lower the buyer's monthly payment. The most popular ways to do this are **buydowns** and **adjustable rate mortgages (ARMs)**. We'll also look at some alternative mortgages: bi-weekly mortgages, growth equity mortgages, reduction option mortgages, and reverse mortgages.

DISCOUNT POINTS

Before discussing alternative financing tools, you need to understand discount points (often referred to as just "points"). **Discount points** are an amount paid to a lender when a loan is made to make up the difference between the current market interest rate and the rate a lender gives a borrower on a note. Points increase a lender's return on loans with lower-than-market interest rates. So by paying a lender a one-time fee, a borrower can get a discount on a loan's interest rate.

A **point** is simply one percent of the *loan* amount. So on a $100,000 loan, the borrower would have to pay an additional $1,000 for every point the lender charged. Points can be charged for many reasons. For example, a lender may charge 2 points as a **loan origination fee**, 3 points as a closing fee, and 6 more points as discount points for the borrower to get a lower interest rate. The lender is being paid an additional 11 percent (2+3+6) of the loan amount for various fees and services. Only 6 points in our example are actually *discount* points which lower the interest rate, but they're all called "points."

EFFECT OF DISCOUNT POINTS. Discount points have the effect of adding to the **lender's yield**. The **lender's yield** is essentially the total amount of money the lender can make from a loan. When figuring the lender's yield, the source of the money doesn't matter. The lender is interested in the total amount of money—the total yield—it will make from the loan.

If the lender can get more cash from a borrower at the beginning of the loan via discount points, the lender can give the borrower a lower interest rate and lower monthly payments because the lender's total yield will be the same. Remember, when the lender is figuring its yield, early money from points counts just like money received over time from monthly payments. The lender has the points figured, so the yield is the same regardless of which option the borrower picks.

PURPOSE OF DISCOUNT POINTS. Discount points have traditionally been associated with FHA and VA loans. In addition, paying points for conventional loans has become a common way to increase a lender's yield from the interest rate the borrower is willing or able to pay to the rate the lender requires as a yield on its loans.

While who pays points is open to negotiation, in most cases the seller pays points to reduce the interest rate to be paid by the buyer making the property more marketable. It's far easier to sell a property if the interest rate is affordable. When points are paid to reduce the buyer's interest rate, it's called a **buydown**.

BUYDOWN PLANS

A **buydown** means additional funds in the form of points are paid to a lender at the beginning of a loan to lower the interest rate and monthly payments for that loan. The buydown is an easy way to make loans less expensive. By lowering the buyer's monthly mortgage payments, the buyer is able to qualify for the loan easily because the lender evaluates the buyer on the basis of the reduced payment.

The seller, builder, or any other person—even the buyer—can make a lump sum payment to the lender when a loan is made to reduce the borrower's payments early in a loan (**temporary buydown**) or for the life of a loan (**permanent buydown**).

TEMPORARY BUYDOWN. A **temporary buydown** means points are paid to the lender to reduce the interest rate and payments early in a loan. When interest rates are high, temporary buydowns are a popular way to reduce buyers' payments. Many buyers feel they'll grow into larger payments but need time to get established.

PERMANENT BUYDOWN. A **permanent buydown** means points are paid to a lender to reduce the interest rate and loan payments for the entire life of the loan. With a permanent buydown, the promissory note will state the reduced interest rate.

CALCULATING BUYDOWNS. The best way to be completely accurate when determining temporary and permanent buydowns is to get a quote from the lender. (You can also get a discount/yield table from a lender and learn to use it.)

For permanent buydowns, a rough estimate is that 8 points equals 1 percent of interest reduction. Sample calculations appear in the Math Appendix in the back of this book.

Temporary buydowns are a little more involved to calculate. Since the lower interest rate is only for a short period of time, figure the payment with and without the subsidy. Get a quote from the lender to be accurate.

ADJUSTABLE RATE MORTGAGES (ARMS)

An **adjustable rate mortgage (ARM)** is a mortgage that permits the lender to periodically adjust the interest rate, so the rate accurately reflects fluctuations in the cost of money. ARMs are made primarily by banks and mortgage companies.

The big advantage to ARMs is that mortgage loans start out with lower interest rates and lower payments. Lenders normally charge a lower rate for ARMs than for fixed-rate loans because with ARMs, the risk of interest rate fluctuations is shifted to the borrower who's affected by interest rate movements. If rates climb, the borrower's payments go up; if rates decline, payments go down. Although the majority of borrowers prefer the security of a fixed rate (provided the rate is not too high), ARMs are perhaps the most popular and widely accepted form of alternative financing. Generally, as interest rates rise, so does ARM popularity.

HOW ARMS WORK. The borrower's interest rate is determined initially by the cost of money at the time the loan is made. Once the rate has been set, it's tied to one of several widely recognized and published indexes; thus, future interest rate adjustments are based on the upward and downward movements of the index. If the selected index rises, the lender has the option of increasing the borrower's interest rate or leaving it the same, but if the index falls, a reduction in the rate is mandatory.

ELEMENTS OF ARM LOANS. There are many elements to ARM loans, including:

1. Index
2. Margin
3. Rate adjustment period
4. Mortgage payment adjustment period
5. Interest rate cap (if any)
6. Mortgage payment cap (if any)
7. Negative amortization cap (if any)
8. Conversion option (if any)

INDEX. An **index** is a statistical report that is generally a reliable indicator of the approximate change in the cost of money. Any widely recognized and published index can be chosen by the lender when the loan is made, but Fannie Mae began purchasing ARMs using the cost-of-funds index (i.e., average interest rates savings and loans pay for deposits and other borrowings) making this index more widely used for ARMs.

MARGIN. The **margin** is the difference between the index value and the interest rate charged to the borrower. In essence, this is the lender's gross profit that must also be used to cover the lender's expenses. As the index fluctuates, the margin remains constant. The index plus the margin equals the adjustable interest rate.

RATE ADJUSTMENT PERIOD. This refers to the intervals at which a borrower's interest rate is adjusted as stated in the mortgage or note. Any period can be selected, but annual rate adjustments are most common.

MORTGAGE PAYMENT ADJUSTMENT PERIOD. This refers to the intervals at which a borrower's actual principal and interest payments are changed. It's possible these changes don't coincide with rate adjustments. For example, the loan agreement may call for rate adjustments every six months, but mortgage payment changes only every three years. When principal and interest payment remains constant but the loan's interest rate has steadily risen during that time, too little interest will be paid in the interim. If this happens, the difference is added to the loan balance. When a loan balance grows because of deferred interest, it's called **negative amortization.**

INTEREST RATE CAP. An **interest rate cap** is a limit placed on the number of percentage points an interest rate can be increased during the term of a loan. This is one mechanism that lenders use to limit the magnitude of payment changes that occur with ARMs. Today, most ARMs have caps of some kind.

MORTGAGE PAYMENT CAP. A **mortgage payment cap** is a limit placed on the amount a mortgage payment can increase. This can be a yearly amount or an amount over the life of the loan. This is another mechanism that lenders use to limit the magnitude of payment changes that occur with ARMs because unrestricted increases could create hardships for many borrowers. Some lenders use both rate and payment caps to keep payment adjustments within a manageable range for the borrower.

NEGATIVE AMORTIZATION CAP. **Negative amortization** means a loan balance grows because of deferred interest when payments are not covering the interest portion of the loan. A cap on this is a limit like that for rates and payments. Negative amortization is most likely to occur where there are frequent rate changes (e.g., every six months) and infrequent payment adjustments (e.g., every three years).

CONVERSION OPTION. A conversion option in an ARM gives the borrower the right to convert from an adjustable-rate loan to a fixed-rate loan. ARMs with a conversion option usually limit the time period to choose the conversion option, charge a fee for conversion, and often have a higher interest rate than a straight ARM.

FANNIE MAE/FREDDIE MAC GUIDELINES FOR ARMS. Fannie Mae and Freddie Mac have established stricter LTV guidelines for ARMs than for fixed-rate loans. Fannie Mae and Freddie Mac LTV ratios may not exceed 90 percent and require owner occupancy for all ARMs.

ARM STANDARDIZATION. Initially, there were more than 200 different ARM loan programs. Now that the secondary mortgage markets are purchasing ARMs on a widespread basis, lenders are following uniform underwriting standards and secondary market guidelines, so they can resell ARMs just as they do fixed-rate loans.

ARM DISCLOSURES. Lenders offering residential financing, including ARMs, must comply with federal guidelines under **Regulation Z** of the **Truth-in-Lending Act** requiring certain disclosures be made to borrowers. The rules require a **general brochure** be given to borrowers, **certain specific disclosures** be made if relevant to the specific ARM program, and disclosure of the **annual percentage rate (APR).**

General Brochure. A lender may comply with this requirement by giving the loan applicant a booklet called *Consumer Handbook on Adjustable Rate Mortgages* prepared by the Federal Reserve and the Federal Home Loan Bank Board.

DISCLOSURES. Disclosures must be provided to the borrower when the loan application is made or before payment of any nonrefundable fee, whichever occurs first. The following disclosures must be made, if appropriate, to the loan applied for:

1. The index used to determine the interest rate
2. Finding the index
3. An explanation of how the interest rate and payment will be determined
4. A suggestion that the borrower ask the lender about the current margin and interest rate
5. If the initial rate is discounted, a disclosure of that fact and a suggestion that the borrower inquire as to the amount of the discount
6. The rate and payment adjustment periods and any rate and payment caps
7. Statement that rate or payment caps may result in negative amortization
8. Statement that the loan has a demand or "call" provision
9. Description of the information that will be contained in the adjustment notice and when such notices will be provided
10. Statement that disclosure forms are available for lender's other ARM loans
11. The maximum interest rate and payment
12. The initial interest rate and payment
13. Conversion option details

The lender must give the borrower advance notice of any change in payment, interest rate, index, or loan balance. Such disclosures must be given at least 25 days, but not more than 120, before a new payment level takes effect. The lender must also give the borrower an example, based on a $10,000 loan, showing how the payments and loan balance would be affected by changes in the index to be used.

ANNUAL PERCENTAGE RATE (APR). Regulation Z disclosures regarding the annual percentage rate (APR) cannot be made based solely on an ARM's initial rate. The disclosure of the APR must be based on the initial rate plus the lender's margin and should reflect a composite annual percentage rate based on the lower rate for a certain number of years and the higher rate for the remaining years on the loan term. The calculation is not important; a lender must disclose more than the initial low rate. The APR as a composite rate is designed to let consumers comparison shop for rates among lenders since all lenders must calculate APR the same way.

ADDITIONAL REGULATION Z RULES. Regulation Z rules as they relate to other aspects of real estate financing and advertising will be covered later in this chapter, and Regulation Z will be covered in depth in your *Ohio Real Estate Finance* textbook.

WHAT AGENTS NEED TO KNOW ABOUT ARMS. Real estate salespeople are expected to be knowledgeable. Expect clients to ask some of these questions about ARM financing:

1. *What will my interest rate be?*

2. *How often will my interest rate change?*
3. *How often will my payment change?*
4. *Is there any limit to how much my interest rate can be increased?*
5. *Is there any limit to how much my payment can be increased at any one time?*
6. *What is the probability of runaway negative amortization?*
7. *Can my ARM be converted to a fixed-rate loan?*

Your textbook discusses these questions in detail. Most of these questions can be answered by asking the lender.

BI-WEEKLY MORTGAGES

A **bi-weekly mortgage** is a fixed-rate mortgage set up similarly to a standard 30-year conventional loan. The main difference is that payments are made every two weeks instead of every month. This alternative financing saves interest because 26 payments are made each year—equal to one extra monthly payment. Bi-weekly loans are usually paid off in about 20 to 21 years instead of 30 years. They do require more servicing for lenders, and they can be an extra burden for borrowers. Many regular monthly loans allow borrowers to make extra payments, but it requires discipline on the part of the borrower to maintain a schedule of voluntary extra payments.

GROWTH EQUITY MORTGAGES (GEMS)

A **growth equity mortgage (GEM)** is a fixed-rate mortgage set up similarly to a 30-year conventional loan, but the payments increase regularly like an ARM. This alternative financing pays off the loan faster and saves interest because the fixed interest rate allows 100 percent of the annual payment increases to reduce the principal balance. GEMs have many variations, but they all work in a similar manner. GEMs are also called building equity mortgages (BEMs) or rapidly amortizing mortgages (RAMs).

REDUCTION OPTION MORTGAGES

A **reduction option mortgage** is a fixed-rate loan that gives the borrower a limited opportunity to reduce the interest rate of the loan without paying refinancing costs. The **Freddie Mac**-approved program is a 30-year, fixed-rate loan with the option to reduce the interest rate once between the 13th and 59th month of the loan. Market interest rates must decline at least 2 percent before the borrower may opt to reduce the rate. The fee to reduce the rate is much lower than points usually charged to refinance, and other costs, such as appraisals and credit checks, are also avoided.

REVERSE MORTGAGES (OR HOME EQUITY CONVERSION MORTGAGES)

A **reverse mortgage** means a homeowner mortgages his or her home to a bank or savings and loan association and in return receives a monthly check from the lender. Reverse equity mortgages are designed to help elderly homeowners achieve financial security by converting their home equity into cash. A reverse mortgage borrower must be over age 62 and own a home with little or no outstanding mortgage.

VII. GOVERNMENT FINANCING

Government financing refers to loans that are insured, guaranteed, or in some way sponsored by government dollars. (Do not confuse this with secondary markets!) The two basic government finance programs are loans insured by **FHA** (Federal Housing Administration), and loans guaranteed by **VA** (Veterans Administration).

FHA-INSURED LOANS

The Federal Housing Administration (FHA) is part of the Department of Housing and Urban Development (HUD). FHA's primary function is to **insure** loans; FHA does **not** make loans or build homes. As a federal mortgage insurance agency, FHA insures approved lenders against losses from borrower defaults on FHA loans. Loans are made by approved lenders up to maximum loan guarantee amounts, which vary by county

FHA's insurance program is called the **Mutual Mortgage Insurance Plan.** Under the plan, lenders approved by FHA to make insured loans submit applications from prospective borrowers to the local FHA office or, if authorized by FHA, perform the underwriting functions themselves (review of appraisal, credit, etc.). As the insurer, FHA incurs full liability for losses from default or foreclosure. In turn, FHA regulates many conditions of the loan. FHA regulations have the force and effect of law. FHA regulations, procedures, and practices shape real estate finance.

FHA LOANS VERSUS CONVENTIONAL LOANS. FHA loans have a number of features that distinguish them from conventional loans. The most significant differences are that FHA requires a minimum investment of 3 percent to be paid by the borrower in cash with no secondary financing; mortgage insurance (MIP) is required on all FHA loans; all FHA loans are assumable (with credit checks if loan was made after December 1, 1986), and FHA loans don't have prepayment penalties.

ADVANTAGES OF FHA-INSURED LOANS. Attractive features of FHA-insured loans are low down payments; all FHA loans are assumable (with credit checks if loan was made after December 1, 1986), less stringent qualifying requirements, and FHA loans don't have prepayment penalties.

FHA LOAN PROGRAMS. FHA has several loan programs: FHA standard loans, rural properties, rehabilitation loans, condominium loans, graduated payment loans, and ARM loans. All of these are covered in depth in the *Ohio Real Estate Finance* textbook. Here we'll look at the two most popular loans: FHA standard Section 203(b) loans and FHA ARM loans.

FHA STANDARD SECTION 203(B) LOANS. HUD limits maximum loan amounts for 203(b) loans, depending on median range housing costs for each area. Different loan ceilings apply for single-family and two-, three-, or four-unit dwellings. Limiting the maximum loan amount ensures that FHA loans help low- and middle-income families. Check with local lenders for current maximum loan amounts, which change periodically to reflect area housing costs.

FHA ARM LOANS. FHA ARM loans are limited to one- to four-family dwellings or condominiums. Using an ARM with an FHA mortgage does *not* affect maximum mortgage limits, LTV ratios, MIP, or borrower qualifications. ARM loans are also restricted to owner occupants. There's only one FHA ARM plan available.

VA-GUARANTEED LOANS

The Veterans Administration (VA) **guarantees** repayment of certain residential loans made to eligible veterans. VA loans can be used to buy single-family homes or multi-family residences up to four units. There are no investor loans guaranteed by the VA. With single-family units, the veteran must intend to occupy it as his or her residence; with multi-family dwellings, the veteran must occupy one of the units.

ADVANTAGES OF VA-GUARANTEED LOANS. Attractive features of VA-guaranteed loans are that VA loans may be obtained with no down payment; secondary financing is permitted; all VA loans are assumable (with credit checks if loan was made after March 1988), and VA loans don't have prepayment penalties. Also, there's no MIP or PMI, but there is a variable funding fee that may be financed.

VA LOAN GUARANTY AMOUNT. VA loan guaranty amounts are determined by the Certificate of Reasonable Value (CRV), which is issued by VA based on an appraisal of the property. There's no overall maximum VA loan amount, but the CRV states the maximum amount that a VA loan may be on that property. Only a portion of the loan will be guaranteed by the VA. The VA rarely makes loans; it only guarantees lenders against losses for the loan guaranty amount.

VA LOAN ELIGIBILITY. Eligibility for VA loans is based on the length of continuous active service in the U.S. armed forces. Eligibility is determined by the discharge papers (DD214) summarized as follows:

1. 90 days of continuous active duty for veterans who served any part of their active duty during WWII, the Korean War, Vietnam War, or Persian Gulf War.
2. 181 days of continuous active duty for veterans who enlisted before September 7, 1980 but did not serve any part of their active duty during a war.
3. 24 months of continuous active duty for veterans who enlisted after September 7, 1980 but did not serve any active duty during the Persian Gulf War.

4. 6 years of service in the Reserves or National Guard, and meet certain conditions. Eligibility for Reservists expires in 2003.
5. Spouses who have not remarried, if other spouse was a veteran who died on active duty from service-related causes, MIAs, POWs, or were part of WWII.

CERTIFICATE OF ELIGIBILITY. A **Certificate of Eligibility** is issued by the VA to those who qualify for VA loans. This is required by a lender to establish the amount and status of the veteran's eligibility under the program.

PARTIAL ELIGIBILITY. When a veteran has unused entitlement, the remaining eligibility may be used for a new loan. The maximum guaranty amount is still used to determine the entitlement, so the guaranty amount for the original loan must be subtracted from the maximum guaranty amount for the new loan.

VA LOAN ASSUMPTIONS. Veterans who have VA-guaranteed loans are legally obligated to reimburse VA for any claim paid under the guaranty. This liability continues for the life of the loan even if the property is sold, and foreclosure is from default of a subsequent owner. It is VA's policy not to pursue secondary liability against a veteran unless the seller participated in fraud against the VA.

It's important that veterans who sell property with a VA loan that won't be paid off at closing be aware they can be released from liability on the loan only if the loan is current; the buyer is an acceptable credit risk; VA approves the buyer, and the buyer agrees, in writing, to assume the veteran's liability and reimbursement obligation on the loan. (The assuming veteran must also have unused eligibility.)

VIII. SELLER FINANCING

Sometimes the only way sellers can make a deal is to finance all or part of the purchase price themselves. Of course, the seller must not need all cash immediately from the sale. The seller is taking a risk, but this may enable the property to be sold or sold at a higher price. A seller can charge below market interest rates or offer financing to a buyer considered a credit risk by other lenders since a seller isn't bound by institutional policies on loan ratios, interest rates, or qualifying standards.

PURCHASE MONEY MORTGAGES

A **purchase money mortgage** is seller financing for which the seller finances all or part of the sale of property for the buyer. The seller retains a mortgage as security, and title passes to the buyer.

UNENCUMBERED PROPERTY. **Unencumbered property** means a seller has clear title to property free of mortgages or other liens. This is the simplest form of purchase money mortgage financing; buyer and seller negotiate the amount and terms of financing and have documents drawn up. Purchase money financing may take any of the forms listed earlier (e.g., variable interest rates) with almost no limits.

ASSUMPTIONS. An **assumption** of a loan means a buyer agrees to take over payments of a seller's debt with terms of the note staying unchanged. The property is still security for the loan, but the buyer becomes primarily liable for repayment.

An assumption might be an agreement strictly between buyer and seller. The buyer assumes responsibility for the loan, but the seller is not completely released from liability; he or she remains **secondarily liable**. If the lender can't recover the loan amount from the buyer or via foreclosure, it may still sue the seller for the rest. To be relieved of liability, the seller must get a **release** from the lender accepting the buyer as new mortgagor and releasing the seller from all mortgage obligations.

A loan is not assumable if it contains an **alienation clause** that gives the lender the right to exercise certain rights upon transfer of the property such as declare the entire loan balance immediately due and payable (a **due-on-sale clause** or **acceleration clause**). The lender may also exercise other rights stated in the contract like raising interest rates or charging assumption fees. To determine if a loan is assumable, always ask the lender or a real estate attorney.

WRAPAROUND FINANCING. **Wraparound financing** means a seller keeps the existing loan and continues to pay on it while giving the buyer another loan. Essentially, the buyer pays the seller who in turn pays the original mortgage lender, so the seller can pass on the low interest rate of the existing mortgage even if the buyer can't or won't directly assume the loan. Sometimes this is done instead of an assumption to get around alienation clauses (which limit the loan's assumability), but if a lender learns of this arrangement, the alienation clause can be enforced.

PURCHASE MONEY SECOND MORTGAGE. A **purchase money second mortgage** means a seller finances only part of the sale of a piece of real estate for the buyer with the seller retaining a second mortgage as security. This second mortgage is always inferior to a primary lender's position, so the primary lender gets paid first if there's a foreclosure. If a buyer can get financing from a primary lender or there's an assumable loan, the seller may still need to provide financing if the buyer doesn't have enough for a down payment or can't borrow enough to buy the property.

LAND CONTRACTS

A **land contract** is a real estate installment agreement where the buyer (**vendee**) makes payments to the seller (**vendor**) in exchange for the right to occupy, use, and enjoy the land, but no deed or title transfers until all, or a specified portion of, payments have been made. Advantages to land contracts are the same as purchase money mortgages, like lower qualifying standards. The seller actually holds title to the land not just a mortgage. The main disadvantage is that land contracts usually can't be resold except to private investors.

UNENCUMBERED PROPERTY. **Unencumbered property** means a seller has clear title to property free of mortgages or other liens. A land contract is simplest when it's made by a seller who owns his or her property free and clear. The seller negotiates terms and interest rate of the contract along with any down payment, and has documents drawn up. Land contracts may contain any of the financing elements discussed earlier like variable interest rates.

LAND CONTRACT SUBJECT TO AN EXISTING MORTGAGE. It's rare to find a seller whose property doesn't have a mortgage lien. If this is the case, the existing mortgage(s) must be taken into account. The simplest way to do this is to make the contract **subject to** the existing mortgage. This means that the buyer takes the property along with the mortgage without being personally liable.

The land contract can be written for the full purchase price, but the buyer's property rights under the contract are subject to the rights of the seller's mortgagee. The seller remains liable to make payments on the loan, so the land may be foreclosed if the seller defaults. This is an obvious problem for buyers, so most land contracts allow buyers to make payments directly to the lender. The *Ohio Real Estate Finance* textbook discusses ways to ensure that payments are kept current.

LAND CONTRACT WITH ASSUMPTION OF EXISTING MORTGAGE. If a seller doesn't want to remain liable for mortgage payments, but the buyer can't (or won't) refinance the debt, the buyer may be able to assume the seller's mortgage and pay the balance of the sale price under a land contract. In this arrangement, the buyer becomes liable to the lender for payment of the mortgage and separately liable to the seller for the land contract. The buyer makes one payment to the lender and another payment to the seller. This is attractive if the mortgage is at a lower interest rate; plus, the seller is relieved of responsibility for making the payments to the original lender (but often seller is secondarily liable if new buyer defaults, so ask the lender).

LEASE/OPTION

The **lease/option** plan is comprised of two elements: a **lease** and an **option to purchase** the property within a specific time period (usually within the term of the lease). Obviously, a lease/option is not equal to a sale, but there's a strong possibility that a sale will eventually take place under the terms of the lease/option. An **option** is an agreement to keep open an offer to purchase or sell property for a predetermined period of time and at a predetermined price. The seller/lessor leases the property to the buyer/tenant for a specific term (e.g., one year) with the provision that part of the rent payments be applied to the purchase price if the tenant decides to buy before the lease expires. This can be done if a buyer wants to "try out" the property, can't qualify for a loan now, or wants to have the option as a speculative investment.

IX. FEDERAL REGULATIONS ON REAL ESTATE FINANCE

There are several state and federal laws that regulate various aspects of the real estate financing process. These include laws prohibiting discrimination in real estate transactions and laws requiring certain financial disclosures to be made.

DISCRIMINATION

Both the state and federal governments have enacted laws prohibiting discriminatory behavior in the real estate industry. Federal legislation includes the Civil Rights Act of 1866 and the Federal Fair Housing Act of 1968 also referred to as Title VIII. State legislation includes the Ohio Civil Rights Law. This is important to know for your real estate practice and the licensing exam. These laws and related topics are covered in depth in Chapter 11 of this book, and the *Ohio Real Estate Law* and *Ohio Real Estate Finance* textbooks.

REDLINING. **Redlining** is the refusal to make loans on property located in certain areas for discriminatory reasons including race, color, religion, sex, national origin, handicap, familial status, age, marital status, or receipt of public assistance. Redlining is illegal under Federal Fair Housing Act, and discrimination is illegal under state and federal laws.

FINANCIAL DISCLOSURES

Federal regulations also impose disclosure requirements on real estate financial transactions. The two most pertinent are **Regulation Z** of the **Truth-in-Lending Act** and the **Real Estate Settlement Procedures Act (RESPA)**. These Acts require institutional lenders to make disclosures to borrowers at the time of loan application and prior to the close of escrow.

TRUTH-IN-LENDING ACT. The **Truth-in-Lending Act** requires lenders to disclose consumer credit costs in order to promote informed use of consumer credit. The idea is to let consumers know exactly what they're paying for credit, enabling them to compare credit costs and shop around for the best credit terms. The Act is implemented by **Regulation Z**. While it does not set limits on interest rates or other finance charges, it does regulate the disclosure of these items. Disclosures are required in two general areas: when lenders offer credit/funds to borrowers and when credit terms are advertised to potential customers.

COVERAGE OF THE ACT. The Act applies to lenders who offer or extend credit to consumers for personal, family, or household purposes. The act covers all real estate loans made to consumers, regardless of amount, if the loan is not business related.

DISCLOSURES. Lenders who offer credit, including real estate credit, must make certain disclosures to the consumer before the credit transaction is completed. Lenders of residential mortgages must make a good faith estimate of required disclosures no later than three business days after the lender receives the buyer's written application. Most lenders give the applicant the disclosure statement when applying for a real estate loan. If any of the estimated figures change over the course of the transaction, new disclosures must be made before settlement.

For residential mortgages, the most important disclosure required is the **annual percentage rate (APR)**. The **APR explains** the total cost of financing the loan in percentage terms as a relationship of the total finance charges to the total amount financed. If the buyer must pay points and a loan fee, the APR will be higher than just the interest rate. For example, a loan with an 11 percent interest rate may have an APR of 11 ½ percent, representing the total cost of the loan including all finance charges spread over the life of the loan. Even though different interest rates may apply during the loan term (e.g., ARMs), the loan still only has one APR.

The APR and other required disclosures are made to the borrower in the form of a disclosure statement. The disclosure statement must include:

1. Lender's name
2. Amount financed
3. Notice of right to receive an itemization of amount financed
4. Total finance charges
5. Finance charges expressed as APR
6. Number, amount, and due dates of payments
7. New payment, late payment, and prepayment provisions
8. Description and identification of security (i.e., mortgaged property)
9. Assumption of the loan

RIGHT TO RESCIND. Under the Act, consumers have the right to rescind any credit transaction where a security interest (mortgage) is given in their principal residence except for the initial purchase or construction of a home, so consumers can rescind home equity loans, home improvement loans, refinances, etc. The right to rescind extends until midnight of the third business day after a transaction closes. Lenders must inform consumers of their right to rescind using a separate document.

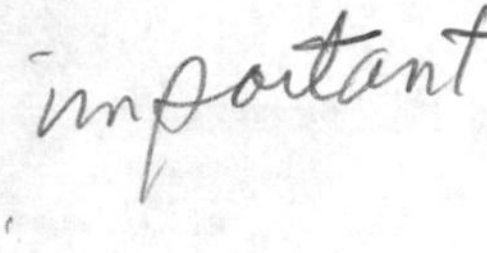

ADVERTISEMENT. The Truth-in-Lending Act also contains provisions that apply to advertising. If an ad contains any of the terms specified in the Act, the ad must also include required disclosures. The lender can't simply state a low interest rate amount or other specific attractive feature of a loan without telling the borrower the whole story. If an ad uses a "trigger" phrase detailing some aspect of the loan, disclosures are needed to tell everything about the loan; if an ad doesn't use a "trigger," no disclosures are needed. Anyone placing consumer credit or lease ads must comply with the Act including real estate salespeople placing home ads.

The "triggering" terms for real estate advertisements include:

- The amount of the down payment (e.g., "20 percent down")
- The amount of any payment (e.g., "Pay less than $700 per month")
- The number of payments (e.g., "only 360 monthly payments")
- The period of repayment (e.g., "30-year financing available")
- The amount of any finance charge (e.g., "1 percent finance charge")

Some examples of terms that do **not** trigger the required disclosures are:

- No down payment
- 12 percent annual percentage rate loan available here
- Easy monthly payments
- VA and FHA financing available" or "100 percent VA financing available"
- Terms to fit your budget

If any triggering terms are used in an ad, *all* of these disclosures must be made:

1. The amount or percentage of down payment
2. The terms of repayment
3. The annual percentage rate using that term spelled out in full. If the APR may increase (e.g., for adjustable rate mortgages), that fact must also be disclosed.

Chapter 12 Summary

1. Finance is affected by government influences through secondary markets, government programs, and regulations. Secondary markets buy and sell lenders' mortgages. *Fannie Mae*: privately owned; biggest residential mortgage investor. *Ginnie Mae*: government owned; guarantees FHA, VA loans. *Freddie Mac*: no mortgage guarantees; buys and sells S and L mortgages. Secondary market sets loan standards, and lenders follow so they can sell loans to secondary market. Different lenders include commercial banks, S and Ls, and mortgage companies.

2. *Conventional financing*: long-term, fully amortized, fixed rate loans; 80 percent LTV ratio plus 20 percent down was norm before PMI. Now 90 percent, 95 percent loans but at least 5 percent down from buyer's own cash; stricter requirements, higher fees for high LTV. PMI shares lender's risk of default but only insures upper part of loan. PMI must be cancelled and interest rate lowered if borrower-paid appraisal shows LTV below 80 percent. Loans are assumable if no alienation clause. Fannie Mae/Freddie Mac have no prepayment penalties. Conforming loans meet Fannie Mae/Freddie Mac criteria, can sell to secondary market; nonconforming loans (e.g., jumbo loans) don't.

3. *Alternative financing*: buydowns, ARMs. Buydown pays points to reduce rate early or for life of loan. Point is 1 percent of loan amount. ARMs usually start at low rate; the lender can adjust. Index is used to check cost of money, adjust rate. Rate or payment can be capped. Negative amortization: balance grows if payments don't keep up with rate change. Need ARM disclosures. Other mortgages: bi-weekly—26 payments=13 months/year; growth equity—fixed interest rate, payments go up so paid faster; reduction option—reduce rate once during loan; reverse—home mortgaged to lender, get monthly check.

4. *Government financing*: FHA-insured loan, VA-guaranteed loan. FHA has own mortgage insurance: MIP; VA has no MIP but funding fee. FHA: low down payment, less stringent qualifying, no prepayment penalties. VA loans: can be no down payment, secondary financing allowed, can finance funding fee. VA eligibility depends on when served in military, prior VA loan amounts. FHA and VA loans are assumable (with credit check now) and have no prepayment penalty. Certificate of Eligibility from VA shows amount/status of veteran's eligibility.

5. *Seller financing*: purchase money mortgage for all or part. Seller secondarily liable on assumptions if no release from lender. Alienation clause may bar assumptions, raise rate, or have fee. Wraparounds may avoid this; buyer pays seller; seller pays lender, but lender can stop if it finds out. Land contracts have buyer make payments to use property, but seller holds title until all or part is paid. Lease/options lease property to tenant with all or part of rent applied to price if tenant buys before lease ends. Option locks in sale price for set time.

6. *Federal regulations*: Federal Fair Housing Act outlaws redlining—lenders not making loans in some areas for discriminatory reasons. Truth-in-Lending Act doesn't limit rates but requires disclosures: APR of loan, right to rescind and ad rules. APR shows total cost of financing—interest rate and fees, charges. Right to rescind is 3 days from close but only home equity loans, etc. Ads with finance details must tell all—down payment, terms, and APR spelled out.

Chapter 12 Quiz

1. *All of the following are functions of the secondary market,* except:

a. Making loans to low-income families
b. Giving primary lenders a place to invest surplus funds
c. Buying and selling mortgages of primary lenders
d. Establishing loan standards

2. *Which of the following secondary market players is government owned?*

a. Federal Home Loan Mortgage Corporation
b. Federal Reserve Board
c. Federal National Mortgage Association
d. Government National Mortgage Association

3. *Which of the following secondary market players is the largest?*

a. Federal Home Loan Mortgage Corporation
b. Federal Reserve Board
c. Federal National Mortgage Association
d. Government National Mortgage Association

4. *A fully amortized loan means that the loan will be paid off:*

a. In equal monthly installments over 30 years
b. In equal monthly installments with a balloon payment
c. In monthly installments covering interest only
d. In monthly installments that pay off the entire balance during the loan term

5. ***Joe wants to buy a $100,000 home with a conventional loan but can't come up with the required minimum 5 percent down payment he needs from his own cash reserves. Joe has also used up his VA loan eligibility. What options does Joe have?***
   a. Ask the seller to do some secondary financing
   b. Pay more points at closing to lower the interest rate
   c. Buy more PMI (private mortgage insurance)
   (d.) Start looking at cheaper houses

6. ***The purpose of private mortgage insurance is to:***
   a. Share all of a lender's risk of default by insuring the entire loan amount
   (b.) Share some of a lender's risk of default by insuring part of the loan amount
   c. Share none of a lender's risk of default but check the borrower's credit
   d. Take over all of the lender's risk of default by servicing the loan

7. ***A conforming loan is one that:***
   (a.) Follows the criteria established by national secondary market investors, primarily Fannie Mae and Freddie Mac
   b. Follows the criteria and guidelines of the lender making the loan
   c. Follows the criteria established by FHA and VA
   d. Follows the Truth in Lending Act

8. ***A discount point costs:***
   a. One percent of the sale price
   (b.) One percent of the loan amount
   c. One percent of the appraised value
   d. One percent of the down payment

9. ***Which one of the following would not be a reason for charging points?***
   a. Because the lender wants to make extra money
   b. To lower the interest rate
   c. For loan origination fees
   (d.) To give the broker extra commission

10. ***A buydown means:***
   a. The seller helps the buyer with a down payment
   (b.) The lender charges extra points to lower the interest rate
   c. The buyer buys mortgage insurance
   d. The lender has special rates because of the Community Reinvestment Act

11. ***Of the following, which is* not *characteristic of adjustable rate mortgages?***
   a. An index is stated in the contract that will determine the interest rate adjustment
   b. The lender will add a margin to the index to determine the interest rate
   (c.) Negative amortization can never occur because of federal regulations
   d. The rate or payment changes can be capped

12. ***The annual percentage rate (APR) is:***
   a. The interest rate being charged on the loan only
   b. The fees being charged on the loan only
   (c.) Both the interest rate and fees being charged on the loan
   d. Neither the interest rate nor the fees being charged on the loan

13. ***Which of the following lender practices is outlawed by Federal Fair Housing Act?***

a. Blockbusting
b. Steering
c. Redlining
d. Conversion

14. ***An ad for a home says, "No Down Payment." What other disclosures are required?***

a. The terms of repayment
b. The annual percentage rate
c. Both a and b
d. Neither a nor b

13 MORTGAGE BASICS

CHAPTER OVERVIEW

Now that you have an understanding of real estate finance, it's time to apply that knowledge. As you work with clients and customers who need mortgages, it's important that you know about the different types of finance instruments. We'll then go through the loan process. Whether the broker's clients are buyers or sellers, salespeople need to understand the process people go through to get a mortgage.

KEY TERMS

Acceleration Clause
Contract clause that gives a lender the right to declare entire loan balance due immediately because of borrower default (or other reason).

Alienation Clause
Contract clause that gives the lender certain stated rights when there's a transfer of ownership in property.

Defeasance Clause
Clause used to defeat or cancel a certain right upon the occurrence of a specific event (e.g., upon final payment, words of grant in mortgage are void, and the mortgage is thereby cancelled and title is re-vested to mortgagor).

Equitable Right of Redemption
The right of a debtor to save or redeem the property from foreclosure proceedings prior to the confirmation of sale.

Holder in Due Course
One who acquires a negotiable instrument in good faith and for consideration and has certain rights beyond those of the original payee.

Land Contract
Real estate installment agreement where buyer makes payments to seller in exchange for the right to occupy and use the property, but no deed or title is transferred until all, or a specified portion of, the payments have been made.

Mortgage
Instrument that creates a lien against real property as security for a note.

Negotiable Instrument
Promissory note (or other financial instrument) that is freely transferable from one party to another.

PITI
Principle, **I**nterest, **T**axes, and **I**nsurance; typical payment on a mortgage loan.

KEY TERMS *cont.*

Promissory Note
Instrument that is evidence of a promise to pay a specific debt.

Residual Income
The amount of income a borrower has left after subtracting taxes, housing expense, and all recurring debt and expense obligations.

Security Instrument
Gives the creditor the right to have the collateral sold to satisfy the debt if the debtor fails to pay according to the terms of the agreement.

Subordination Clause
Contract clause that gives a mortgage recorded at a later date the right to take priority over an earlier recorded mortgage.

Trust Deed
Instrument held by a third party as security for the payment of a note.

I. GETTING A MORTGAGE

As clients and customers begin to go through the financing process to get a mortgage, it's important to understand the types of finance instruments available and the loan process in general so you can answer questions intelligently. We'll go through a brief overview of finance instruments and discuss the loan process and buyer qualification process.

II. TYPES OF REAL ESTATE INSTRUMENTS

Our discussion of finance instruments will focus on some of the more common written documents used as an integral part of most real estate financing transactions. **Instruments** are simply written legal documents that establish the rights and duties of the parties. We'll discuss **promissory notes**, **mortgages**, **trust deeds**, **land contracts**, and some of the typical clauses found in those documents.

This section is only an introduction to real estate finance instruments. It is **not** intended as a substitute for competent professional or legal advice. It should **not** be used as a basis for personal action nor to advise clients or customers regarding the operation of any documents. Always consult an attorney for current, local advice.

PROMISSORY NOTES

Simply stated, a promissory note is a written promise to pay money. Before a lender will finance the purchase of a house, the borrower must promise to repay the funds. The one promising to pay the money is called the **"maker"** of the note and is usually the homebuyer. The one who is promised payment is called the **"payee,"** usually the lender, who can also be the seller.

Promissory notes are basic evidence of debt showing who owes how much to whom. They're usually simple documents often less than a page long, that state:

- Date
- Names of the parties
- Amount of the debt
- How and when the money is to be paid
- What happens in the event of default
- Signature of the maker

Promissory Note

FOR VALUE RECEIVED, maker promises to pay to order of BEARER

THE SUM OF $ ____________________

PAID AS FOLLOWS: $ ____________________ a week, month, year, or more starting ____________________, including interest at ______% per annum.

ACCELERATION: In the event of default, payee or bearer can declare all sums due and payable at once.

____

Maker/Borrower Date

NEGOTIABLE INSTRUMENTS. **Negotiable instruments** are promissory notes that are freely transferable from one party to another. Most promissory notes used in real estate are negotiable instruments. When a note is freely transferable, a bank or other creditor can sell the note to obtain immediate cash. The sale is usually at a discount, meaning the note is sold for a cash amount less than the note's face value.

Negotiable instruments are governed by the **Uniform Commercial Code (UCC)**. The UCC sets out certain requirements for negotiable instruments. If any of these elements are missing from the promissory note, it may still be valid between the parties, but it may not be valid if the note is transferred to another party. This is important since most real estate lenders sell their real estate loans to the secondary market. Secondary market investors will buy only a promissory note that is negotiable because they want to be a **holder in due course** of the note. A **holder in due course** is one who acquires a negotiable instrument in good faith and for consideration and has certain rights beyond those of the original payee.

An example of a holder in due course would be Fannie Mae purchasing a note from a lender for a fair price when there is no indication of any irregularity in the note. By contrast, if Sue gives a promissory note to her brother for his birthday, the brother is not a holder in due course because no valuable consideration was paid for the note.

A holder in due course will get paid in circumstances where the original payee may not have been paid. For example, if there was fraud in the inducement because the original payee convinced the maker to sign the note by making false statements, a holder in due course could still go after the maker to get paid; whereas, the original payee couldn't. On the other hand, if there's forgery or material alteration of the note, neither a holder in due course nor the original payee could force the maker to pay.

TYPES OF NOTES. Four types of notes usually used in real estate transactions are:

1. **Straight note:** calls for payments of interest only during the term of the note with a balloon payment at the end of loan term to pay off the principal amount.

2. **Installment note:** calls for periodic payments of the principal amount only with a balloon payment at the end of the loan term to pay off the balance due.
3. **Fully amortized installment note:** calls for regular payment of principal and interest calculated to pay off the entire balance by the end of loan term.
4. **Adjustable rate note:** has an interest rate that varies up or down depending on the cost of money as determined by an index.

MORTGAGES

Mortgages are instruments that create a lien against real property as security for the payment of a note. A mortgage is a type of security instrument where the borrower (called the **mortgagor**) pledges his or her property to the lender (called the **mortgagee**) as collateral for the debt. A promissory note is almost always accompanied by a security instrument since the **security instrument** gives the creditor the right to have the collateral sold to satisfy the debt if the debtor fails to pay according to the terms of the agreement.

With a mortgage as security, the collateral is real estate, so the procedure in the event of default is **judicial foreclosure**. **Judicial foreclosure** under a mortgage requires a court-ordered sheriff's sale of the property to repay the debt.

FORECLOSURE PROCEDURE. When a borrower is in **default** on a loan, the lender **accelerates** the due date of the debt to the present and gives the debtor a **notice of default** demanding that the debtor pay off the entire outstanding balance of the loan at once. If the debtor fails to do so, the lender starts a lawsuit, called a **foreclosure action** in Common Pleas Court where the land is located. If the court determines that the lender is rightfully owed the money, a judge will issue an **order of execution** directing an officer of the court to seize and sell the property.

The officer of the court, usually the county sheriff, notifies the public of the place and date of the sale through **advertising** that runs for three consecutive weeks in a newspaper circulated in the county. On the sale date, a **public auction** is held at the courthouse where anyone can bid on the property. The minimum bid is two-thirds of the appraised value as determined by three disinterested appraisers who live in the county. The property is sold to the highest bidder with proceeds used to pay costs of the sale and to pay off the mortgage. Any surplus funds go to the debtor.

After the sale, a document called a **confirmation of sale** is filed to finalize the sale. The officer then makes out a **sheriff's deed** to the purchaser of the property, which is executed, acknowledged, and recorded just like any other deed. If the property does not bring enough money at the sale to pay off the mortgage, the creditor may be able to obtain a deficiency judgment against the debtor for the remaining debt. A deficiency judgment requires a separate court action.

REDEMPTION. The debtor can redeem (save) the property from the time the foreclosure action is brought up until the confirmation of the foreclosure sale. This is done by paying the court what is due, which may include court costs and attorneys' fees. This right, used in Ohio, to save or redeem the property prior to the confirmation of sale is called the **equitable right of redemption.** Some other states use the statuary right of redemption which allows debtors to redeem themselves after the final sale. Once the redemption is made, the court will set aside the sale, pay the parties, and the debtor has title to the property again.

In Ohio, after the confirmation of sale, the transfer of the property is final. The debtor no longer has the right to redeem the property by paying what is due.

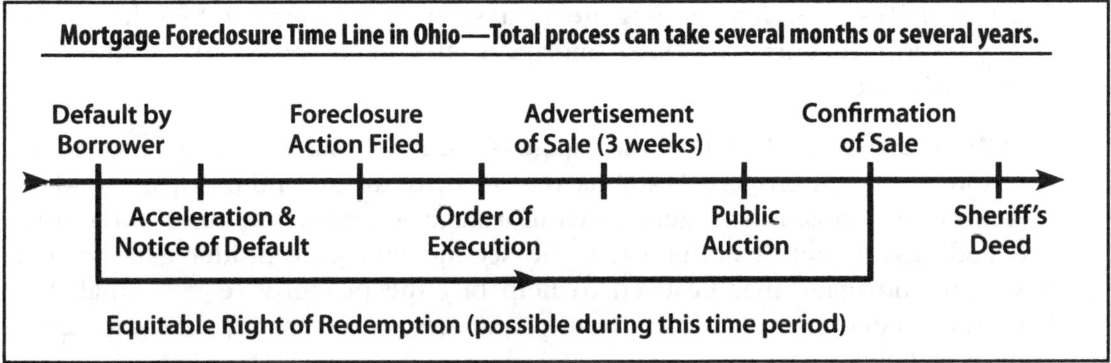

One other option to avoid foreclosure is for a debtor to make a **voluntary conveyance** (also called **deed in lieu of foreclosure**). Debtors still lose the property, but by returning it voluntarily before final court action, they avoid having a foreclosure on their credit report. After confirmation of sale, it's too late.

ADVANTAGES AND DISADVANTAGES OF MORTGAGES. For the lender, the main advantage of a mortgage is the right to accelerate the entire debt in the event of default. The main disadvantage is the time and expense involved with judicial foreclosure. Legal fees and court costs may reach several thousand dollars, which the lender may or may not recover from the sale, and the process can take a long time.

For the borrower, the advantages and disadvantages of a mortgage correspond to those of the lender but in reverse. The lender's right of acceleration may mean that a homeowner who misses one or two payments will be faced with the prospect of having to pay off the entire debt to save the home. On the other hand, the debtor usually has a long time to get money together due to the length of court proceedings.

TRUST DEEDS

Trust deeds are instruments held by a third party as security for the payment of a note. They're also called **deeds of trust**. This is another type of security instrument. Trust deeds are a three-party device. The borrower is called the **trustor**; the lender is called the **beneficiary**, and there is an independent third party called the **trustee**. The creditor has the right to force the sale of the property if the debtor defaults on payments under the note or trust deed. Upon default, the creditor may begin a **non-judicial foreclosure** action authorized by a **power of sale clause** that allows the trustee to sell the property without court supervision. Trust deeds are rarely used in Ohio because the foreclosure is not backed by a judicial decree. (Also note that trust deeds are different than *trustee's deeds,* which convey real estate of a trustee as proscribed in a trust agreement or a will.)

MORTGAGE TYPES AND MORTGAGE TERMS

Although mortgages are primarily security devices, the word "mortgage" is often prefaced with adjectives that serve to describe the particular function the mortgage is serving or the nature of the circumstances surrounding its use. For example, a "construction mortgage" is a mortgage used to secure a construction loan. We'll look at a few of the more common mortgage types and mortgage terms here.

FIRST MORTGAGE. A **first mortgage** is a security instrument that has a first lien position meaning the first mortgage holder is paid first if there's a foreclosure sale.

SECOND MORTGAGE. A **second mortgage** is a security instrument in a second lien position. Although property is still used as security, the second mortgage lender is in a more risky position because a first mortgage gets paid first out of foreclosure proceedings. If there's nothing left, the second mortgage holder gets nothing. A second mortgage may be used to help buy the property (e.g., a small loan from the seller), or it could be a home equity loan used for repairs or to send a child to college.

SENIOR MORTGAGE/JUNIOR MORTGAGE. A **senior mortgage** is any mortgage that has a higher lien position than another. A **junior mortgage** is any mortgage that has a lower lien position than another. So, a second mortgage is a junior mortgage to a first mortgage but a senior mortgage to a third mortgage.

Lien status is important in the event of foreclosure because the proceeds from a foreclosure sale pay the first lien in its entirety; if any money remains, the second lien is paid; then the third is paid, and so on, until the money is gone. Obviously, it's best to have a first lien.

PURCHASE MONEY MORTGAGE. A purchase money mortgage is where the seller finances all or part of the sale price of a piece of property for a buyer. Here the seller retains a mortgage and title passes to the buyer.

CONVENTIONAL MORTGAGE. A **conventional mortgage** is a mortgage loan that is not insured or guaranteed by a government entity or agency.

ADJUSTABLE RATE MORTGAGE (ARM). An **adjustable rate mortgage** permits a lender to periodically adjust the interest rate, so the rate reflects fluctuations in the cost of money as indicated by a chosen index.

BUDGET MORTGAGE. A **budget mortgage** is a mortgage agreement where payments are set up to include principal and interest on the loan plus one-twelfth of the year's property taxes and hazard insurance premiums. Most home loans are secured by budget mortgages because this is the safest and most practical way for the lender to make sure that property taxes and insurance are paid on time.

REVERSE EQUITY MORTGAGE. A **reverse equity mortgage** means a qualified senior citizen mortgages his or her home to a lender and in return gets a monthly check from the lender. Mortgage is repaid when the home is sold or the borrower dies.

WRAPAROUND MORTGAGE. A **wraparound mortgage** means a seller keeps the existing loan and continues to pay on it while giving the buyer another mortgage.

The total debt (new loan plus existing loan) is treated as a single obligation by the buyer with one payment made on the entire debt. Essentially, buyer pays the seller who, in turn, pays the original lender (done when buyer can't or won't assume loan).

PACKAGE MORTGAGE. A **package mortgage** means personal property, like appliances, are included in a property sale and financed together with one contract.

BLANKET MORTGAGE. A **blanket mortgage** covers more than one parcel or lot and is usually used to finance subdivision developments. These loans usually have a partial release clause allowing the borrower to pay a certain amount of money to release one or more lots with the mortgage continuing to cover the other lots.

CONSTRUCTION MORTGAGE. A **construction mortgage** is a temporary loan used to finance the construction of buildings on land. When construction is complete, the loan is replaced by permanent financing called a **takeout** loan.

LAND CONTRACTS

Land contracts are real estate installment agreements where the buyer (**vendee**) makes payments to the seller (**vendor**) in exchange for the right to occupy and use the property, but no deed or title is transferred until all, or a specified portion of, payments have been made. The seller actually holds title to land as security not just a mortgage lien. Since actual title will be transferred by deed at a future date, the buyer's present interest in a land contract is called **equitable title**.

In Ohio, a land contract must be executed in duplicate, recorded within 20 days of execution, and must include:

1. Names and address of all parties
2. Date each party signed
3. Legal description of the property
4. Price of the property
5. Charges or fees for services, separate from the contract price
6. Down payment amount
7. Principal amount owed
8. Amount and due date of each payment
9. Interest rate and method of computing the interest rate
10. Encumbrances against the property
11. Requirement that the vendor delivers a general warranty deed
12. Requirement that the vendor provides evidence of title
13. Provision for vendor's default
14. Requirement that the vendor records the contract

Because the seller still retains title to the property, there's some risk that the seller could go out and mortgage the property for an amount greater than his or her interest in the property. Under Ohio law, the seller can't mortgage the property for more than the balance due under the land contract without the buyer's consent. This protects the buyer's interest in the property. The seller must also give the buyer a statement, at least once a year or as requested, showing the amount of payments that have been credited to principal and interest and the balance due under the contract.

BUYER DEFAULT. If the contract has been in effect for **less than five years** or the buyer has paid **less than 20 percent** of the purchase price before default, the seller may initiate **forfeiture** proceedings 30 days after the buyer's default by giving the buyer written notice of the default and of the seller's intent to declare the contract forfeited unless the buyer corrects the default. The buyer has ten days to correct the default to reinstate contract terms and retain his or her rights under the contract. If the buyer fails to remedy the default within the ten-day notice period, he or she loses all rights to the property as well as all payments made up to that point.

If the contract has been in effect for **five or more years** or the buyer has paid **20 percent or more** of the price, upon default, the seller must use **foreclosure** proceedings the same as under a mortgage in order to protect the buyer's substantial investment.

ADVANTAGES AND DISADVANTAGES OF LAND CONTRACTS. For the seller, the main advantage of land contracts is the right to hold title as security. The main disadvantage is the expense and time required for foreclosure after the five-year period.

For the buyer, the main advantage is that a land contract is typically easier to qualify for than a conventional loan. The main disadvantage is the lack of ownership making it difficult to obtain financing for the equity built up or for improvements.

OHIO DIVISION OF REAL ESTATE. The Ohio Division of Real Estate's position on listing properties sold by land contract is to remind the licensee to exercise extreme caution since a licensee cannot give legal advice on any questions regarding validity of title or other legal issues that may arise from listing or selling property with a land contract. An attorney should always be consulted by all parties involved, and a licensee must never draft any documents relating to this or any other, real estate transaction. *Such actions can be grounds for license suspension or revocation.*

Typical Clauses in Finance Instruments

We'll now look briefly at some clauses used in real estate finance instruments.

ACCELERATION. An **acceleration clause** in a contract gives the lender the right to declare the entire loan balance due immediately because of borrower default or for violation of other contract provisions. Most promissory notes, mortgages, trust deeds, and many land contracts contain an acceleration clause allowing the lender to accelerate the debt upon default as defined in the contract. A debtor who missed one payment may discover that he or she doesn't owe just two payments next month but rather the entire loan balance. Most lenders will wait until payments are at least 90 days delinquent before enforcing an acceleration clause.

ALIENATION. An **alienation clause** in a contract gives the lender certain stated rights when there's a transfer of ownership in the property. This is designed to limit the debtor's right to transfer the property without permission of the creditor. Upon sale of, or even a transfer of significant interest in the property, the lender will often have the right to accelerate the debt (here called a **due-on-sale clause**), change the interest rate, or charge a hefty assumption fee. (FHA and VA loans cannot have this.)

DEFEASANCE. A **defeasance clause** is a clause used to defeat or cancel a certain right upon the occurrence of a specific event. For example, upon final payment, words of grant in a mortgage are void, and the mortgage is thereby cancelled, and the title is re-vested to mortgagor. A defeasance clause is often used in mortgages in title theory states whereby the mortgagee agrees to deed property to the mortgagor after all terms of the contract have been performed satisfactorily. (A defeasance clause may also be used to give a borrower the right to redeem real estate after default on a note by paying the full amount due plus fees and court costs.)

PREPAYMENT. A **prepayment clause** in a contract gives the lender the right to charge the borrower a penalty for paying off the loan early and essentially depriving the lender of further interest income. (FHA and VA loans cannot have this.)

SUBORDINATION. A **subordination clause** in a contract gives a mortgage recorded at a later date the right to take priority over an earlier recorded mortgage. Normally with mortgages, trust deeds, and other real estate contracts, the first to get recorded gets lien priority. In some situations, however, the parties may desire that a later recorded instrument have priority over an earlier recorded instrument. This is particularly common in construction financing. Because of the high-risk nature of construction loans, construction lenders frequently refuse to lend any money unless they can be assured of first lien priority. Since the developer, in many circumstances, has already purchased the land on some sort of deferred payment plan, there is often a security instrument (mortgage, trust deed, or contract) that has already been recorded. For the later construction loan mortgage or trust deed to take priority over the earlier instrument, the earlier instrument must contain a subordination clause.

III. PRE-QUALIFICATION VERSUS PRE-APPROVAL

There's a growing trend toward pre-approving buyers for loans because, among other things, pre-approval can be a useful negotiating tool. This is *not* the same as pre-qualifying buyers. The two terms are *not* interchangeable.

Pre-qualification is the process by which an agent or lender reviews potential borrowers to determine if they are likely to get approved for a loan and for approximately how much money. *Pre-qualification of a buyer is not binding on the lender*, and this is why the distinction is very important. In fact, many agents do a simple pre-qualification of prospective clients by asking them general questions about income, expenses, and debts so they do not waste time showing prospects homes they cannot afford.

Pre-approval is the process by which a lender determines that potential borrowers can be financed through the lender for a certain amount of money. A real estate agent can't give a buyer a pre-approval (unless perhaps she or he is also a mortgage broker). For pre-approval, a buyer generally goes through most of the loan process. Furthermore, with a pre-approval the lender is stating the prospective buyer has been evaluated, and providing that all circumstances stay generally the same, the lender is willing to loan a person up to a certain amount of money.

IV. THE LOAN PROCESS

Clients will most likely be interested in the loan process. Of course, these steps can be done quickly and conveniently using electronic means, but we'll examine the five traditional steps in the loan process:

1. Meeting with the lender
2. Filling out the loan application
3. Analyzing the borrower and property
4. Processing the loan application
5. Closing the loan

MEETING WITH THE LENDER

During the initial meeting with the lender, the buyer will learn about the various types of financing programs offered by the lender usually 30-year, 15-year, fixed rate, and adjustable rate mortgages. The buyer will decide which program best suits his or her needs. The lender will require a deposit to cover the expenses of the credit report, property appraisal, and preliminary title report. This deposit will assure the lender these fees will be paid even if the loan does not close.

If there is a purchase agreement, it will be examined at this interview. The lender wants to be sure that the terms of the agreement are consistent with the loan terms the lender can offer (e.g., interest rate, loan term). The closing date is critical. If the closing date is too early for the lender to meet, a more feasible date can be agreed upon to avoid frustration later.

The potential homebuyer must also attend this lender meeting with lots of personal and financial data that will be the basis of the lender's decision.

FILLING OUT THE LOAN APPLICATION

The typical loan application is designed for those who will follow through and actually borrow funds (provided the loan is approved), so there's a lot of required information. Missing data must be supplied later, so it will likely delay the loan process. The information a buyer should take to the interview includes:

1. Purchase and sales agreement for the house the borrower wants to buy
2. Residence history:
   - Where the buyer has lived for the past two years
   - If renting, landlord or rental agent's name, address, and phone number
   - If owns home, lender's name, address, phone number, and type of loan

3. Employment history:

   - Names, addresses, and phone numbers of employers for last two years; position held; full time, part time, or temporary; and income earned

   - If self-employed or fully commissioned, tax returns for past two years plus a year-to-date income and expense statement

   - If a major stockholder in a corporation (owns 25 percent or more of the stock), three years of corporate tax returns

4. Income information:

   - Amount and sources, including regular salary and secondary sources such as pensions, social security, disability, child support, alimony, etc

   - Benefits statement from income sources; child support or alimony requires copy of divorce decree (but need not be disclosed if not counted)

5. List of assets:

   - Names, addresses, and account numbers for all bank accounts

   - Value of personal property; make, model, year, and value of cars

   - Cash and face value of insurance policies or other assets (e.g., stocks)

   - Address, description, and value of any other real estate owned; (income properties should have a spreadsheet showing relevant data)

6. List of liabilities:

   - Name, address, and phone number for each creditor and the balance, monthly payment, and account number

   - Copy of divorce decree if paying any child support or alimony

7. Copy of a gift letter if a gift is the source of down payment or closing costs:

   - Letter must be signed and state that funds are not to be repaid

8. Certificate of Eligibility for VA loans

9. If selling present home:

   - Net dollar amount from sale (after commissions and expenses)

   - A letter from an employer stating what relocation costs it will cover

10. Any other relevant documentation requested by the lender

THE LOAN APPLICATION. The buyer typically fills out a loan application at the initial interview with the lender. Lenders expect the loans to be repaid in a timely manner without collection, servicing, or foreclosure. That's why they require the borrower to supply so much information. A sample loan application used in Ohio for conventional loans is shown on the following pages.

Uniform Residential Loan Application

This application is designed to be completed by the applicant(s) with the Lender's assistance. Applicants should complete this form as "Borrower" or "Co-Borrower," as applicable. Co-Borrower information must also be provided (and the appropriate box checked) when ☐ the income or assets of a person other than the Borrower (including the Borrower's spouse) will be used as a basis for loan qualification or ☐ the income or assets of the Borrower's spouse or other person who has community property rights pursuant to state law will not be used as a basis for loan qualification, but his or her liabilities must be considered because the spouse or other person has community property rights pursuant to applicable law and Borrower resides in a community property state, the security property is located in a community property state, or the Borrower is relying on other property located in a community property state as a basis for repayment of the loan.

If this is an application for joint credit, Borrower and Co-Borrower each agree that we intend to apply for joint credit (sign below):

Borrower ____________ Co-Borrower ____________

I. TYPE OF MORTGAGE AND TERMS OF LOAN

Mortgage Applied for:	☐ VA ☐ FHA	☐ Conventional ☐ USDA/Rural Housing Service	☐ Other (explain):	Agency Case Number	Lender Case Number
Amount $	Interest Rate %	No. of Months	Amortization Type:	☐ Fixed Rate ☐ GPM	☐ Other (explain): ☐ ARM (type):

II. PROPERTY INFORMATION AND PURPOSE OF LOAN

Subject Property Address (street, city, state & ZIP)	No. of Units
Legal Description of Subject Property (attach description if necessary)	Year Built

Purpose of Loan ☐ Purchase ☐ Construction ☐ Other (explain): ☐ Refinance ☐ Construction-Permanent

Property will be: ☐ Primary Residence ☐ Secondary Residence ☐ Investment

Complete this line if construction or construction-permanent loan.

Year Lot Acquired	Original Cost	Amount Existing Liens	(a) Present Value of Lot	(b) Cost of Improvements	Total (a + b)
	$	$	$	$	$ 0.00

Complete this line if this is a refinance loan.

Year Acquired	Original Cost	Amount Existing Liens	Purpose of Refinance	Describe Improvements ☐ made ☐ to be made
	$	$		Cost: $

Title will be held in what Name(s)	Manner in which Title will be held	Estate will be held in: ☐ Fee Simple ☐ Leasehold (show expiration date)

Source of Down Payment, Settlement Charges, and/or Subordinate Financing (explain)

III. BORROWER INFORMATION

Borrower				Co-Borrower			
Borrower's Name (include Jr. or Sr. if applicable)				Co-Borrower's Name (include Jr. or Sr. if applicable)			
Social Security Number	Home Phone (incl. area code)	DOB (mm/dd/yyyy)	Yrs. School	Social Security Number	Home Phone (incl. area code)	DOB (mm/dd/yyyy)	Yrs. School
☐ Married ☐ Separated	☐ Unmarried (include single, divorced, widowed)	Dependents (not listed by Co-Borrower) no.	ages	☐ Married ☐ Separated	☐ Unmarried (include single, divorced, widowed)	Dependents (not listed by Borrower) no.	ages
Present Address (street, city, state, ZIP)	☐ Own	☐ Rent ____No. Yrs.		Present Address (street, city, state, ZIP)	☐ Own	☐ Rent ____No. Yrs.	
Mailing Address, if different from Present Address				Mailing Address, if different from Present Address			

If residing at present address for less than two years, complete the following:

Former Address (street, city, state, ZIP)	☐ Own	☐ Rent ____No. Yrs.	Former Address (street, city, state, ZIP)	☐ Own	☐ Rent ____No. Yrs.

IV. EMPLOYMENT INFORMATION

Borrower			Co-Borrower		
Name & Address of Employer	☐ Self Employed	Yrs. on this job	Name & Address of Employer	☐ Self Employed	Yrs. on this job
		Yrs. employed in this line of work/profession			Yrs. employed in this line of work/profession
Position/Title/Type of Business	Business Phone (incl. area code)		Position/Title/Type of Business	Business Phone (incl. area code)	

If employed in current position for less than two years or if currently employed in more than one position, complete the following:

Freddie Mac Form 65 7/05 Page 1 of 5 Fannie Mae Form 1003 7/05

Borrower			IV. EMPLOYMENT INFORMATION (cont'd)	Co-Borrower		
Name & Address of Employer	☐ Self Employed	Dates (from – to) Monthly Income $	Name & Address of Employer	☐ Self Employed		Dates (from – to) Monthly Income $
Position/Title/Type of Business	Business Phone (incl. area code)		Position/Title/Type of Business		Business Phone (incl. area code)	
Name & Address of Employer	☐ Self Employed	Dates (from – to) Monthly Income $	Name & Address of Employer	☐ Self Employed		Dates (from – to) Monthly Income $
Position/Title/Type of Business	Business Phone (incl. area code)		Position/Title/Type of Business		Business Phone (incl. area code)	

V. MONTHLY INCOME AND COMBINED HOUSING EXPENSE INFORMATION

Gross Monthly Income	Borrower	Co-Borrower	Total	Combined Monthly Housing Expense	Present	Proposed
Base Empl. Income*	$	$	$ 0.00	Rent	$	
Overtime			0.00	First Mortgage (P&I)		$
Bonuses			0.00	Other Financing (P&I)		
Commissions			0.00	Hazard Insurance		
Dividends/Interest			0.00	Real Estate Taxes		
Net Rental Income			0.00	Mortgage Insurance		
Other (before completing, see the notice in "describe other income," below)			0.00	Homeowner Assn. Dues		
				Other:		
Total	$ 0.00	$ 0.00	$ 0.00	**Total**	$ 0.00	$ 0.00

* **Self Employed Borrower(s) may be required to provide additional documentation such as tax returns and financial statements.**

Describe Other Income *Notice:* **Alimony, child support, or separate maintenance income need not be revealed if the Borrower (B) or Co-Borrower (C) does not choose to have it considered for repaying this loan.**

B/C		Monthly Amount
		$

VI. ASSETS AND LIABILITIES

This Statement and any applicable supporting schedules may be completed jointly by both married and unmarried Co-Borrowers if their assets and liabilities are sufficiently joined so that the Statement can be meaningfully and fairly presented on a combined basis; otherwise, separate Statements and Schedules are required. If the Co-Borrower section was completed about a non-applicant spouse or other person, this Statement and supporting schedules must be completed about that spouse or other person also.

Completed ☐ Jointly ☐ Not Jointly

ASSETS Description	Cash or Market Value	**Liabilities and Pledged Assets.** List the creditor's name, address, and account number for all outstanding debts, including automobile loans, revolving charge accounts, real estate loans, alimony, child support, stock pledges, etc. Use continuation sheet, if necessary. Indicate by (*) those liabilities, which will be satisfied upon sale of real estate owned or upon refinancing of the subject property.		
Cash deposit toward purchase held by:	$			
List checking and savings accounts below		**LIABILITIES**	**Monthly Payment & Months Left to Pay**	**Unpaid Balance**
Name and address of Bank, S&L, or Credit Union		Name and address of Company	$ Payment/Months	$
Acct. no.	$	Acct. no.		
Name and address of Bank, S&L, or Credit Union		Name and address of Company	$ Payment/Months	$
Acct. no.	$	Acct. no.		
Name and address of Bank, S&L, or Credit Union		Name and address of Company	$ Payment/Months	$
Acct. no.	$	Acct. no.		

Freddie Mac Form 65 7/05 Page 2 of 5 Fannie Mae Form 1003 7/05

VI. ASSETS AND LIABILITIES (cont'd)

Assets		Liabilities		
Name and address of Bank, S&L, or Credit Union		Name and address of Company	$ Payment/Months	$
Acct. no.	$	Acct. no.		
Stocks & Bonds (Company name/ number & description)	$	Name and address of Company	$ Payment/Months	$
		Acct. no.		
Life insurance net cash value	$	Name and address of Company	$ Payment/Months	$
Face amount: $				
Subtotal Liquid Assets	$ 0.00			
Real estate owned (enter market value from schedule of real estate owned)	$			
Vested interest in retirement fund	$			
Net worth of business(es) owned (attach financial statement)	$	Acct. no.		
Automobiles owned (make and year)	$	Alimony/Child Support/Separate Maintenance Payments Owed to:	$	
Other Assets (itemize)	$	Job-Related Expense (child care, union dues, etc.)	$	
		Total Monthly Payments	$	
Total Assets a.	$ 0.00	Net Worth (a minus b) ▸ $ 0.00	**Total Liabilities b.**	$ 0.00

Schedule of Real Estate Owned (If additional properties are owned, use continuation sheet.)

Property Address (enter S if sold, PS if pending sale or R if rental being held for income) ▼		Type of Property	Present Market Value	Amount of Mortgages & Liens	Gross Rental Income	Mortgage Payments	Insurance, Maintenance, Taxes & Misc.	Net Rental Income
			$	$	$	$	$	$
		Totals	$ 0.00	$ 0.00	$ 0.00	$ 0.00	$ 0.00	$

List any additional names under which credit has previously been received and indicate appropriate creditor name(s) and account number(s):

Alternate Name	Creditor Name	Account Number

VII. DETAILS OF TRANSACTION

a.	Purchase price	$
b.	Alterations, improvements, repairs	
c.	Land (if acquired separately)	
d.	Refinance (incl. debts to be paid off)	
e.	Estimated prepaid items	
f.	Estimated closing costs	
g.	PMI, MIP, Funding Fee	
h.	Discount (if Borrower will pay)	
i.	Total costs (add items a through h)	0.00

VIII. DECLARATIONS

If you answer "Yes" to any questions a through i, please use continuation sheet for explanation.	**Borrower** Yes	No	**Co-Borrower** Yes	No
a. Are there any outstanding judgments against you?	☐	☐	☐	☐
b. Have you been declared bankrupt within the past 7 years?	☐	☐	☐	☐
c. Have you had property foreclosed upon or given title or deed in lieu thereof in the last 7 years?	☐	☐	☐	☐
d. Are you a party to a lawsuit?	☐	☐	☐	☐
e. Have you directly or indirectly been obligated on any loan which resulted in foreclosure, transfer of title in lieu of foreclosure, or judgment? (This would include such loans as home mortgage loans, SBA loans, home improvement loans, educational loans, manufactured (mobile) home loans, any mortgage, financial obligation, bond, or loan guarantee. If "Yes," provide details, including date, name, and address of Lender, FHA or VA case number, if any, and reasons for the action.)	☐	☐	☐	☐

Freddie Mac Form 65 7/05 — Page 3 of 5 — Fannie Mae Form 1003 7/05

VII. DETAILS OF TRANSACTION		
j.	Subordinate financing	
k.	Borrower's closing costs paid by Seller	
l.	Other Credits (explain)	
m.	Loan amount (exclude PMI, MIP, Funding Fee financed)	
n.	PMI, MIP, Funding Fee financed	
o.	Loan amount (add m & n)	0.00
p.	Cash from/to Borrower (subtract j, k, l & o from i)	

VIII. DECLARATIONS	Borrower Yes	Borrower No	Co-Borrower Yes	Co-Borrower No
If you answer "Yes" to any questions a through i, please use continuation sheet for explanation.				
f. Are you presently delinquent or in default on any Federal debt or any other loan, mortgage, financial obligation, bond, or loan guarantee? If "Yes," give details as described in the preceding question.	☐	☐	☐	☐
g. Are you obligated to pay alimony, child support, or separate maintenance?	☐	☐	☐	☐
h. Is any part of the down payment borrowed?	☐	☐	☐	☐
i. Are you a co-maker or endorser on a note?	☐	☐	☐	☐
j. Are you a U.S. citizen?	☐	☐	☐	☐
k. Are you a permanent resident alien?	☐	☐	☐	☐
l. **Do you intend to occupy the property as your primary residence?** If "Yes," complete question m below.	☐	☐	☐	☐
m. Have you had an ownership interest in a property in the last three years?	☐	☐	☐	☐
(1) What type of property did you own—principal residence (PR), second home (SH), or investment property (IP)?	______		______	
(2) How did you hold title to the home—solely by yourself (S), jointly with your spouse (SP), or jointly with another person (O)?	______		______	

IX. ACKNOWLEDGEMENT AND AGREEMENT

Each of the undersigned specifically represents to Lender and to Lender's actual or potential agents, brokers, processors, attorneys, insurers, servicers, successors and assigns and agrees and acknowledges that: (1) the information provided in this application is true and correct as of the date set forth opposite my signature and that any intentional or negligent misrepresentation of this information contained in this application may result in civil liability, including monetary damages, to any person who may suffer any loss due to reliance upon any misrepresentation that I have made on this application, and/or in criminal penalties including, but not limited to, fine or imprisonment or both under the provisions of Title 18, United States Code, Sec. 1001, et seq.; (2) the loan requested pursuant to this application (the "Loan") will be secured by a mortgage or deed of trust on the property described in this application; (3) the property will not be used for any illegal or prohibited purpose or use; (4) all statements made in this application are made for the purpose of obtaining a residential mortgage loan; (5) the property will be occupied as indicated in this application; (6) the Lender, its servicers, successors or assigns may retain the original and/or an electronic record of this application, whether or not the Loan is approved; (7) the Lender and its agents, brokers, insurers, servicers, successors, and assigns may continuously rely on the information contained in the application, and I am obligated to amend and/or supplement the information provided in this application if any of the material facts that I have represented herein should change prior to closing of the Loan; (8) in the event that my payments on the Loan become delinquent, the Lender, its servicers, successors or assigns may, in addition to any other rights and remedies that it may have relating to such delinquency, report my name and account information to one or more consumer reporting agencies; (9) ownership of the Loan and/or administration of the Loan account may be transferred with such notice as may be required by law; (10) neither Lender nor its agents, brokers, insurers, servicers, successors or assigns has made any representation or warranty, express or implied, to me regarding the property or the condition or value of the property; and (11) my transmission of this application as an "electronic record" containing my "electronic signature," as those terms are defined in applicable federal and/or state laws (excluding audio and video recordings), or my facsimile transmission of this application containing a facsimile of my signature, shall be as effective, enforceable and valid as if a paper version of this application were delivered containing my original written signature.

Acknowledgement. Each of the undersigned hereby acknowledges that any owner of the Loan, its servicers, successors and assigns, may verify or reverify any information contained in this application or obtain any information or data relating to the Loan, for any legitimate business purpose through any source, including a source named in this application or a consumer reporting agency.

Borrower's Signature	Date	Co-Borrower's Signature	Date
X		X	

X. INFORMATION FOR GOVERNMENT MONITORING PURPOSES

The following information is requested by the Federal Government for certain types of loans related to a dwelling in order to monitor the lender's compliance with equal credit opportunity, fair housing and home mortgage disclosure laws. You are not required to furnish this information, but are encouraged to do so. The law provides that a lender may not discriminate either on the basis of this information, or on whether you choose to furnish it. If you furnish the information, please provide both ethnicity and race. For race, you may check more than one designation. If you do not furnish ethnicity, race, or sex, under Federal regulations, this lender is required to note the information on the basis of visual observation and surname if you have made this application in person. If you do not wish to furnish the information, please check the box below. (Lender must review the above material to assure that the disclosures satisfy all requirements to which the lender is subject under applicable state law for the particular type of loan applied for.)

BORROWER ☐ I do not wish to furnish this information	CO-BORROWER ☐ I do not wish to furnish this information
Ethnicity: ☐ Hispanic or Latino ☐ Not Hispanic or Latino	Ethnicity: ☐ Hispanic or Latino ☐ Not Hispanic or Latino
Race: ☐ American Indian or Alaska Native ☐ Asian ☐ Black or African American ☐ Native Hawaiian or Other Pacific Islander ☐ White	Race: ☐ American Indian or Alaska Native ☐ Asian ☐ Black or African American ☐ Native Hawaiian or Other Pacific Islander ☐ White
Sex: ☐ Female ☐ Male	Sex: ☐ Female ☐ Male

To be Completed by Interviewer	Interviewer's Name (print or type)	Name and Address of Interviewer's Employer
This application was taken by: ☐ Face-to-face interview ☐ Mail ☐ Telephone ☐ Internet	Interviewer's Signature — Date	
	Interviewer's Phone Number (incl. area code)	

CONTINUATION SHEET/RESIDENTIAL LOAN APPLICATION

Use this continuation sheet if you need more space to complete the Residential Loan Application. Mark **B** f or Borrower or **C** for Co-Borrower.	Borrower:	Agency Case Number:
	Co-Borrower:	Lender Case Number:

I/We fully understand that it is a Federal crime punishable by fine or imprisonment, or both, to knowingly make any false statements concerning any of the above facts as applicable under the provisions of Title 18, United States Code, Section 1001, et seq.

Borrower's Signature	Date	Co-Borrower's Signature	Date
X		X	

Freddie Mac Form 65 7/05 Page 5 of 5 Fannie Mae Form 1003 7/05

ANALYSIS OF THE BORROWER AND PROPERTY

Once the application has been completed, the lender can begin gathering other pertinent information about the buyer. Verification forms will be sent out to the buyer's employer, banks, other lenders, and any previous mortgage lender. A credit report will be ordered, and a preliminary title report will be prepared. An approved appraiser will also be contacted to appraise the property. After examining the application, the lender may also ask the buyer to submit further information such as:

- Investment account records or other documentation
- Tax returns (if buyer is self-employed or living on investment income)
- Any other documents relevant to a buyer's income or credit status

The lender will also be concerned with the source of the buyer's down payment. Savings, the previous sale of a home, or gifts are all acceptable sources of down payment, but the buyer is usually not allowed to use borrowed funds.

CREDIT SCORING. **By credit scoring,** the lender makes certain determinations regarding the credit of potential borrowers. While this is often not the only means of analysis, it provides a benchmark to compare the relative value of the borrower's qualifications. Credit scoring involves the lender assigning specified numerical values to different aspects of the borrower. These numbers are adjusted up and down based on the strength or weakness of a particular borrower's qualification. For example, a lengthy employment history with the same company would score higher than a person who just joined a new firm. The numbers are added up from all the different categories scored, and the borrower's application is given a credit score based on these various criteria and their respective scores.

EQUAL CREDIT OPPORTUNITY ACT. The Federal Equal Credit Opportunity Act prohibits discrimination in lending based on age, sex, race, marital status, color, religion, national origin, or receipt of public assistance. All people must be considered for credit equally on the basis of income adequacy, sufficient net worth, job stability, and satisfactory credit rating. The Equal Credit Opportunity Act states that a borrower need disclose to the lender only the amount of income he or she has which is necessary to obtain the loan. Lenders must apply their credit guidelines to each potential borrower in the same manner. (Note that age, marital status, and receipt of public assistance are protected classes under this law but not under the Federal Fair Housing Act.)

PROCESSING THE LOAN APPLICATION

When the credit report, verification forms, preliminary title report, and appraisal have all been received by the lender, a loan package is put together and submitted to the underwriting department. Loan underwriters thoroughly examine the loan package and then decide to approve, reject, or approve the loan with conditions. Conditional approval usually requires additional information, such as:

- Closing statement from the sale of the buyer's previous home
- Pay stubs to verify income
- A final inspection report

- A commitment for private mortgage insurance (which is always a condition for approving conventional loans with less than 20 percent down payment)

CLOSING THE LOAN

After the loan is approved and all conditions are met, the necessary documents are prepared for closing. The closing process ordinarily takes about one week if everything goes smoothly. Although the closing process is detailed in Chapter 12 of this book, we'll mention the highlights here.

The mechanics of closing are normally the responsibility of an escrow agent. This escrow agent may be an "in-house" escrow department of the lender, an independent escrow company, or a title insurance company. The escrow agent simultaneously follows the instructions of both buyer and seller. A certified copy of the escrow instructions must be provided to the lender. The escrow agent gathers all necessary documents (e.g., promissory note, mortgage, deed, etc.), making sure they're properly signed and calculates the various prorations, adjustments, and fees charged to each party. Finally, each party is given a settlement (closing) statement.

If there are no unforeseen problems during closing (e.g., the seller did not really have title to the property), loan papers are signed and sent to the lender's funding department. This department makes one final check to be sure that everything is in order. Loan funds are then disbursed to the proper parties accordingly.

V. QUALIFYING THE BUYER

Before making real estate loans, lenders evaluate borrowers to make sure they meet minimum qualifying standards. Qualifying standards can vary from lender to lender, but with lenders' increased dependence on selling their loans to the national secondary mortgage markets, a high degree of standardization has developed. The majority of lenders have incorporated Fannie Mae and Freddie Mac standards into their own conventional loan underwriting criteria.

Since most lenders use Fannie Mae and Freddie Mac conventional underwriting standards, it's important for real estate salespersons to know those standards to pre-qualify buyers and properties. If a loan is being considered as an FHA-insured or VA-guaranteed loan, different standards would apply. We'll discuss Fannie Mae and Freddie Mac qualifying standards for conventional loan underwriting first and take a look at differences between FHA and VA guidelines.

FANNIE MAE AND FREDDIE MAC QUALIFYING STANDARDS

According to Freddie Mac, "underwriting mortgage loans is an art, not a science. It can't be reduced to mathematical formulas, but requires sensitive weighing of many aspects of the loan." These aspects of a borrower's loan application include **income**, **net worth**, and **credit history**. In addition, math is involved.

INCOME. A borrower's income is considered adequate for a mortgage loan if the proposed payment of principal, interest, taxes, and insurance **(PITI) does not exceed 28 percent of stable monthly income**. This is called the **housing**

expense ratio. Stable monthly income is the borrower's gross monthly income from primary base employment and any secondary income considered reliable and likely to endure.

> **Example:**
>
> | | |
> |---|---|
> | $2,900 | stable monthly income |
> | x 0.28 | (28 percent maximum housing expense ratio) |
> | $ 812 | maximum PITI mortgage payment allowed |
>
> Proposed mortgage payment = $700, including PITI and PMI—**Acceptable.**

A second but equally important concern is that the **total borrower's debt does not exceed 36 percent of stable monthly income**. This is called a **total debt service ratio**. Total debt includes housing expenses (PITI and PMI), all installment debts with more than ten payments remaining, and alimony or child support.

> **Example:**
>
> | | |
> |---|---|
> | $2,900 | stable monthly income |
> | x 0.36 | (36 percent maximum total debt service ratio) |
> | $1,044 | maximum total debt allowed |
>
> | | |
> |---|---|
> | $1,044 | maximum total debt allowed |
> | - 225 | auto payment (18 payments remain) |
> | - 100 | child support |
> | $719 | maximum PITI mortgage payment allowed |
>
> Proposed mortgage payment = $700, including PITI and PMI—**Acceptable.**

The total debt service ratio is usually a more realistic measure of the borrower's ability to make the loan payments (and is usually the smaller number) because it takes into account all of the borrower's financial obligations. Since the borrower must qualify under both ratios, the smaller of the two—usually the total debt service ratio—is the maximum allowable mortgage payment.

FANNIE MAE RATIOS FOR 95 PERCENT LOANS. For loans exceeding 90 percent LTV ratios (95 percent loans), the **total debt service ratio is 33 percent** (the **housing expense ratio remains 28 percent**). These ratios may be exceeded (up to the standard ratio of 36 percent) only if there is sound justification which is documented by the lender.

DO THE MATH!

Qualifying a Buyer for a Conventional 90 Percent Loan

Let's see how easy it is to use the housing expense ratios and total debt service ratios to determine the maximum mortgage payment for which a borrower may qualify.

> **Example:** Susan Day's stable monthly income is $2,800. She has three debts: $190/mo. car payment, $65/mo. personal loan payment, and $35/mo. credit card payment. What's the maximum monthly mortgage payment she'll qualify for?

STEP 1: Take Susan's stable monthly income, and multiply that by the maximum housing expense ratio of 28 percent (0.28).

$2,800 x .28 = $784 This is the maximum mortgage payment (PITI) allowed under the first ratio.

STEP 2a: Take Susan's stable monthly income, and multiply that by the maximum total debt service ratio of 36 percent (0.36).

$2,800 x .36 = $1,008 This is the maximum total debt payments allowed under the second ratio.

STEP 2b: Take this total debt payments amount, and subtract Susan's other monthly long-term debts (not including mortgage payments).

$1,008 ($190 + $65 + $35) = $718 This is the maximum mortgage payment (PITI) allowed under the second ratio.

The maximum monthly mortgage payment Susan would qualify for is **$718**. Remember, Susan must qualify under both ratios, so the lower figure is the most Susan can get. Of course, if she could pay off some of her debts and reduce her total other long-term monthly obligations, she would be able to qualify for a larger mortgage payment.

Note: Mortgage payments determined by calculating total debt service ratio are likely to be smaller than with housing expense ratio because all monthly debts are counted.

Fannie Mae/Freddie Mac Ratios
Conventional, Fixed Rate Loans

Loan-to-Value	Housing Expense Ratio	Total Debt Service Ratio
90% or less LTV (10% or more down)	28%	36%
Fannie Mae: 95% Loan (5% down payment)	28%	33%

STABLE MONTHLY INCOME. Before deciding if there's a sufficient quantity of income, the lender must decide what income is acceptable as *stable* monthly income. **Stable income** is any income that can reasonably be expected to continue for the foreseeable future. This is figured as the **gross** base income of borrower(s); in addition, earnings from acceptable secondary sources are studied for quality (reliability) of income source and durability (probability of continuance) of income.

Secondary sources of income include bonuses, commissions, part-time earnings, overtime, pensions, disability, social security, interest-yielding investments, unemployment, welfare, alimony, child support, maintenance, or rental income.

CO-MORTGAGOR. A co-mortgagor can aid a primary borrower in qualifying for a loan. A co-mortgagor or co-borrower accepts joint liability for the loan by signing the promissory note and mortgage. Like the primary borrower, a co-mortgagor must have earnings, assets, and a credit history that are acceptable to the underwriter.

Keep in mind that co-mortgagors must be able to pay their own housing expense *and* part, if not all, of the proposed housing expense. Marginal co-mortgagors should not be relied on heavily and may do more harm than good to a loan application.

VERIFICATION OF INCOME. Fannie Mae and Freddie Mac now allow income verification by the borrower. The borrower can provide W-2 forms for the previous two years and payroll stubs for the previous 30-day period. Pay stubs must identify the borrower, employer, and the borrower's gross earnings for both the current pay period and year to date. Lenders then confirm employment and earnings by calling the employer.

NET WORTH. **Net worth** is determined by subtracting liabilities from total assets. According to Fannie Mae, "accumulation of net worth is a strong indication of credit worthiness." A borrower who has built up a significant amount of net worth from earnings, savings, and investment activities shows skill in managing financial affairs.

If a borrower has a marginal total debt service ratio, an above average net worth can offset this deficiency. Lenders know that net worth in liquid form can be used to pay unexpected bills or support a borrower when there's an interruption in income.

REQUIRED RESERVES AFTER CLOSING. As a safeguard against unexpected bills or temporary income loss and as an indicator of financial ability, Fannie Mae requires borrowers to have enough cash on deposit, or in highly liquid assets, to cover two months' mortgage payments (PITI and PMI) after paying the down payment and all closing costs. Freddie Mac guidelines require a minimum of two months' payments for owner-occupied loans and three to six months for non-owner-occupant loans.

CREDIT HISTORY. **Credit history** is a record of debt repayment detailing how a person paid credit accounts in the past as a guide to whether he or she is likely to pay accounts on time and as agreed in the future. **Debts** are any recurring monetary obligation that cannot be cancelled. For example, a car lease, student loan, or court-ordered child support are debts. Utilities and insurance premiums are not considered debts because they can be cancelled. Gray areas may involve doctor bills, but a payment schedule (e.g., for braces) makes it a debt. Borrowers must inform a lender of all debts even if they do not appear on a credit report.

As a part of the loan evaluation, underwriters analyze the borrower's (and co-borrower's) credit history by obtaining a credit report from a credit bureau. If the credit history shows a slow payment record or other derogatory credit information (suit, judgment, repossession, collection, foreclosure, or bankruptcy), a loan application could be declined or the borrower put into a high-risk (BC credit) category.

CREDIT SCORING. This is a means of assigning a numerical value to a person's credit history. Using objective numerical criteria is becoming popular as a means of avoiding potential claims of discrimination for using more subjective criteria. Credit scoring can be as simple as the lender assigning numeric values to different aspects of a loan application or as complex as the calculations performed by the various credit bureaus. The term **Beacon score** is used by the Equifax credit reporting agency, and this has become a generic term for all credit bureau reported scores. Numbers typically range from 400 to 900 with a lower score indicating a greater risk of default. As a point of reference, Freddie Mac considers borrowers with a Beacon score of 660 and above to be acceptable credit risks.

Poor credit doesn't always stop loans if credit problems can be explained to a lender's satisfaction.The circumstances causing the problems should have been temporary—such as loss of job, hospitalization, prolonged illness, death in the family, or divorce—and no longer exist. If prior and subsequent credit ratings have been good, the loan application might be approved.

EXPLAINING DEROGATORY CREDIT. When explaining derogatory credit to lenders, it's a mistake to blame misunderstandings on creditors. Borrowers must accept responsibility for their acts because lenders will be concerned that a reluctance to take responsibility for prior credit problems may happen again.

If a borrower's credit report is laced with derogatory credit for a period of years, there's probably little hope for loan approval. Perpetual credit problems could reflect an attitude instead of a circumstance, and lenders may presume this will continue. But credit problems are resolved with time, so never assume a buyer can't qualify for a loan. Refer him or her to a competent lender for an expert's opinion.

BILL CONSOLIDATION, REFINANCING. In the absence of derogatory ratings, other things can be revealed by a credit report that might indicate the borrower is a marginal credit risk. If an individual's credit pattern is one of continually increasing liabilities and periodically "bailing out" through refinancing and debt consolidation, he or she may be classified as a marginal risk. The pattern suggests a tendency to live beyond a prudent level. This is a subjective consideration likely to influence a lender's decision if a borrower is weak in other areas such as income or assets.

FHA QUALIFYING STANDARDS

FHA qualifying standards for net worth and credit history are similar to Fannie Mae and Freddie Mac but more liberal.

FHA allows a maximum housing expense ratio of 29 percent of stable monthly income. This is higher than Fannie Mae and Freddie Mac and allows a higher monthly housing payment. FHA's maximum payment includes PITI and must include monthly homeowner's association dues or assessments (if any) such as condominium fees.

FHA allows a maximum total debt service ratio of 41 percent of stable monthly income. This includes all debt payments owed (with 10 or more payments left) just like Fannie Mae and Freddie Mac.

VA QUALIFYING STANDARDS

VA qualifying standards with regard to net worth and credit history are similar to FHA, Fannie Mae, and Freddie Mac. **VA allows a total debt service ratio of 41 percent** (same as FHA), but VA also uses an additional qualifying component based on residual income. This means that when working with VA-guaranteed loans, two separate figures must be determined and analyzed: *residual income* and *total debt service ratio*.

Residual Income. Residual income is the amount of income a borrower has left after subtracting taxes, housing expense, and all recurring debt obligations. A veteran's residual income must meet VA's minimum requirements. Charts with these regional figures based on family size and loan amount can be obtained from VA.

Overall, FHA and VA guidelines are more liberal than Fannie Mae and Freddie Mac ratios and standards. A borrower who would be considered marginal by Fannie Mae and Freddie Mac standards might qualify more easily for an FHA or VA loan.

QUALIFYING INCOME EXPENSE RATIOS FOR CONVENTIONAL, FHA, AND VA LOANS

	Housing Expense Ratio	Total Debt Service Ratio	Residual Income
FannieMae/Freddie Mac CONVENTIONAL LTV 90% OR LESS	PITI NOT TO EXCEED 28% OF INCOME	Housing + Debts (10 or More PYMTS) NOT TO EXCEED 36% OF INCOME	NOT USED
Fannie Mae 95% LOANS	NOT TO EXCEED 28% OF INCOME	NOT TO EXCEED 33% OF INCOME	NOT USED
FHA	PITI NOT TO EXCEED 29% OF INCOME	HOUSING+DEBTS (10 OR MORE PYMTS) NOT TO EXCEED 41% OF INCOME	NOT USED
VA	NOT USED	HOUSING + ALL Recurring Debt Not to Exceed 41 % of Income	Residual Income Should Equal or Exceed Regional Figures for Family Size And Loan Amount

VI. SUB-PRIME LOANS

Sub-prime loans are loans that have more risks than are allowed in the conforming loan market. (These are also called **B-C Loans** or **B-C Credit**.) These alternative financing tools are growing in use and are filling a need by helping people with questionable credit reach their goal of home ownership. Some lenders and investors are willing to make these riskier loans because they can get much higher rates than they can with other real estate loans. For some people, it's the only way they may be able to buy a house and re-establish their credit. Many sub-prime lenders offer borrowers a chance to refinance their loans at lower interest rates after they pay on time for a given period of time.

With sub-prime lending, criteria for who gets approved—and at what interest rate—can vary greatly. Prime loans are made to customers with good credit. For these loans, borrowers can typically find interest rates posted in the newspaper. For customers with less-than-perfect credit who must get sub-prime loans, however, interest rates are quoted based on the risk that the lender associates with the loan. Sometimes larger down payments or secondary owner financing may be required by lenders who want to ensure the collateral can cover the loan amount.

Sub-prime mortgage rates are really determined in the assessment of the borrower's risk factors. A sub-prime borrower is matched to a series of risk profiles the lender has developed based on past experience by the lender and by the industry. To underwrite a sub-prime loan, the lender is not examining whether the borrower is worthy of credit as much as where he or she belongs on the risk scale. Credit scoring is a helpful factor, and appraisals are also important because the property may be the lender's only recourse in case of default. It takes an experienced underwriter to wade through the risk factors and pick a rate.

Chapter 13 Summary

1. **Real estate lenders** making residential loans are commercial banks, savings and loans, mortgage companies, and small players like mutual savings banks, real estate investment trusts, life insurance companies, pension plans, and individuals. Credit unions are source of home equity/improvement loans.
2. **Real estate finance instruments** are promissory notes, mortgages, trust deeds, and land contracts. Promissory notes are negotiable instruments (freely transferable from one party to another) if they contain all elements required by UCC. A note missing an element is still valid between the parties but may not be valid if transferred. A holder in due course is one who acquires a negotiable instrument in good faith and will get paid in instances where an original payee may not. If the maker signed a note due to fraudulent statements, a holder in due course can still get paid by the maker, but original payee can't. If there's forgery of a note, then holder in due course and payee can't get paid.

3. **Mortgages** are instruments that create a lien against property as security for payment of a note. In case of default, judicial foreclosure is the remedy: a foreclosure action is filed in court; an order of execution authorizes a sheriff's sale; advertising for three weeks before public auction, highest bidder gets confirmation of sale, and sheriff's deed is issued. Debtor can redeem up until confirmation of sale. Process is slow and expensive but has court authority.

4. **Trust deeds**: instruments held by third party as security for payment of note. Upon default, non-judicial foreclosure by power of sale clause. Not used in Ohio because lacks court authority. (Trust deed isn't same as trustee deed—transfer per will or trust document.) **Land contracts**: real estate installment agreements where buyer makes payments to seller for right to occupy and use land, but seller holds title until all, or most of, payments are made. Must be recorded in duplicate within 20 days. Upon default, if less than five years and less than 20 percent paid then forfeiture proceedings; if five plus years or more than 20 percent paid, then foreclosure. With land contract, difficult to borrow against equity.

5. **Clauses** in finance instruments include acceleration clause (entire loan due upon default or some other event, like sale of property), alienation clause (sale or transfer triggers lender rights, like due on sale, interest rate change or assumption fee), prepayment clause (provides penalty if paid off early), and subordination clause (later recorded mortgage takes priority over earlier recorded mortgage—used for land and construction loans.)

6. **Loan process has five steps**: meeting with lender, filling out loan application, analyzing borrower and property, processing loan application, and closing the loan. Employment history is relevant, but ***three most important items are income, net worth, and credit history***. Qualifying buyer for conventional loans, 90 percent LTV or lower: housing expense ratio (PITI) can't exceed 28 percent of stable monthly income, and the total debt service ratio can't exceed 36 percent; for FNMA 95 percent loans: housing expense ratio=28 percent or less, total debt service ratio=33 percent; FHA: housing expense (PITI)=29 percent, total debt service ratio=41 percent; VA loans: housing expense ratio isn't used, total debt service ratio=41 percent, residual income must equal regional figures for family size and loan amount.

Chapter 13 Quiz

1. ***Which of the following are* not *security instruments for real estate?***
   a. Promissory notes
   b. Mortgages
   c. Trust deeds
   d. Land contracts

2. ***To be a holder in due course:***
   a. One must be an original payee on a promissory note
   b. One must be a national secondary market investor such as Fannie Mae
   c. One must acquire a negotiable instrument in good faith for consideration
   d. One must be the original mortgagor

3. ***Upon debtor default, which of the following remedies is available to a mortgagee?***
   a. Non-judicial foreclosure
   b. Judicial foreclosure
   c. Power of sale clause
   d. Forfeiture

4. ***A debtor has an equitable right of redemption until which of the following events?***
   a. Foreclosure action filed
   b. Order of execution issued
   c. Confirmation of sale issued
   d. Sheriff's deed issued

5. ***Which of the following is* not *a typical clause found in real estate mortgage?***
   a. Acceleration clause
   b. Alienation clause
   c. Subordination clause
   d. Subliminal clause

6. ***Qualifying standards for Fannie Mae/Freddie Mac 90 percent LTV conventional loans are:***
   a. Total debt service ratio=28 percent, housing expense ratio=36 percent
   b. Housing expense ratio=28 percent, total debt service ratio=36 percent
   c. Total debt service ratio=33 percent, housing expense ratio=28 percent
   d. Housing expense ratio=29 percent, total debt service ratio=41 percent

7. ***Qualifying standards for FHA loans are:***
   a. Total debt service ratio=28 percent, housing expense ratio=36 percent
   b. Housing expense ratio=28 percent, total debt service ratio=36 percent
   c. Total debt service ratio=33 percent, housing expense ratio=28 percent
   d. Housing expense ratio=29 percent, total debt service ratio=41 percent

8. ***In addition to total debt service ratios, VA loans rely on which of the following?***
   a. Housing expense averaging
   b. Residual housing analysis
   c. Residual income analysis
   d. Cost averaging of housing

14 OVERVIEW OF REAL ESTATE APPRAISAL

CHAPTER OVERVIEW

Now that you understand the real estate market, real estate law, and real estate finance, it's time to discuss the important skill of appraisal. While only a small percentage of real estate agents choose to go into the appraisal field full time, salespeople need a general knowledge of how to value property for the buyers and sellers who are clients (and for the licensing exam).

This chapter will build on knowledge of how overall real estate prices are affected by the real estate market and focus on some specific factors that influence a particular piece of real estate. We'll also discuss the market value of property and some different definitions of value. We'll conclude the chapter by outlining the appraisal process and different types of appraisal reports in preparation for the in-depth discussion of the different approaches to appraisal in the next chapter.

KEY TERMS

Arm's Length Transaction
A transaction that occurred under typical conditions in the marketplace where each party was acting in his or her own best interests.

Conformity
"Rule" that says a particular home (or neighborhood) achieves maximum value when it's surrounded by homes that are similar in style and function.

Contribution
"Rule" that says a particular item or feature of a home is worth only what it actually contributes in value to that piece of property.

Highest and Best Use
The most profitable, legally permitted, feasible, and physically possible use of a piece of property.

Market Price
The price that was paid for a piece of real estate.

Market Value
The price that a piece of real estate is most likely to bring in a typical transaction.

Site
A plot of land with enhancements that make it ready for a building or structure.

Situs
Place where something exists; an area of preference, or preference by people for a certain location giving economic attributes (value) to the property.

Substitution
"Rule" that says an informed buyer will not pay more for a home than a comparable substitute.

I. THE NEED FOR APPRAISAL

Appraisal is an estimate of value of a piece of property as of a certain date. An important element of appraisal is that this estimate or opinion of value be defendable and supported by objective evidence and data.

Appraisals are performed for a variety of reasons. Most people want to know what their property is worth when they're looking to buy or sell, but appraisals are necessary for other reasons like loans, insurance, and taxes.

You must be a trained real estate appraiser for your opinion to count for these third parties. Be careful when dealing with clients so they do not accept your knowledge of appraisal as being a definitive authority in that discipline. It takes years of skill and experience to gain a true understanding of appraisal. The knowledge gained from this chapter and the textbook can help guide clients (and will come in handy on the licensing exam) but should not be used instead of an expert appraisal.

II. FACTORS THAT AFFECT VALUE

As we discussed previously, there are several factors that influence the real estate market. Economic, governmental, and social factors all play different, but important, roles in the value of land. These influence the value of real estate in a given area as well as having an individual effect on a given piece of real estate. A good appraiser is aware of these factors and how to weigh them when subjective criteria must be applied to a given factor in an overall appraisal.

BROAD MARKET FACTORS

The two most important factors we've discussed that may affect a specific piece of property are **supply and demand** and **uniqueness and scarcity**.

SUPPLY AND DEMAND. A quick review of the supply and demand model for the real estate market shows when prices are high due to a temporary housing shortage, the supply of housing in a given area will increase after a short time lag needed for the market to respond. This trend may be noted in an appraisal if the value of the subject home is higher than expected because there is still a housing shortage in the area. Conversely, an appraiser may have to justify lowering the appraisal value of a particular house because there's a temporary glut in the market, such as when a major company closes, which hurts the economic base of an area.

Other reasons for a supply and demand situation that may be noted on an appraisal may be a sharp rise in the appreciation rate for houses in a given area leveling off as more houses became available due to more sellers or increased construction, or an increase in value because of a new company that has announced plans to move to the area.

UNIQUENESS AND SCARCITY. These factors can influence the broad real estate market as well as a particular piece of real estate. Scarcity is tied to the supply and demand model and specifically relates to the fact that there's a limited amount of real estate within a geographical region. When people want to live in a certain area, they must compete with other people who want to live there for the limited supply of land in that area. Scarcity may be noted on a real estate appraisal by indicating the subject property is the last undeveloped lot in a neighborhood, perhaps justifying a slightly higher valuation.

Uniqueness means no two pieces of real estate are exactly the same and it can be good or bad depending on perspective. A "unique" feature of a house could actually make it less desirable. The owner of a custom-built house who had eccentric taste may have included features that other people do not want in their house, or a unique feature that adds character to a house could make it more desirable. These features, and their effect on the appraiser's opinion of value, should be noted on the appraisal form.

PROPERTY SPECIFIC FACTORS

There are additional factors to consider when valuing a specific piece of property like **highest and best use**, **location**, **substitution**, **conformity**, and **contribution**.

HIGHEST AND BEST USE. **Highest and best use** is the most profitable, legally permitted, feasible, and physically possible use of a piece of property. This is the *most important property-specific factor* that an appraiser considers before making a determination of value. A number of factors go into making this determination. With most houses, this determination isn't necessary since they're in the middle of residential neighborhoods. Highest and best use becomes a vital consideration when examining vacant land or land that has changed zoning since the original structure was built.

If a house sits on a widened street, surrounded by commercial buildings, it's very likely that the land would be more valuable if it were put to a commercial use. The zoning laws must permit the intended use, and we must be able to build the proposed structure on the land. All of these factors must be considered when an appraiser is valuing a piece of real estate.

LOCATION. **Location** is the exact position of a piece of real estate. Location can be talked about with respect to a given neighborhood and within the neighborhood itself. It's easy to understand that homes in a growing, popular, and prosperous neighborhood are more desirable than those in other neighborhoods. It's also important to recognize that each individual home's location within that neighborhood affects its value. A home on a corner lot next to the park or in a cul-de-sac would have a higher value than a home next to a railroad track.

Situs is a term used to describe the place where something exists: an area of preference, or preference by people for a certain location thus giving economic attributes (value) to the property. Remember, in real estate the three most important aspects of a house (or land) are *location, location, location*.

"BEST" AND "WORST" HOMES. An important corollary to the concept of location is the effect of surrounding homes on valuation. There are technical terms often used to describe this concept, but the theory needs to be clear. The value of the "worst" home in a given area is positively affected by the other homes in the area. The value of this theoretical "worst" home can only go so low because the desirability of the other homes in the neighborhood will keep it from falling too far. Conversely, the value of the "best" home in a given area is negatively affected by the other homes in the area. The value of this theoretical "best" home can only go so high because, if the other homes in the neighborhood are less expensive, people who can afford this "best" home will be attracted to other neighborhoods.

For example, if all the homes in one neighborhood average $110,000, a run-down home there that might command only $50,000 in another area is positively affected by the fact that people will pay more in this particular neighborhood, with the anticipation that improving the property will provide a higher return on investment. Conversely, in the same neighborhood where the average home price is $110,000, a home that is much larger than the average with a swimming pool and other amenities that would help it command $350,000 in another area is negatively affected by the fact that people who can afford this much for a home probably want to live in a neighborhood surrounded by homes similar in value, and may fear a lower future value there.

SUBSTITUTION. **Substitution** says that an informed buyer will not pay more for a home than a comparable substitute. Although each home is said to be unique, there's a limit to what a buyer will pay. No one really knows where that point is until he or she tries to sell the home for too much, and no one buys it. The theory of substitution can also be applied to items within a home. When an appraiser determines the value of a fireplace in an area where most homes don't have one, the appraiser must take into account that a buyer is not going to pay more for that home than he or she would for a similar home plus the cost of adding a fireplace to it. In other words, if a fireplace costs $2,500 to add to a typical home in the area, an appraiser can't justify adding much more than that to the value of a home.

CONFORMITY. **Conformity** means a particular home achieves its maximum value when surrounded by homes that are similar in style and function. This applies to neighborhoods as well. Neighborhoods, as a whole, are more desirable when there is a general similarity in utility and value for all homes there. A home that stands out as being too different from the rest is worth less than that same home would be if it were in a different, more homogeneous neighborhood.

CONTRIBUTION. **Contribution** means a particular item or feature of a home is worth what it actually contributes in value to that piece of property. If a five- bedroom home is not desirable, putting an addition onto a house to add that fifth bedroom doesn't increase the value of the home. The owner of the house may want or need a fifth bedroom, but he or she should not expect that to add to the value of the home when it's sold. The value of an item or improvement is equal only to what a prospective buyer is willing to pay for it.

III. MARKET VALUE OF PROPERTY

Market value is the theoretical price that a piece of real estate is likely to bring in a typical transaction. A typical transaction may also be referred to as an **arm's length transaction** meaning that the transaction occurred under typical conditions in the marketplace, and each of the parties was acting in his or her own best interests.

Those conditions are:

1. The buyer paid cash for the property at closing or obtained a mortgage through a lender to pay the seller the agreed upon price at closing.
2. The seller did not grant any unusual payment concessions such as untypical financing concessions.
3. The buyer and seller are not related in any way.
4. The buyer and seller are both acting in their own best interests.
5. The buyer and seller are not acting out of undue haste or duress.
6. The buyer and seller are both reasonably informed about the property and its potential uses.
7. The property has been available on the market for a reasonable period of time.

All of these factors should be taken into consideration when determining a property's value. An appraiser may not be able to ascertain all of these points, but the effort is important because these points affect the sale price of a piece of property and its perceived value. If the seller was forced to sell because of a lost job, this would tend to lower the sale price of the subject home. Or if the seller agreed to some type of owner financing, this would allow the sale price to be higher. A good appraiser takes all of these things into account.

DEFINING VALUE

We've defined market value as the theoretical price that a piece of real estate is most likely to bring in a typical transaction. But the *value* of a piece of real estate should not be confused with its *price*. **Market value** is **expected price**; **market price** is **actual price**. Both value and price may have nothing to do with what the property actually *cost* to build.

There are additional types of value that are used for other purposes. The **loan value** is the amount of money a lender is willing let someone borrow to finance a particular piece of property. The **insurance value** is the amount that the property can be insured for, usually only representing the replacement costs of the structure and disregarding any value for the land. The **assessed value** is the amount of value that is used to calculate taxes due, and usually represents a percentage of the market value (e.g., market value x 35 percent = assessed value for taxes).

Furthermore, market value of property should not be confused with property valuation. Property valuation refers to the actual approaches appraisers use to determine market value for a piece of property. These approaches—sales comparison approach, cost approach, and income approach—will be discussed in the next chapter.

IV. APPRAISAL PROCESS

Regardless of the approach used by the appraiser to determine the value of a piece of property, there is a step-by-step procedure that should be followed in all cases. ***The steps*** in the appraisal process are:

1. **Define** the appraisal: state the problem.
2. Define the **data and sources** necessary to do the appraisal.
3. **Collect** and analyze the relevant data.
4. **Determine the highest and best use** for the subject property.
5. Determine the **value of the land** separate from the structures.
6. **Estimate** the value of the subject property using each of the three approaches.
7. **Reconcile** estimates of value using the three approaches.
8. **Report** conclusions of the valuation process including all data used and final value estimate.

DEFINE THE APPRAISAL/STATE THE PROBLEM

Defining the appraisal has several components. First, the subject property must be identified by locating the property physically, checking the legal description, and verifying these against the given street address.

Second, the purpose of the appraisal needs to be identified. This is important because there are different reasons to value property. An insurance appraisal has different goals and requires different criteria than a loan appraisal. Also, the purpose of the appraisal may be a valuation for purposes of selling the entire bundle of rights or for selling some of the rights separately.

Third, the effective date of the appraisal and any other relevant factors should be noted because the estimate of value contained in an appraisal is ***valid only as of that date***. An appraisal is ***not*** a look into the future. The effective date may tell someone else looking at the report whether a particular fact may have been known at the time. For example, if a company has announced a new factory in the area, it could have a significant influence on the value of the subject property. Other relevant factors should be noted on the report so someone looking at the report can tell if it reflects such a fact.

DEFINE THE DATA AND SOURCES NECESSARY

After you've adequately defined the appraisal and all of its components, it's time to decide which data and sources are necessary to carry out the appraisal. Time permitted to complete the appraisal and the number of people devoted to the project may influence your choice of sources. Nevertheless, every effort must be made to be sure the appraisal is not compromised because of lack of time or resources. Typical information necessary for an accurate appraisal includes regional, city, and neighborhood economic data, governmental regulations such as zoning laws, construction cost information for the area, and data on other recent property sales in the area.

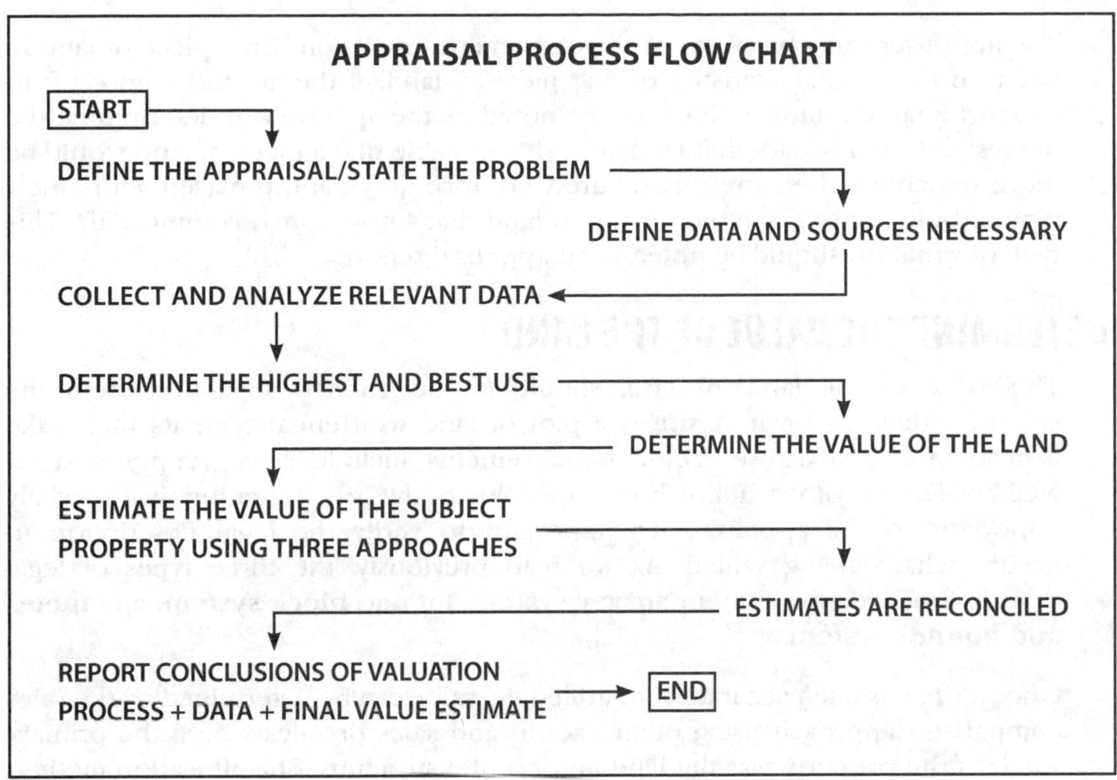

COLLECT AND ANALYZE THE RELEVANT DATA

The experienced appraiser will have access to typical information required for an appraisal since most appraisers work within a given region or area. Professional appraisers keep updated files regarding data on economic trends in an area as well as changes in state and local laws. Expert appraisers also maintain a number of different cost manuals that break down building and construction costs in a given region. Comparable sales data can be obtained from the same resources used by other real estate professionals. Finally, computer databases have become popular methods of regularly updating all these areas of information.

This information is collected and analyzed, giving proper weight to each category depending on the ultimate goals of the appraisal. For example, if an appraisal is for an insurance company, the information provided by the cost manuals would probably be given considerable weight as the cost approach method is most relevant. The cost approach method is still done in conjunction with the other methods, but it does not replace the sales comparison approach or income approach because all methods are used whenever possible.

DETERMINE THE HIGHEST AND BEST USE

Determining the highest and best use for the subject property is an important exercise. The goal is to determine whether the property is being used for its most profitable permitted use. Highest and best use is always considered, although sometimes it is more important than others. With homes in a residential neighborhood, this isn't an issue, but with vacant land in an area that's changing, growing, or expanding, it can be a significant point.

The appraiser must be aware of all government restrictions on a piece of land in addition to the characteristics of that piece of land. If the ground is too soft to support a large building, this must be noted by the appraiser in determining the highest and best use for that land. Also, it's possible that a piece of land would be more valuable if the current structure were torn down and replaced with a new type of building (e.g., an old house on land that's now zoned commercial). This type of situation should be noted in an appraisal report.

DETERMINE THE VALUE OF THE LAND

The value of the land, or **site**, should be determined separately from the structure that sits on it. A **site** is a plot of land with enhancements that make it ready for a structure. These enhancements include sewer, septic system, well, water, or other utility hook ups. When the site valuation is especially important to the appraisal, it's important to verify the legal description to ensure what's being valued. As we read previously, the three types of legal descriptions are **government survey system**, **lot and block system,** and **metes and bounds system**.

Once a site has been accurately identified, its value can be determined by the sales comparison approach using other vacant land sales or sales where the primary value of the property was the land and not the structure. The allocation method can also be used, which takes a ratio of total land value to site value that is typical in the area. For example, the site alone may represent 1/6 of the total value of a piece of real estate, meaning that the building on the land contributes 5/6 of the total value.

ESTIMATE VALUE USING THE THREE APPROACHES

The value of the subject property should be determined using each of the three approaches, which will be discussed in the next chapter. Generally, the sales comparison approach is the most useful and accurate in determining market value. This is especially true for houses. The cost approach is best suited for properties that are unique or not sold often enough for adequate sales comparison data. The income approach is best suited for commercial or investment properties. It's best to use all three approaches.

ESTIMATES ARE RECONCILED

Reconcile estimates of value from all three approaches to arrive at the best estimate of value. Reconciliation involves giving each method an appropriate weight depending on the type of property being analyzed and the amount and accuracy of data available. (The estimates from each of the three approaches are ***never*** averaged.) An appraiser's experience is critical in deciding the importance of the results and conclusions of the overall appraisal effort.

REPORT CONCLUSIONS

The final step of the valuation process is to prepare and submit a report of the conclusions from all data gathered and analyzed. The report should include all data, including specific references to support conclusions and a final value estimate for the subject property. Report types used under the Uniform Standards of Professional Appraisal Practice (USPAP) are the **Self-Contained Appraisal Report**, **Summary Appraisal Report,** and **Restricted Appraisal Report**.

The **Uniform Residential Appraisal Report (URAR)** form is a standard appraisal report form used by lenders and appraisers because it has been developed and approved by secondary mortgage market players Fannie Mae and Freddie Mac. As the name implies, it is used for residential appraisals and is preferred by lenders because it is standardized, allowing residential properties to be compared in a consistent manner.

There are several types of pre-printed **appraisal report forms** available, and appraisers simply fill in the blanks. This makes it easy to do comparisons between properties and handle large volumes of appraisals. Report forms are often used by secondary market players (e.g., Fannie Mae), government entities (e.g., FHA), large lenders, and insurance and tax evaluations. The reports, though simple and concise, must still be supported by strong evidence and data to support the value conclusions. Reports often contain photos and other documentation.

Narrative Format. The **narrative format**, rather than using a form is a thesis format that allows the appraiser to comment fully on the opinions and conclusions of the appraisal. Narrative reports typically contain more complete data and documentation.

V. COMPETITIVE ANALYSIS

A **competitive market analysis (CMA)**, also referred to as a **comparable market analysis**, is a method of determining the approximate market value of a home by comparing the subject property to other homes that have sold, are presently for sale, or did not sell in a given area. This is **not** the equivalent of an appraisal but an exercise performed by real estate agents to assist clients in determining a suggested figure at which they could buy or sell a home.

A typical CMA does not involve the mass collection of data that the other three appraisal approaches use. Furthermore, a CMA tends to be more subjective because it depends on visual impressions of the various properties and does not involve the same amount of detail as a true appraisal. Finally, a CMA gives different weights to properties depending on how quickly they sold or have been for sale on the market.

Uniform Residential Appraisal Report

815
File # 18988

The purpose of this summary appraisal report is to provide the lender/client with an accurate, and adequately supported, opinion of the market value of the subject property.

SUBJECT

Property Address 22 OAKWOOD DRIVE | City WESTERVILLE | State OH | Zip Code 43081

Borrower CHRISTOPHER S. JONES | Owner of Public Record JAMES R. & MARIA S. HOLDER | County FRANKLIN

Legal Description LOT #27, PHASE II, LAKE RIDGE SUBDIVISION

Assessor's Parcel # 62-42316000 | Tax Year 2004 | R.E. Taxes $ 4,397.00

Neighborhood Name LAKE RIDGE SUBDIVISION | Map Reference 45 P40 | Census Tract 0071.93

Occupant [X] Owner [ ] Tenant [ ] Vacant | Special Assessments $ NONE | [ ] PUD | HOA $ N/A [ ] per year [ ] per month

Property Rights Appraised [X] Fee Simple [ ] Leasehold [ ] Other (describe)

Assignment Type [X] Purchase Transaction [ ] Refinance Transaction [ ] Other (describe)

Lender/Client SECOND FEDERAL MORTGAGE | Address 2723 NORTH MAIN STREET, HILLIARD, OHIO

Is the subject property currently offered for sale or has it been offered for sale in the twelve months prior to the effective date of this appraisal? [X] Yes [ ] No

Report data source(s) used, offering price(s), and date(s). THE SUBJECT HAS BEEN LISTED THROUGH THE COLUMBUS MULTIPLE LISTING SERVICE FOR $179,900. THE PROPERTY HAS BEEN LISTED APPROXIMATELY 35 +/- DAYS.

CONTRACT

I [X] did [ ] did not analyze the contract for sale for the subject purchase transaction. Explain the results of the analysis of the contract for sale or why the analysis was not performed. THE CURRENT AGREEMENT TO PURCHASE INCLUDES THE FOLLOWING PERSONALTIES: RANGE, REFRIGERATOR AND MISCELLANEOUS WINDOW COVERINGS. NONE ARE CONSIDERED TO CONTRIBUTE SIGNIFICANT VALUE TO THE TRANSACTION.

Contract Price $ $178,000 | Date of Contract 6/1/2005 | Is the property seller the owner of public record? [X] Yes [ ] No | Data Source(s) FRANKLIN CO. REC.

Is there any financial assistance (loan charges, sale concessions, gift or downpayment assistance, etc.) to be paid by any party on behalf of the borrower? [X] Yes [ ] No

If Yes, report the total dollar amount and describe the items to be paid. $3,000.00 THE SELLER IS PAYING UP TO $3,000 TOWARD THE PURCHASER'S POINTS AND/OR CLOSING COSTS.

NEIGHBORHOOD

Note: Race and the racial composition of the neighborhood are not appraisal factors.

Neighborhood Characteristics				One-Unit Housing Trends				One-Unit Housing			Present Land Use %	
Location	[ ] Urban	[X] Suburban	[ ] Rural	Property Values	[X] Increasing	[ ] Stable	[ ] Declining	PRICE		AGE	One-Unit	90 %
Built-Up	[ ] Over 75%	[X] 25-75%	[ ] Under 25%	Demand/Supply	[ ] Shortage	[X] In Balance	[ ] Over Supply	$ (000)		(yrs)	2-4 Unit	0 %
Growth	[X] Rapid	[ ] Stable	[ ] Slow	Marketing Time	[X] Under 3 mths	[ ] 3-6 mths	[ ] Over 6 mths	155	Low	2	Multi-Family	0 %
								279	High	9	Commercial	0 %
								180	Pred.	5	Other	10 %

Neighborhood Boundaries SPRINGHILL DRIVE TO THE NORTH, STONERIDGE DRIVE TO THE EAST, FLOWER AVENUE TO THE SOUTH, CUSTER DRIVE TO THE WEST.

Neighborhood Description THE IMMEDIATE MARKET AREA IS PREDOMINATELY SINGLE-FAMILY HOUSING OF VARIOUS STYLES WITH SCATTERED UPPER-MID RANGE CUSTOM CONSTRUCTION. PROXIMITY TO SERVICES, EMPLOYMENT, AND RECREATION IS CONSIDERED AVERAGE. OTHER LAND USE IS THE INFLUENCE OF A PUBLIC PARK WITHIN THE DEFINED NEIGHBORHOOD.

Market Conditions (including support for the above conclusions) INTEREST RATES APPEAR TO BE STABLE AND REMAIN FAVORABLE, WITH MANY FINANCING AVENUES AVAILABLE. ONGOING NEW CONSTRUCTION SUPPORTS STEADY TO RAPID GROWTH PATTERN OF THE OVERALL MARKET. EXISTING HOUSING RESALES COUPLED WITH NEW CONSTRUCTION MAINTAIN SUPPLY/DEMAND IN BALANCE.

SITE

Dimensions 110' X 150' | Area 16,500 SQ.FT. | Shape RECTANGULAR | View RESID. HOUSING

Specific Zoning Classification R-4 | Zoning Description LOW DENSITY RESIDENTIAL DISTRICT

Zoning Compliance [X] Legal [ ] Legal Nonconforming (Grandfathered Use) [ ] No Zoning [ ] Illegal (describe)

Is the highest and best use of subject property as improved (or as proposed per plans and specifications) the present use? [X] Yes [ ] No If No, describe

Utilities	Public	Other (describe)		Public	Other (describe)	Off-site Improvements - Type	Public	Private
Electricity	[X]	[ ]	Water	[X]	[ ]	Street ASPHALT	[X]	[ ]
Gas	[X]	[ ]	Sanitary Sewer	[X]	[ ]	Alley NONE	[ ]	[ ]

FEMA Special Flood Hazard Area [ ] Yes [X] No | FEMA Flood Zone X | FEMA Map # 39049C0069H | FEMA Map Date 4/21/1999

Are the utilities and off-site improvements typical for the market area? [X] Yes [ ] No If No, describe

Are there any adverse site conditions or external factors (easements, encroachments, environmental conditions, land uses, etc.)? [ ] Yes [X] No If Yes, describe

NO ADVERSE SITE CONDITIONS OR ENCROACHMENTS HAVE BEEN NOTED. FLOOD INFORMATION IS PER FLOODSOURCE FLOOD MAPPING SERVICE, AND IS NOT TO BE RELIED UPON FOR FLOOD INSURANCE DETERMINATION. THE CLIENT SHOULD RELY UPON THEIR FLOOD CERTIFICATION SOURCE FOR FINAL DETERMINATION.

IMPROVEMENTS

General Description		Foundation		Exterior Description	materials/condition	Interior	materials/condition
Units [X] One [ ] One with Accessory Unit		[ ] Concrete Slab	[X] Crawl Space	Foundation Walls	POURED CONC.	Floors	WOOD/CRPT/CER
# of Stories	2	[ ] Full Basement	[X] Partial Basement	Exterior Walls	VINYL/BRICK	Walls	DRYWALL
Type [X] Det. [ ] Att. [ ] S-Det./End Unit		Basement Area	642 sq.ft.	Roof Surface	DIM. SHINGLE	Trim/Finish	STND. OAK
[X] Existing [ ] Proposed [ ] Under Const.		Basement Finish	75 %	Gutters & Downspouts	ALUMINUM	Bath Floor	CERAMIC
Design (Style)	COLONIAL/2ST	[ ] Outside Entry/Exit	[X] Sump Pump	Window Type	DOUBLE HUNG	Bath Wainscot	CERAMIC
Year Built	1999	Evidence of [ ] Infestation		Storm Sash/Insulated	INSULATED	Car Storage [ ] None	
Effective Age (Yrs)	3 YEARS	[ ] Dampness [ ] Settlement		Screens	YES	[X] Driveway # of Cars	2
Attic	[ ] None	Heating [X] FWA [ ] HWBB [ ] Radiant		Amenities	[ ] Woodstove(s) #	Driveway Surface	CONCRETE
[ ] Drop Stair	[ ] Stairs	[ ] Other	Fuel NAT. GAS	[X] Fireplace(s) # 1	[X] Fence WD. PRIV.	[X] Garage # of Cars	2
[ ] Floor	[X] Scuttle	Cooling [X] Central Air Conditioning		[X] Patio/Deck REAR	[X] Porch FRONT	[ ] Carport # of Cars	
[ ] Finished	[ ] Heated	[ ] Individual	[ ] Other	[ ] Pool	[X] Other B-I SPA	[X] Att. [ ] Det.	[ ] Built-in

Appliances [P] Refrigerator [P] Range/Oven [X] Dishwasher [X] Disposal [X] Microwave [ ] Washer/Dryer [X] Other (describe) TRASH COMPACTOR

Finished area **above** grade contains: 7 Rooms 3 Bedrooms 2.1 Bath(s) 1,952 Square Feet of Gross Living Area Above Grade

Additional features (special energy efficient items, etc.). MONITORED SECURITY AND FIRE ALARM SYSTEM. GARAGE HAS FINISHED INTERIOR, 2 ELECTRIC DOOR OPENERS AND BUILT-IN STORAGE AREA.

Describe the condition of the property (including needed repairs, deterioration, renovations, remodeling, etc.). THE SUBJECT WAS FOUND TO BE IN OVERALL ABOVE AVERAGE CONDITION AND REASONABLY MAINTAINED. THE EFFECTIVE AGE IS SLIGHTLY LESS THAN ACTUAL DUE TO OVERALL CONDITION.

Are there any physical deficiencies or adverse conditions that affect the livability, soundness, or structural integrity of the property? [ ] Yes [X] No If Yes, describe

Does the property generally conform to the neighborhood (functional utility, style, condition, use, construction, etc.)? [X] Yes [ ] No If No, describe

Freddie Mac Form 70 March 2005 | Page 1 of 6 | Fannie Mae Form 1004 March 2005

Uniform Residential Appraisal Report

815
File # 18988

There are 7 comparable properties currently offered for sale in the subject neighborhood ranging in price from $ 174,900 to $ 192,500 .

There are 12 comparable sales in the subject neighborhood within the past twelve months ranging in sale price from $ 168,500 to $ 191,000 .

SALES COMPARISON APPROACH

FEATURE	SUBJECT	COMPARABLE SALE # 1		COMPARABLE SALE # 2		COMPARABLE SALE # 3	
Address	22 OAKWOOD DRIVE WESTERVILLE, OH 43081	21 VALLEYVIEW COURT WESTERVILLE, OHIO		337 CHRIS COURT WESTERVILLE, OHIO		321 PEARSON DRIVE WESTERVILLE, OHIO	
Proximity to Subject		0.37 MILE NORTHEAST		0.33 MILE NORTH		0.62 MILE SOUTHEAST	
Sale Price	$ $178,000		$ 180,000		$ 185,000		$ 172,000
Sale Price/Gross Liv. Area	$ 91.19 sq.ft.	$ 89.82 sq.ft.		$ 97.16 sq.ft.		$ 99.48 sq.ft.	
Data Source(s)		FRANKLIN CO. AUDITOR		FRANKLIN CO. AUDITOR		FRANKLIN CO. AUDITOR	
Verification Source(s)		COLS. MLS, BROKER		COLS. MLS, BROKER		COLS. MLS, BROKER	
VALUE ADJUSTMENTS	DESCRIPTION	DESCRIPTION	+(-) $ Adjustment	DESCRIPTION	+(-) $ Adjustment	DESCRIPTION	+(-) $ Adjustment
Sales or Financing Concessions		CONV NONE		CONV SELLER PAID	-5,000	CONV NONE	
Date of Sale/Time		4/30/2005		3/5/2005		5/14/2005	
Location	INSIDE LOT	INSIDE LOT		INSIDE LOT		INSIDE LOT	
Leasehold/Fee Simple	FEE SIMPLE	FEE SIMPLE		FEE SIMPLE		FEE SIMPLE	
Site	16,500 SQ.FT.	17,200 SQ. FT.		15,740 SQ. FT		13,650 SQ. FT.	
View	RES/AVG	RES/AVG		PARK/GOOD	-2,500	RES/AVG	
Design (Style)	COLONIAL/2ST	COLONIAL/2ST		COLONIAL/2ST		COLONIAL/2ST	
Quality of Construction	AVERAGE	AVERAGE		AVERAGE		AVERAGE	
Actual Age	6 YEARS	5 YEARS		6 YEARS		8 YEARS	
Condition	GOOD	GOOD		GOOD		AVERAGE	+2,500
Above Grade Room Count (Total / Bdrms. / Baths)	7 / 3 / 2.1	6 / 3 / 2.1		8 / 3 / 2.1		7 / 3 / 2	+500
Gross Living Area	1,952 sq.ft.	2,004 sq.ft.	-500	1,904 sq.ft.	+500	1,729 sq.ft.	+2,200
Basement & Finished Rooms Below Grade	642 Sq.Ft. 2 RMS, F BA	1,002 SQ. FT. UNFINISHED	-2,000 +3,000	700 SQ. FT. 1 RM. FIN	+2,000	600 SQ. FT. 2 RMS, F BA	
Functional Utility	AVERAGE	AVERAGE		AVERAGE		AVERAGE	
Heating/Cooling	GFA/CENTRAL	GFA/CENTRAL		GFA/CENTRAL		GFA/CENTRAL	
Energy Efficient Items	TYPICAL	TYPICAL		TYPICAL		TYPICAL	
Garage/Carport	2-C ATT GAR	2-C ATT GAR		2-C ATT GAR		2-C ATT GAR	
Porch/Patio/Deck	PORCH, PATIO	PORCH, DECK		PORCH, PATIO		PORCH,DECK	
	B-I SPA	NONE	+500	IN-GRD POOL	-500	B-I SPA	
	WD PRIV FNC	WD PRIV FNC		WD PRIV FNC		NONE	+500
	FIREPLACE	FIREPLACE		2 FIREPLACES	-1,000	FIREPLACE	
Net Adjustment (Total)		☒ + ☐ -	$ 1,000	☐ + ☒ -	$ -6,500	☒ + ☐ -	$ 5,700
Adjusted Sale Price of Comparables		Net Adj. 0.6 % Gross Adj. 3.3 %	$ 181,000	Net Adj. 3.5 % Gross Adj. 6.2 %	$ 178,500	Net Adj. 3.3 % Gross Adj. 3.3 %	$ 177,700

I ☒ did ☐ did not research the sale or transfer history of the subject property and comparable sales. If not, explain

My research ☐ did ☒ did not reveal any prior sales or transfers of the subject property for the three years prior to the effective date of this appraisal.

Data Source(s) FRANKLIN COUNTY AUDITOR

My research ☒ did ☐ did not reveal any prior sales or transfers of the comparable sales for the year prior to the date of sale of the comparable sale.

Data Source(s) FRANKLIN COUNTY AUDITOR

Report the results of the research and analysis of the prior sale or transfer history of the subject property and comparable sales (report additional prior sales on page 3).

ITEM	SUBJECT	COMPARABLE SALE #1	COMPARABLE SALE #2	COMPARABLE SALE #3
Date of Prior Sale/Transfer	NONE IN 36 MONTHS	9/23/2004	NONE IN 12 MONTHS	NONE IN 12 MONTHS
Price of Prior Sale/Transfer		$155,000		
Data Source(s)		FRANKLIN CO AUDITOR		
Effective Date of Data Source(s)		6/3/2005		

Analysis of prior sale or transfer history of the subject property and comparable sales RESEARCH REVEALED THAT SALE #1 TRANSFERRED ON 9/23/2004 FOR $155,000. FURTHER INQUIRY WITH THE SELLER IN THE MOST RECENT TRANSACTION REVEALED THAT THE PURCHASE WAS VIA SHERRIFF'S AUCTION. COSMETIC RENOVATIONS WERE PERFORMED PRIOR TO THE PROPERTY BEING RE-MARKETED.

Summary of Sales Comparison Approach THE SALES REFLECT A REASONABLE VALUE RANGE. ALL SALES ARE FROM THE IMMEDIATE MARKET AREA. CORRELATION IS TOWARD THE UPPER PART OF THE VALUE RANGE, WITH TWO OF THE THREE SALES INDICATING THAT DIRECTION. THESE SALES ARE THE MOST RECENT AND REQUIRE THE FEWEST NET ADJUSTMENTS.

Indicated Value by Sales Comparison Approach $ 178,000

RECONCILIATION

Indicated Value by: Sales Comparison Approach $ 178,000 **Cost Approach (if developed) $** 182,822 **Income Approach (if developed) $** N/A

THE COST APPROACH LENDS SUPPORT AS THE UPPER RANGE OF VALUE. THE SALES COMPARISON APPROACH HAS BEEN GIVEN THE MOST WEIGHT AS IT REFLECTS THE ACTIONS OF BUYERS AND SELLERS IN THE MARKETPLACE. THE SALES COMPARISON APPROACH IS TYPICALLY CONSIDERED TO BE THE MOST RELIABLE IN ASSIGNMENTS OF SINGLE-FAMILY DWELLINGS.

This appraisal is made ☒ "as is", ☐ subject to completion per plans and specifications on the basis of a hypothetical condition that the improvements have been completed, ☐ subject to the following repairs or alterations on the basis of a hypothetical condition that the repairs or alterations have been completed, or ☐ subject to the following required inspection based on the extraordinary assumption that the condition or deficiency does not require alteration or repair:

Based on a complete visual inspection of the interior and exterior areas of the subject property, defined scope of work, statement of assumptions and limiting conditions, and appraiser's certification, my (our) opinion of the market value, as defined, of the real property that is the subject of this report is $ 178,000 **, as of** JUNE 3, 2005 **, which is the date of inspection and the effective date of this appraisal.**

Freddie Mac Form 70 March 2005 Page 2 of 6 Fannie Mae Form 1004 March 2005

Chapter 14 Summary

1. **Appraisal** is an estimate or opinion of value of a piece of property as of a certain date. *The appraisal is valid only for that date*. An appraisal is not a look into the future. Estimate or opinion of value must be supported by objective evidence and data. Appraisals are performed for a variety of reasons including loans, insurance, and taxes, and each of these can lead to a different opinion of value.

2. Factors that affect the value of a particular piece of real estate include many of the same economic, governmental, and social factors that influence the broad real estate market. Some of the most relevant broad market factors influencing the value of a particular piece of real estate include *supply and demand* and *uniqueness and scarcity*. Property specific factors include *highest and best use, location, substitution, conformity, and contribution*.

3. **Market value** is the theoretical price a piece of real estate is most likely to bring in a typical transaction—not to be confused with market price, which is the actual selling price of a piece of real estate. A typical real estate transaction is often referred to as an *arm's length transaction* meaning the transaction occurred under typical conditions in the marketplace with each of the parties acting in his or her own best interests. *Those conditions are*: buyer paid cash; seller did not offer financing or unusual terms; buyer and seller aren't related; buyer and seller are acting in their own best interests; buyer and seller aren't acting out of undue haste or duress; both are reasonably informed about the property, and the property has been on the market for a reasonable period of time.

4. **Property valuation** refers to the actual approaches appraisers use to determine market value for a piece of property. These are sales comparison approach, cost approach, and income approach. Regardless of the approach used, the appraisal process is basically the same. *The five steps and three sub-steps are*: define the appraisal; define data and sources needed; collect and analyze relevant data; determine highest and best use; determine value of the land; estimate value of the property using each of the three approaches; reconcile estimates from the approaches, and report conclusions of the valuation process including all data used and final value estimate.

5. **Defining appraisal/stating problem** involves different parts: identify subject property; identify purpose of the appraisal, and note the date and other relevant factors. Identifying the subject property or determining value of the land may include verifying the legal description. Legal descriptions can be government survey system, lot and block system, or metes and bounds system.

6. Report types used under the Uniform Standards of Professional Appraisal Practice (USPAP) are Self-Contained Appraisal Report, Summary Appraisal Report, and Restricted Appraisal Report. The Uniform Residential Appraisal Report (URAR) form is a standard appraisal report form used by lenders and appraisers. Format types are appraisal report form (standard fill-in-the blanks form—easy for comparisons and large volumes), or narrative format (usually more detailed).

Chapter 14 Quiz

1. ***An appraisal is valid:***
   a. For 30 days after it's completed
   b. For 1 year from the date stated on the appraisal report
   c. Indefinitely until a new appraisal is performed
   d. As of the effective date of the report

2. ***Which of the following statements is true about appraisals?***
   a. An appraisal can always determine market price
   b. An appraisal is completely subjective in defining market value
   c. An appraisal is only an opinion of value supported by objective data
   d. An appraisal is completely objective

3. ***Which of the following best describes an example of a piece of real estate being put to its highest and best use?***
   a. A parking lot in downtown Columbus
   b. A house in a residential subdivision
   c. An old house on a major highway surrounded by commercial development
   d. A vacant lot

4. ***Which house will hold its value best?***
   a. The "best" house in the "worst" neighborhood
   b. The "worst" house in the "best" neighborhood
   c. A $500,000 house in an area of apartment complexes
   d. A $50,000 house that overlooks a huge landfill

5. ***What would not be a typical condition in the marketplace?***
   a. Buyer pays cash for real estate
   b. Buyer and seller are not related
   c. Buyer and seller are reasonably informed about the property
   d. Property has been on the market for 7 years

6. ***The first step in the appraisal process is:***
   a. Define the appraisal
   b. Collect data
   c. Determine the highest and best use
   d. Estimate value

7. ***Determining the highest and best use for a piece of property must take into account which of the following?***
   A. Governmental regulations
   b. Characteristics of the piece of land
   c. Whether the current structure should be torn down
   d. All of the above

8. ***When an appraiser is finished calculating the estimate of value using the three approaches, how are these figures presented?***
   a. All three are presented objectively, allowing the client to pick whichever is the most favorable outcome
   b. The three figures are averaged together
   c. The three figures are reconciled, giving each an appropriate weight depending on the type of appraisal and its goals
   d. The three figures are written down at random

9. ***Which of the following appraisal report formats is usually the most comprehensive?***

a. Appraisal report form
b. Letter of opinion
c. Narrative report
d. Oral report

10. ***Which of the following appraisal report formats allows the appraiser to customize the presentation?***

a. Appraisal report form
b. Letter of opinion
c. Narrative report
d. Oral report

11. ***Complete the following statement. A competitive market analysis is __________ the equivalent of an appraisal.***

a. Never
b. Always
c. Usually
d. Sometimes

15 PROPERTY VALUATION

CHAPTER OVERVIEW

Now that you have some background on the basics of appraisal, we'll go into an in-depth discussion of the three different approaches to appraisal. We'll discuss the criteria and data used for the sales comparison approach, cost approach, and income approach. Our analysis will also show the mechanics of how to perform each type of appraisal. While your own assessment can't replace a professional appraisal, it will be a valuable tool in advising clients on price. Plus, these topics are covered on the licensing exam. We'll conclude the chapter by comparing appraisal with the competitive market analysis, which is more widely used by real estate agents.

KEY TERMS

Capitalization Rate
Percentage rate of return used by investors to calculate the present value of future income. Also called **rate**.

Comparables
Other similar properties sold in a certain area. Also called **comps**.

Cost Manuals
Books that give estimated construction costs for various types of buildings and structures in different regions of the country.

Depreciation
Loss in value of a piece of property for any reason.

Effective Age
Age of a structure based on the actual wear and tear that the building shows and not necessarily the structure's age.

Effective Gross Income
Potential gross income minus a figure for vacancy and collection losses. (Should also add any other miscellaneous income.)

Gross Income
Income before expenses.

Net Income
Income after expenses.

Potential Gross Income
The income possibly produced by a property in an ideal situation with no vacancies and no collection losses. (No miscellaneous income here.)

Replacement
Building the functional equivalent of the original building, usually with one of the same size, layout, quality, and utility as the original building.

Reproduction
Building an exact replica of the original building giving the new structure the exact same look and feel as the original building.

Subject Property
Property for which a value estimate is sought. The subject of an appraisal to which all other properties are compared.

I. THREE APPROACHES TO PROPERTY VALUATION

Property valuation is a process of gathering and analyzing information to determine the market value of a piece of property. Remember that the general process and resulting reports are the same *regardless of which approach is used.*

The three approaches to appraisal are the **sales comparison approach**, **cost approach,** and **income approach**. Each has advantages and disadvantages, and some are preferable for certain types of properties. Our final analysis will compare these three approaches with the competitive market analysis (CMA), which is typically performed by the real estate sales agent.

II. SALES COMPARISON APPROACH

The **sales comparison approach** is an appraisal method that estimates the value of real estate by performing a market analysis of the area where the **subject property** is located. The **subject property** is the property being appraised or for which an appraisal value estimate is sought. With the sales comparison approach, the value of the subject property, is estimated by comparing it to other properties, called **comparables** or **comps,** sold recently in the area. Properties currently on the market aren't included as comps since a final selling price hasn't yet been determined for them.

COMPARABLES

The sales comparison approach uses between three and five comps to arrive at a value figure. A minimum of three comps is required by most secondary market lenders to ensure an accurate appraisal from sufficient data. These comps should be as recent as possible, usually having been sold no more than six months or a year prior to the date the current appraisal is being performed, and as similar as possible to the subject property.

If there aren't enough properties that have been sold recently in a given area, the appraiser may look in another similar area or make price adjustments up or down, depending on market conditions at the time of the sale. The preferable route is to find another similar area. In either case, the appraiser must make note in the appraisal report of the fact that a different area or older comps were used and explain why this was done.

The ideal situation is to find recently sold comps in the same area as the subject property. The comps must be close in style and other features to the subject property. For example, a two-story house should not be compared to a single-story ranch home. Furthermore, the comps should share as many features as possible with the subject property. It's often difficult to find properties that are the same as the subject property in all respects. Therefore, the sales comparison approach gives us a method of adjusting these properties so that meaningful comparisons and analysis can be performed.

ADJUSTING PROPERTIES

Adjusting properties is the process of making the chosen comps come as close as possible in features to the subject so meaningful price comparisons can be made. The sales comparison approach is able to approximate the value of the subject property based on objective data readily available in the marketplace.

The rule for adjusting properties is simple. The subject property is the starting point. Each comp is compared to the subject. **The subject never changes**, so if a comp is missing something the subject has, you need to add something to the comp to make them equal. If the comp has something extra the subject doesn't have, you need to take away from the comp to make them equal. Let's look at an example property adjustment picking one feature to adjust. (From a separate comparative analysis, we've determined that $5,000 is the going rate in this neighborhood for garages.)

PROPERTY ADJUSTMENT EXAMPLE SCENARIO FOR ONE FEATURE

Subject Property	Comp #1	Comp #2	Comp #3
1-Car Garage	No Garage	1-Car Garage	2-Car Garage
Never Adjust!	Missing Something so Must Add More to Make Equal to Subject	Equal to Subject, so Don't Adjust	Has More, so Must Take Away to Make Equal to Subject
	Comp #1 Value= $90,000 +5,000 Added for Missing Garage	Comp #2 Value= $97,000	Comp #3 Value= $110,000 -5,000 Subtracted for extra Garage
Final Value= $100,000	Final Value= $95,000	Final Value= $97,000	Final Value= $105,000

This scenario is repeated for each significant feature that's different between the subject property and the comps on the day they were sold. Changes to the comps after they were sold don't count because these would not be reflected in the sale price. Now let's discuss which features are "significant" and how much of a value adjustment for each comp we add or subtract for them.

SIGNIFICANT FEATURES. These are features of the properties themselves but can also refer to features of the transaction such as when the transaction occurred or financing terms offered. Furthermore, some of these features are objective—the number of bedrooms in the subject and each comp—while other features are subjective—rating the overall condition of the subject and each comp. Finally, note that important features can change from area to area. For example, a house in a golf course community may include such things as a view of the golf course, or a house on riverfront property with access to the waterway.

Here's a partial list of features usually considered for most homes:

1. Date the sale took place—an older sale could have appreciated, or a supply and demand situation changed since the comp was sold.
2. Property location—e.g., corner lot versus middle lot, cul-de-sac versus main road.
3. Size of lot—lot frontage is worth more than lot depth, and an overall bigger lot also is worth more, but the amount depends on the area.
4. Condition—upkeep and overall quality, e.g., is painting or landscaping needed to meet the condition of the average home in the neighborhood.
5. Age—a newer home is usually worth a little more.
6. Style and construction of home—adjustments should be made if homes are different styles or made from different materials, e.g., wood versus stone.
7. Size of home/square footage—usually only counts livable space, not basements, and finished basements are often a separate point to compare.
8. Total number of rooms—dining rooms or breakfast nooks should be noted.
9. Number of bedrooms—include master bedroom, lack of master bedroom, any rooms that may double as bedrooms, and an office or den.
10. Number of full/half bathrooms—half baths are sometimes referred to as lavs (just toilet and sink); also note special features like all-tile walls.
11. Basement—note kind of basement, e.g., full, half, or walk-out, whether any finishing has been done, and quality of work.
12. Garage—note not only size but also attached or detached.
13. Heating/cooling/water—note presence, size, and type of cooling or heating system (e.g., heat pump), and well water or septic tank versus city utilities.
14. Other—note unique features, e.g., patio, deck, porch, breezeway, fireplace, built-in shelves, walk-in closets, hot tubs, swimming pools, etc.
15. Terms of sale—special financing arrangements or other conditions.

Every feature doesn't need to be considered every time since the object is to find comps that are already as close as possible to the subject. Furthermore, if differences in features between the comps did not result in differences in sale prices, only those features that appeared to contribute to any price differences should be noted.

EXAMPLE Suppose we have three comps and our subject. The subject and two comps have four bedrooms, but one of the comps has only three bedrooms. The two comps with four bedrooms sold for almost exactly the same price, even though one had central air conditioning and one had a heat pump. Since they sold for almost the same price, we can conclude that the presence of central air or a heat pump didn't have a significant effect on the price. Therefore, we don't need to consider this fact when comparing the three comps to the subject.

Value Adjustments. Value adjustments for each feature that's missing or is additional in a comp depends on a number of factors. The figures are usually different in different areas and may seem arbitrary, but an experienced appraiser can make a fairly accurate determination as to how much a particular feature affects the value of a house. Much of the basis for these figures is computed from a matched pair analysis of sales data for houses sold in the area. By looking at sales data in the area where (ideally) only one feature is different, a comparison of the sale prices will reveal the amount that feature added to the price. In our next math exercise, we'll do a sales comparison exercise using value adjustments for a fictitious neighborhood.

DO THE MATH!

Sales Comparison Approach Math Adjustments to Comps

FEATURE	SUBJECT PROPERTY	COMP #1 ADJ.	COMP #2 ADJ.	COMP #3 ADJ.
Address	61 Lake Ave.	127 Dock St.	39 Lake Ave.	168 Shore Dr.
Sale Price	?	$137,900	$149,500	$142,700
Date	—	21 days 0	60 days +$1,495	85 days +$2,854
1. Location	waterfront	waterfront 0	waterfront 0	waterfront 0
2. Lot Size	100'x115'	105'x110' 0	130'x130' -$3,000	105'x125 -$1,000
3. Condition	good	ave. +$2,000	good 0	good 0
4. Age	20 yrs.	17 yrs. 0	24 yrs. 0	21 yrs. 0
5. Style/Construct.	brick	brick 0	stone -$3,000	stucco -$1,000
6. Size/Sq. Ft.	1,750 s.f.	1675 s.f.+$750	1875 s.f. -$1,250	1800 s.f. -$500
7. # Total Rooms	7	6 +$1,000	8 -$1,000	7 0
8. # Bedrooms	3	3 0	3 0	3 0
9. # Bathrooms	2 1/2	2 1/2 0	3 -$500	2 +$500
10. Basement	full	full	full	full
11. Garage	2-car, att.	2-car,att. 0	2-car,att. 0	2-car,att. 0
12. Heat/Cool/Water	N/A	N/A	N/A	N/A
13. Other	none	none	pool -$2,500	deck -$2000
14. Terms of Sale	--	VA -$1,000	conv. 0	oan assump. -$1,000
Total Adjustments	--	+$2,750	-$9,755	-$2,146
Adjusted Values		$140,650	$139,745	$140,554

Final Value Estimate.: $140,500

III. COST APPROACH

The **cost approach** is an appraisal method that estimates the value of real estate by figuring the cost of building the house or other improvement on the land, minus depreciation, plus the value of the vacant land. We'll discuss how to value each of these components, starting with the land, then the building, then depreciation.

LAND VALUATION

Vacant land is called a **site** when it has enhancements making it ready for building. Land valuation, or site valuation, can be determined by using the sales comparison approach discussed in the previous section of this chapter. If only vacant land is available in the area with no site enhancements, the cost of adding these enhancements to the vacant land should be added to determine the true site value of a piece of real estate.

COST OF BUILDING AN IMPROVEMENT

The cost of building a house or improvement on a piece of land can be determined several different ways. The two most common methods are **cost manuals** and **quantity survey**. It's important to know whether the cost estimate is for *replacing* or *reproducing* the building. There's a significant difference: **replacement** of a structure is building the functional equivalent of the original building; **reproduction** of a structure is building an exact replica of the original building. Usually cost estimates are done for replacing a building with one that's similar in size, layout, quality, and utility. For most buildings, it makes sense that a similar building is an acceptable substitute since this is less expensive. Cost estimates for reproducing a building are typically done for historical buildings where it's important for a new structure to have the exact look and feel as the original.

COST MAUALS. The typical method for determining the cost of replacing a building relies on **cost manuals**. **Cost manuals** are books that give estimated construction costs for various types of buildings and structures in different regions of the country. Once the proper book is selected for the type of building (e.g., house cost manual), the appraiser matches the subject property with the closest type and features that can be found in that manual. Once located, this will give the appraiser an estimated cost per square foot to build that type of structure with those features in that part of the country. The appraiser then makes any necessary adjustments for variations in materials used or other features not reflected in the cost manual.

QUANTITY SURVEY. A second method used less frequently to estimate replacement costs (but is often used with the less common reproduction cost estimates) is the **quantity survey**. The **quantity survey** has the appraiser count the number of each type of part and material used to construct the building. The total cost for all of these components is added together with an appropriate charge for the labor to put everything together: builder's profit, cost of permits, etc.

Both of these methods are supplemented with an appropriate list of additional features, such as a hot tub, with a corresponding price and cost of installation.

DEPRECIATION

Depreciation is a loss in value of a piece of real estate for any reason. Keep in mind that the land itself is never said to depreciate although the enhancements to the land that make it a site could. For the most part, depreciation refers to the building or structure on the land.

There are several kinds of depreciation. One used for accounting purposes takes a set amount of depreciation as a loss each year during the useful life of a building. This usually is not equal to the actual number of years the building would be expected to last and often doesn't consider actual wear on a building but rather is a form of tax incentive. We'll focus on **effective age-life depreciation** and different kinds of **observable depreciation**.

EFFECTIVE AGE-LIFE DEPRECIATION. **Effective age-life depreciation**, or **age-life depreciation,** is a depreciation method that takes the total new cost of the building times a depreciation percentage. This depreciation percentage is derived using the building's effective age, which considers the physical, functional, and external obsolescence. The effective age of the structure is divided by the total expected (economic) life to determine the percentage of depreciation to apply to the building.

EXAMPLE

- 20 years effective age / 50 years economic life = 0.40 or 40% depreciation.

OBSERVABLE DEPRECIATION. **Observable depreciation** is any loss of value that the appraiser can attribute to one of three main causes: **physical deterioration, functional obsolescence,** and **economic obsolescence**. The amount of depreciation calculated for each category varies.

Physical Deterioration. **Physical deterioration** is actual wear and tear on something due to age, the elements, or other forces. Regular maintenance can slow the process, and most physical deterioration is repairable or **curable**. A depreciation figure for physical deterioration is calculated by taking the new price of the item and subtracting a percentage for the wear and tear actually used. For example, if a furnace costs $5,000 new, and wear and tear makes it appear that it's used up about 20 percent of its life, then $1,000 ($5,000 x 20 percent) is the amount of depreciation that should be attributed to that item. If an item must be replaced, the new cost is used.

Functional Obsolescence. **Functional obsolescence** means a building is less desirable because of something inherent in the structure itself. Some examples are an outdated home style, outdated fixtures, or only one bathroom. These undesirable features may be **curable**, that is fixed at a reasonable cost, or **incurable**, something that can't be fixed without major cost or renovations. A depreciation figure for functional obsolescence is determined by the cost of curing the undesirable feature or, for incurables, by comparing the difference in sale prices from a property with the feature and one without it.

Economic Obsolescence. **Economic obsolescence** occurs when something outside the control of the property makes it less desirable. Some examples are the general decline in a neighborhood, the closing of a plant that was important to the economic base of an area, a nearby landfill, or the construction of a new highway that creates noise or re-routes traffic. These external causes are usually **incurable**. A depreciation figure for economic obsolescence is determined by comparing the difference is sale prices from a property with the feature and one without the feature.

In our next math excercise, we'll look at a cost approach appraisal example that uses the cost manuals method and calculates depreciation using both straight depreciation and observable depreciation.

DO THE MATH!

COST APPROACH: CALCULATING DEPRECIATION & TOTAL VALUE

Subject Property: 61 Lake Ave., 1,750 sq. ft., 20 yrs. old, brick

Example #1: Age-Life Depreciation

A. Site Valuation:

From a sales comparison, we've determined that the value of the site is... **$27,000**

[plus]

B. Building Valuation:

The cost manuals tell us that building a two-story house, with features that match our subject property, currently costs about...

$65 per sq. ft. x 1,750 sq. ft. = $113,750
cost manual x house size [plus]

C. Age-Life Depreciation:

The house has an estimated total economic life of 65 years and an estimated effective age of 10 years, so...

10 / 65 = 15%
$113,750 x 15% = $17,063
(minus)

D. Other Extras

Here we add the cost of things not included above (landscaping, driveway, etc.) and come up with a total... **$18,750**

[plus]

TOTAL ESTIMATE: $142,437

Example #2: Observable Depreciation

A. Site Valuation:

From a sales comparison, we've determined that the value of the site is... **$27,000**

[plus]

B. Building Valuation:

The cost manuals tell us that building a two-story house, with features that match our subject property, currently costs about...

$65 per sq. ft. x 1,750 sq. ft. = $113,750
cost manual x house size [plus]

C. Observable Depreciation:

Physical deterioration—
Condition: House=good, roof=poor, etc.
To calculate: value x % used up=deprec.
House: **$113,750 x 10%=$11,375**
Roof: **$ 6,000 x 80%=$ 4,800**
(minus)

Functional Obsolescence—
Master bedroom only has shower stall, not bathtub, so... **$3,000**
(minus)

Economic Obsolescence— $ 0

D. Other Extras

Here we add the cost of things not included above (landscaping, etc.) and come up with a total... **$18,750**

[plus]

TOTAL ESTIMATE: $140,325

IV. INCOME APPROACH

The **income approach** is an appraisal method that estimates the value of real estate by analyzing the amount of revenue, or income, the property currently generates or could generate often comparing it to other similar properties. This approach is most widely used with commercial or investment properties. There are many ways to analyze real estate income depending on the purpose. The two most common methods are **capitalization rate** and **gross rent multiplier**.

Capitalization Rate

The **capitalization rate** is a percentage rate used by investors to calculate the present value of future income. We'll use the capitalization rate, or **rate**, to estimate the value of real estate. This rate is essentially equal to the interest rate an investor would expect money to earn in a real estate investment. Since the capitalization rate for a real estate investment is not guaranteed, an investor will expect a larger rate of return than he or she can get from safer investments. In other words, for the same investment, the investor would expect to earn more future income, *or* for the same future income, the investor would expect to make a smaller investment. Both of these desired results are achieved by an investment with a higher capitalization rate.

We can estimate the value of a real estate investment using three variables: **future income** of the investment, **capitalization rate** of return paid on the investment, and **price of that particular investment (value)**. If we know any two of the variables, we can use a math equation to find the third variable.

In our equation, we can find any of the variables, but usually we are solving to find the value of the investment. **Value** is the amount we would need to spend to buy the investment. The **income** is the future income we hope the property will have but is usually based on the present income of the property. The **rate**, or capitalization rate, is a percentage rate representing the amount of profit return the investor expects in order to be willing to risk his or her money in the investment.

EXAMPLE We can find any of the variables. Suppose you wanted to buy a property that already was listed at a certain price (value). You could get the income figures and find out what your rate of return would be on the investment. Or if you knew the price (value) and wanted to make a higher rate of return on your investment, you could use the equation to find out how high you would need to raise the property's income level to receive the higher rate of desired return. We'll do some examples in our math exercise and the Math Appendix in the back of the book.

INCOME. **Income** is the amount of money that comes from a property. This income can come from many sources. In addition to rents, there's miscellaneous income from parking fees, vending machines, and other sources. All of this is added together to come up with a **gross income**—income *before* expenses. There's an important distinction between **potential gross income** and **effective**

gross income. **Potential gross income** is the income that could be produced by the property in an ideal situation with no vacancies and no collection losses. **Effective gross income** is the potential gross income of a property plus other miscellaneous income minus a figure for **vacancy and collection losses**. **Vacancy and collection losses** are an estimate as to how much future income may be lost when the building is not full, or tenants do not pay their rent. A typical number for this falls in the 2-10 percent range.

In the capitalization rate method of income appraisal, we're interested only in the **net income** or **net operating income**—income *after* expenses. This is important because an investor doesn't receive money that pays expenses.

The formula is:

Gross **I**ncome (annual)	—	**V**acancy and collection losses	—	**E**xpenses (annual)	=	**N**et Operating Income (NOI)

In figuring net operating income (NOI), add the total *annual* income from all sources. When you subtract expenses, subtract *annual* **operating expenses**. **Operating expenses** include such things as repairs, maintenance, trash removal, property taxes, etc., but operating expenses do **not** include any debt payments (called **debt service**) owed on the property and do **not** include depreciation.

exam will include debt service as expen – ignore

RATE. **Rate**, or **capitalization rate**, is the percentage rate of return used by investors to calculate the present value of future income. The actual amount of return desired by an investor is arbitrary but must be relative to other investments. For example, an investor could want a 50 percent return on investment but would have extreme difficulty finding one. Another investor may be happy with a 5 percent return. Two equally informed investors could look at the same property and be happy with different rates. One may look at the property and want a 15 percent return while another investors is happy with a 12 percent return on his money for the same property.

As the rate of return an investor desires goes up, the value of the property goes down. This can be looked at mathematically or intuitively. Mathematically, you are dividing by the rate of return, and as you divide by a larger number, you get a smaller answer. Intuitively, as you expect to get a higher rate of return (with the same expected property income), you must value your money more and value the property less.

VALUE. **Value** is the worth of the investment. This is how much someone is willing to pay for a piece of real estate at a given moment in time. The value is dependent on the expected future income of the property. We say expected because everyone could move out when his or her lease is up. We can be reasonably sure if the property's income is fair in the marketplace, the income stream is likely to continue into the future (minus a small percentage for vacancy and collection losses).

This value figure does not take into account the fact that the real estate may appreciate in the future. Most investors buy real estate with this in mind, but since this is an uncertain event, it is not included in an appraisal.

DO THE MATH!

INCOME APPROACH: CAPITALIZATION RATE METHOD

INCOME ÷ RATE = VALUE *[Remembered easily as IRV}*

This is the basic formula for calculating value using the income approach to appraisal. By knowing any two of the variables you can find the third using this equation. Of course, if you're not into math, we'll show you an easier way.

EXAMPLE #1: Let's look at a standard problem. You're given the following:

Gross Income	=$250,000
Expenses	=$130,000
Depreciation	=$ 50,000
Debt Service	=$ 25,000
Cap Rate	= 15%

You're told to find the **value** of the property. So we use our standard formula:

INCOME ÷ RATE = VALUE

Now remember two important things:

1. ALWAYS USE **NET INCOME**,
   Net Income=Gross Income - Expenses
2. DEPRECIATION and DEBT SERVICE
   DON'T COUNT AS EXPENSES

As is common on the test, this question is trying to confuse you with extra information you don't need. Sometimes the expenses are a list of items that you must add together, or they may be one figure like in this example. Either way, *ignore depreciation and debt service numbers*. Figure your answer as follows:

INCOME ÷ RATE	=	VALUE
($250,000 - $130,000) ÷ 15%	=	?
$120,000 ÷ 15%	=	**$800,000**

EXAMPLE #2: Let's look at a less common problem with similar information:

Gross Income	=$250,000
Expenses	=$130,000
Depreciation	=$ 50,000
Debt Service	=$ 25,000
Value	=$800,000

Here we're finding the property's **cap rate**. Same NET income rules, but we use a different formula:

INCOME	÷	VALUE	=	RATE
($250,000-$130,000)	÷	$ 800,000	=	?
$120,000	÷	$800,000	=	**0.15 = 15%**

EXAMPLE #3: A final variation might go like this:

Value	=$800,000
Cap Rate	= 15%

Here, we're given the property's value and the cap rate that our investor desires. We must find the **net income** needed to achieve this return.

Formula

VALUE x RATE = INCOME

$800,000 x 15% = **$120,000**

GROSS RENT MULTIPLIER

The **gross rent multiplier (GRM;** sometimes also referred to as *GMRM or gross monthly rent multiplier*) is a number derived from comparable rental properties in an area that is used to estimate the value of a piece of real estate (the gross rent multiplier is used for only one- to four-unit residential properties). The GRM is based on the total gross monthly rent of a particular piece of real estate. With this method, no deduction allowance is made for expenses, vacancies, or collection losses.

The gross rent multiplier is most useful in determining the value of residential homes in areas where there are many other rental properties. The GRM identifies the subject property's ranking within the market of similar properties by giving a means of comparing gross monthly rent and sale prices or value. This method can help support a value estimate derived from other appraisal methods. The GRM gives no consideration to a property's profitability since it does not take into account expenses or losses. Rather, the GRM is a benchmark to gauge the property's *potential* profitability by analyzing the potential gross income against the investment dollars needed to buy the future income stream.

DERIVING THE GRM. The GRM is derived with a very simple formula. Data are collected on a number of rental properties sold recently in a certain area. The selling price for each is divided by the gross monthly rent (or income) the property commanded in the marketplace, thus arriving at a GRM figure:

Rental Home Sale Price ÷ Gross Monthly Rent = GRM

GRMs are calculated for a number of comps that are similar to the subject property. The GRMs are then analyzed and weighted (*never* averaged), giving the most consideration to homes most like the subject property. From these comps, a GRM figure is selected to apply to the subject property to estimate a value.

USING THE GRM. The GRM arrived at for the subject property is then put into another simple formula to arrive at an estimate of value. The gross monthly rent (or expected monthly rent) from the subject property is multiplied by the GRM derived in the first step to give an estimate of value for the subject property:

Gross Monthly Rent (or Expected Monthly Rent) x GRM = Estimated Value

This value is not intended to stand alone, but rather it is intended to be used as supporting evidence for other appraisal methods. In fact, many times there are not enough residential rentals in an area to derive a value using this method.

The GRM is not held to be as reliable as the capitalization rate method to perform an income approach appraisal for a piece of real estate because the GRM does not take into account expenses and losses. Nevertheless, the GRM is a good method for doing a quick comparison when there are many properties available in the marketplace and is useful to double check other appraisal methods.

We'll go through an example for deriving a GRM and using a GRM to calculate property value in our next math exercise. **Also note:** The state exam requires slightly different math calculations than the real-life calculations presented here. The state exam uses *annual* income figures. For a sample problem similar to the exam, please refer to the Math Appendix at the end of this book.

DO THE MATH!

INCOME APPROACH: GROSS RENT MULTIPLIER METHOD

Deriving the Gross Rent Multiplier (GRM):

Note: You must be given the home sale price and rent figure to derive GRM.

	Rental Home Sale Price	÷	Gross Monthly Rent (or Income)	= GRM
Comp #1—	$137,900	÷	$865	= 159.42
Comp #2—	$149,500	÷	$950	= 157.37
Comp #3—	$142,700	÷	$900	= 158.56

Our analysis of the GRM says that our subject property is most similar to comp #1, then comp #3, then comp #2 (see the Do the Math! chart on page 274 for specific information on the comps and subject property), so we conclude the GRM should be about **159**.

Using the Gross Rent Multiplier (GRM):

Note: Use the GRM figure you derived above, and you must be given the home rent figure.

	Gross Monthly Rent (or Expected Monthly Income)	x GRM	=	Estimated Value
Subject Property—	$885	x 159	=	$140,715

[Note that this estimate of value is very close to the same value we derived using the sales comparison approach and the cost approach previously.]

OTHER IMPORTANT NOTES AND REMINDERS:

1. Be careful: if you are given yearly rental or income figures for residential property, make sure you divide the figure by twelve to get a *monthly* rent figure.
2. If you are given a problem involving commercial or investment property, use annual income figures. This is a GIM/Gross Income Multiplier (the state exam will call it a GRM /gross rent multiplier). Either way, be sure that income figures for all comps are stated using the same time frame; all income figures must be yearly or all monthly.

The math appendix at the back of this book goes over some examples using annual income figures, similar to the license exam questions.

V. ANALYZING THE THREE APPRAISAL APPROACHES

As we went through each of the appraisal approaches, you could probably see some of the advantages and disadvantages to each. Each of these strengths and weaknesses also make the approaches more or less suitable for particular kinds of real estate. We'll summarize that analysis here.

Pros and Cons of the Three Approaches

As we discussed the three appraisal approaches in detail, it may have occurred to you that we always referred to the value of the subject property as an estimate. It's important to remember that even with all of the extensive research and calculations that go into appraisal, we are only able to estimate, not determine, the value of a piece of property. Only the marketplace can truly tell us the value of a piece of real estate. In fact, real estate has no value until someone is willing to buy it at a given price.

Nevertheless, appraisal is still an important function that allows us to compare the relative worth of different pieces of property. Even if we cannot determine an absolute value, we can still make relative comparisons. These comparisons are enhanced by the knowledge and experience of the appraiser. All of the appraisal approaches are important because each can serve as a check against the other two. Let's look at the specific pros and cons to each appraisal approach.

SALES COMPARISON APPROACH. The sales comparison approach is the most accurate of the three appraisal methods (if you have good data). Its biggest advantage is that it relies on information deeply rooted in marketplace activity. Furthermore, it attempts to make adjustments to comps so they more closely approximate the actual features and conditions of the subject property. Finally, sales comparison approach works for most types of residential or commercial property.

The main disadvantage to the sales comparison approach is that it requires properties to have been sold recently in the area. A proper and meaningful sales comparison analysis cannot be performed without this data, so the sales comparison approach is not suitable for special-purpose properties such as schools, churches, etc., and other unusual or unique properties for which there aren't recent sales data to analyze. Finally, the sales comparison approach fails to take into account properties currently for sale which may skew results.

COST APPROACH. The cost approach is a very useful and accurate estimate of value for special-purpose properties. Schools, churches, and other unique properties can be analyzed this way. The main advantage is its use of extensive data. The cost approach is excellent for new properties and for insurance purposes.

The main disadvantage to the cost approach is the cost of a building does not necessarily equal its value. Anyone looking at a cost approach appraisal must keep in mind there are a number of market factors that must be taken into account to make an accurate estimate of value.

Among the cost approach methods, the cost manuals method is best for value estimates when the property being analyzed is a "typical" structure. The quantity survey method is best for value estimates when the property is a "unique" structure.

INCOME APPROACH. The income approach is most useful when analyzing income-producing properties such as commercial or investment real estate. The main advantage to the income approach is we can solve for any variable we desire. Furthermore, it gives us a method of analyzing the value of a future income stream.

The income approach is seldom useful for residential property due to lack of data. Another problem is that income figures and expenses are about *past* income performance of the property. Attempts to introduce vacancy, collections, and other losses into the equation are merely a guess. Also, the income approach doesn't account for depreciation, building condition, and other factors.

The capitalization rate method is best for commercial properties. The gross rent multiplier is best for single-family residences, but a GRM analysis can be difficult due to lack of comps. Finally, remember that **capitalization rate** method uses **net income,** and **gross rent multiplier** method uses **gross income**.

VI. COMPETITIVE MARKET ANALYSIS

A **competitive market analysis (CMA)**, also called a **comparable market analysis**, is a method of determining the approximate market value of a home by comparing the subject property to other homes that have sold, are presently for sale, or did not sell in a given area. This is similar to, but not equal to, a sales comparison appraisal. Both follow a similar presentation format consisting of a table of facts comparing features of the subject property to a series of comps. Let's look at some of the similarities and differences.

CMA VERSUS SALES COMPARISON APPRAISAL

The typical CMA is a simplified version of the sales comparison appraisal. The goal is for the sales agent to assist the client by providing a range of probable selling prices for a given home. This is done by comparing the subject property with other houses in the area. The main difference is the CMA doesn't go into as much detail as a sales comparison appraisal. A CMA compares only the main features of the houses when finding comps. Size and style are two of the more important criteria in a typical CMA. Size compares lot size, square footage of the houses, and room counts. Style looks at number of stories, construction, and other visible attributes.

The CMA is primarily concerned with the observable differences between houses that would draw a buyer to one house over another. If the subject property is lacking a significant feature that's present in the comps, the agent may suggest a lower price to attract buyers to look at the house. If a feature is present in the subject property that is not in any comps, a higher price may not scare off potential buyers because they may be interested in that feature.

PROS AND CONS. A CMA is preferable to a sales comparison appraisal when a client is trying to get an idea of what his or her property is worth without doing a costly appraisal. Furthermore, a CMA analyzes multiple listing services and other sources for houses currently for sale or that did not sell that could yield additional insight into market conditions affecting the sale price of the subject property. A CMA, however, is much less detailed than an appraisal and cannot replace an appraisal for many "official" purposes, such as bank loans.

Chapter 15 Summary

1. Property valuation is the process of gathering and analyzing information to estimate a property's market value. Process and reports for appraisal approaches—sales comparison approach, cost approach, income approach—are the same.

2. Sales comparison takes a market analysis of the location of the subject property. Subject property is property being appraised for value estimate. Subject is compared to other properties (comparables or comps) recently sold in the area. Three to five comps are usually used and should be close in features to subject. Comp sale prices are adjusted to compensate for features lacking or extra when compared to subject. *Subject never changes*; adjustments are made only to comps. Value is added to comps for missing features; value is subtracted from comps for extra features.

3. Cost approach figures the cost of building a structure, minus depreciation, plus value of land. Sales comparison determines land/site value. Building can be replacement (functional equivalent of original) or reproduction (exact replica). Replacements are more common. Cost manuals give costs of construction for different types of buildings. Book figure is multiplied by structure's square footage to estimate costs. Quantity survey method counts type and number of parts in a building, adds their costs, plus labor, profit, etc. Depreciation is loss in value for any reason (physical deterioration, functional obsolescence, economic obsolescence) and can be curable, fixed at reasonable cost, or incurable—requires major cost or renovations.

4. Income approach analyzes revenue or income a property generates. The capitalization rate is used most. Cap rate, or rate, is a percentage used by investors to calculate present value of future income. Net income divided by rate equals value of property. Income is annual net income arrived at by taking gross income, minus percentage for vacancy and collection losses, minus operating expenses. Debt payments aren't included in operating expenses. Rate reflects risk and varies among investors but compares relative investment risk. Income approach #3 is gross rent multiplier (GRM). Prices of other rentals, usually homes, are divided by monthly rent to get GRM. GRM is multiplied by subject's rent to get a value.

5. Sales comparison is most accurate. *Advantages*: relies on market information, adjusts comps to be like subject. *Disadvantages*: needs properties recently sold, can't use for unique properties, doesn't count properties currently for sale. Cost approach is accurate and useful for special or new properties. *Advantages*: uses extensive data, good for insurance. *Disadvantages*: cost doesn't always equal value. Income approach is best for commercial/investment properties. *Advantages*: analyzes income, finds any variable. *Disadvantages*: value does not count future ups and downs, uses past income, not useful for residential.

6. Competitive market analysis (CMA) is similar to sales comparison, but counts homes currently for sale or that didn't sell without using as much detail. CMA focuses on observable differences. Not equal to appraisal; not for official uses.

Chapter 15 Quiz

1. ***Which of the following is not an approach to appraisal?***
   a. Comparable market analysis
   b. Sales comparison
   c. Cost approach
   d. Income approach

2. ***In the sales comparison approach to appraisal, comps are compared to the subject property by:***
   a. Adjusting the features of the subject property to match the comps
   b. Adjusting the features of the comps to match the subject property
   c. Only using comps that are an exact match to the subject property
   d. Using any comps, without regard to features, as long as they were sold recently and are from the same area

3. ***Which features are adjusted in the sales comparison approach?***
   a. Any feature that's different between the subject property and the comps, even if that feature had no affect on the sale price of the comp
   b. Any significant feature that's different between the subject property and the comps, including features changed up to the day of the appraisal
   c. Any significant feature that's different between the subject property and the comps, but only features as of the day the comps were sold
   d. Any feature that's different between the subject property and the comps, up until the day of the appraisal report

4. ***Indicate the correct adjusted values for each comp in this abbreviated example.***

	Subject Property	Comp A	Comp B	Comp C
Price:	?	$92,700	$87,900	$99,500
Size:	1,750 Sq. Ft.	1,800 Sq. Ft.	1,675 Sq. Ft.	1,875 Sq. Ft.
Rooms:	7	7	6	8

   Adjustments are $10 per square foot, and $1,000 per room. Adjusted values are:

   a. Comp A=$93,200, Comp B=$89,650, Comp C=$101,750
   b. Comp A=$92,200, Comp B=$86,150, Comp C=$97,250
   c. Comp A=$93,200, Comp B=$86,150, Comp C=$101,750
   d. Comp A=$92,200, Comp B=$89,650, Comp C=$97,250

5. ***Which of the following is not an element that must be determined for the cost approach to appraisal?***
   a. Cost of the building or other improvement on the land
   b. Depreciation of the building
   c. Depreciation of the land
   d. Value of the vacant land/site

6. ***Observable depreciation does not include:***
   a. Physical deterioration
   b. Wear and tear to the land
   c. Functional obsolescence
   d. Economic obsolescence

7. ***The formula for estimating property value using the cost approach is:***

a. Site value + (cost per square foot x land size) - depreciation + extras
b. Building cost using quantity survey method + depreciation + site value
c. Building cost using cost manuals method + site value + depreciation
d. Site value + building cost - depreciation + extras

8. ***For estimating property value using the income approach, we must know which of the following variables?***

a. Gross income, cap rate, and value
b. Net income, cap rate, and value
c. Any two of the gross income, cap rate, or value
d. Any two of net income, cap rate, or value

IRV

9. ***All of the following are considered operating expenses* except:**

a. Interest payments
b. Repairs and maintenance
c. Lawn service
d. Trash removal

10. ***What must we have to calculate the gross rent multiplier?***

a. Recent sales of any residential homes in the area
b. Recent sales of rental comps with income figures
c. Rental rate of the subject property only
d. Rental rates of the comps only

11. ***Which appraisal approach is most accurate?***

a. Sales comparison approach
b. Cost approach
c. Income approach
d. Comparable market approach

12. ***Which appraisal approach is best for commercial/investment property?***

a. Sales comparison approach
b. Cost approach
c. Income approach
d. Comparable market approach

13. ***A competitive market analysis (CMA) and sales comparison appraisal differ how?***

a. A CMA doesn't go into as much detail as a sales comparison because a CMA is most interested in observable differences
b. A CMA analyzes homes currently for sale; sales comparison doesn't
c. Neither a nor b
d. Both a and b

APPENDIX
MATH MODULE

INTRODUCTION

An extensive review of student performance on the state exam has indicated that many students, even those with "math anxiety," have little difficulty with math on the state exam after attending classes at Hondros College. We have identified the primary information needed on the state exam and created instructional methods that convey this information as simply as possible. This module will help you in both areas.

THE FORMULAS

The formulas were created to address three basic needs:

1. The formulas were designed to *only teach the math currently on the state exam*. If you note something that is absent, it is probably no longer on the state exam. A substantial amount of research as well as discussion with the Ohio Division of Real Estate has gone into confirming the accuracy of this information.
2. Through the formulas, we have you deal with words more than numbers. Many people feel that they can't "do" math, but when math is presented as words, much of that anxiety is diminished. The formulas won't magically eliminate math anxiety overnight, but they are a great start.
3. The formulas were created to use the simplest approach to each math calculation. They are not always the shortest method as, typically, they do not omit even the smallest step. However, they do break down calculations to a more easily understood process. There may be another way to solve the problem. Always use the formula with which you are most comfortable.

This section contains the basic formulas you need to know to answer the math questions on the real estate sales license exam. Sample problems will be worked in class. Following this section are additional math exercises and a math quiz with answers to test your skill.

For additional study help, Hondros Learning's *Real Estate Math Crammer*, Exam Prep Software and Practice Workbook, is available in our bookstore.

FORMULA 1: PERCENT PROBLEMS

Many questions on the state exam require the ability to calculate various percent problems. Two approaches are presented here. Adopt whichever method you find most comfortable.

Line Approach

- Sale Price or Loan Amount x Percentage = Part or Annual Interest
- Part or Interest ÷ Percent = Sale Price or Loan Amount
- Sale Price or Loan Amount ÷ Percentage = Part or Interest

T (Circle) Approach

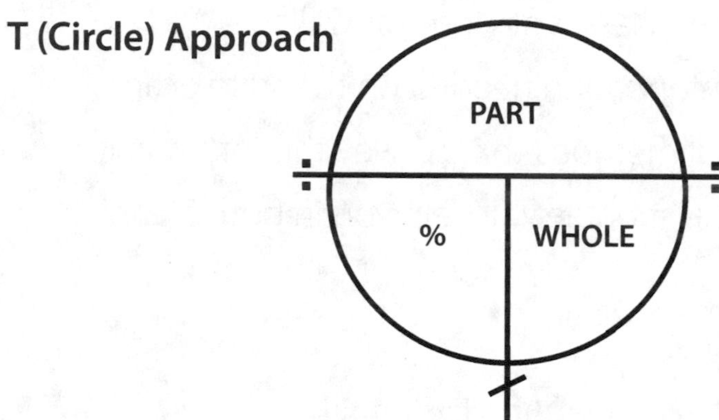

Same Formula as Line Approach

- Part ÷ Whole = % (TGIF…Top Goes In First)
- Part ÷ % = Whole (TGIF)
- Whole x % = Part

For Example:

Read the question carefully.

Boss Realty sold its listing for $105,000. If a 6% commission was charged, what commission would they earn?

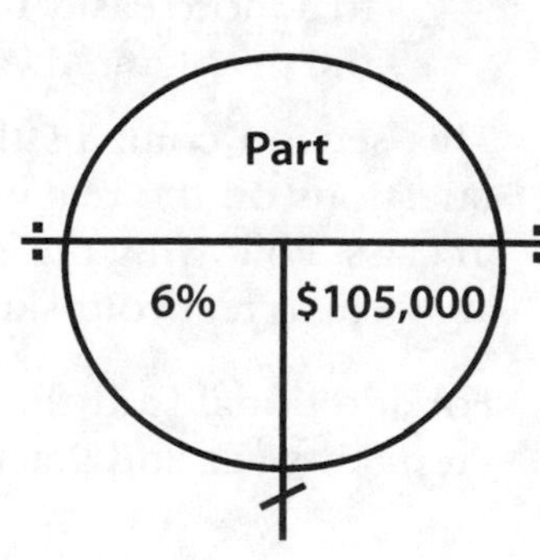

Solve the problem.

Part (Commission) = 6 % x $105,000

0.06 x 105,000 = 6,300

The commission earned was $6,300.

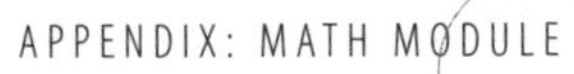

SAMPLE PROBLEMS **(to be worked in class):**

1. A property listed for $100,000 sold in a co-op transaction for $90,000. If the commission rate was seven percent and the brokerages split evenly, how much did each company get?
2. A company sold another company's listing. It received 50% of a six percent commission. If the company receive $2,250, what was the price of the home?
3. If the sales agent received half of the total commission, of $5,122 and the home sold for $157,600, what rate did the broker charge for commission?

FORMULA 2: POINTS

A point is defined as *one percent of the mortgage*, or loan, amount. On the exam, points may be referred to as "discount points" or "loan origination fees."

You will need to calculate the loan amount (sales price – down payment). The question may also give you the sales price on a VA transaction. Since *VA requires no down payment,* the sales price and mortgage amount are the same.

For Example:

Read the question carefully.

A buyer is purchasing a property for $250,000 and will make a $60,000 down payment. If charged two points, how much will be owed in points?

Solve the problem.

Part = Whole x %

First: $250,000 – $60,000 = $190,000; amount of the loan

Part = $190,000 x 2%

Second: 0.02 (2%) x $190,000 = $3,800

The points owed are $3,800.

SAMPLE PROBLEMS **(to be worked in class).**

1. A buyer is purchasing a property for $100,000 and will make a 20% down payment. If charged two points, how much will be owed in points?
2. A property is being VA financed. If the sales price is $75,000 and the points are four, the points will total what dollar amount?
3. John is purchasing a property for $125,000 and received an 80% loan. He paid $3,000 for points. How many points did John pay?

FORMULA 3: PROPERTY TAXES

The question on the state exam will ask you to calculate the property taxes on real estate.

You will receive three pieces of information:

1. **The market value or appraised value of the property**
2. **The assessment level**
   - **Property taxes are referred to as *ad valorem* taxes. Ad valorem means "as per value" and taxes are based on the assessed value of a property.**
3. **"Mills"**
   - **One mill equals one dollar per thousand dollars of assessed value (1 mill = *1/1,000 or* 0.001).**

For Example:

Read the question carefully.

A property is appraised at $380,000 and assessed for tax purposes at 35% of value. Calculate the annual taxes if the mills total 65.

Solve the problem.

Part = Whole x %

35% x $380,000 = $133,000 assessed value

$133,000 ÷ 1,000 (mill = $1 per $1,000) = $133 cost of 1 mill

$133 x 65 mills = $8,645

or

Part = Whole x %

$133,000 x 0.065 = $8,645

The annual taxes are $8,645.

SAMPLE PROBLEMS **(to be worked in class).**

1. **A property is appraised at $150,000 and assessed for tax purposes at 35% of value. Calculate the annual taxes if the mills total 80.** 4200
2. **The assessed value of a property is $35,000 and the annual taxes are $2,380. How many mills were charged on this property?** 68 Mills
3. **A home is valued at $100,000 and assessed for tax purposes at 35% of value. If mills are 47.5, calculate the annual taxes.** 1662.50

2 questions on proration

FORMULA 4: PRORATIONS

First, a simple definition of **proration** is: ***the cost of a financial item divided between two parties, such that each pays a share of it***. On the exam, the financial item will usually either be property taxes (between buyer and seller), insurance premiums (between seller and insurance company), or mortgage interest (between seller and lender).

There are two types of years used in proration:

1. A **calendar**, or 365-day year
   - In these problems, the first step is to calculate the *daily cost* of the item in question. Always take the daily rate to four places past the decimal point. Next, calculate the actual number of days in question. Finally, multiply the daily rate by the number of days.
2. A **statutory**, or 360-day year
   - In these questions a monthly rate is used so your first step is to calculate the *monthly rate*. You should again calculate to four places past the decimal point. Next, calculate the number of months in question. The problem will use simple closing dates, like the 15th or 30th, so you can use a whole or half month. Finally, multiply the monthly rate by the number of months.

Remember these rules:

1. Always use a 365-day year unless the exam says otherwise.
2. Always calculate the math to 4 places past the decimal point, then adjust the final answer.
3. The seller always pays for day of closing.
4. Property taxes are an accrued item in Ohio. This means taxes are paid in arrears, or after use. Taxes are a minimum six months behind. If the question does not say that the previous six months are paid, you must calculate the number of days in that six-month period, as well.

For Example:

Read the question carefully.

The sale of a property will close on May 10, 2006. Taxes are $3,600 per year and are paid through the last half of 2005. Calculate the seller's share of taxes using a 365-day year.

Solve the problem.

Step 1: Daily Tax Rate = 3,600 ÷ 365 = 9.8630 daily rate

Step 2: Number of Days = Jan. 31 + Feb. 28 + Mar. 31 + Apr. 30 + May 10 = 130 days

Step 3: Amount Owed = 130 x 9.8630 = 1282.19 The seller owes $1,282.19 in taxes.

SAMPLE PROBLEMS **(to be worked in class).**

1. **The sale of a property will close April 30, 2006. Taxes are $1,575 per year, and are paid through the last half of 2005. Calculate the seller's share of taxes using a 360-day year.**
2. **Property taxes on a home are $2,200 per year. They are paid through the first half of the year. The property has been sold and the closing will take place August 1 of the same year. What amount of prorated taxes will be due to the buyer?**
3. **The premium for two-year insurance coverage on a home is $460. If the policy was purchased and paid for August 1, 2004 and a closing will take place June 2, 2006, Using a 365-day year, calculate the seller's credit.**

FORMULA 5: LOT MEASUREMENTS

Questions on the state exam use different types of measurements relating to building lots, fencing, and concrete.

The five types of measurements you need to know are:

1. **Front Feet**: The portion of the lot that faces the street. In a measurement, front feet is always the *first* number (65' x 150' lot; 65' frontage).
2. **Square Feet:** Length times width (65' x 150' = 9,750 sq. ft.).
3. **Acreage:** There are 43,560 square feet in an acre. Calculate the square feet of the lot, then divide that number by 43,560 (65' x 150' = 9,750 ÷ 43,560 = 2.2382 acres).
4. **Linear Footage:** This is simply the length in feet (20' x 30' garden will take 100 linear feet of fencing).
5. **Cubic Feet/Yards:** Length times width times depth equals cubic feet. Cubic feet divided by 27 cubic feet gives you cubic yards. (120' x 10' x 0.3333' = 399.96 cubic feet ÷27 = 14.8133 cubic yards).

For Example:

Read the question carefully.

A property measures 230 feet x 310 feet. If it sells for $14,000 per acre and the commission is 6.5%, how much is the commission?

Solve the problem.

l x w = sq. ft.

230' x 310' = 71,300 square feet

Sq. ft. ÷ 43,560 sq. ft. = acres

71,300 ÷ 43,560 = 1.6368 acres

1.6368 x $14,000 = $22,915.517

Part = Whole x %

22,915.517 x .065 = 1,489.5086

The commission earned is $1,489.51.

SAMPLE PROBLEMS **(to be worked in class).**

1. What would a commercial lot, 150' x 600', priced at $2,000 per front foot cost? What would it cost at $2.50 per square foot?

2. If a bag of concrete makes 1 cu. yd., how many bags will it take to pour a 60' x 4' x 4" sidewalk?

3. A lot measures 80' across the back, 50' deep, and 110' across the front. What are the sq. ft. of the lot?

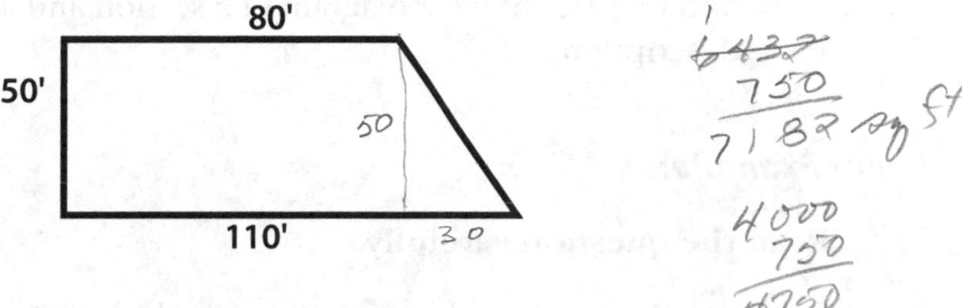

FORMULA 6: TRANSFER TAX (CONVEYANCE FEE)

Transfer tax is a tax charged to the seller based on the sale price. The exam uses the mandatory state tax, which is $1 per thousand dollars of sales price. *Note:* Exam questions try to obscure the sale price by adding down payment, mortgage, or other information to the question that you do not need. ***Use sales price only***.

For Example:

Read the question carefully.

A seller is selling his home for $160,000. The buyer will make a $20,000 down payment and borrow $140,000 from the bank. What is the transfer tax?

Solve the problem.

$160,000 ÷ 1,000 = $160 taxable parts

The transfer tax is $160.00.

SAMPLE PROBLEMS **(to be worked in class).**

1. A buyer is purchasing a home for $150,000. He will make a $25,000 down payment and will borrow $125,000 from a local savings and loan. What will the amount of the transfer tax be?

2. A home is sold for $147,500. The seller has agreed to carry a second mortgage for the buyer in the amount of $20,000. Calculate the transfer tax.

FORMULA 7: SECTIONS

The rectangular (government, military) survey system is one method of property description. It uses terms such as sections and townships.

There are two types of math problems on sections:

1. You will be given a description and asked to calculate the number of acres in that particular area. Here, it is important to remember that the *total number of acres in a section is 640.*
2. You may be shown a diagram of a section and asked to write the description.

For Example:

Read the question carefully.

Calculate the number of acres in the parcels described as the NW ¼, NE ¼ of section 32, and the NW ¼, NE ¼, NE ¼ of Section 33.

Solve the problem.

$640 \div 4 \div 4 = 40$

$640 \div 4 \div 4 \div 4 = 10$

$40 + 10 = 50$

There are 50 acres total in the two parcels.

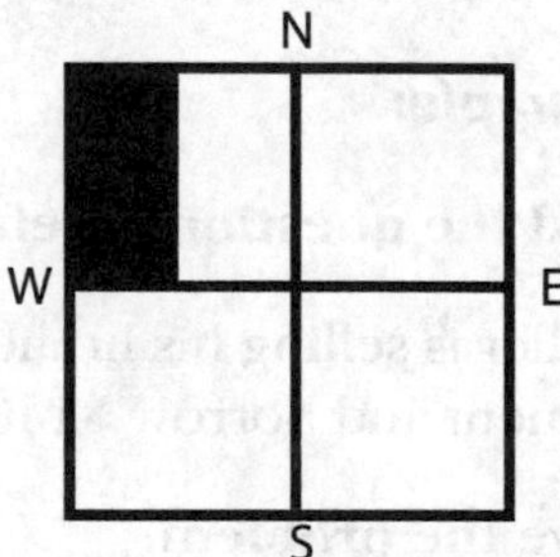

Write the description for the shaded area.

This description for the shaded area would read W 1/2, NW 1/4 of the section.

SAMPLE PROBLEMS **(to be worked in class).**

1. Write a description for the shaded area:
2. Calculate the number of acres in the parcels described as the N 1/2, NW ¼, and the SW 1/4, NW 1/4, NE 1/4 of Section 33.
3. A parcel described as the S 1/2, NE 1/4, NW 1/4 sells for $31,500 per acre. If the commission rate is 6%, calculate the commission.

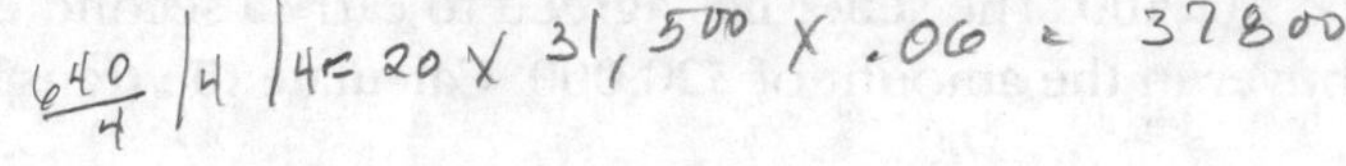

FORMULA 8: CAPITALIZATION

With capitalization and the GRM, you will be required to calculate the value of the property based on its ability to generate income. Capitalization uses ***net income***. You may be required to use different steps to find net income, depending on the question. Be familiar with the following terms, which you may see in some of the questions.

- **Potential Gross Income:** The income a property would generate if every unit was occupied 100% of the time.
- **Effective Gross Income**: Potential gross income, minus vacancy and collection losses.
- **Net Income**: Effective gross income, minus building expenses.
- **Capitalization Rate**: The rate of return on an investment.

Note: Depreciation and annual debt service (monthly payment) are ***not*** considered building expenses, and should ***not*** be used if they are included in the problem. They are owner expenses. These problems only use operating expenses.

The formula for capitalization is remembered as ***IRV.***

(Net) Income ÷ Rate = Value

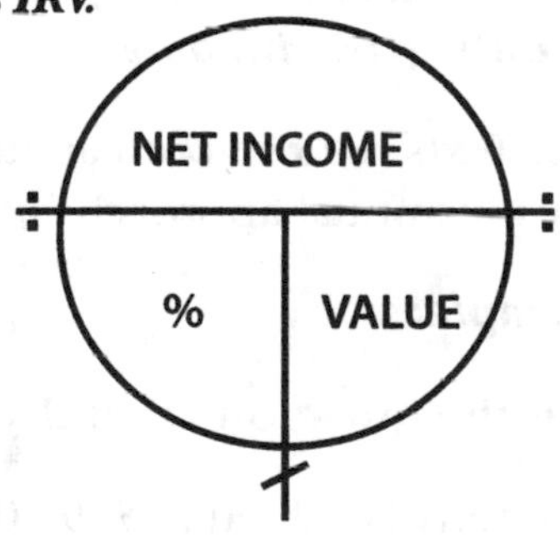

For Example:

Read the question carefully.

A property could generate $200,500 in annual income. The building has an 8% collection loss, monthly expenses of $4,200 and the capitalization rate is 9%. What is the value of the property?

Solve the problem.

Potential income $200,500 – losses 8% ($16,040) = effective income of $184,460

Effective income – annual operating expenses ($4,200 x 12) $50,400 = net income of $134,060

Net income $134,060 ÷ *rate* 9% = *value* $1,489,555.5555

The value of the property is $1,489,556.

SAMPLE PROBLEMS **(to be worked in class).**

1. A property has an annual income of $50,000 and monthly building expenses of $2,500. Annual debt service is $16,000 and depreciation is 3% of value. Using a capitalization rate of 8%, determine the value of the building.
2. An apartment building has 10 units, each of which rents for $600 per month. The building has an occupancy rate of 90%, monthly building expenses are $500, and depreciation is 2%. Determine the highest price the investor will pay if he demands a 9% rate of return on his investments.

FORMULA 9: GRM

Unlike capitalization in the previous formula, GRM uses gross income.

Value ÷ Gross Annual Income = Gross Rent Multiplier

Some questions refer to the value as the sale price and/or to the gross annual income as gross rents. Expect the question to include information, such as expenses, that will attempt to direct you to net income...*ignore it*! Remember to ***use only gross income***.

Note: Texts refer to both annual and monthly income, but the state exam uses ***only*** the annual approach.

For Example:

Read the question carefully.

A property is valued at $195,000 and generates an annual income of $24,000. Building expenses run $1,100 per month, leading to a net income of $10,800. Calculate the gross rent multiplier.

Solve the problem.

195,000 ÷ 24,000 = 8.125

The GRM is 8.

SAMPLE PROBLEMS **(to be worked in class).**

1. A property is valued at $150,000 and generates annual income of $30,000. Building expenses run $1,500 per month, leading to a net income of $12,000. Calculate the gross rent multiplier.
2. A property generates gross rents of $40,000 yearly. It recently sold for $300,000. If it has a vacancy rate of 10% and expenses are $1,200 per month, calculate the gross rent multiplier.
3. Calculate the gross rent if a property valued at $900,000 had a GRM of 9.5.

FORMULA 10: PROFIT/LOSS/RETURN ON INVESTMENT

This type of problem will give you both the original purchase price of the property and the eventual sale price. You will be asked to calculate the return on investment or percent of profit—both are the same figure!

A simple formula expressed as a "poem" comes in handy:

What You Made ÷ What You Paid = Percentage of Profit

or

What You Lost ÷ What It Cost = Percentage of Loss

For Example:

Read the question carefully.

A parcel of land is purchased for $100,000 and later sold for $115,000. What is the percent of profit?

Solve the problem.

Divide what you made by what you paid:

15,000 ÷ 100,000 = 0.15

The percent of profit is 15%.

SAMPLE PROBLEMS **(to be worked in class).**

1. A man purchases land for $50,000. He divides it into three lots that are sold for $20,000 each. What is his return on investment?
2. You purchase an investment property for $125,000. You later sell it at a loss of $20,000. What is your percent of loss?
3. Bill sold his real estate for $234,900 and made a nice 28% profit. What did he originally pay for that property?

FORMULA 11: SELLER PRICING/NET TO OWNER

These questions are one of the few types of questions where one or two words will not identify the type of question for you. You'll need to read the entire question to recognize it.

In the problem, an owner is selling a home. You will be given a number of cost items, including brokerage commission. Your task is to determine the ultimate selling price.

"Selling price" may also be called "listing price," "sales price," or "minimum offer."

1. Total the money that the seller must get. This is the part.
2. Divide it by the percentage of the sale that it represents. This is the %.
3. The answer is the whole.

For Example:

Read the question carefully.

Laney wants to sell her home. She must pay off her existing $35,000 mortgage and pay $3,200 in closing costs. She wants to have $40,000 left so she can buy another home. If she pays a 6.5% commission, what is the minimum offer she can accept?

Solve the problem.

Whole = Part ÷ %

78,200 ÷ 0.935 (93.5%) = 83,636.3636

Laney must sell her house for a minimum of $83,636.36.

SAMPLE PROBLEMS **(to be worked in class).**

1. **Joan is selling her home. She needs to pay off a $65,000 first mortgage, a $15,000 second mortgage, and wants $10,000 in cash for herself. If her closing costs will total $1,200 and she must pay a seven percent commission, how much must she sell the property for?**
2. **The Jones are considering an offer on their home. They must pay off a $115,000 loan, pay closing costs of $1,000, and a survey fee of $425. Their broker is charging them a five percent commission. Determine the minimum acceptable offer.**

MATH EXERCISES

1. A seller must pay off an existing $42,000 mortgage and pay $1,700 in closing costs. If the seller wants to net $22,000 after paying a brokerage fee of 7%, for how much must the home be sold?

2. An individual purchased two lots last year for $10,000 each. The lots just sold for a total of $25,000. What is the percent of profit?

3. A property is currently valued at $3,500,000. If it generates an annual income of $175,000 and annual expenses total $40,000, what is the gross rent multiplier?

4. An apartment building generates $150,000 in yearly income. Building expenses total $2,000 per month. Using a capitalization rate of 9%, what's the building's value?

5. A lot is listed for sale at $1,500 per acre. Calculate the listing price for the parcel described as the S 1/2, SE 1/4, NE 1/4 of Section 33.

6. A buyer agrees to purchase a property for $150,000. The buyer will make a cash down payment of $30,000, the seller will carry a second mortgage of $10,000, and the buyer will get a first mortgage in the amount of $110,000 from a local savings and loan. How much is the transfer tax?

7. You are going to build a building. It will be 40' x 40' and consist of two floors. If the price per square foot of the building is $90, and the cost of a 150' x 500' lot is $100 per front foot, what is the total cost of the project?

8. A property is appraised for tax purposes at $150,000 and assessed for tax purposes at 35% of value. Using a total of 95 mills, calculate the annual taxes.

9. In the previous question, the property has been sold and will close on October 15, 2006. If the taxes for the first half of the year are paid, using a calendar year, how much in prorated taxes will be due the buyer at closing?

10. A buyer is purchasing a home for $100,000 and will finance it with a VA loan. If the lender is charging three points, how much will be owed in points?

11. A property is sold and will close on September 15, 2006. The annual taxes, last paid for 2005, are $2,436. Calculate the buyer's credit using a 365-day year.

12. A developer purchased a lot that measures 348' x 1,000'. If the land cost $5,000 per acre, what was the total cost?

13. A home is appraised at $130,000 and is insured for 80% of value. The premium for two-year coverage is $5 per thousand. The seller purchased and paid for the two-year policy on August 1, 2004. The property has been sold and will close on May 15, 2006. Calculate the seller's credit.

14. A house sold for $165,000 and the commission paid was $5,775. What was the rate of commission?

15. Laura paid $265,000 for her new home. She is putting 45% down, paying 3 points, and $2,650 in closing costs. How much money will she need to bring to the closing?

16. A property was listed for $150,000 and sold for 90% of the listing price. Commission was 7% and was split 50/50 between two brokerages. The listing broker then split his portion evenly with a listing salesperson. How much did the selling company get?

17. A property is valued at $125,000 and is assessed at 35% of value for tax purposes. Taxes are calculated at $5 per $100 of assessed value. Using a 365-day year, calculate the daily rate of taxes.

18. The apartments in a 12-unit apartment building rent for $475 per month. Vacancy and collection losses total 5% and monthly building expenses are $4,000. Calculate the effective gross income.

MATH QUIZ

1. *Your home is appraised at $125,000. The assessment level is 35%. There are a total of 40 mills in your taxing area. What are your annual taxes?*

a. $1,750
b. $3,215
c. $1,853
d. $2,361

2. *How many acres are there in the shaded area? What is the correct description for this section?*

a. 10 acres, N 1/2, NE 1/4, SE 1/4
b. 20 acres, N 1/2, NW 1/4, SE 1/4
c. 10 acres, N 1/2, NW 1/4, SW 1/4
d. 20 acres, N 1/2, NW 1/4, SW 1/4

3. *Mr. and Mrs. Davis sold their home for $182,000 and it is due to transfer on August 13, 2006. The buyer, Miss Fairchild, took out a loan for $162,000 and is planning on moving in on August 15. Who pays the conveyance fee and how much is it?*

a. Mr. and Mrs. Davis—$20
b. Miss Fairchild—$182
c. Miss Fairchild—$20
d. Mr. and Mrs. Davis—$182

4. *Bill expects a return of 8% on his investments and is considering a property with an asking price of $670,000. The records show a potential income of $6,200 a month, expenses of $1,500 a month, and a vacancy factor of 10%. With this information in mind, what would Bill's highest bid be?*

a. $343,250
b. $612,000
c. $137,000
d. $818,250

5. *Arnold wants to net $132,000 for his home. He has to pay off an existing mortgage of $19,700. His closing costs will run $5,400 and he owes the broker a fee of 7%. For Arnold to get the net figure he wants, what must he sell the home for?*

a. $157,100
b. $141,935
c. $163,118
d. $168,925

6. *Mr. and Mrs. Williams want to net $90,000 when they sell their home. They have to pay closing costs of $3,200 and the broker a 6% commission What's the least the home can sell for to net $90,000?*

a. $99,149
b. $93,200
c. $98,945
d. $99,500

7. *A house costs $100,000. The buyer is making a down payment of $32,000 and getting a $68,000 loan. If there are 4 points, how much money will be paid out of the closing for the points?*

a. $4,000
b. $2,720
c. $1,280
d. $400

8. *Mrs. Wilson got an interest-only loan for $12,500 at 8.75%. She has made 15 monthly payments of $91.15. What is her balloon payment?*

a. $12,045
b. $11,133
c. $12,500
d. $11,252

9. *How many square feet are there in the S 1/2, SW 1/4, NE 1/4 of Section 28?*

a. 720,480
b. 435,600
c. 136,125
d. 871,200

10. *Mr. and Mrs. Jason sold the lot adjoining their home for $15,000. If the lot measures 300 feet by 500 feet, how much did they get per front foot?*

a. $30
b. $50
c. $300
d. $500

11. *A property has a gross monthly income of $12,600 and a vacancy and collection loss rate averaging 11%, with monthly expenses of $1,500 and depreciation of 6% a year. What would be the highest counteroffer the prospective buyer should come up with if the buyer insists on a 15% rate of return and the asking price is $850,000?*

a. $777,120
b. $730,493
c. $723,293
d. $833,293

MATH EXERCISES ANSWER KEY

1. $70,645.16
2. 25%
3. 20
4. $1,400,000
5. $30,000
6. $150
7. $303,000
8. $4,987.50
9. $1,462.09
10. $3,000
11. $1,721.89
12. $39,945
13. $54.85
14. 3.5%
15. $126,272.50
16. $4,725
17. $5.99
18. $64,980

MATH QUIZ ANSWER KEY

1. a
2. b
3. d
4. b
5. d
6. a
7. b
8. c
9. d
10. b
11. a

FINAL EXAM 1

1. The first step in the appraisal process is to:
   a. Reconcile data
   b. Gather data
   c. Define the problem
   d. Inspect the property
2. An appraiser is appraising a single-family residence. The most weight would probably be given to which of the following methods?
   a. Sales comparison approach
   b. CMA
   c. Income approach
   d. Cost approach
3. A property has gross annual income of $250,000, monthly expenses of $8,000, and has recently sold for $2 million. What is the gross rent multiplier?
   a. 12.5%
   b. 12.5
   c. 8
   d. 12.9
4. An income-producing property generates $50,000 in gross annual income and has monthly expenses of $1,500. Depreciation is 3.64% per year and annual debt service is $18,000. Using a capitalization rate of 9%, calculate the value of the property.
   a. $45,000
   b. $535,555
   c. $155,556
   d. $355,556
5. The mortgage would be acknowledged by the:
   a. Notary
   b. Mortgagors
   c. Mortgagee
   d. Closing officer
6. A house costs $100,000 and the buyer is making a 20% down payment. The lender will charge 2 points. How much is that?
   a. $2,000
   b. $1,600
   c. $20,000
   d. $200
7. Of the 30 hours of continuing education, how many can be on computer-related subjects?
   a. 15 hours
   b. 6 hours
   c. 9 hours
   d. 8 hours
8. Chris passes the sales exam on June 2, 2006, his license is issued by the Division of Real Estate on June 15, 2006. Chris's birthday is September 16th. What is Chris's first continuing education due date?
   a. 01/01/2009
   b. 06/02/2009
   c. 06/15/2009
   d. 09/16/2009
9. The maximum number of hours of post-licensing instruction that can be taken in one day is:
   a. 8 hours
   b. 10 hours
   c. 5 hours
   d. 6 hours
10. The maximum number of hours of basic computer courses that may be included in the required 30 hours of continuing education is:
    a. 15 hours
    b. 6 hours
    c. 9 hours
    d. No limit
11. A salesperson's license must:
    a. Be displayed at the broker's office
    b. Be on file and available for inspection at the appropriate branch office
    c. Be on file and available for inspection at the broker's principal location
    d. Be carried in card form for inspection
12. Which of the following would have first priority?
    a. First mortgage
    b. IRS tax lien
    c. Ad valorem taxes
    d. Mechanic's lien

13. The state has decided to widen the highway in front of your home. It will be necessary to use 15 feet of your front yard to do so. The taking of that land by the state is termed:
    a. Eminent domain
    b. Confiscation
    c. Condemnation
    d. Right-of-way

14. In Ohio, it is presumed by statute that a buyer is represented by:
    a. Nobody
    b. Broker
    c. Selling salesperson
    d. None of the above

15. In Ohio, it is presumed by statute that a seller is represented by:
    a. Nobody
    b. Listing broker
    c. Listing broker and salespersons
    d. Listing broker and listing salesperson

16. Pat wishes to purchase an investment property and share ownership with two children. Pat will retain two-thirds ownership and the children will have one-third ownership. Pat and the children will take ownership as:
    a. Tenants by the entireties
    b. Joint tenants with the right of survivorship
    c. Tenants in common
    d. Tenants in a survivorship deed

17. Abandoned private property redeemed by local government is an example of:
    a. Police power
    b. Eminent domain
    c. Taxation
    d. Escheat

18. Which of the following would not be a fixture?
    a. Wall-to-wall carpet installed over plywood subflooring
    b. Built-in dishwasher
    c. Patio stones
    d. Light bulbs

19. Property held by a trust is going to be sold. The document necessary to convey the property is called:
    a. General warranty deed
    b. Trustee's deed
    c. Deed of trust
    d. Executor's conveyance certificate

20. A contract is entered into on fraudulent terms introduced by the seller. Upon discovery of the fraud by the buyers, the contract is:
    a. Void
    b. Voidable by the buyer
    c. Voidable by the seller
    d. Valid

21. Earnest money is:
    a. Determined by local custom
    b. Determined by the real estate broker/salesperson
    c. Fixed by law
    d. Not required for a valid purchase agreement

22. Excluding potential tenants based on which of the following criteria is a violation of federal fair housing laws?
    a. Sexual orientation
    b. Poor credit history
    c. Possession of pets
    d. Having of children

23. Which of the following is an exception to compliance by a property owner with fair housing laws in Ohio?
    a. Owner refusing to rent based on race
    b. Apartment owner taking into consideration a tenant's family status
    c. Landlord refusing reasonable accommodations based on handicap
    d. Religious organization renting space in its campground only to members of its church

24. All of the following documents are required to be in writing. Which one is not covered by the statute of frauds?
    a. Purchase agreement
    b. Listing agreement
    c. Option
    d. Five-year commercial lease

25. A parcel of ground described as the N 1/2, SE 1/4 of a section sells for $5,000 per acre. If the commission is 7% and it is split 50/50 between two brokerage companies, how much did each company receive?
    a. $14,000
    b. $28,000
    c. $7,000
    d. $1,400

26. Which of the following listings is discouraged in Ohio?
    a. Net listing
    b. Open listing
    c. Exclusive listing
    d. Exclusive right of sale listing

27. While Ohio law doesn't specifically permit or prohibit answering specific questions about the racial or ethnic composition of a neighborhood, the Ohio Division of Real Estate generally considers answering such questions:
    a. A violation
    b. Acceptable
    c. OK with the client's permission
    d. Permissible depending on the agency relationship

28. A homeowner enters into a listing agreement with a brokerage company. Several days into the listing but before the broker begins actively marketing the property, the homeowner sells the property to a close friend. If the homeowner stills owes the broker a commission, what type of listing was it?
    a. Exclusive listing
    b. Net listing
    c. Open listing
    d. Exclusive right to sell listing

29. A salesperson is acting as a dual agent. If the buyer is a family member, how must the salesperson disclose this fact?
    a. Disclosure is not necessary
    b. In the purchase contract
    c. On the Consumer Guide To Agency Relationships
    d. On the Agency/Dual Agency Disclosure form

30. A buyer attends an open house on October 4. The salesperson at the open house sets an appointment to meet with the buyer and does so on October 6, discussing at that time the buyer's motivation, urgency, and financial capabilities. They visit property on October 9 and submit an offer on October 10. What date must the Consumer Guide to Agency Relationships have been provided to the purchaser?
    a. October 4
    b. October 6
    c. October 9
    d. October 10

31. The owner of a large, vacant manufacturing facility must sell it. Rather than select just one broker, the owner extends an offer to a number of local commercial real estate brokers to invite their participation in the marketing of the property. The most likely type of listing here is:
    a. Net listing
    b. Open listing
    c. Exclusive right of sale listing
    d. Exclusive agency listing

32. In an in-house transaction, one salesperson represents the buyer and another salesperson represents the seller. In this transaction, the broker would be described as:
    a. An agent
    b. A subagent
    c. A dual agent
    d. A designated agent

33. In a real estate transaction, the principal would best be described as:
    a. The seller
    b. The buyer
    c. The person you represent
    d. All of the above

34. Consumer Guide to Agency Relationships must be given to a seller:
    a. At the time of the listing
    b. Prior to the marketing or showing
    c. At the first meeting
    d. At the first substantive meeting

35. **Two agents from the same company are involved in an in-house transaction. If one represents the seller and the other represents the buyer and neither are dual agents, they are best described as:**
    a. Split agents
    b. Undisclosed dual agents
    c. Disclosed dual agents
    d. Subagents

36. **An agent takes a property listing and, per company policy, is representing the seller. Another salesperson in the same firm is representing the buyer who wishes to make an offer on the seller's home. The agent for the buyer inadvertently discloses information about the buyer that's beneficial to the seller. What's the buyer's agent's responsibility?**
    a. Maintain composure and act as if nothing happened
    b. Act in an unbiased manner
    c. Disclose to the buyer that a breach has occurred and offer to withdraw as agent
    d. Act as a disclosed dual agent

37. **Using the information in the previous question, if the broker learned of the information in question, the broker's responsibility would be to:**
    a. Maintain the confidentiality of the information
    b. Act in a biased manner
    c. Act as an undisclosed dual agent
    d. Fire the buyer's agent

38. **A brokerage company represents the buyer in a co-op transaction. The company is informed that the buyer's earnest money deposit check has been returned for insufficient funds. What is its responsibility to the co-op company?**
    a. Disclose the information immediately
    b. Ask the buyer if it's OK to disclose the problem
    c. Maintain confidentiality of the information
    d. Give the buyer reasonable time to resolve the problem before calling the co-op

39. **Conventional loans are:**
    a. Never insured
    b. Insured by FHA
    c. Guaranteed by VA
    d. Not insured by the federal government

40. **A brokerage company receives an offer on a listing they have. This offer is accepted, contingent upon the buyer obtaining financing and a satisfactory home inspection. If another brokerage wants to show the property, what is the listing broker's responsibility?**
    a. Disclose the existing offer
    b. Disclose the existing offer only if the seller gives permission
    c. Maintain confidentiality of the information
    d. Refuse to return calls of the agent involved so as not to have to make a decision

41. **If a duly appointed representative of the Ohio Division of Real Estate wants to audit your company's files, trust account records, etc., the broker's responsibility is to:**
    a. Require a subpoena
    b. Ask for legal counsel
    c. Require an advance list of the files sought
    d. Make files and records readily available

42. **A real estate salesperson wishes to purchase property personally. By law, how must the salesperson disclose his or her status as a licensee?**
    a. By disclosing it in all relevant documents
    b. By writing it in the agency disclosure form
    c. In writing on the offer before entering into a binding agreement for the sale of the property
    d. Verbally as soon as the agent meets the seller

43. **A real estate salesperson wishes to sell a personal residence. It will be listed with the salesperson's brokerage company. By law, how must the salesperson disclose his or her status as a licensee?**
    a. In the listing contract
    b. In the Multiple Listing Service
    c. In all marketing materials and on the purchase contract
    d. In writing before entering into a binding agreement for the sale of the property

44. A salesperson decides not to continue in the real estate business and instructs the broker to return his or her license to the Ohio Division of Real Estate. The license will be termed:

a. In escrow
b. On deposit
c. Inactive
d. On hold

45. A brokerage company has the listing on a property. It receives two offers on the property from two separate co-op brokers. What is the brokerage company's responsibility to the other two brokerages?

a. Disclose the multiple offers
b. Disclose the multiple offers only with the seller's permission
c. Disclose the multiple offers as required by the Canons of Ethics
d. Disclose the multiple offers as required by the Code of Ethics

46. A buyer and seller agree in a purchase contract to have the earnest money deposit held in an interest-bearing account with the interest split between buyer and seller. This is:

a. OK, if the buyer and seller make this request since it is part of the contract
b. Not OK, because the deposit must be kept in the sales agent's non-interest trust account
c. OK, if a separate account is created in the broker's name to hold the deposit
d. Not OK, and the broker should inform the buyer and seller that they cannot do this

47. Who needs a real estate license?

a. An attorney handling real estate in an estate
b. A salesperson working on a commission basis for a production builder
c. A property management company
d. A friend selling a neighbor's house for $100

48. An agent, in making an agency disclosure to a buyer or seller, must provide which of the following?

a. Agency/dual agency disclosure form
b. Agency/dual agency disclosure form and a copy of company policy
c. Agency/dual agency disclosure form and the Consumer Guide to Agency Relationships
d. Agency/dual agency disclosure form and residential property disclosure form

49. A consumer sues a real estate salesperson for a major problem and wins a $50,000 judgment. The licensee has few assets and the consumer asks to be compensated from the Real Estate Recovery Fund. The maximum amount that the consumer can collect from the fund is:

a. $40,000
b. $50,000
c. $10,000
d. $1,000,000

50. A salesperson, holding an open house on a rainy day, learns that when it rains, the windows leak. The seller made no mention of it on the Residential Disclosure Form. What is the salesperson's duty as a licensee?

a. Tell the sellers they must correct the form
b. Disclose the leaks to prospective buyers
c. Tell the sellers to disclose the leaks
d. Maintain confidentiality of the information since the seller is your client

FINAL EXAM 2

1. **What is the primary purpose of a deed?**
   a. Transfer of title
   b. Proof of ownership
   c. Recordation
   d. Legal evidence

2. **A seller's counteroffer would be considered which of the following?**
   a. An amended listing contract
   b. An amended offer to purchase
   c. A change
   d. A new contract

3. **All of the following are essential to a valid contract, except:**
   a. Consideration
   b. Duress
   c. Offer and acceptance
   d. Legality of object

4. **An act by a creditor to receive payment on a defaulted loan is called:**
   a. Redemption
   b. Escrow
   c. Foreclosure
   d. Assignment

5. **The type of mortgage that encompasses more than one property is:**
   a. Package mortgage
   b. Wraparound mortgage
   c. Blanket mortgage
   d. Construction mortgage

6. **A landlord-tenant relationship can be which of the following?**
   a. Periodic
   b. Severalty
   c. Tenancy by the entireties
   d. Freehold estate

7. **Which lease tenancy is engaged in by a holdover tenant?**
   a. Tenancy at sufferance
   b. Tenancy for life
   c. Estate for years
   d. Periodic tenancy

8. **Title to real property may be obtained by means of:**
   a. License
   b. Easement
   c. Encroachment
   d. Adverse possession

9. **Section 36 of a township is found where?**
   a. NE corner of the township
   b. NW corner of the township
   c. SE corner of the township
   d. SW corner of the township

10. **The responsibility for recording a deed lies with the:**
    a. Grantor
    b. Grantee
    c. County
    d. State

11. **A latent defect is best described as:**
    a. A defect that the prudent buyer can see
    b. An old defect
    c. A defect that is hidden from view
    d. A breach of contract by the seller

12. **A real estate salesperson must:**
    a. Always be affiliated with a broker
    b. Never refuse to accept a listing
    c. Display his or her own salesperson's license in the broker's place of business
    d. Have a personal trust account

13. **An offeror may withdraw his or her offer until:**
    a. The closing date
    b. The deed is recorded
    c. The offer is signed
    d. He or she is notified that the offer has been accepted

14. **If the mortgagor defaults on the note:**
    a. The mortgagor is given a six-month grace period to bring the account current
    b. The mortgage becomes due and payable
    c. The mortgagee may begin a non-judicial foreclosure proceeding immediately
    d. The mortgagor may redeem the property after the confirmation

15. **What type of ownership does a condominium owner hold?**
    a. Fee simple
    b. Estate in trust
    c. Proprietary lease
    d. Group ownership

16. **The government of a municipality holds control over real property through all of the following, except:**
   a. Taxation
   b. Assessments
   c. Encumbrances
   d. Eminent domain

17. **Which of the following is an example of an easement appurtenance?**
   a. A shared driveway
   b. Power lines
   c. License
   d. Landlocked land

18. **A gas station was built in 1960 in an area that was rezoned to residential in 1990. The gas station constitutes:**
   a. A variance
   b. A nonconforming use
   c. Spot zoning
   d. A violation

19. **The government regulations that most affect the value of property are:**
   a. Zoning ordinances
   b. Covenants of deed restrictions
   c. Laws of escheat
   d. Federal Housing Authority regulations

20. **When a lessee assigns his or her lease to another, the lessee:**
   a. Gives up the remainder of the lease
   b. Retains a portion of the lease
   c. Terminates his or her own lease
   d. Has created a novation

21. **Land can be taken by adverse possession if:**
   a. The adverse claimant cultivates crops
   b. The land is possessed in a manner hostile to the owner
   c. The land is possessed with the owner's knowledge and consent
   d. The owner receives rent

22. **Functional obsolescence is due to:**
   a. Normal wear and tear
   b. Poor design or floor plan
   c. Poor location
   d. External factors

23. **To the owner of the land it runs across, an easement is:**
   a. An appurtenance
   b. An encumbrance
   c. A common interest
   d. An attachment

24. **The legal description of the shaded area in the diagram is:**
   a. NW 1/4 of SW 1/4
   b. SW 1/4 of NE 1/4
   c. SW 1/4 of NW 1/4
   d. SW 1/4 of SW 1/4 of NW 1/4

25. **Deed restrictions are considered to be:**
   a. General liens
   b. Escheat
   c. Encumbrances
   d. Enforceable only by the property owner

26. **Which of the following persons cannot be held to a contract?**
   a. A minor
   b. An elderly person
   c. A widow or widower
   d. A divorced couple

27. **It is mandatory that a listing contract:**
   a. Have a termination date
   b. Be signed by the purchasers
   c. Be executed in triplicate
   d. Have a legal description of the property being sold

28. **Money for FHA financing is provided by:**
   a. Any government agency
   b. FDIC
   c. Any qualified lending institution
   d. The Federal Housing Administration

29. **A second mortgage taken on real property:**
   a. Has precedence over the first mortgage
   b. Is subordinate to any previously issued or recorded mortgage on the property
   c. Is paid second, after real estate taxes, in foreclosure proceedings
   d. Can exist only with approval of the first mortgagee

30. Discount points are charged by lending institutions:

a. To lower the closing costs
b. To help a mortgagor with a down payment
c. To lower the interest rate
d. To help cover closing costs

31. The definition of depreciation is:

a. A loss in value
b. Mortgage foreclosures
c. Loss from scarcity of a product
d. Negative amortization

32. A property is sold and will close on April 12, 2006. The seller's have paid taxes through the first half of 2006. If annual taxes are $3,400, what amount of pro-rated taxes will be debited the seller at closing?

a. $1,250.14
b. $2,650.14
c. $2,691.67
d. $2,664.12

33. What is the fullest estate a property owner can have?

a. Fee simple divisible
b. Full unity of possession
c. Tenancy for years
d. Fee simple absolute

34. The Fair Housing Act prohibits all of the following except:

a. Discrimination in housing because of race
b. Discrimination in housing due to religion
c. Discrimination in residential renting
d. Discrimination in housing based on marital status

35. Identification objects used by surveyors to establish description points are referred to as:

a. Metes and bounds
b. Base lines
c. Monuments
d. Meridians

36. A warranty deed guarantees against all of the following, except:

a. The grantor's heirs
b. Easements of record
c. Mortgages
d. Judgment liens

37. Meeting of the minds refers to:

a. The consummation of a contract
b. The consideration
c. The offer and acceptance
d. The closing of a contract

38. The person who hires another to represent him or her is known as:

a. A customer
b. A client
c. A broker
d. An agent

39. Conventional loans are:

a. Never insured
b. Insured by FHA
c. Guaranteed by VA
d. Can be insured

40. The lender in a mortgage arrangement is the:

a. Mortgagee
b. Mortgagor
c. Trustee
d. Beneficiary

41. A note, as opposed to a mortgage, is a:

a. Lien
b. Personal obligation
c. Second mortgage
d. Judgment

42. If a lessor dies, the lease is:

a. Cancelled
b. Renegotiated
c. Unchanged
d. Rescinded

43. Upon signing a management contract with an owner, a broker becomes a:

a. Trustee
b. Receiver
c. Management director
d. Fiduciary

44. The value of property can be lowered by:

a. Open market operations
b. Options
c. Order of execution
d. Obsolescence

45. **Under the housing discrimination laws, it is illegal to refuse to show real property to all of the following, except:**
    a. A single person
    b. A minority group member
    c. A foreigner
    d. A person of another religion

46. **Essential items for a deed include:**
    a. Signatures of grantor and grantee
    b. Words of conveyance
    c. Recording
    d. Property address

47. **An agency relationship is created between a principal and a real estate broker by a:**
    a. Purchase agreement
    b. Listing contract
    c. Purchase offer
    d. Land contract

48. **If personal property is included in the sale of real property, which of the following documents should be used?**
    a. Purchase agreement
    b. Bill of sale
    c. Deed
    d. All of the above

49. **Which permits the seller to subsidize the buyer's interest rate so that the first few years require lower payments from the buyer?**
    a. Open-end mortgage
    b. Balloon payment
    c. Temporary buydown
    d. Blanket mortgage

50. **For a deed to be conveyed, it must be:**
    a. Signed by the grantee
    b. Accepted
    c. Mortgaged
    d. Recorded

CHAPTER ANSWER KEYS

Chapter 1
The Real Estate Profession

1. c
2. d
3. b
4. a
5. b
6. a
7. a
8. d
9. a

Chapter 2
Getting a Real Estate License

1. d
2. b
3. c
4. d
5. c
6. d
7. a
8. a

Chapter 3
Keeping your Real Estate License

1. a
2. d
3. d
4. a
5. b
6. d
7. a
8 b

Chapter 4
The Real Estate Industry

1. c
2. a
3. c
4. d
5. d
6. b
7. a

Chapter 5
Overview of Real Estate Law

1. b
2. a
3. c
4. d
5. b
6. d
7. d
8. d
9. b
10. d
11. c
12. c
13. d
14. c

Chapter 6
Brokers, Salespeople, and the Agency Relationship

1. c
2. c
3. a
4. b
5. b
6. d
7. a
8. a
9. d
10. b
11. a
12. c
13. d
14. b
15. a
16. d

Chapter 7
Real Estate Contracts, Agreements, and Documents

1. d
2. c
3. b
4. c
5. c
6. a
7. c
8. c
9. a
10. d
11. b
12. c
13. d
14. b

Chapter 8 Deeds and Ownership

1. c
2. c
3. b
4. a
5. c
6. b
7. a
8. c
9. a
10. a
11. b

Chapter 9 Real Estate Closings

1. c
2. d
3. a
4. c
5. b
6. b
7. c
8. c
9. d
10. a

Chapter 10 Real Estate Practice

1. d
2. c
3. b
4. c
5. b
6. d
7. d
8. b

Chapter 11 Fair Housing

1. c
2. c
3. a
4. b
5. a
6. b
7. c
8. d
9. a
10. d
11. c
12. a

Chapter 12 Overview of Real Estate Finance

1. a
2. d
3. c
4. d
5. d
6. b
7. a
8. b
9. d
10. b
11. c
12. c
13. c
14. d

Chapter 13 Mortgage Basics

1. a
2. c
3. b
4. c
5. d
6. b
7. d
8. c

Chapter 14 Overview of Real Estate Appraisal

1. d
2. c
3. b
4. b
5. d
6. d
7. a
8. d
9. c
10. c
11. a

Chapter 15
Property Valuation

1.	a	8.	d
2.	b	9.	a
3.	c	10.	b
4.	d	11.	a
5.	c	12.	c
6.	b	13.	d
7.	d		

Final Exam Answer Key
Exam 1

1.	c	26.	a
2.	a	27.	a
3.	c	28.	d
4.	d	29.	d
5.	b	30.	b
6.	b	31.	b
7.	a	32.	c
8.	d	33.	c
9.	d	34.	b
10.	b	35.	a
11.	c	36.	c
12.	c	37.	a
13.	c	38.	a
14.	a	39.	d
15.	d	40.	b
16.	c	41.	d
17.	d	42.	c
18.	d	43.	c
19.	b	44.	c
20.	b	45.	b
21.	d	46.	a
22.	d	47.	a
23.	d	48.	c
24.	b	49.	a
25.	a	50.	b

Final Exam Answer Key
Exam 2

1.	a	26.	a
2.	c	27.	a
3.	b	28.	c
4.	c	29.	b
5.	c	30.	c
6.	a	31.	a
7.	a	32.	d
8.	d	33.	d
9.	c	34.	d
10.	b	35.	c
11.	c	36.	b
12.	a	37.	c
13.	d	38.	b
14.	b	39.	d
15.	a	40.	a
16.	c	41.	b
17.	a	42.	c
18.	b	43.	d
19.	a	44.	d
20.	a	45.	a
21.	b	46.	b
22.	b	47.	b
23.	b	48.	b
24.	c	49.	c
25.	c	50.	b

GLOSSARY

The definitions given here represent how these terms are used in real estate. Some terms have additional meanings, which can be found in a standard dictionary.

Abandonment The failure to occupy and use property, which may result in a loss of rights.

Abstract of Title A brief, chronological summary of the recorded documents affecting title to a particular parcel of real property. *Compare:* **Title Report**.

Acceleration Clause A contract clause giving the lender the right to declare the entire loan amount due immediately because of borrower's default, or other reasons as stated in the contract.

Acceptance 1. Agreeing to the terms of an offer to enter into a contract, thereby creating a binding contract. 2. Taking delivery of a deed.

Accession The acquisition of title to land by its addition to real estate already owned, through human actions or natural processes. *See:* **Accretion; Annexation; Reliction**.

Accord and Satisfaction An agreement to accept something different (usually less) than what the original contract required.

Accretion A gradual addition to dry land by the forces of nature, as when the tide deposits waterborne sediment on shoreline property. *See:* **Accession; Alluvion**.

Acknowledgment A person who signing a document and formally declaring to an authorized official (usually a notary public) that he or she signed voluntarily. The official certifies that the signature is voluntary and genuine. *Compare:* **Attestation**.

Act *See:* **Statute**.

Actionable Fraud *See:* **Fraud, Actionable**.

Actual Annexation *See:* **Annexation, Actual**.

Actual Authority *See:* **Authority, Actual**.

Actual Damages *See:* **Damages, Actual**.

Actual Eviction *See:* **Eviction, Actual**.

Actual Fraud *See:* **Fraud, Actual**.

Actual Notice *See:* **Notice, Actual**.

Ad Valorem A Latin phrase meaning "according to value"; refers to taxes assessed on property value.

Adjustable Rate Mortgage A mortgage that permits the lender to periodically adjust the interest rate so that the rate reflects fluctuations in the cost of money. Also called **ARM**.

Adjustment Period, Mortgage Payment The interval at which a borrower's actual mortgage payments change with an ARM (adjustable rate mortgage).

Adjustment Period, Rate The interval at which a borrower's actual interest rate changes with an ARM (adjustable rate mortgage).

Administrative Agency A government agency (federal, state, or local) that administers a complex area of law, adopting and enforcing detailed regulations that have the force of law.

Administrator A person appointed by the probate court to manage and distribute the estate of a deceased person when no executor is named in the will or there is no will.

Adverse Possession Acquiring title to someone else's real property by possession of it. The possession must be open and notorious, hostile and adverse, exclusive, and continuous, for more than 21 years. *Compare:* **Prescription**.

Affiant A person who makes an affidavit.

Affidavit A sworn statement that has been written and acknowledged; may be submitted as evidence in a trial.

Affirm An appeals court ruling that the lower court's decision was correct, rejecting the appellant's arguments.

After-Acquired Title *See:* **Title, After-Acquired**.

Age of Majority *See:* **Majority, Age of**.

Agency A relationship of trust created when one person (the principal) gives another person (the agent) the right to represent the principal in dealings with third parties.

Agency, Apparent 1. When someone who has not been authorized to represent another acts as if he or she is that person's agent. 2. When an agent acts beyond the scope of his or her authority, giving a third party the impression that the acts are authorized. Also called **ostensible agency**.

Agency, Dual A broker or salesperson representing both parties (buyer and seller) in a transaction, ***and*** all management-level licensees at a brokerage.

Agency, Exclusive *See:* **Listing, Exclusive Agency**.

Agency, Ostensible *See:* **Agency, Apparent**.

Agency Coupled with an Interest A situations in which the agent has a personal interest in the subject of the agency, as when one co-owner has been authorized by the others to sell their property.

Agency Disclosure Statement Form that states whether an agent is representing the seller or the buyer, or both, in a transaction.

Agent A person licensed to represent another in a real estate transaction; or a person authorized to represent another (the principal) in dealings with third parties.

Agent, Dual A licensee who represents both the seller and buyer in the same transaction.

Agent, General An agent authorized to handle all of the principal's affairs in one area or in specified areas.

Agent, Special An agent with limited authority to do a specific thing or conduct a specific transaction.

Agent, Split A licensee assigned by a broker to represent a buyer or seller in a transaction, usually in an in company dual agency situation.

Agent, Universal An agent authorized to do everything that can be lawfully delegated to a representative.

Agreement *See:* **Contract**.

Air Rights The right to undisturbed use and control of the airspace over a parcel of land (within reasonable limits for air travel); may be transferred separately from the land.

Alienation The transfer of ownership or an interest in property from one person to another, by any means.

Alienation, Involuntary The transfer of an interest in property against the will of the owner, or without action by the owner, occurring through operation of law, natural processes, or adverse possession.

Alienation, Voluntary An owner voluntarily transferring an interest to someone else.

Alienation Clause A contract clause that gives the lender certain stated rights when there's a transfer of ownership in the property. Upon sale of, or even a transfer of, significant interest in the property, the lender will often have the right to accelerate the debt (here called a **due on sale clause**), change the interest rate, or charge a hefty assumption fee (FHA and VA loans cannot have this) .

Allodial System The system of land ownership under which anyone can own land.

Alluvion The solid material deposited along a shore by accretion. Also called **alluvium**.

Amortization Provision In a zoning law, a provision that places time limits on nonconforming uses. Not permitted in Ohio.

Amortized Loans Loans for which payments are applied to principal and interest.

Amount in Controversy The amount of money at issue in a lawsuit; used as a limitation on the jurisdiction of some courts.

Ancillary Trustee A trustee appointed by the Ohio Real Estate Commission to wrap up the brokerage business of a broker who dies.

Annexation Attaching personal property to land so that the law views it as part of the real property. *See:* **Fixture**.

Annexation, Actual A physical attachment of personal property to land. *See:* **Fixture**.

Annexation, Constructive Personal property associated with real property in such a way that the law treats it as a fixture, even though it is not physically attached to the real property.

Annual Percentage Rate The total cost of financing a loan in percentage terms, as a relationship of the total finance charges to the total amount financed.

Answer Document that a defendant must file with the court in response to the plaintiff's complaint.

Anticipatory Repudiation When one party to a contract informs the other before the time set for performance that he or she does not intend to perform as agreed. *See:* **Tender**.

Apparent Agency *See:* **Agency, Apparent**.

Apparent Authority *See:* **Authority, Apparent**.

Appeal The process in which a higher court reviews the decision of a lower court or an administrative tribunal.

Appellant The party (also called the **petitioner)** who files an appeal because of dissatisfaction with the trial court's decision.

Appellate Jurisdiction *See:* **Jurisdiction, Appellate.**

Appellee In an appeal, the party (also called the **respondent)** who did *not* file the appeal.

Appraisal An estimate or opinion of the value of property as of a certain date. Also called **valuation.**

Appraisal Report Form A type of appraisal report that the appraiser fills in blanks to complete.

Appraiser A person who appraises property, especially an expert qualified to do so by education and experience.

Appropriation Taking private property for public use, through the government's power of eminent domain. Also called **condemnation.**

Appropriative Rights Water rights allocated by government permit, according to an appropriation system. It is not necessary to own property beside the body of water in order to apply for an appropriation permit. *Compare:* **Littoral Rights, Riparian Rights.**

Appurtenance A right that goes along with ownership of real property; usually transferred with the property, but may be sold separately.

Appurtenance, Intangible An appurtenant right that does not involve ownership of physical objects, for example, easements (as opposed to mineral rights, which involve tangibles).

Appurtenant Easement *See:* **Easement, Appurtenant.**

APR *See:* **Annual Percentage Rate.**

Arbitration An alternative to a court proceeding where the parties agree to submit facts and evidence to an impartial third party.

Area Variance *See:* **Variance, Area.**

ARM *See:* **Adjustable Rate Mortgage.**

Arm's Length Transaction A transaction that occurred under typical conditions in the marketplace, with each party acting in his or her own best interest.

Artificial Person An entity created by law, as distinguished from a natural person, a human being; usually refers to a corporation.

"As Is" Clause A provision in a purchase agreement stating that the buyer accepts the property in its present condition.

Assessed Value *See:* **Value, Assessed.**

Assessment 1. A government's valuation of property for tax purposes; 2. A special assessment.

Assessment, Special *See:* **Special Assessment.**

Assessor An official who determines the value of property for taxation.

Assign 1. To transfer a right or interest to another; 2. A tenant transferring his or her right of possession, or other interest in leased property, to another for the remainder of the lease term. *Compare:* **Sublease.**

Assignee Person to whom a right or interest has been assigned.

Assignment *See:* **Assign.**

Assignor A person who assigns a right or interest to another.

Associate Broker *See:* **Broker, Associate.**

Assumption One party taking over responsibility for the loan of another party; usually lender approval is needed.

Attachment Court-ordered seizure of property belonging to a defendant in a lawsuit, so it will be available to satisfy a judgment. In the case of real property, attachment creates a lien. *See:* **Lien, Attachment.**

Attachments, Man-made *See:* **Fixture.**

Attachments, Natural Things growing on a piece of land, such as trees, shrubs, or crops. *See:* **Fructus Industriales; Fructus Naturales.** *Compare:* **Fixture.**

Attestation Witnesses signing a legal document to affirm that the parties' signatures are real; the act of witnessing the execution of a legal document (such as a deed or will). *Compare:* **Acknowledgment.**

Attorney in Fact Any person authorized to act for another by a power of attorney (not necessarily a lawyer who is an attorney at law).

Authority, Actual Authority intentionally given to an agent by the principal, either expressly or by implication.

Authority, Apparent *See:* **Agency, Apparent.**

Authority, Express Authority expressly communicated, in words or in writing, by the principal to the agent.

Authority, Implied Authority indirectly given to an agent to do everything reasonably necessary to carry out the principal's express orders.

Balloon Payment A final payment at the end of a loan term to pay off the entire remaining balance of principal and interest not covered by payments during the loan term.

Bargain and Sale Deed *See:* **Deed, Bargain and Sale**.

Base *See:* **Subject Property**.

Base Lines Main east-west lines designated and named throughout the country for use with the government survey system.

Bequeath To transfer personal property to another by a will.

Bequest Personal property transferred by a will.

Bi-Weekly Mortgage *See:* **Mortgage, Bi-Weekly**.

Bilateral Contract *See:* **Contract, Bilateral**.

Bill A proposed law, formally submitted to a legislature for consideration.

Bill of Sale A document used to transfer title to personal property from one person to another.

Binding Precedent *See:* **Precedent, Binding**.

Blanket Mortgage *See:* **Mortgage, Blanket**.

Blockbusting The illegal practice of inducing owners to sell their homes (often at a deflated price) by suggesting that the ethnic or racial composition of the neighborhood is changing, with the implication that property values will decline as a result. Also called **panic selling**.

Bona Fide In good faith; genuine.

Bond-type Securities Mortgage backed securities issued by Ginnie Mae, which are long term, pay interest semi-annually, and provide for repayment at a specified date.

Boundary The perimeter or border of a parcel of land; the dividing line between one piece of property and another.

Breach Violation of an obligation, duty, or law.

Breach, Material A breach of contract important enough to excuse the non-breaching party from performing his or her contractual obligations.

Breach of Contract An unexcused failure to perform according to the terms of a contract.

Broker One who is licensed to represent one of the parties in a real estate transaction, for compensation.

Broker, Associate One who has qualified as a real estate broker but works for another broker.

Brokerage A broker's business.

Budget Mortgage *See:* **Mortgage, Budget**.

Building Code Regulations establishing minimum standards for construction and materials.

Bump Clause A provision in a purchase agreement that allows the seller to keep the property on the market until a condition in the contract is fulfilled.

Bundle of Rights All real property rights that are conferred with ownership, including right of use, right of enjoyment, and right of disposal.

Burden of Proof *See:* **Proof, Burden of**.

Business Compulsion *See:* **Duress, Economic**.

Business Cycles General swings in business activity, resulting in expanding and contracting activity during different phases of the cycle.

Business Name Certificate Partnership document listing the names and addresses of all partners, which must be filed in the county where the partnership office is located before property can be held in a partnership's name.

Buydown Additional funds in the form of points paid to a lender at the beginning of a loan to lower the interest rate and monthly payments on a loan.

Buydown, Permanent When points are paid to a lender to reduce the interest rate and loan payments for the entire life of the loan.

Buydown, Temporary When points are paid to a lender to reduce the interest rate and payments early in a loan, with interest rate and payments rising later.

Buyer's Market A situation in the housing market giving buyers a large selection of properties from which to choose.

Call Provision Clause that lets lender demand full payment of a loan immediately (verb: **call a note**).

Cancellation Termination of a contract without undoing the acts already performed under it. *Compare:* **Rescission**.

Cap, Interest Rate A limit on the amount of interest rate increase that can occur with an adjustable rate mortgage.

Cap, Mortgage Payment A limit on the amount of mortgage payment increase that can occur with an adjustable rate mortgage.

Cap, Negative Amortization A limit on the amount of negative amortization that can occur with an adjustable rate mortgage.

Capacity Legal ability to perform some act, such as enter into a contract or execute a deed or will. *See:* **Competent; Minor**.

Capitalization Rate A percentage rate of return used by investors to calculate the present value of future income; used for an income approach to appraisal. Also called **rate**.

Capture, Rule of *See:* **Rule of Capture**.

Carryover Clause *See:* **Extension Clause**.

Case Law Rules of law developed in court decisions, as opposed to constitutional law, statutory law, or administrative regulations.

Caveat Emptor A Latin phrase meaning "let the buyer beware." The rule that says a buyer is expected to examine property carefully instead of relying on the seller to point out problems.

CC&Rs A declaration of covenants, conditions, and restrictions; usually recorded by a developer to create a general plan of private restrictions for a subdivision.

Cease and Desist Order A court order requiring certain activities be stopped.

Certificate of Eligibility Certificate issued by the Veteran's Administration to establish the status and amount of a veteran's eligibility to qualify for a guaranteed loan.

Certificate of Judgment A summary of the provisions of a court judgment; when recorded, it creates a lien on all real property of the debtor in the county where recorded.

Certificate of Title A document prepared by an attorney stating the attorney's opinion of the status of the title to a piece of property, after performing a title search and reviewing the public records.

Certificate of Transfer A document issued by a probate court showing a transfer of title from a deceased person to his or her heirs or devisees.

Chain of Title *See:* **Title, Chain of**.

Chattel A piece of personal property.

Chattel Real Personal property that is closely associated with real property, such as a lease.

Checker Person working with the fair housing organization who pretends to be interested in buying or renting property from someone suspected of unlawful discrimination. Also called a **tester**.

Choate Dower *See:* **Dower Rights, Choate**.

Civil Law The body of law concerned with the rights and liabilities of one individual in relation to another; includes contract, tort, and property law. *Compare:* **Criminal Law**.

Civil Litigation A lawsuit in which one person sues another for compensation.

Civil Rights Fundamental rights guaranteed to all persons by the law. The term is primarily used in reference to constitutional and statutory protections against discrimination based on race, religion, sex, or national origin.

Civil Wrong *See:* **Tort**.

Client Person who employs a broker, lawyer, or other professional. Real estate clients can be sellers, buyers, or both. *See:* **Fiduciary**.

Closing Transfer of real property ownership from seller to buyer, according to terms and conditions in a sales contract or escrow agreement; the final stage in a real estate transaction.

Closing Costs Expenses incurred in the transfer of real estate in addition to the purchase price; for example, the appraisal fee, title insurance premiums, broker's commission, transfer tax.

Closing Statement *See:* **Settlement Statement**.

Cloud on Title A claim, encumbrance, or defect that makes the title to real property unmarketable. *See:* **Marketable Title**.

CMA *See:* **Competitive Market Analysis**.

Codicil Addition to or revision of a will (must be executed with the same formalities as a will) .

Codification Collection and organization of various laws into a comprehensive statutory code.

Collusion An agreement between two or more persons to defraud someone.

Color of Title Title that appears to be good but that, in fact, is not.

Commercial Banks Financial institutions that provide a variety of financial services.

Commercial Property Property zoned and used for business purposes, such as warehouses, restaurants, and office buildings (as distinguished from residential, industrial, or agricultural property).

Commingling Illegally mixing money held in trust on behalf of a client with personal funds. *See:* **Conversion**.

Commission Compensation paid to a broker for services in a real estate transaction; usually a percentage of sale price, rather than a flat fee.

Common Areas The land and improvements in a condominium, planned unit development, or cooperative that all residents use and own as tenants in common, such as the parking lot, hallways, and recreational facilities; individual apartment units or homes are not included.

Common Grantor A person who owned two or more neighboring properties and then sold them to different buyers.

Common Law 1. Early English law. 2. Long established rules based on English law, still followed in many states. 3. Case law.

Common Law Marriage When two people of the opposite sex hold themselves out to the world as being married, such as through the use of a joint checking account, even though no formal marriage decree has been issued by a court. No longer available in Ohio.

Common Law Remedy *See:* **Legal Remedy**.

Community Property In some states, property is owned jointly by a married couple. Only Arizona, California, Idaho, Louisiana, Nevada, New Mexico, Texas, and Washington have community property system laws. *Compare:* **Separate Property.**

Comparable Market Analysis *See:* **Competitive Market Analysis**.

Comparables Other similar properties that have sold in a certain area. Also called **Comps**.

Comparative Negligence Rule When parties share liability based on their partial fault or negligence in causing the injury or tort.

Compensatory Damages *See:* **Damages, Compensatory**.

Competent 1. Of sound mind, for the purposes of entering a contract or executing a will; not suffering from mental illness, retardation, or senility. 2. Of sound mind and having reached the age of majority.

Competitive Market Analysis A method of determining the approximate market value of a home by comparing the subject property to other homes that have sold, are presently for sale, or did not sell in a given area.

Complaint The document a plaintiff files with the court to begin a lawsuit.

Comprehensive Plan Long-range plan for development of a city or region.

Comps *See:* **Comparables**.

Compulsion, Business *See:* **Duress, Economic**.

Concurrent Jurisdiction *See:* **Jurisdiction, Concurrent**.

Concurrent Ownership *See:* **Co-ownership**.

Condemnation 1. Taking private property for public use, through the government's power of eminent domain. Also called **Appropriation**. 2. A declaration that a structure is unfit for occupancy and must be closed or demolished.

Condition A provision in a contract or deed that makes the parties' rights and obligations depend on the occurrence (or nonoccurrence) of a particular event. Also **Contingency Clause**.

Conditional Fee *See:* **Fee, Conditional**.

Conditional Use A land use that does not comply with the general zoning rules for the zone in which it's located, but is permitted because it benefits the public; for example, a hospital in a residential neighborhood. Also called a **Special Exception**.

Condominium A property developed for co-ownership, with each co-owner having a separate interest in an individual unit, combined with an undivided interest in the common areas of the property. *Compare:* **Cooperative.**

Condominium Association *See:* **Unit Owners Association.**

Condominium Declaration The document that must be filed for record when property is developed as, or converted to, a condominium.

Confirmation of Sale A document filed by the court to finalize the sale of property at foreclosure, and after which time the equitable right of redemption is no longer available to the original defaulting borrower.

Conforming Loans Loans that meet Fannie Mae/Freddie Mac standards and, thus, can be sold on the secondary market.

Conformity A "rule" that says a particular house achieves maximum value when it's surrounded by homes similar in style and function.

Consequential Damages *See:* **Damages, Consequential**.

Consideration Anything of value, such as money, services, goods, or promises, given to induce another to enter into a contract. Sometimes called **Valuable Consideration**.

Consideration, Adequate Consideration that is comparable in value to the consideration the other party to the contract is giving. A contract is enforceable even if the consideration is inadequate, but a court cannot order specific performance in that case.

Constitution A fundamental document that establishes a government's structure and sets limits on its power.

Constitutional 1. Pertaining to or based on a constitution. 2. Not in violation of the U.S. Constitution or a state constitution.

Constitutional Law Law derived from the Constitution.

Construction, Statutory *See:* **Statutory Construction**.

Construction Mortgage *See:* **Mortgage, Construction**.

Constructive Annexation *See:* **Annexation, Constructive**.

Constructive Eviction *See:* **Eviction, Constructive**.

Constructive Fraud *See:* **Fraud, Constructive**.

Constructive Notice *See:* **Notice, Constructive**.

Consumer Guide to Agency Relationships Form that states the agency relationships permitted in Ohio and the agency relationships that your broker practices, payment to/from brokers who do not represent the broker's client, and required fair housing language.

Contingency Clause *See:* **Condition**.

Contract An agreement between two or more parties to do, or not do, a certain thing. The requirements for an enforceable contract are **capacity**, **mutual consent**, **lawful objective**, and **consideration**. In addition, certain contracts must be in writing to be enforceable.

Contract, Bilateral A contract in which each party promises to do something. *Compare:* **Contract, Unilateral**.

Contract, Breach *See:* **Breach of Contract**.

Contract, Executed A contract under which both parties have completely performed their contractual obligations.

Contract, Executory A contract under which one or more parties have not yet completed performance of their obligations, as they may be in the process of carrying out their duties.

Contract, Express A contract that has been put into words, either spoken or written.

Contract, Implied A contract that has not been put into words, but is implied by the actions of the parties.

Contract, Land A real estate installment agreement where buyer makes payment to seller in exchange for right to occupy and use property, but no deed or title transfers until all, or a specified portion of, payments have been made. Also called **installment land contract**, **installment sales contract**, **land sales contract**, **real estate contract**, and other names.

Contract, Oral A spoken agreement, as opposed to a written one.

Contract, Unenforceable A contract that a court would refuse to enforce. For example, a contract may be unenforceable because its contents cannot be proven, or because it is not in writing, or because the statute of limitations has run out.

Contract, Unilateral When only one party makes a legally binding promise and the other has not. The promise will become legally binding if the other party chooses to accept it (similar to an offer). *Compare:* **Contract, Bilateral**.

Contract, Valid A binding, legally enforceable contract.

Contract, Void A contract that is not an enforceable contract because it lacks one or more of the requirements for contract formation, or is defective in some other respect.

Contract, Voidable A contract that one of the parties can disaffirm, without liability, because of a lack of legal capacity or a negative factor such as fraud or duress.

Contribution A "rule" that says a particular item or feature of a house is only worth what it actually contributes in value to that piece of property.

Conventional Loan Loan not insured or guaranteed by a government entity.

Conventional Mortgage *See:* **Mortgage, Conventional**.

Conversion 1. Misappropriating property or funds belonging to another. 2. Changing an existing rental apartment building into a condominium.

Conversion Option A right a borrower has to convert from an adjustable rate mortgage to a fixed rate mortgage one time during the loan term, provided certain conditions are met.

Conveyance The transfer of title to real property from one person to another by means of a written document, such as a deed.

Conveyance, Voluntary *See:* **Deed in Lieu of Foreclosure**.

Conveyance, Words of *See:* **Words of Conveyance**.

Cooperative A building owned by a corporation, where the residents are shareholders in the corporation; each shareholder receives a proprietary lease on an individual unit and the right to use the common areas. *Compare:* **Condominium**.

Co-ownership Any form of ownership in which two or more people share title to a piece of property, holding undivided interests. Also called **co-tenancy** or **concurrent ownership**. *See:* **Community Property; Tenancy, Joint; Tenancy, Statutory Survivorship; Tenancy by the Entireties; Tenancy in Common; Tenancy in Partnership**.

Corporation An association, organized according to strict regulations, in which individuals purchase ownership shares; regarded by the law as an artificial person, separate from the individual shareholders. *Compare:* **Partnership**.

Corporation, Domestic A corporation doing business in the state in which it was created.

Corporation, Foreign A corporation doing business in one state, but created (incorporated) in another state.

Correction Deed *See:* **Deed, Correction**.

Cost, Replacement *See:* **Replacement**.

Cost, Reproduction *See:* **Reproduction**.

Cost Approach An appraisal method that estimates the value of real estate by figuring the cost of building the house or other improvement on the land, minus depreciation, plus the value of the vacant land.

Cost Inflation An increase in the cost of goods or services. *Compare:* **Demand Inflation**.

Cost of Money The interest rate that people or businesses pay to use another's money for their own purposes.

Cost Manuals Books that give estimated construction costs for various types of buildings/structures in different regions of the country.

Cost Manuals Method Cost approach appraisal method that uses cost manuals to arrive at an estimate of value for property.

Co-tenant Anyone who shares ownership of a property with another. In Ohio, a co-tenant may be a joint tenant, a statutory survivorship tenant, a tenant in common, a tenant by the entireties, or a tenant in partnership.

Counteroffer A counteroffer represents a change. It is a response to an offer to enter into a contract, changing some of the terms of the original offer. A counteroffer is a rejection of the original offer (not a form of acceptance), and does not create a binding contract unless the new counteroffer is accepted by the original offeror (the counterofferee).

Coupled with an Interest, Agency *See:* **Agency Coupled with an Interest**.

Covenant 1. A contract. 2. A promise. 3. A guarantee (express or implied) in a document such as a deed or lease. 4. A restrictive covenant.

Covenant, Restrictive *See:* **Restrictive Covenant**.

Covenant of Quiet Enjoyment A guarantee that a buyer or tenant has the right to exclusive, undisturbed possession of a leasehold estate, and will not be disturbed by the previous owner, the lessor, or anyone else claiming an interest in the property.

Covenants, Conditions, and Restrictions *See:* **CC&Rs**.

Credit Scoring A means by which the lender makes certain determinations regarding the creditworthiness of potential borrowers. This involves a lender assigning specified numerical values to different aspects relating to a borrower.

Creditor A person or other entity, such as a bank, who is owed a debt.

Creditor, Judgment *See:* **Judgment Creditor**.

Creditor, Secured A creditor with a lien on specific property that enables him or her to foreclose and collect the debt from the sale proceeds if it is not otherwise paid.

Credits A sum of money that is to be received.

Criminal Law The body of law concerned with crimes, an individual's actions against society. *Compare:* **Civil Law**.

Criminal Litigation A lawsuit in which the government sues someone to punish the wrongdoer and protect society.

Cure To remedy a default, by paying money that is overdue or fulfilling other obligations.

Curtesy At common law, a husband's interest in his wife's property; in Ohio, curtesy has been abolished and replaced by dower rights. *See:* **Dower Rights**.

Customer A party in a transaction to whom an agent does not have a fiduciary duty or relationship, but to whom an agent must still be fair and honest.

Damages An amount of money a defendant is ordered to pay to a plaintiff.

Damages, Actual *See:* **Damages, Compensatory**

Damages, Compensatory Damages award, usually of money, intended to compensate the plaintiff for harm caused by the defendant's act or failure to act, including personal injuries (physical and mental), property damage, and financial losses.

Damages, Consequential Damages compensating for losses that were not the direct result of the defendant's wrongful act, but which were a foreseeable consequence of it.

Damages, Exemplary *See:* **Damages, Punitive**.

Damages, Liquidated A sum of money that the parties to a contract agree in advance (at the time of entering into the contract) will serve as compensation in the event of a contract breach.

Damages, Punitive Damages award that is added to compensatory damages, to punish the defendant for malicious or outrageous conduct and discourage others from engaging in similar acts.

Debits Any sum of money that is owed.

Debt Recurring monetary obligation that cannot be cancelled.

Debtor A person or other entity, such as a company, who owes money to another.

Debtor, Judgment *See:* **Judgment Debtor**.

Decedent A person who has died.

Deceit *See:* **Fraud, Actual**.

Declaration, Condominium *See:* **Condominium Declaration**.

Declaration of Restrictions *See:* **CC&Rs**.

Dedication A gift of private property for public use; may transfer ownership or simply create a public easement.

Dedication, Common Law Dedication resulting from the owner's intention to donate land for public use, along with the government's acceptance of the donation. Common law dedication is actually involuntary in some cases; if an owner acquiesces to public use of his or her property for a long time, intention to dedicate the property may be implied.

Dedication, Statutory A dedication required by law; for example, dedication of property for streets and sidewalks as a prerequisite of subdivision approval.

Deed An instrument that conveys grantor's interest, if any, in real property.

Deed, Bargain and Sale A deed that implies the grantor owns the property and has the right to convey it, but does not carry any warranties.

Deed, Correction A deed used to correct minor mistakes in an earlier deed, such as misspelled names or errors in the legal description of the property.

Deed, Fiduciary A deed executed by a trustee, executor, or other fiduciary, conveying property that the fiduciary does not own but is authorized to manage.

Deed, General Warranty A deed in which the grantor warrants title against defects that might have arisen before or during his or her period of ownership. *Compare:* **Deed, Limited Warranty**.

Deed, Gift A deed that is not supported by valuable consideration; often lists "love and affection" as the consideration.

Deed, Limited Warranty A deed in which the grantor warrants title only against defects arising during the time he or she owned the property, and not against defects arising before that time of ownership. Also called a **special warranty deed**. *Compare:* **Deed, General Warranty**.

Deed, Quitclaim A deed that conveys any interest in a piece of real property the grantor has at the time the deed is executed. This type of deed is often used to clear up a cloud on the title. It contains no warranties of any kind.

Deed, Special Warranty *See:* **Deed, Limited Warranty**.

Deed, Warranty A deed carrying warranties (guarantees) of clear title and the grantor's right to convey. *See:* **Deed, General Warranty; Deed, Limited Warranty**.

Deed, Wild A recorded deed that will not be discovered using the grantor-grantee indexes because of a break in the chain of title (*See:* **Title, Chain of**) . A mortgage or other document can also be "wild."

Deed in Lieu of Foreclosure A deed given by a borrower to the lender to satisfy the debt and avoid foreclosure.

Deed of Trust An instrument held by a third party as security for the payment of a note (rarely used in Ohio). Like a mortgage, it creates a voluntary lien on real property to secure repayment of a debt. The parties to a deed of trust are the grantor or trustor (borrower), beneficiary (lender), and trustee (neutral third party). Unlike a mortgage, a deed of trust includes a power of sale, allowing the trustee to foreclose non-judicially. Also called a **Trust Deed**. *Compare:* **Mortgage**.

Deed Restriction *See:* **Restrictive Covenant**.

Default Failure to fulfill an obligation, duty, or promise, as when a borrower fails to make payments, a tenant fails to pay rent, or a party to a contract fails to perform.

Defeasance Clause A clause used to defeat or cancel a certain right upon the occurrence of a specific event (e.g., on final payment, words of grant in a mortgage are void and the mortgage is thereby cancelled and title is revested to mortgagor). This clause may also be used to give a borrower the right to redeem real estate after default on a note, by paying the full amount due plus fees and court costs.

Defeasible Fee *See:* **Fee Simple Defeasible.**

Defect, Latent *See:* **Latent Defect**.

Defect, Patent *See:* **Patent Defect**.

Defendant 1. Person being sued in a civil lawsuit. 2. Accused person in criminal lawsuit.

Deferment Permission to delay fulfillment of an obligation (e.g., paying taxes) until a later date.

Delivery The legal transfer of a deed (or other instrument). A valid deed does not convey title until it has been delivered to the grantee. *See:* **Donative Intent**.

Demand Inflation Too much money chasing too few goods. *Compare:* **Cost Inflation**.

Deposit 1. Money offered as an indication of good faith regarding the future performance of a purchase agreement; also called earnest money. 2. A tenant's security deposit.

Deposit, On *See:* **License on Deposit**.

Deposit, Security *See:* **Security Deposit**.

Deposition In a lawsuit, the formal, out-of-court testimony of a witness or a party taken before the trial; used as part of the discovery process to determine facts of a case, or if witness is not able to attend trial. A transcript of a deposition can be introduced as evidence in the trial.

Depreciate To decline in value.

Depreciation A loss in value of a piece of property for any reason.

Depreciation, Observable Any loss of value that the appraiser can attribute to physical deterioration, functional obsolescence, or economic obsolescence.

Depreciation, Straight Line Simple depreciation method that takes the total cost of a building and divides that by the number of years the building is expected to be useful.

Dereliction *See:* **Reliction**.

Designated Heir Chosen heir. By filing a document with probate court, a person can choose anyone to be his or her heir in the eyes of the law.

Detainer Action *See:* **Unlawful Detainer Action**.

Detrimental Reliance *See:* **Estoppel, Promissory**.

Devise 1. (Noun) Real property transferred in a will. 2. (Verb) To transfer real property by will. *Compare:* **Bequest; Bequeath; Legacy**.

Devisee A recipient of real property under a will. *Compare:* **Legatee**.

Difficulties, Practical *See:* **Practical Difficulties**.

Direct Index *See:* **Index, Direct**.

Disaffirm The act of asking a court to terminate a voidable contract.

Discount Points An amount paid to a lender when a loan is made to make up the difference between the current market interest rate and the rate a lender gives a borrower on a note. Discount points increase a lender's yield on a note, allowing the lender to give a borrower a lower interest rate. *See also:* **Points**.

Discovery, Pretrial Using depositions and interrogatories to learn about disputed facts in a case from opposing parties and reluctant witnesses; when opposing parties in a lawsuit must disclose requested info and evidence to the other side and are allowed to examine the other side's witnesses who will testify at trial.

Discrimination Treating people unequally because of their race, religion, sex, national origin, age, or some other characteristic of a protected class, in violation of civil rights law.

Disparate Impact When a law that isn't discriminatory on its face value has a greater impact on a minority group than it has on other groups.

Distinguished When the facts of a case differ from a precedent.

Diversity Jurisdiction *See:* **Jurisdiction, Diversity**.

Doctrine of Emblements *See:* **Emblements, Doctrine of**.

Domicile The state in which a person has a permanent home.

Dominant Tenant *See:* **Tenant, Dominant**.

Dominant Tenement *See:* **Tenement, Dominant**.

Donative Intent An intent to transfer title immediately and unconditionally.

Dower Rights In Ohio (and some other states), the interest held by a married person in the real property owned by a spouse in fee simple during their marriage. At common law, dower referred only to the wife's interest in her husband's property, while the husband's interest in his wife's property was called **curtesy**. Now dower refers to either spouse's interest in the other's property.

Dower Rights, Choate Dower rights that have vested in a person, creating a statutory life estate. This occurs because the person's spouse sold the property without a dower release and subsequently died.

Dower Rights, Inchoate Dower rights that have not yet vested, but have the potential to do so; held by a married person in real property currently owned by a spouse, or (if the spouse is still alive) in real property the spouse sold without a dower release. Also called **contingent dower rights**.

Dual Agency *See:* **Agency, Dual**.

Dual Agent *See:* **Agent, Dual**.

Due on Sale Clause Mortgage clause that prohibits assignment by making the entire mortgage balance due when property is sold.

Due Process A fair hearing before an impartial judge. Under the U.S. Constitution, no one may be deprived of life, liberty, or property without due process of law.

Duress Threatening violence against or unlawfully confining someone to force the person to sign a document; or threatening or confining a signer's spouse, child, or other close relative.

Duress, Economic Threatening to take some action that will be financially harmful to a person, to force him or her to sign a document; for example, threatening to breach a contract. Also called **business compulsion**.

Earnest Money *See:* **Deposit**.

Earnest Money Agreement *See:* **Purchase Agreement**.

Easement A right to use some part of another person's real property for a particular purpose. An easement is irrevocable and creates an interest in the property. *Compare:* **License**.

Easement, Appurtenant An easement that benefits a particular piece of property (dominant tenement). *Compare:* **Easement in Gross**.

Easement, Implied *See:* **Easement by Implication**.

Easement, Negative An easement that prevents the servient tenant from using his or her own land in a certain way (as opposed to allowing the dominant tenant to use it). Essentially the same as a **restrictive covenant**.

Easement, Positive An easement that allows the dominant tenant to use the servient tenement in a particular way.

Easement, Prescriptive *See:* **Easement by Prescription**.

Easement by Express Grant An easement granted to another in a deed or other document.

Easement by Express Reservation An easement created in a deed when a landowner is dividing the property, transferring the servient tenement but retaining the dominant tenement.

Easement by Implication An easement created by operation of law (not express grant or reservation) when land is divided, if there is a longstanding, apparent use that is reasonably necessary for enjoyment of the dominant tenement. Also called an **implied easement**.

Easement by Necessity A special kind of easement by implication that occurs when the dominant tenement would be completely useless without an easement, even if it is not a longstanding, apparent use.

Easement by Prescription An easement acquired by prescription. Also called a **prescriptive easement**. *See:* **Prescription**.

Easement in Gross An easement that benefits a person instead of a piece of land; there is a dominant tenant, but no dominant tenement. *Compare:* **Easement, Appurtenant**.

ECOA *See:* **Equal Credit Opportunity Act**.

Economic Base The main business or industry in an area that a community uses to support and sustain itself. A good economic base is critical for home values.

Effective Age The age of a structure based on the actual wear and tear that the building shows, not necessarily the structure's age.

Effective Gross Income Potential gross income, less a figure for vacancy and collection losses.

Egress *See:* **Ingress and Egress**.

EIS *See:* **Environmental Impact Statement**.

Eligibility, Certificate of *See:* **Certificate of Eligibility**.

Emblements, Doctrine of The rule that allows an agricultural tenant to re-enter the land to harvest crops if the lease ends, through no fault of the tenant, before the crop can be harvested (applies only to the first crop).

Eminent Domain The government's constitutional power to take (appropriate or condemn) private property for public use, as long as the owner is paid just compensation.

Employee Someone who works under the direction and control of another. *Compare:* **Independent Contractors**.

Encroachment A physical object intruding onto neighboring property, often due to a mistake regarding the boundary.

Encumbrance A non-possessory interest in property; a lien, easement, or restrictive covenant, burdening the property owner's title.

Enjoin To prohibit an act, or command performance, by court order; to issue an injunction.

Enjoyment *See:* **Quiet Enjoyment**.

Entireties, Tenancy by the *See:* **Tenancy by the Entireties**.

Environmental Impact Statement Study required by the National Environmental Policy Act for all federal and federally related projects that details a development project's impact on energy use, sewage systems, drainage, water facilities, schools, and other environmental, economic, and social areas.

Equal Credit Opportunity Act (ECOA) Federal law that prohibits discrimination in granting credit to people based on sex, age, marital status, race, color, religion, national origin, or receipt of public assistance.

Equal Protection Requirement Under the fifth and fourteenth amendments to the U.S. Constitution, all citizens are entitled to equal protection of the laws; no law may arbitrarily discriminate between different groups, or be applied to groups in a discriminatory manner.

Equitable Lien *See:* **Lien, Equitable.**

Equitable Remedy A judgment granted to a plaintiff that is something other than an award of money (damages); for example, an injunction, quiet title, rescission, and specific performance. *Compare:* **Legal Remedy.**

Equitable Right of Redemption The right of a debtor to save (redeem) property from foreclosure proceedings prior to confirmation of sale. *Compare:* **Statutory Redemption.**

Equitable Title *See:* **Title, Equitable.**

Equity 1. An owner's unencumbered interest in property; the difference between the value of the property and the liens against it. 2. A judge's power to soften or set aside strict legal rules, to bring about a fair and just result in a particular case.

Erosion A gradual loss of soil due to the action of wind or water.

Error, Harmless A mistake by a trial judge that is determined not to have affected the final judgment in a case.

Error, Prejudicial A mistake by a trial judge that may have affected the final judgment in a case. Also called **reversible error,** because it is grounds for reversing the trial court's decision.

Errors and Omissions Insurance Professional liability insurance that protects real estate licensees from mistakes or negligence.

Escheat When property reverts to the state after a person dies without leaving a valid will and without heirs. (Property also reverts to the state after abandonment.)

Escrow The system in which things of value (e.g., money or documents) are held on behalf of parties to a transaction by a disinterested third party (called an escrow agent), until specific conditions have been satisfied.

Escrow Account Account in which the lender maintains the borrower's extra 1/12, monthly deposits to cover next year's insurance and tax payments. Also called **Reserve Account.**

Escrow Closing A closing by a disinterested third party, often an escrow agent.

Escrow Instructions The contract that authorizes an escrow agent to deliver items deposited in escrow once the parties have complied with specified conditions. Can be the real estate purchase contract or a separate document.

Estate 1. A possessory interest in real property; either a freehold estate or a leasehold estate. 2. The real and personal property left by someone who has died.

Estate for Life *See:* **Life Estate.**

Estate for Years A leasehold estate set to last for a definite period (e.g., one week, three years), after which it t automatically terminates. Also called a **term tenancy.** *Compare:* **Tenancy, Periodic; Tenancy at Will.**

Estate in Fee Simple *See:* **Fee Simple.**

Estate in Remainder *See:* **Remainder.**

Estate in Reversion *See:* **Reversion.**

Estate of Inheritance An estate that can be willed or descend to heirs, such as a fee simple estate.

Estoppel A legal doctrine that prevents a person from asserting rights or facts that are inconsistent with earlier actions or statements, when he or she failed to object (or to "stop") another person's actions.

Estoppel, Promissory A doctrine applied when someone makes a technically unenforceable promise, but another person acts in reasonable reliance on the promise. If the person who relied on the promise will suffer harm unless it is enforced, a court may enforce it. Also called **Doctrine of Detrimental Reliance.**

Eviction Dispossessing or expelling someone from real property. *See:* **Unlawful Detainer Action.**

Eviction, Actual Physically forcing someone off of property, preventing someone from re-entering property, or using the legal process to make someone leave. *Compare:* **Eviction, Constructive.**

Eviction, Constructive When a landlord's act (or failure to act) interferes with the tenant's quiet enjoyment of the property, or makes the property unfit for its intended use, to such an extent that the tenant is forced to move out.

Eviction, Retaliatory When a landlord evicts a tenant in retaliation for complaining about code violations or violations of the Landlords and Tenants Act, or for participating in a tenants' rights group.

Eviction, Self-help When a landlord uses physical force, a lockout, or a utility shutoff to remove a tenant, instead of the legal process.

Eviction, Wrongful When a landlord evicts a tenant in violation of the tenant's rights.

Evidence Testimony, documents, and objects submitted in a lawsuit as proof of a fact.

Exclusionary Zoning *See:* **Zoning, Exclusionary**.

Exclusive Agency *See:* **Listing, Exclusive Agency**.

Exclusive Jurisdiction *See:* **Jurisdiction, Exclusive**.

Exclusive Right to Sell *See:* **Listing, Exclusive Right to Sell**.

Exculpatory Clause A clause in a contract or lease providing that one of the parties will not be liable in the event the other party (or someone else) is injured. This type of clause is void in residential leases in Ohio.

Execute 1. To sign. 2. To perform or complete. *See:* **Contract, Executed**.

Execution, Order of The legal process in which a court orders an official (such as a sheriff) to seize and sell the property of a judgment debtor to satisfy a judgment lien.

Execution, Writ of *See:* **Writ of Execution**.

Executive The head of a government, such as a president, governor, or mayor.

Executor/Executrix A person appointed in a will to carry out the provisions of the will. If a man is appointed, he is called an **executor**; if a woman is appointed, she is called an **executrix**. *Compare:* **Administrator**.

Executory Contract *See:* **Contract, Executory**.

Executrix *See:* **Executor/Executrix**.

Exemplary Damages *See:* **Damages, Punitive**.

Exemption A provision holding that a law or rule does not apply to a particular person, entity, or group (e.g., a company with a property tax exemption does not have to pay property taxes).

Exhibit 1. Documents or physical evidence submitted at trial. 2. Attachment to legal document.

Expert Witness *See:* **Witness, Expert**.

Express Stated in words (spoken or written).

Express Grant *See:* **Easement by Express Grant**.

Express Reservation *See:* **Easement by Express Reservation**.

Express Contract *See:* **Contract, Express**.

Extension Clause Listing agreement clause providing for a specified time period after a listing expires, when a broker will still be entitled to a commission if the property is sold to someone the broker dealt with during the listing term. Also called **Carryover Clause** or **Safety Clause**.

Fact, Material *See:* **Material Fact**.

Fact Witness *See:* **Witness, Fact**.

Failure of Purpose When the intended purpose of an agreement or arrangement can no longer be achieved; in most cases, this releases the parties from their obligations.

Fair Market Value *See:* **Value, Fair Market**.

Familial Status A protected group under the Federal Fair Housing Act and Ohio Civil Rights Law, making it illegal to discriminate against a person because he or she is the parent or guardian of a child less than 18 years of age.

Fannie Mae *See:* **Federal National Mortgage Association**

Farming an Area A marketing technique of working a specific area over a period of time.

Federal Discount Rates The interest rate charged by Federal Reserves banks on loans to member commercial banks.

Federal Funds Rate The Federal Reserve's target for short-term interest rates.

Federal Home Loan Mortgage Corporation (Freddie Mac) Nonprofit, federally chartered institution that functions as a buyer and seller of savings and loan residential mortgages.

Federal Housing Administration (FHA) Government agency that insures mortgage loans.

Federal National Mortgage Association (Fannie Mae) The nation's largest, and privately owned, investor in residential mortgages.

Federal Open Market Committee (FOMC) A body that controls the Fed's sale and purchase of government securities. The body is made up of the seven members of the Federal Reserve Board, plus the President of the Federal Reserve Bank of New York, and four other Federal Reserve Bank presidents.

Federal Question Legal issue involving U.S. Constitution, treaty, or federal statute. Federal courts have jurisdiction over federal questions, but can also be decided in state court.

Federal Reserve Board (the Fed) Body responsible for U.S. monetary policy, maintain economic stability and regulating commercial banks.

Fee An estate of inheritance; title to real property that can be willed or descend to heirs.

Fee, Conditional A type of defeasible fee; title may be terminated by former owner if conditions stated in deed are not met. Former owner has a power of termination. Also called **Fee Simple Subject to a Condition Subsequent**. *Compare:* **Fee Simple Determinable.**

Fee Simple *See:* **Fee Simple Absolute**.

Fee Simple Absolute The greatest estate one can have in real property; freely transferable and inheritable, and of indefinite duration, with no conditions on the title. Often called **Fee Simple** or **Fee Title**.

Fee Simple Defeasible A fee estate in real property that may be defeated or undone if certain events occur or conditions aren't met. Also called a **Defeasible Fee**. *See:* **Fee, Conditional; Fee Simple Determinable**.

Fee Simple Determinable A defeasible fee that's terminated automatically if certain conditions occur. Grantor (or his or her heirs) has a possibility of reverter. Also called a **Determinable Fee**. *Compare:* **Fee, Conditional.**

Fee Simple Subject to a Condition Subsequent *See:* **Fee, Conditional**.

Fee Title *See:* **Fee Simple Absolute**.

Feudal System The system of land ownership under which a king or queen owns all of the land and all other people are merely tenants.

FHA Federal Housing Administration; government agency that insures mortgage loans.

Fiduciary Person in a position of trust, held by law to high standards of good faith and loyalty.

Fiduciary Deed *See:* **Deed, Fiduciary**.

Fiduciary Relationship A relationship of trust and confidence, in which one party owes the other (or both parties owe each other) loyalty and a higher standard of good faith than is owed to third parties. For example, an agent is a fiduciary in relation to the principal; husband and wife are fiduciaries in relation to each other. Can be referred to as a **client**.

Financing Statement A brief document that, when recorded, gives constructive notice of a creditor's security interest in an item of personal property.

Finder's Fee A referral fee paid for directing a buyer or seller to a real estate agent.

First Lien Position The spot held by the lien with highest priority, when there's more than one mortgage or other debt or obligation secured by the property.

First Mortgage *See:* **Mortgage, First**.

Fiscal Policy The government's plan for spending, taxation, and debt management.

Fixed Rate Loan Loan with an interest rate that remains constant for the duration of the loan.

Fixed Term A period of time with a definite ending date.

Fixture A man-made attachment; an item of personal property that has been attached to or closely associated with real property in such a way that it has legally become part of the real property.

Fixtures, Trade *See:* **Trade Fixtures**.

Forcible Detainer Action *See:* **Unlawful Detainer Action**.

Foreclosure When a lienholder causes property to be sold so the unpaid debt secured by the lien can be satisfied from the sale proceeds.

Foreclosure, Judicial A lawsuit filed by a lender or other creditor to foreclose on a mortgage or other lien; a court ordered sheriff's sale of the property to repay the debt.

Foreclosure, Nonjudicial Foreclosure by a trustee under the power of sale clause in a deed of trust, without the involvement of a court. Not used in Ohio.

Foreclosure, Strict Foreclosure with a strict deadline, past which a mortgagor can no longer reclaim interest in the real property out of the foreclosure proceedings by bringing the mortgage current.

Foreclosure Action A lawsuit filed by a creditor to begin foreclosure proceedings.

Foreign Corporation *See:* **Corporation, Foreign**

Foreign Real Estate Any real estate situated outside the state of Ohio.

Foreign Real Estate Broker/Salesperson Any real estate broker/salesperson licensed to engage exclusively in real estate sales for land situated outside the state of Ohio.

Forfeiture Loss of a right or something of value as a result of failure to perform an obligation or condition.

Forward Commitment Purchase Program Program where a commitment is made by Freddie Mac to buy mortgages for 68 months, with delivery of mortgages at the option of seller.

Four Unities *See:* **Unities, Four.**

Fraud An intentional or negligent misrepresentation or concealment of a material fact; making statements that a person knows, or should realize, are false or misleading.

Fraud, Actionable Fraud that meets certain criteria, so that a victim can successfully sue. Victim/plaintiff must prove the defendant concealed material facts or made false statement (intentionally or negligently) with intent to induce the victim to enter a transaction, and that the victim was harmed by relying on these misrepresentations.

Fraud, Actual An intentional misrepresentation or concealment of a material fact; when a person actively conceals material information, or makes statements that are known to be false or misleading.

Fraud, Constructive A negligent misrepresentation or concealment of a material fact; when a person carelessly fails to disclose material information, or makes statements that he or she should realize are false or misleading.

Frauds, Statute of *See:* **Statute of Frauds.**

Freddie Mac *See:* **Federal Home Loan Mortgage Corporation.**

Freehold A possessory interest in real property of uncertain (and often unlimited) duration; an ownership estate in real property; either a fee simple or life estate. Holder of freehold estate has title. *Compare:* **Leasehold Estate.**

Fructus Industriales Plants planted and cultivated by people ("fruits of industry").

Fructus Naturales Naturally occurring plants ("fruits of nature").

Fully Amortized Loans Loans for which the total payments over the life of the loan pay off the entire balance of principal and interest that is due at the end of the loan term.

Future Interest An interest in real property that may become or will become a possessory interest at some point in the future. *See:* **Remainder; Reversion.**

Garnishment Legal process by which a creditor gains access to a debtor's personal property or funds in the hands of a third party. If a debtor's wages are garnished, the employer pays part of the paycheck direct to a creditor.

General Agent *See:* **Agent, General.**

General Jurisdiction *See:* **Jurisdiction, General.**

General Lien *See:* **Lien, General.**

General Partner *See:* **Partner, General.**

General Partnership *See:* **Partnership, General.**

General Warranty Deed *See:* **Deed, General Warranty.**

GIM *See:* **Gross Income Multiplier.**

Ginnie Mae *See:* **Government National Mortgage Association.**

GMRM. *See:* **Gross Rent Multiplier.**

Good Faith Improver *See:* **Occupying Claimant.**

Government National Mortgage Association (Ginnie Mae) Government-owned corporation that guarantees payment of principal and interest to investors that buy its mortgage-backed securities on the secondary markets.

Government Survey System Legal description for land referencing principal meridians and base lines designated throughout the country. Also **Government Rectangular Survey**.

Grant To transfer or convey an interest in real property by means of a written instrument.

Grantee Person receiving a grant of real property.

Granting Clause Deed clause stating a grantor's intent to transfer an interest in real property.

Grantor Person who grants an interest in real property to another.

Grantor, Common *See:* **Common Grantor**.

Grantor/Grantee Index *See:* **Index, Direct; Index, Reverse**.

GRM *See:* **Gross Rent Multiplier**.

Gross Income Income before expenses.

Gross Income Multiplier (GIM) A variation of the GRM that is used for commercial properties, but uses *annual* income figures.

Gross Lease Lease for which the landlord pays all property taxes, insurance, etc.

Gross Rent Multiplier (GRM) A number derived from comparable rental properties in an area, which is then used to estimate the value of a piece of real estate. The GRM is only used for one- to four-unit residential properties. *Compare:* **Gross Income Multiplier**, which is a variation used for commercial properties that uses *annual* income.

Guardian Court-appointed person who administers the affairs of a minor or incompetent person.

Habendum Clause Clause included after granting clause in many deeds; begins "to have and to hold," describing the type of estate granted.

Harmless Error *See:* **Error, Harmless**.

Heir Someone entitled to inherit another person's real or personal property under the laws of intestate succession.

Heir, Designated *See:* **Designated Heir**.

Highest and Best Use The most profitable, legally permitted, feasible, and physically possible use of a piece of property.

Holder in Due Course One who acquires a negotiable instrument in good faith and for consideration and, thus, has certain rights above the original payee.

Holdover Tenant *See:* **Tenant, Holdover**.

Holographic Will *See:* **Will, Holographic**.

Home Rule A rule that says a city or village that has adopted a charter is not required to comply with state zoning procedures.

Homeowners Association A nonprofit association comprised of homeowners in a subdivision, responsible for enforcing the subdivision's CC&Rs and managing other community affairs.

Homestead Protection Limited protection for a debtor against claims of judgment creditors; applies to property of the debtor's residence (very limited in Ohio).

Hostile and Adverse Possession or use of land without the owner's permission and against the owner's interests; one condition necessary for an easement by prescription and adverse possession.

HUD The Department of Housing and Urban Development; government agency that deals with housing issues.

Hung Jury A jury that cannot agree on a verdict after deliberating for a long time; thus, the case must be retried with a new jury.

Hypothecate To make property the security for a loan without giving up possession of it (as with a mortgage). *Compare:* **Pledge**.

Identifiable Grantee The person to whom real property interest is to be conveyed, identified in such a way so as to reasonably separate that person from all others in the world.

Immediate Delivery Program Freddie Mac Program giving sellers up to 60 days to deliver mortgages that Freddie Mac has agreed to buy on the secondary market.

Immobility A physical characteristic of real estate referring to the fact that real estate can't move from one place to another. (Customers are somewhat immobile also.)

Implied Authority *See:* **Authority, Implied**.

Implied by Law Required by law to be part of an agreement, and treated by a court as part of an agreement even if it contradicts the express terms agreed to by the parties.

Implied Contract *See:* **Contract, Implied.**

Implied Easement *See:* **Easement by Implication.**

Implied Warranty *See:* **Warranty, Implied.**

Implied Warranty of Habitability An implied guarantee that the property is safe and fit for human habitation; treated by law as an implicit provision in every residential lease, regardless of the express terms of the lease.

Improvements Man-made additions to real property; substantial fixtures, such as buildings.

In Escrow *See:* **Escrow.**

In Gross *See:* **Easement in Gross.**

Inactive License *See:* **License Inactive.**

Inchoate Dower *See:* **Dower Rights, Inchoate.**

Income, Residual *See:* **Residual Income.**

Income, Stable *See:* **Stable Income.**

Income Approach An appraisal method that estimates the value of real estate by analyzing the amount of revenue, or income, the property currently generates or could generate, often comparing the subject property to other similar properties.

Incompetent Not legally competent; not of sound mind; mentally ill, senile, or feebleminded.

Independent Contractors Self-employed people paid based on jobs completed rather than hours worked, and who are responsible for setting their own hours and paying their own taxes. *Compare:* **Employee.**

Index A statistical report that is generally a reliable indicator of the approximate change in the cost of money, and is thus often used to adjust the interest rate in ARMs.

Index, Direct An index kept by the county recorder, with each recorded document listed in alphabetical order according to grantor's last name. Also called a **grantor/grantee index.**

Index, Reverse An index kept by the county recorder, with each recorded document listed in alphabetical order according to the last name of the grantee. Also called a **grantee/grantor index.**

Index, Sectional An index that lists recorded documents under the tax parcel number of the property they apply to, grouping together all recorded documents affecting a particular piece of property. Also called a **tract index.**

Inflation An increase in the cost of goods or services; or, too much money chasing too few goods.

Inflation, Cost An increase in the cost of goods or services.

Inflation, Demand Too much money chasing too few goods.

Ingress and Egress Entering and exiting; usually refers to a road or other means of access to a piece of property. An easement for ingress and egress is one that gives the dominant tenant access to the dominant tenement.

Inherit In strict legal usage, to acquire property by intestate succession; commonly used to mean acquiring property either by intestate succession or by will.

Injunction A court order prohibiting an act or compelling an act to be done. *See:* **Enjoin; Equitable Remedy.**

Innocent Improver *See:* **Occupying Claimant.**

Inquiry Notice *See:* **Notice, Inquiry.**

Installment Note A note that calls for payments of principal only during the term of the note, with a balloon payment to pay off the balance.

Instrument Any document that transfers title (such as a deed), creates a lien (such as a mortgage), or gives a right to payment (such as a contract).

Insurance Value *See:* **Value, Insurance.**

Intangible Appurtenance *See:* **Appurtenance, Intangible.**

Integration Clause A provision in a contract document stating that the document contains the entire agreement between the parties.

Intent, Objective A person's manifested intention; what he or she appears to intend, whether or not that is what is intended.

Intent, Subjective What a person actually intends, whether or not it is apparent to others.

Interest 1. A right or share in something (such as a piece of real estate). 2. A charge a borrower pays to a lender for the use of the lender's money.

Interest, Non-possessory *See:* **Non-possessory Interest**.

Interest, Possessory *See:* **Possessory Interest**.

Interest, Security *See:* **Security Interest**.

Interest, Successor in *See:* **Successor in Interest**.

Interest, Undivided A co-tenant's interest, giving him or her the right to possession of the whole property, rather than a particular section of it. *See:* **Unity of Possession**.

Interest, Unity of *See:* **Unity of Interest**.

Interest Rate Cap *See:* **Cap, Interest Rate**.

Interpleader A court action filed by someone who is holding funds that two or more people are claiming. The holder turns the funds over to court; the court resolves the dispute and delivers the money to whoever is entitled to it.

Interrogatories Written questions submitted to the opposing party in a lawsuit during discovery, which he or she is required to answer in writing and under oath.

Intestate Dying without leaving a will.

Intestate Succession Distribution of property to the heirs of a person who died intestate.

Invalid Not legally binding or legally effective; not valid.

Inverse Condemnation Action A court action by a private landowner against the government, seeking compensation for damage to property that resulted from government action.

Inverted Pyramid A way of visualizing ownership of real property; theoretically, a property owner owns all the earth, water, and air enclosed by a pyramid that has its tip at the center of the earth and extends up through the property boundaries into the sky.

Involuntary Alienation *See:* **Alienation, Involuntary**.

Involuntary Lien *See:* **Lien, Involuntary**.

Issue Person's lineal descendants—children, grandchildren, great-grandchildren, and so on.

Joint Tenancy *See:* **Tenancy, Joint**.

Joint Venture Two or more individuals or companies joining together for one project or a series of related projects, but not as an ongoing business. *Compare:* **Partnership**.

Judgment 1. A court's binding determination of the rights and duties of the parties in a lawsuit. 2. A court order requiring one party to pay the other damages.

Judgment Certificate *See:* **Certificate of Judgment**.

Judgment Creditor A person who is owed money as a result of a being awarded a judgment in a lawsuit.

Judgment Debtor A person who owes money as a result of a judgment in a lawsuit.

Judgment Lien *See:* **Lien, Judgment**.

Judicial Foreclosure *See:* **Foreclosure, Judicial**.

Judicial Opinion *See:* **Opinion, Judicial**.

Judicial Partition *See:* **Partition, Judicial**.

Judicial Review When a court considers whether a statute or regulation is constitutional.

Junior Mortgage *See:* **Mortgage, Junior**.

Jurisdiction The extent of a particular court's authority; a court can't hear a case that's outside its jurisdiction.

Jurisdiction, Appellate The authority to hear an appeal (as opposed to conducting a trial). *Compare:* **Jurisdiction, Original**.

Jurisdiction, Concurrent When there is more than one court with jurisdiction over a case and a plaintiff may choose in which court to file suit. *Compare:* **Jurisdiction, Exclusive**.

Jurisdiction, Diversity The federal court's power to hear cases in which a citizen of one state sues a citizen of another state (or country) in a dispute concerning more than $50,000.

Jurisdiction, Exclusive When there is only one court in which a particular type of case can be filed, that court has exclusive jurisdiction. *Compare:* **Jurisdiction, Concurrent**.

Jurisdiction, General When a court's subject matter jurisdiction is not limited to specific types of cases.

Jurisdiction, Original The authority to conduct a trial (as opposed to hearing an appeal). *Compare:* **Jurisdiction, Appellate**.

Jurisdiction, Personal A court's authority over a particular individual; usually obtained by service of process.

Jurisdiction, Subject Matter The types of cases a particular court has authority to hear. *Compare:* **Jurisdiction, General**.

Jurisdiction, Territorial The geographical area over which a particular court has authority.

Just Compensation Appropriate or fair value for private land taken by the government for public use. *See:* **Eminent Domain**.

Land Contract *See:* **Contract, Land**.

Land Lease Lease under which the tenant leases only the land from the owner, but the tenant owns the building.

Land Use Controls Public or private restrictions on how land may be used (e.g., zoning).

Landlocked Property 1. Land without access to a road or highway. 2. Land not beside water.

Landlord A landowner who has leased his or her property to another. Also called a **lessor**.

Latent Defect A defect that is not visible or apparent; a hidden defect that would not be discovered in a reasonably thorough inspection of property. *Compare:* **Patent Defect.**

Lateral Support *See:* **Support, Lateral**.

Law, Case *See:* **Case Law**.

Law, Constitutional *See:* **Constitutional Law**.

Law, Statutory *See:* **Statutory Law**.

Lawful Objective A legal purpose.

Lease Conveyance of a leasehold estate from the fee owner to a tenant; a contract where one party pays the other rent in exchange for possession of real estate. *See:* **Gross Lease; Net Lease; Percentage Lease; Land Lease**.

Lease/Option When a seller leases property to someone for a specific term, with an option to buy the property at a predetermined price during the lease term, usually with a portion of the lease payments applied to the purchase price.

Leasehold Estate An estate that gives the holder (tenant) a temporary right to possession, without title. Also called **less-than-freehold estate**.

Legacy Receiving money by will.

Legal Description A precise description of a piece of property. *See:* **Lot and Block Description; Metes and Bounds Description; Government Survey System**.

Legal Title *See:* **Title, Legal**.

Legal Remedy Money awarded to the plaintiff in a civil lawsuit; damages. Also called a **remedy at law** or **common law remedy**. *Compare:* **Equitable Remedy**.

Legatee A person who receives money (a legacy) under a will.

Legislature The arm of a government that has primary responsibility for passing laws.

Lender's Yield *See:* **Yield**.

Lessee A person who leases property; a tenant.

Lessor A person who leases property to another; a landlord.

Less-than-freehold Estate *See:* **Leasehold Estate**.

Letter of Opinion 1. Type of appraisal report that is simply a business letter on the appraiser's stationery that identifies the facts and conclusions of the appraisal. 2. A letter issued by an attorney regarding the status of title to a piece of property.

Levy 1. Verb: to impose a tax. 2. Noun: the tax itself.

Liable Legally responsible.

License 1. Official permission to do a particular thing that the law does not allow everyone to do. 2. Revocable, non-assignable permission to enter another person's land for a particular purpose. *Compare:* **Easement**.

License Inactive License status of any salesperson who returns his or her license to Division of Real Estate to pursue non-real estate activities. License may remain inactive indefinitely if it is renewed each year and continuing education requirements are met.

License on Deposit 1. A special license status that is only available to brokers who wish to return their broker's license to the Division of Real Estate to reactivate their license as a salesperson. A broker's license may remain on deposit indefinitely if it is renewed each year and continuing education requirements are met. 2. A special license status available to any broker or salesperson who enters the armed services. Licenses may remain on deposit until the next renewal date after military discharge.

Lien A non-possessory interest in property giving a lienholder the right to foreclose if the owner does not pay a debt owed the lienholder; a financial encumbrance on the owner's title.

Lien, Attachment A lien intended to prevent property transfer pending the outcome of litigation.

Lien, Equitable A lien arising out of fairness, instead of agreement or operation of law.

Lien, General A lien against all property of a debtor, instead of a particular piece of property.

Lien, Involuntary A lien that arises by operation of law, without the consent of the property owner. Also called a **Statutory Lien**.

Lien, Judgment A general lien against a judgment debtor's property, which the judgment creditor creates by recording a certificate of judgment in county where property is located.

Lien, Materialman's Similar to a mechanic's lien, but based on a debt owed to someone who supplied materials, equipment, or fuel for a project (as opposed to labor).

Lien, Mechanic's A specific lien claimed by someone who performed work on the property (construction, repairs, or improvements) and has not been paid. This term is often used in a general sense, referring to materialmen's liens as well as actual mechanics' liens.

Lien, Specific A lien that attaches only to a particular piece of property (as opposed to a general lien, which attaches to all of the debtor's property).

Lien, Statutory *See:* **Lien, Involuntary**.

Lien, Tax A lien on real property to secure the payment of taxes.

Lien, Vendor's A lien to secure payment of the purchase price balance, held by a real estate seller if the buyer does not pay the seller in full at closing (unless the buyer gives the seller a mortgage for the balance).

Lien, Voluntary A lien placed against property with the consent of the owner; a mortgage (or, in other states, a deed of trust).

Lien Priority The order in which liens are paid off out of the proceeds of a foreclosure sale. Tax liens always have the highest priority.

Lien Theory States States in which a mortgagee only holds a lien against property (not actual title) until the loan is repaid, and the mortgagor holds the actual title. *Compare:* **Title Theory States**.

Lienholder, Junior Secured creditor with a lower priority lien than another lien on the same land.

Life Estate A freehold estate that lasts only as long as a specified person lives. That person is referred to as the **measuring life**.

Life Estate, Statutory A life estate held by a person whose dower rights have vested (because a person's spouse sold property without a dower release, and subsequently died).

Life Estate Pur Autre Vie A life estate "for the life of another," where the measuring life is someone other than the life tenant.

Life Tenant Someone who owns a life estate; the person entitled to possession of the property during the measuring life.

Limitations, Statute of *See:* **Statute of Limitations**.

Limited Partner *See:* **Partner, Limited**.

Limited Partnership *See:* **Partnership, Limited**.

Limited Real Estate Broker/Salesperson Person licensed exclusively to sell cemetery interment rights for a fee.

Limited Warranty Deed *See:* **Deed, Limited Warranty**.

Lineal Descendants A person's children, grandchildren, great-grandchildren, and so on.

Liquidated Damages *See:* **Damages, Liquidated**.

Lis Pendens A recorded notice stating that a lawsuit is pending that may affect title to the defendant's real estate.

Listing A written agency contract between a seller and a real estate broker, stating that the broker will be paid a commission for finding (or attempting to find) a buyer for the seller's real property. *Compare:* **Listing, Exclusive Agency; Listing, Exclusive Right to Sell**.

Listing, Exclusive Agency A listing agreement that entitles the broker to a commission if anyone other than the seller finds a buyer for the property during the listing term.

Listing, Exclusive Right to Sell A listing agreement that entitles the broker to a commission if anyone, including the seller, finds a buyer for the property during the listing term.

Listing, Net A listing agreement in which the seller sets a net amount that is acceptable for the property; if the actual selling price exceeds that amount, the broker is entitled to keep the excess as commission. Net listings are discouraged in Ohio.

Listing, Open A nonexclusive listing, given by a seller to as many brokers as he or she chooses. If the property is sold, a broker is only entitled to a commission if he or she is the procuring cause of the sale.

Litigant A party to a lawsuit; a plaintiff or defendant.

Litigation A lawsuit (or lawsuits).

Littoral Rights The water rights of a landowner whose property is adjacent to a lake or contains a lake; often called riparian rights (although that term refers only to the water rights of a landowner on a river). *Compare:* **Appropriative Rights; Riparian Rights**.

Loan Origination Fee Points charged to a borrower to cover the costs of issuing a loan.

Loan-to-Value Ratio The amount of money borrowed, compared to the value (or price) of the property.

Loan Value *See:* **Value, Loan**.

Location The exact position of a piece of real estate.

Location Survey A survey that determines if a property's buildings encroach on adjoining property, or any adjoining property's buildings encroach on the subject property.

Lot A parcel of land; especially, in a subdivision.

Lot and Block Description The type of legal description used for platted property. The description states only the property's lot and block numbers in a particular subdivision. To find the exact location of the property's boundaries, the plat map for that subdivision must be consulted at the county recorder's office.

LTV *See:* **Loan-to-Value Ratio**.

Mailbox Rule An acceptance of a contract offer is effective the moment it's mailed, even though the other party has not yet received it.

Majority, Age of The age at which a person gains legal capacity; in Ohio, 18 years old. *Compare:* **Minor**.

Maker One promising to pay money in a note.

Man-made Attachments *See:* **Fixtures**.

Mansion House The family home and the land on which it is located; referred to in this way when it is part of a deceased person's estate.

Margin The difference between the index value and the interest rate charged to the borrower with an ARM loan.

Market Price The price for which a piece of real estate actually sold.

Market Value The theoretical price that a piece of real estate is most likely to bring in a typical transaction.

Marketable Record Title Under the Marketable Title Act, an unbroken chain of recorded title going back at least 40 years.

Marketable Title Title free and clear of objectionable encumbrances or defects, so that a reasonably prudent person with full knowledge of the facts would not hesitate to purchase the property.

Marketable Title Act An Ohio law that extinguishes certain old, dormant claims against a title to simplify the title search process.

Marriage, Common Law *See:* **Common Law Marriage**.

Material Breach *See:* **Breach, Material**.

Material Fact An important fact; one that is likely to influence a decision.

Materialman A person who supplies materials, equipment, or fuel for a construction project. *See:* **Lien, Materialman's**. *Compare:* **Mechanic**.

Measuring Life A person whose life determines the length of a life estate. *See:* **Life Estate**.

Mechanic A person who performs work (construction, remodeling, repairs, or demolition) on real property. *See:* **Lien, Mechanic's**. *Compare:* **Materialman**.

Mediation The process whereby cases already filed with the court are accelerated by referring certain matters to a court referee.

Meeting of Minds *See:* **Mutual Consent**.

Merger Uniting two or more properties by transferring ownership of them all to one person.

Metes and Bounds Description A legal description that starts at an easily identifiable point of beginning, then describes the property's boundaries in terms of courses (compass directions) and distances, ultimately returning to the point of beginning.

Mineral Rights Rights to the minerals located beneath the surface of a piece of property.

Minor A person who has not yet reached the age of majority; in Ohio, a person under 18.

Misrepresentation A false or misleading statement. *See:* **Fraud**.

Mistake, Mutual When both parties to a contract were mistaken about a fact or a law.

Mistake, Unilateral When only one of the parties to a contract was mistaken about a fact or a law.

Mitigation When the non-breaching party takes action to minimize the losses resulting from a breach of contract.

MLS *See:* **Multiple Listing Service**.

Monetary Policy The means by which the government can exert control over the supply and cost of money.

Monuments Fixed physical objects stated as points of reference in a metes and bounds description.

Mortgage An instrument that creates a voluntary lien on real property to secure repayment of a debt. The parties to a mortgage are the mortgagor (borrower) and mortgagee (lender).

Mortgage, Adjustable Rate *See:* **Adjustable Rate Mortgage**.

Mortgage, Bi-weekly A fixed rate mortgage, similar to a standard mortgage, but with payments every two weeks instead of every month, resulting in an extra payment made each year.

Mortgage, Blanket 1. Mortgage that covers more than one parcel of real estate. 2. Mortgage that covers an entire building or development, rather than an individual unit or lot.

Mortgage, Budget A mortgage agreement where payments include principal and interest on the loan, plus 1/12 of the year's property taxes and hazard insurance premiums as well.

Mortgage, Construction A temporary loan used to finance the construction of a building on land. Replaced with a takeout loan.

Mortgage, Conventional A loan that is not insured or guaranteed by a government entity.

Mortgage, First A security instrument with a first lien position, meaning the first mortgage holder is paid first from a foreclosure sale.

Mortgage, Junior Any mortgage that has a lower lien position than another mortgage.

Mortgage, Package A mortgage where personal property, like furniture, is included in the property sale and financed together with one loan.

Mortgage, Purchase Money A mortgage where the seller finances all or part of the sale price of property for a buyer. Here the seller retains a mortgage and title passes to the buyer.

Mortgage, Reduction Option A fixed rate mortgage that gives the borrower a limited opportunity to reduce the interest rate once during the course of the loan, provided certain conditions are met.

Mortgage, Reverse When a homeowner over age 62 with little or no outstanding liens, mortgages his or her home to a lender and, in return, receives a monthly check.

Mortgage, Satisfaction of The document a mortgagee gives the mortgagor when the mortgage debt has been paid in full, acknowledging that the debt has been paid and the mortgage is no longer a lien against the property.

Mortgage, Second A security instrument in a second lien position.

Mortgage, Senior Any mortgage that has a higher lien position than another mortgage.

Mortgage, Wraparound *See:* **Wraparound Financing**.

Mortgage Companies Institutions that function as the originators and servicers of loans on behalf of large investors, such as insurance companies, pension plans, or Fannie Mae.

Mortgage Markets *See:* **Primary Mortgage Markets** or **Secondary Mortgage Markets**.

Mortgage Payment Adjustment Period *See:* **Adjustment Period, Mortgage Payment**.

Mortgage Payment Cap *See:* **Cap, Mortgage Payment**.

Mortgagee A lender who accepts a mortgage as security for repayment of the loan.

Mortgagor A person who borrows money and gives a mortgage to the lender as security.

Multiple Listing Service A listing service whereby local member brokers agree to share listings and commissions on properties sold jointly. Referred to as **MLS**.

Mutual Consent When all parties freely agree to the terms of a contract, without fraud, undue influence, duress, or mistake. Mutual consent is achieved through offer and acceptance; it is sometimes referred to as a "**meeting of the minds**."

Mutual Mortgage Insurance Plan The name of FHA's insurance program for residential mortgages.

Mutual Mistake *See:* **Mistake, Mutual**.

NAR National Association of REALTORS®.

Narrative Report A type of appraisal report that is the most detailed analysis, as it allows the appraiser to comment fully on the opinions and conclusions of the appraisal.

Natural Attachments *See*: Attachments, Natural.

Natural Person A real human being (as opposed to an artificial person such as a corporation).

Necessity, Easement by *See:* **Easement by Necessity**.

Negative Amortization When the balance of a loan grows because of deferred interest.

Negative Amortization Cap *See:* **Cap, Negative Amortization**.

Negative Easement *See:* **Easement, Negative**.

Negligence Conduct that falls below the standard of care a reasonable person would exercise under the circumstances; an unintentional breach of a legal duty resulting from carelessness, recklessness, or incompetence. *See:* **Tort**. *Compare:* **Strict Liability**.

Negligent Misrepresentation *See:* **Fraud, Constructive**.

Net Income Income after expenses.

Net Listing *See:* **Listing, Net**.

Net Lease Lease for which tenants pay all taxes, insurance, etc., plus utilities and rent.

Net to Seller An estimate of the money a seller should receive from a real estate transaction, based on a certain selling price after all costs and expenses have been paid.

Net Worth Value of a person's assets after subtracting liabilities from total assets.

Nonconforming Loans Loans that do not meet Fannie Mae/Freddie Mac standards and, thus, cannot be sold on the secondary market.

Nonconforming Use Property use that doesn't conform to current zoning laws, but is allowed because the property was being used that way before the new zoning law was passed.

Nonhomogeneity *See:* **Uniqueness**.

Nonjudicial Foreclosure *See:* **Foreclosure, Nonjudicial**.

Non-possessory Interest An interest in property that does not include the right to possess and occupy the property; an encumbrance, such as a lien or an easement.

Notary Public An official whose primary function is to witness and certify the acknowledgment made by one signing a legal document.

Note *See:* **Promissory Note**.

Notice, Actual Actual knowledge of a fact, rather than knowledge imputed or inferred by law.

Notice, Constructive Knowledge of a fact imputed to a person by law. A person is held to have constructive notice of something when he or she should have known it, even if he or she did not know it. Everyone is held to have constructive notice of the contents of recorded documents, since everyone is expected to protect their interests by searching the public record.

Notice, Inquiry When circumstances should have alerted someone to a possible problem prompting further investigation, a person may be held to have had notice of the problem even if he or she does not have actual knowledge of it.

Notice to Quit A notice to a tenant, demanding that the tenant vacate the leased property. Also called a **Notice to Vacate**.

Notice to Vacate *See:* **Notice to Quit**.

Novation 1. When one party to a contract withdraws and a new party is substituted, with the consent of all parties, relieving the withdrawing party of liability. 2. The substitution of a new obligation for an old one.

Nuisance Interference with the right of quiet enjoyment of property.

Nuncupative Will *See:* **Will, Nuncupative**.

Objective Intent *See:* **Intent, Objective**.

Occupying Claimant Someone who makes improvements to real property in the good faith, but mistaken belief, that he or she has title to it. Also called a **Good Faith Improver** or **Innocent Improver**.

Offer When one person proposes a contract to another and that offer is accepted, a binding contract is formed. *See:* **Acceptance**. *Compare:* **Counteroffer**.

Offeree A person who receives an offer or to whom an offer is made.

Offeror A person who makes an offer.

Open and Notorious When possession or use of land is obvious and unconcealed; one of the conditions necessary for easement by prescription.

Open Listing *See:* **Listing, Open**.

Open Market Operations When the Federal Reserve Board sells or buys government securities (or U.S. dollars) as a means of controlling supply and demand and confidence in those items.

Operating Expenses Costs of running a building, such as repairs and maintenance, but not including debt service or depreciation.

Opinion, Judicial A judge's written statement of a court case decision, outlining the facts of the case and explaining the legal basis for the decision.

Option A contract giving one party the right to do something within a designated time period, without obligation to do it. *Compare:* **Right of Preemption**.

Optionee Person to whom an option is given.

Optionor Person who gives an option.

Option to Purchase A contract giving the optionee the right, but not the obligation, to buy property owned by the optionor at an agreed price during a specified period.

Oral Contract *See:* **Contract, Oral**.

Oral Report A type of appraisal report given in person or over the phone, often without supporting documentation.

Order of Attachment *See:* **Attachment**.

Order of Execution *See:* **Execution, Order of**

Ordinance A law passed by a local legislative body; in Ohio, more specifically, a law passed by a city council or village council. *Compare:* **Resolution**.

Original Jurisdiction *See:* **Jurisdiction, Original**.

Ostensible Agency *See:* **Agency, Apparent**.

Ownership Title to property, dominion over property; the rights of possession and control of real or personal property.

Ownership, Concurrent Ownership by more than one person; co-ownership.

Ownership in Severalty Ownership by a single individual, as opposed to co-ownership.

Package Mortgage *See:* **Mortgage, Package**.

Panic Peddling *See:* **Blockbusting**.

Panic Selling *See:* **Blockbusting**.

Parcel A lot or piece of real estate, particularly a specified part of a larger tract.

Parol Evidence Evidence concerning negotiations or oral agreements that were not included in a written contract, altering or contradicting the terms of the written contract.

Partition, Judicial A court action to divide real property among its co-owners, so that each owns part of it in severalty, or (if it's not practical to physically divide the property) each gets a share of the sale proceeds.

Partition, Voluntary When co-owners agree to terminate their co-ownership, dividing the property so each owns a piece of the property in severalty.

Partner, General A partner who has the authority to manage and contract for a general or limited partnership, and who is personally liable for the partnership's debts.

Partner, Limited A partner in a limited partnership who is primarily an investor and does not participate in the management of the business, and who is not personally liable for the partnership's debts.

Partnership Association of two or more people to carry on business for profit. Law generally regards a partnership as a group of individuals, not as an entity separate from its owners. *Compare:* **Joint Venture; Corporation**.

Partnership, General A partnership in which each member has an equal right to manage the business and share in the profits, as well as equal responsibility for partnership's debts. All partners are considered general partners.

Partnership, Limited A partnership comprised of one or more general partners and one or more limited partners.

Partnership Property All property partners bring into the business at the outset or later acquire for their business; property owned as tenants in partnership. *See:* **Tenancy in Partnership**.

Part Performance A legal doctrine that allows a court to enforce an oral agreement that should have been in writing, when the promisee has taken irrevocable steps to perform his or her side of the bargain, and failure to enforce the contract would result in an unjust benefit for the promisor.

Pass-through Securities Mortgage backed securities issued by Ginnie Mae, which are more common, pay interest and principal payments on a monthly basis.

Patent The instrument used to convey government land to a private individual.

Patent Defect A visible, apparent defect that can be seen in a reasonably thorough inspection of property. *Compare:* **Latent Defect**.

Payee The one promised payment in a note.

Percentage Lease Lease under which a tenant pays a percentage of gross sales in addition to rent.

Performance, Part *See:* **Part Performance**.

Performance, Specific *See:* **Specific Performance**.

Performance, Substantial *See:* **Substantial Performance**.

Performance, Tendering *See:* **Tender**.

Periodic Tenancy *See:* **Tenancy, Periodic**.

Permanent Buydown *See:* **Buydown, Permanent**.

Permit System System used by state and local governments to monitor compliance with and enforce building codes and other regulations.

Personal Jurisdiction *See:* **Jurisdiction, Personal**.

Personal Property Any property that is not real property; movable property not affixed to land. Also called **Chattels** or **Personalty**.

Personalty Personal property.

Petitioner 1. An **appellant**. 2. A **plaintiff** (in some actions, such as dissolution of marriage).

PITI Principle, interest, taxes, and insurance; typical payment on a mortgage loan.

Plaintiff The party who brings or starts a civil lawsuit; the one who sues.

Planned Unit Development (PUD) A special type of subdivision that may combine nonresidential uses with residential uses, or otherwise depart from ordinary zoning and subdivision regulations; some PUDs have lot owners co-own recreational facilities or open spaces as tenants in common.

Planning Commission A local government agency responsible for preparing a community's comprehensive development plan.

Plat A detailed survey map of a subdivision, recorded in the county where the land is located. Subdivided property is often called platted property. Also called a **Plat Map**.

Plat Book A large book containing subdivision plats and kept at the county recorder's office.

Pledge When a debtor transfers possession of property to the creditor as security for repayment of the debt. *Compare:* **Hypothecate**.

PMI *See:* **Private Mortgage Insurance**.

Point of Beginning (POB) The starting point and ending point for a metes and bounds description.

Points One percent of a loan amount. Points can be charged for any reason, but are often used for buydowns (also called **Discount Points**).

Police Power The constitutional power of state and local governments to enact and enforce laws that protect the public's health, safety, morals, and general welfare.

Positive Easement *See:* **Easement, Positive.**

Possession 1. The holding and enjoyment of property. 2. Physical occupation of real property.

Possession, Adverse *See:* **Adverse Possession.**

Possession, Unity of *See:* **Unity of Possession.**

Possession, Writ of *See:* **Writ of Possession.**

Possessory Interest An interest in property that entitles the holder to possess and occupy the property, now or in the future; an estate, which may be either a freehold or leasehold.

Possibility of Reverter The interest held by a grantor (or grantor's heirs) who has transferred a fee simple determinable. *Compare:* **Power of Termination.**

Potential Gross Income The income that could be produced by a property in an ideal situation, with no vacancy and collection losses.

Power of Attorney An instrument authorizing one person (called an attorney in fact) to act as another's agent, to the extent stated in the instrument.

Power of Sale Clause A clause that allows the trustee to sell trust deed property, without court supervision, when terms of the trust deed are not kept.

Power of Termination The right to terminate a conditional fee estate if the estate holder fails to meet the required conditions. Also called a **Right of Re-entry**. *See:* **Fee, Conditional.** *Compare:* **Possibility of Reverter.**

Practical Difficulties Reason for a zoning area variance, because the zoning prevents owner from making a permitted use of the property.

Pre-approval Process by which a lender determines that potential borrowers can be financed through the lender for a certain amount of money.

Pre-qualification Process by which an agent or lender reviews potential borrowers to determine if they are likely to get approved for a loan, and for approximately what amount.

Precedent A previously decided case concerning the same facts as a later case; a published judicial opinion that serves as authority for determining a similar issue in a later case. *See:* **Stare Decisis.**

Precedent, Binding A precedent that a particular court is required to follow because it was decided by a higher court in the same jurisdiction.

Pre-emption *See:* **Right of Pre-emption.**

Prejudicial Error *See:* **Error, Prejudicial.**

Prepayment Penalties Additional money charged by a lender to the borrower for paying off a loan early.

Prescription Acquiring an interest in property (usually an easement) by using it openly and without the owner's permission for at least 21 years. In contrast to adverse possession, prescriptive use doesn't have to be exclusive (the owner may be using the property, too), and user does not acquire title to the property. *See:* **Easement by Prescription.** *Compare:* **Adverse Possession.**

Prescriptive Easement *See:* **Easement by Prescription.**

Pretrial Discovery *See:* **Discovery, Pretrial.**

Primary Mortgage Markets Lenders who make mortgage loans directly to borrowers. Also called **Primary Markets**. *Compare:* **Secondary Mortgage Markets.**

Principal 1. A person who grants another person (an agent) authority to represent him or her in dealings with third parties. 2. One of the parties to a transaction (such as a buyer or seller), as opposed to those who are involved as agents or employees (such as a broker or escrow agent). 3. With regard to a loan, the amount originally borrowed, as opposed to the interest.

Principal Meridians Main north-south lines designated and named throughout the country for use with government survey system.

Prior Appropriation *See:* **Appropriative Rights.**

Private Mortgage Insurance Insurance offered by private companies to insure a lender against default on a loan by a borrower.

Private Restriction *See:* **Restriction, Private.**

Probate A judicial proceeding in which the validity of a will is established and the executor is authorized to distribute the estate property; or, when there is no valid will, a judicial proceeding in which an administrator is appointed to distribute the estate to heirs according to the laws of intestate succession.

Probate Court A court that oversees the distribution of property under a will or intestate succession.

Procedural Law A law that establishes a legal procedure for enforcing a right. *Compare:* **Substantive Law**.

Process, Service of *See:* **Service of Process**.

Procuring Cause The real estate agent who is primarily responsible for bringing about a sale, such as by introducing the buyer to the property or by negotiating the agreement between the buyer and seller. Sometimes more than one agent contributes to a sale. *See:* **Listing, Open**.

Promisee A person who has been promised something; a person who is supposed to receive the benefit of a legally binding contractual promise.

Promisor A person who has made a contractual promise to another.

Promissory Estoppel *See:* **Estoppel, Promissory**.

Promissory Note A written, legally binding promise to repay a debt.

Proof, Burden of The responsibility for proving or disproving a particular issue in a lawsuit. The plaintiff usually has the burden of proof.

Proof, Standard of The extent to which plaintiff or prosecutor must convince a jury or judge to win a case. In most civil suits, a preponderance of evidence must support plaintiff's case. In criminal action, prosecutor must prove the case beyond a reasonable doubt.

Property 1. The rights of ownership in a thing, such as the right to use, possess, transfer, or encumber the thing. 2. Something that is owned—real or personal.

Property Manager A person hired by a real property owner to administer, market, merchandise, and maintain property, especially rental property.

Property Tax *See:* **Tax, Property**.

Proprietary Lease Exclusive, longer term lease given to a person who lives in a cooperative and owns stock in the cooperative.

Proration The allocation of expenses between buyer and seller in proportion to their actual usage of an item represented by the expense.

Public Nuisance A land use that threatens public health, safety, morals, or welfare, or constitutes a substantial annoyance to the public.

Public Record The official collection of legal documents that individuals have filed with the county recorder to make the information contained in them public. *See:* **Notice, Constructive; Recording**.

Public Restriction *See:* **Restriction, Public**.

Puffing Superlative statements about the quality of a property that should not be considered assertions of fact. "The best buy in town," or "a fabulous location" are examples of puffing.

Punitive Damages *See:* **Damages, Punitive**.

Pur Autre Vie *See:* **Life Estate Pur Autre Vie**.

Purchase Agreement A contract in which a seller promises to convey title to real property to a buyer in exchange for the purchase price. Also called a **Purchase and Sale Agreement**, a **Purchase Contract**, or an **Earnest Money Agreement**.

Purchase and Sale Agreement *See:* **Purchase Agreement**.

Purchase Contract *See:* **Purchase Agreement**.

Purchase Money Mortgage *See:* **Mortgage, Purchase Money**.

Quantity Survey Method A cost approach appraisal method that has the appraiser count the number and type of each part and material used to construct the building, plus adding a cost for labor, profit, permits, etc.

Question of Fact In a lawsuit, a question about what actually occurred, as opposed to a question about the legal consequences of what occurred (a question of law).

Question of Law In a lawsuit, a question about what the law is on a particular point; what the legal rights and duties of the parties were.

Quiet Enjoyment Use and possession of real property without interference from the previous owner, the lessor, or anyone else claiming title. *See:* **Covenant of Quiet Enjoyment**.

Quiet Title Action A lawsuit to determine who has title to a piece of property, or to remove a cloud from the title.

Quitclaim Deed *See:* **Deed, Quitclaim**.

Race/Notice Rule When the same property has been sold to two different buyers, if the second buyer records the deed before the first buyer, then the second buyer has good title to the property as long as he or she did not have notice of the first buyer's interest.

Range Lines North-south lines that run parallel to principal meridians at six-mile intervals in the government survey system.

Rate Adjustment Period *See:* **Adjustment Period, Rate**.

Ratification Later confirmation or approval of an act not authorized when it was performed.

Ready, Willing, and Able Making an offer to purchase on terms acceptable to the seller, and having the financial ability to complete the purchase.

Real Estate Contract 1. A purchase agreement. 2. A land contract. 3. Any contract having to do with real property.

Real Estate Cycles General swings in real estate activity, resulting in increasing or decreasing activity and property values, during different phases of the cycle.

Real Estate Investment Trust (REIT) A real estate investment business with at least 100 investors, organized as a trust.

Real Estate Settlement Procedures Act Federal law dealing with real estate closings that sets forth specific procedures and guidelines for disclosure of settlement costs.

Real Estate Taxes *See:* **Property Tax**.

Real Estate Transfer Tax *See:* **Tax, Real Estate Transfer**.

Real Property Land and everything attached to it or appurtenant to it. *Compare:* **Personal Property**.

Realtist A real estate licensee who is a member of National Association of Real Estate Brokers.

REALTOR® Any real estate licensee who is a member of the National Association of REALTORS® and its affiliate boards. Only members may use the term REALTOR® as it's a registered trademark of the NAR.

Realty Real property.

Receiver A person appointed by a court to manage and look after property or funds involved in litigation.

Reconciling The process of giving each number an appropriate weight depending on its importance to the overall assessment.

Reconveyance Instrument that releases security property from the lien created by a deed of trust; equivalent of satisfaction of mortgage.

Record, Public *See:* **Public Record**.

Record Title, Marketable *See:* **Marketable Record Title**.

Recording Filing a document at the county recorder's office so it will be placed in the public record.

Recording Numbers The numbers stamped on documents when they are recorded, used to identify and locate public record documents.

Rectangular Survey System *See:* **Government Survey System**.

Redemption *See:* **Equitable Right of Redemption**. *Compare:* **Statutory Redemption**.

Redlining When a lender refuses to make loans secured by property in a certain neighborhood because of the racial or ethnic composition of the neighborhood.

Reduction Option Mortgage *See:* **Mortgage, Reduction Option**.

Referendum When citizens vote on an issue.

Reformation A legal action to correct a mistake, such as a typographical error, in a deed or other document. The court will order the execution of a correction deed.

Regulation 1. A rule adopted by an administrative agency. 2. Any governmental order having the force of law.

Regulation Z Federal guidelines under the Truth-in-Lending Act that require full disclosure of all credit terms for consumer loans.

Release 1. To give up a legal right. 2. A document in which a legal right is given up.

Reliction When a body of water gradually recedes, exposing land that was previously under water. Also called **Dereliction**.

Remainder A future interest that becomes possessory when a life estate terminates, and that's held by someone other than the grantor of the life estate; (reversion is a future interest held by the grantor). *Compare:* **Reversion**.

Remainderman The person who has an estate in remainder.

Remand When an appellate court orders further trial proceedings in a case, sending the case back to the court that originally tried it, or to a different trial court.

Remedy *Compare:* **Equitable Remedy** and **Legal Remedy**.

Renewal Premium Recurring fee to continue an insurance policy.

Rent Consideration paid by tenant to landlord in exchange for possession and use of property.

Rent Control Governmental restrictions on how much rent a landlord can charge.

Renunciation When someone who has been granted something or has accepted something later gives it up or rejects it; as when an agent withdraws from the agency relationship. *Compare:* **Revocation**.

Repair and Deduct Remedy When a tenant is paying rent to the court, the judge may allow the tenant to use some of the rent money to pay for necessary repairs.

Replacement Building the functional equivalent of the original building, usually with one that is the same size, layout, quality, and utility as the original.

Report *See:* **Appraisal Report Form; Letter of Opinion; Narrative Report; Oral Report.**

Reproduction Building an exact duplicate of the original building, giving the new structure the same look and feel as the original.

Repudiation *See:* **Anticipatory Repudiation**.

Res Judicata The legal doctrine holding that once a lawsuit between two parties has been tried and a final judgment has been issued, neither one can sue the other over the same dispute again.

Rescission When a contract is terminated and each party gives anything acquired under the contract back to the other party (verb form is **rescind**) . *Compare:* **Cancellation**.

Reservation A right retained by a grantor when conveying property; for example, mineral rights, an easement, or a life estate can be reserved in the deed.

Reserve Account Account in which the lender maintains the borrower's extra 1/12, monthly deposits to cover next year's insurance and tax payments. Also called **Escrow Account**.

Reserve Requirements The percentage of customers' deposits that commercial banks are required to keep on deposit, either on hand at the bank or in the bank's own accounts—in other words, money the bank can't lend to other people.

Residual Income The amount of income a borrower has left after subtracting taxes, housing expense, and all recurring debts and obligations (used for VA loan qualifying) .

Resolution In Ohio, a law passed by a county board of commissioners or a board of township trustees. *Compare:* **Ordinance**.

Resolution, Corporate Action passed by a corporation authorizing the sale or purchase of real estate.

RESPA *See:* **Real Estate Settlement Procedures Act**.

Respondent 1. An **appellee**. 2. In a dissolution of marriage, party who did not file the action.

Restitution Restoring something to a person that he or she was unjustly deprived of.

Restriction A limitation on the use of real property. *Compare:* **Restriction, Public** and **Restriction, Private**.

Restriction, Deed Restrictive covenant in a deed that limits or curtails certain specified uses of the land.

Restriction, Private A restriction imposed on property by a previous owner or the subdivision developer; a restrictive covenant or a condition in a deed.

Restriction, Public A law or regulation limiting or regulating the use of real property.

Restrictive Covenant A restriction on real property use, imposed by a former owner; promise to do or not do an act relating to real property; usually an owner's promise not to use property in a particular way. May or may not run with the land.

Retaliatory Eviction *See:* **Eviction, Retaliatory**.

Reverse To overturn a lower court's decision on appeal, ruling in favor of the appellant. *Compare:* **Affirm**.

Reverse Equity Mortgage *See:* **Mortgage, Reverse**.

Reverse Index *See:* **Index, Reverse**.

Reverse Mortgage *See:* **Mortgage, Reverse**.

Reversible Error *See:* **Error, Prejudicial**.

Reversion A future interest that becomes possessory when a temporary estate (such as a life estate) terminates, and that is held by the grantor (or grantor's successors in interest). *Compare:* **Remainder**.

Reverter *See:* **Possibility of Reverter**.

Revocation When someone who granted or offered something withdraws it, as when a principal withdraws the authority granted to the agent, an offeror withdraws the offer. *Compare:* **Renunciation**. 2. Also, when the Real Estate Commission permanently withdraws a real estate agent's license. *Compare:* **Suspension**.

Rezone An amendment to a zoning ordinance, usually changing the uses allowed in a particular zone. Also called a **Zoning Amendment.** *Compare:* **Zoning, Spot**.

Right of Disposal A right to transfer all or some of a person's ownership interest in real property.

Right of Enjoyment A right to enjoy the benefits of land ownership without outside interference. *See:* **Quiet Enjoyment**.

Right of First Refusal *See:* **Right of Pre-emption**.

Right of Pre-emption A right to have the first chance to buy or lease property if the owner decides to sell or lease it. Also called a **Right of First Refusal**. *Compare:* **Option**.

Right of Survivorship A characteristic of statutory survivorship tenancy, joint tenancy, and tenancy by the entireties; surviving co-tenants automatically acquire a deceased co-tenant's interest in the property.

Right of Use A right of land ownership to make property productive (part of bundle of rights).

Right of Way Easement that gives the holder the right to cross another person's land.

Right to Rescind The right of a consumer to rescind any credit transaction involving his or her principal residence as collateral (except first mortgages), lasting up to midnight of the third business day after the transaction.

Riparian Rights The water rights of a landowner whose property is adjacent to or crossed by a river (or any body of water). *Compare:* **Appropriative Rights; Littoral Rights**.

Root of Title *See:* **Title, Root of**.

Roundtable Closing A closing conducted with all parties present.

Rule of Capture A legal principle that grants a landowner the right to all oil and gas produced by wells on his or her land, even if it migrated from underneath land belonging to another.

Running with the Land Binding or benefiting the successive owners of a piece of property, rather than terminating when a particular owner transfers his or her interest. Usually refers to easements or restrictive covenants.

S&Ls *See:* **Savings and Loan Associations**.

Safety Clause *See:* **Extension Clause**.

Sales Associate Any licensed real estate salesperson associated with a broker.

Salesperson Any licensed agent associated with a broker and, as such, who may perform most of the acts a broker, on behalf of the broker.

Satisfaction and Accord *See:* **Accord and Satisfaction**.

Satisfaction of Mortgage *See:* **Mortgage, Satisfaction of**.

Savings and Loan Associations Institutions that specialize in taking savings deposits and making mortgage loans.

Scarcity Characteristic of real property that says there is a limited supply of real estate.

Second Mortgage *See:* **Mortgage, Second**.

Secondarily Liable When a party is not completely released from liability on an obligation; thus if the lender cannot recover the loan amount from the new party, the original party who is secondarily liable may still be pursued.

Secondary Mortgage Markets Private investors and government agencies that buy and sell mortgages. Also called **Secondary Market**. *Compare:* **Primary Mortgage Markets**

Secret Profit A financial benefit an agent takes from a transaction without authority from the principal, nor informing the principal of the benefit retained. *See:* **Self-dealing**.

Section Part of a township, one-mile by one-mile square. Used for the government survey system; one section equals 640 acres, 36 sections equal one township.

Sectional Index *See:* **Index, Sectional**.

Secured Creditor *See:* **Creditor, Secured**.

Security Agreement An instrument that creates a voluntary lien on property to secure repayment of a loan. Real property security agreement are mortgages or trust deeds.

Security Deposit Money a tenant gives a landlord at the beginning of tenancy to ensure that the tenant will comply with the terms of the lease. The landlord may retain all or part of the deposit to cover unpaid rent, repair costs, or other damage at the tenancy's end.

Security Interest The interest a creditor may acquire in the debtor's property to ensure that the debt will be paid.

Seizen The possession of a freehold estate; ownership. Also spelled **Seisin** or **Seizin**.

Self-dealing When a real estate agent buys the principal's property (or sells it to a relative, friend, etc., or to a business the agent has an interest in), without disclosing that fact to principal, then sells it for a profit.

Self-help Eviction *See:* **Eviction, Self-help**.

Seller Financing When a seller extends credit to a buyer to finance the purchase of the property; this can be instead of or in addition to the buyer obtaining a loan from a third party, such as an institutional lender.

Seller's Market Situation in the housing market when sellers can choose from a large number of buyers looking for houses in an area.

Senior Mortgage *See:* **Mortgage, Senior**.

Separate Property In states with a community property system, any property owned by a married person that is not held jointly with the spouse as community property.

Service of Process Delivery of a legal document, especially a summons to a person according to the rules of statute, so that he or she is held to have legally received the document (even if he or she actually didn't).

Servient Tenant *See:* **Tenant, Servient**.

Servient Tenement *See:* **Tenement, Servient**.

Setback Requirements Provisions in a zoning ordinance that do not allow structures to be built within a certain distance of property lines.

Settlement 1. An agreement between the parties to a civil lawsuit, in which the plaintiff agrees to drop the suit in exchange for a sum of money or the defendant's promise to do or refrain from doing something. 2. Closing.

Settlement Statement A document that presents a final, detailed accounting for a real estate transaction, listing each party's debits and credits and the amount each will receive or be required to pay at closing. Also called a **Closing Statement**.

Severable When one part or provision in a contract can be held unenforceable without making the entire contract unenforceable.

Severalty *See:* **Ownership in Severalty**.

Shareholders Stockholders in a corporation.

Sheriff's Deed A deed issued by the court to a property purchaser from a foreclosure sale.

Sheriff's Sale A foreclosure sale held after a judicial foreclosure. Sometimes called an **Execution** or an **Execution Sale**.

Side Yard The area between a building and one side boundary of the lot on which it is located.

SIP *See:* **State Implementation Plan**.

Site A plot of land with enhancements that make it ready for a building or structure.

Situs Place where something exists; an area of preference or preference by people for a certain location, thus giving economic attributes (value) to the property.

Special Agent *See:* **Agent, Special**.

Special Assessment A tax levied only against properties that benefit from a public improvement (e.g., a sewer or street light), to cover the cost of the improvement; creates a **special assessment lien**, (an involuntary lien).

Special Exception *See:* **Conditional Use**.

Special Warranty Deed *See:* **Deed, Special Warranty**.

Specific Lien *See:* **Lien, Specific**.

Specific Performance A legal remedy in which a court orders someone who has breached a contract to perform as agreed, rather than simply paying monetary damages.

Specific Tax Policies Tax laws enacted by government that can encourage or discourage a particular behavior or activity.

Sphere of Influence People you know (and whom you can ask for referrals).

Spot Zoning *See:* **Zoning, Spot**.

Stable Income Income that can reasonably be expected to continue in the future.

Standard of Proof *See:* **Proof, Standard of**.

Standing to Sue Generally, meaning that a lawsuit can only be filed by someone who was personally harmed by the potential defendant's action. The Supreme Court has interpreted this very broadly with regard to housing discrimination lawsuits.

Stare Decisis Legal doctrine requiring judges to follow precedents (from the same jurisdiction) to make law consistent and predictable.

State Action In constitutional law, action by a government (federal, state, or local) rather than by a private party.

State Implementation Plan Study required by Federal Environmental Protection Agency to help states meet national air quality standards.

Statute A law enacted by a state legislature or the U.S. Congress. *See:* **Statutory Law**. *Compare:* **Ordinance; Resolution**.

Statute of Frauds A law that requires certain types of contracts to be in writing and signed to be enforceable.

Statute of Limitations A law requiring a particular type of lawsuit to be filed within a specified time after the event giving rise to the suit occurred.

Statutory Construction When, in the course of resolving a lawsuit, a judge interprets and applies a statute.

Statutory Dedication *See:* **Dedication, Statutory**.

Statutory Law Laws adopted by a legislative body (Congress, state legislature, or a county or city council), as opposed to constitutional law, case law, or administrative regulations.

Statutory Lien *See:* **Lien, Involuntary**.

Statutory Life Estate *See:* **Life Estate, Statutory**.

Statutory Redemption This lets a mortgagor redeem property for a set period of time after a foreclosure sale, regardless of the timing of other events. Time frames for **statutory right of redemption** vary by state. NOT USED IN OHIO. *Compare:* **Equitable Right of Redemption**.

Statutory Right of Redemption *See:* **Statutory Redemption**.

Statutory Survivorship Tenancy *See:* **Tenancy, Statutory Survivorship**.

Steering Channeling prospective buyers or tenants to particular neighborhoods based on their race, religion, national origin, or ancestry.

Stock Cooperative *See:* **Cooperative**.

Straight Note A note that calls for payments of interest only during the term of the note, with a balloon payment at the end to pay off the principal balance.

Strict Foreclosure *See:* **Foreclosure, Strict**.

Strict Liability When someone is held legally responsible for an injury to another, even though he or she did not act negligently. *Compare:* **Negligence**.

Subagent An agent of an agent; a person that an agent has delegated authority to, so that the subagent can assist in carrying out the principal's orders.

Subdivision 1. A piece of land divided into two or more parcels. 2. A residential development.

Subdivision Plat *See:* **Plat**.

Subdivision Regulations State and local laws that must be complied with before land can be subdivided.

Subjacent Support *See:* **Support, Subjacent**.

Subject Matter Jurisdiction *See:* **Jurisdiction, Subject Matter**.

Subject Property Property for which a value estimate is sought.

Subject To When property is transferred to a buyer along with an existing mortgage or lien, but without the buyer accepting personal responsibility for the debt. The buyer must make the payments to keep the property, but only loses his or her equity in the event of default. *Compare:* **Assumption; Novation**.

Subjective Intent *See:* **Intent, Subjective**.

Sublease When a tenant transfers only part of his or her right of possession or other interest in leased property to another person for part of the remaining lease term (as opposed to an assignment, where the tenant gives up possession for the entire remainder of the lease term). *Compare:* **Assignment**.

Subordination Clause A contract clause that gives a mortgage recorded at a later date the right to take priority over an earlier recorded mortgage.

Subpoena Document ordering a person to appear at a deposition or court proceeding to testify or produce evidence.

Subsequent Good Faith Purchasers Later grantees of a deed who actually paid consideration for it (as such, they are given some protection from claims not recorded).

Substantial Performance When a promisor does not perform all of his or her contractual obligations, but does enough so the promisee is required to fulfill his or her side of the bargain. *Compare:* **Breach, Material.**

Substantive Law A law that establishes a right or duty. *Compare:* **Procedural Law.**

Substitution A "rule" that says an informed buyer will not pay more for a house than a comparable substitute.

Successor in Interest A person (such as a buyer or an heir) who has acquired property previously held by someone else.

Sufferance, Tenancy at *See:* **Tenancy at Sufferance.**

Summons A document informing a defendant that a lawsuit has been filed against him or her, and directing the defendant to file an answer to the plaintiff's complaint with the court.

Supply and Demand Law of economics that says for all products, goods, and services, when supply exceeds demand, prices will fall, and when demand exceeds supply, prices will rise.

Support, Lateral The support that piece of land receives from the land adjacent to it.

Support, Subjacent The support that the surface of a piece of land receives from the land beneath it.

Support Rights The right to have one's land supported by the land adjacent to and beneath it.

Surrender Giving up an estate (such as a life estate or leasehold) before it has expired.

Survey The process of precisely measuring the boundaries and determining the area of a parcel of land.

Survivorship *See:* **Right of Survivorship.**

Survivorship Tenancy *See:* **Tenancy, Statutory Survivorship.**

Suspension A real estate agent's license being temporarily withdrawn. Usually, reactivation is automatic the day after the suspension is lifted. *Compare:* **Revocation.**

Syndicate An association of people or entities formed to operate an investment business. A syndicate is not a recognized legal entity; can be organized as a corporation, partnership, or trust.

Tacking When successive periods of use or possession by more than one person are added together to equal the 21 years required for prescription or adverse possession.

Takeout Loan A loan that is used to pay off a construction loan when construction is complete.

Taking When the government acquires private property for public use by appropriation, it is called "a taking." Term is also used in inverse condemnation lawsuits, when a government action has made private property useless.

Tax, General Real Estate *See:* **Tax, Property.**

Tax, Property An annual tax levied on the value of real property.

Tax, Real Estate Transfer A tax levied on the transfer of a piece of real property.

Tax Lien *See:* **Lien, Tax.**

Tax Sale Sale of property after foreclosure of a tax lien.

Taxation The process of a government levying a charge on people or things.

Temporary Buydown *See:* **Buydown, Temporary.**

Tenancy Lawful possession of real property; an estate.

Tenancy, Joint A form of co-ownership in which the co-owners have equal undivided interests and the right of survivorship. In Ohio, joint tenancy has been replaced by the statutory survivorship tenancy; joint tenancies established before 1985 still exist, but no new ones may be created. Joint tenancy must have the four unities present. *See:* **Unities, Four.**

Tenancy, Periodic A leasehold estate that continues for successive periods of equal length (such as from week to week or month to month), until terminated by proper notice from either party. Also called a month-to-month (or week-to-week, etc.,) tenancy. *Compare:* **Estate for Years.**

Tenancy, Statutory Survivorship A form of co-ownership created by the Ohio General Assembly to replace joint tenancy and tenancy by the entireties in Ohio; each co-tenant has an equal undivided interest in real property and the right of survivorship.

Tenancy, Term *See:* **Estate for Years**.

Tenancy at Sufferance Possession of property by a holdover tenant.

Tenancy at Will When a tenant is in possession with the owner's permission, but with no definite lease term and no rent being paid (or rent is not paid on a regular basis); e.g., a landlord lets a holdover tenant remain on the premises without paying rent until a new tenant is found.

Tenancy by the Entireties A form of property co-ownership by husband and wife, in which each spouse has an undivided one-half interest and the right of survivorship, with neither spouse able to convey or encumber his or her interest without the other's consent. In Ohio, tenancy by the entireties has been replaced by statutory survivorship tenancy; tenancies by the entireties from before 1985 still exist, but no new ones may be created.

Tenancy in Common A form of co-ownership in which two or more persons each have an undivided interest in the entire property (unity of possession), but no right of survivorship.

Tenancy in Partnership The form of co-ownership in which general partners own partnership property, whether or not title to the property is in the partnership's name. Each partner has an equal undivided interest, but no right to transfer the interest to someone outside the partnership.

Tenant Someone in lawful possession of real property, especially, someone who has leased property from the owner; can also refer to sublessees.

Tenant, Dominant A person who has easement rights on another's property; either the owner of a dominant tenement, or someone who has an easement in gross.

Tenant, Holdover A lessee who remains in possession of property after the lease has expired; a tenant who refuses to surrender possession of property at the tenancy's end.

Tenant, Life *See:* **Life Tenant**.

Tenant, Servient The owner of a servient tenement; that is, someone whose property is burdened by an easement.

Tender An unconditional offer by one party to a contract to perform his or her part of the agreement; made when the offeror believes the other party will breach to establish the offeror's right to sue if the other party doesn't accept it. Also called **Tender Offer**.

Tendering Performance *See:* **Tender**.

Tenement, Dominant Property that receives the benefit of an appurtenant easement.

Tenement, Servient Property burdened by an easement. In other words, the owner of the servient tenement (the servient tenant) is required to allow someone who has an easement (the dominant tenant) to use his or her property.

Tenements Everything of a permanent nature associated with a piece of land and ordinarily transferred with the land. Tenements are both tangible (buildings, for example) and intangible (air rights, for example).

Term A prescribed period of time; especially, the length of time a borrower has to pay off a loan, or the duration of a lease.

Term Tenancy *See:* **Tenancy, Term**.

Testament *See:* **Will**.

Testamentary Capacity A person making a will who is of sound mind and memory, and at least 18 years of age.

Testamentary Intent A person making a will that intends to do so, and can understand the consequences of his or her actions.

Testate Refers to someone who has died and left a will. *Compare:* **Intestate**.

Testator A man who makes a will.

Testatrix A woman who makes a will.

Tester *See:* **Checker**.

Time, Unity of *See:* **Unity of Time**.

Time is of the Essence A contract clause that means performance on the exact dates specified is an essential element of the contract; failure to perform on time is a material breach.

Time Share An ownership interest that gives the owner a right to possession of the property only for a specific, limited period each year.

Title Actual lawful ownership of real property. (This is ***not*** a document, but rather a concept or theory dealing with ownership.)

Title, Abstract of *See:* **Abstract of Title.**

Title, After-acquired Title acquired by a grantor after he or she attempted to convey property he or she did not own.

Title, Chain of The chain of deeds (and other documents) transferring title to a piece of property from one owner to the next, as disclosed in the public record.

Title, Clear Title that is free of encumbrances or defects; marketable title.

Title, Cloud on *See:* **Cloud on Title.**

Title, Color of *See:* **Color of Title.**

Title, Equitable An interest created in property upon the execution of a valid sales contract, whereby actual title will be transferred by deed at a future date (closing). Also, the vendee's (buyer's) interest in property under a land contract. Also called an **Equitable Interest**. *Compare:* **Title, Legal.**

Title, Legal The interest in property held by the rightful owner. Also, the vendor's (seller's) interest in property under a land contract. *Compare:* **Title, Equitable.**

Title, Marketable *See:* **Marketable Title.**

Title, Root of Under the Marketable Title Act, the deed (or other document of conveyance) that, 40 years earlier, was most recently recorded.

Title, Unity of *See:* **Unity of Title.**

Title Company A title insurance company.

Title Insurance Insurance that indemnifies against losses resulting from undiscovered title defects and encumbrances.

Title Plant A duplicate (usually microfilmed) of a county's public record, maintained by a title company at its offices for use in title searches.

Title Report A report issued by a title company, disclosing the condition of the title to a specific piece of property.

Title Search An inspection of the public record to determine all rights and encumbrances affecting title to a piece of property.

Title Theory States States in which a mortgagee holds actual title to property until the loan is repaid. *Compare:* **Lien Theory States.**

Torrens System Title registration system administered by the state; adopted in Ohio and other states, but is costly and rarely used.

Tort A breach of the standards of reasonable conduct imposed by law (as opposed to a duty voluntarily taken on in a contract) that causes harm to another person, giving the injured person the right to sue the one who breached the duty. Also called a **Civil Wrong** (in contrast to a criminal wrong, a crime). *See:* **Negligence; Strict Liability.**

Touch and Concern the Land Legal doctrine that says restrictive covenants must be related to actual land use to be enforceable.

Townships Square divisions of land, 6 miles by 6 miles, in the government survey system. One township contains 36 sections.

Township Lines East-west lines that run parallel to base lines at six-mile intervals in the government survey system.

Tract Index *See:* **Index, Sectional.**

Trade Fixtures Equipment a tenant installs for use in his or her trade or business, and which can be removed by the tenant before the lease expires.

Transfer, Certificate *See:* **Certificate of Transfer.**

Trespass An unlawful physical invasion of property owned by another.

Trial The fundamental court proceeding in a lawsuit, in which a judge (and in some cases, a jury) hears evidence presented by the plaintiff and defendant and issues a judgment. *Compare:* **Appeal.**

Trial Record All documents and transcripts from a trial.

Trier of Fact The one who decides questions of fact in a lawsuit. In a jury trial, it's the jury; in a non-jury trial, it's the judge. Questions of law are always decided by the judge, whether or not there is a jury.

Trust A legal arrangement in which title to property (or funds) is vested in one or more trustees who manage the property (or invest the funds) on behalf of the trust's beneficiaries, in accordance with instructions set forth in the document establishing the trust.

Trust Account A bank account, separate from a real estate broker's personal and business accounts, used to segregate trust funds from the broker's own funds.

Trust Deed *See:* **Deed of Trust**.

Trustee A person appointed to manage a trust on behalf of the beneficiaries.

Trustee's Sale A non-judicial foreclosure sale under a deed of trust.

Trust Funds Money or things of value received by an agent, not belonging to the agent but being held for the benefit of others.

Truth-in-Lending Act Act that requires lenders to disclose consumer credit costs to promote informed use of consumer credit.

UCC *See:* **Uniform Commercial Code**.

Unconscionable Provision Contract provision so unfair that it shocks the conscience of the court and, as such, a court will not enforce it.

Unconstitutional Violating a provision of the U.S. Constitution or a state constitution.

Undivided Interest *See:* **Interest, Undivided**.

Undue Influence Exerting excessive pressure on someone to overpower the person's free will and prevent him or her from making a rational or prudent decision; often involves abusing a relationship of trust.

Unencumbered Property Property whose seller has clear title free of mortgages or other liens

Unenforceable Contract *See:* **Contract, Unenforceable**.

Uniform Commercial Code Sets out certain requirements for negotiable instruments.

Uniform Residential Appraisal Report (URAR) A standard appraisal report form used by lenders and appraisers because it has been developed and approved by secondary mortgage market players Fannie Mae and Freddie Mac.

Uniform Standards of Professional Appraisal Practice (USPAP) Professional appraisal standards developed by The Appraisal Foundation, and now recognized throughout the United States as accepted standards of appraisal practice.

Unilateral Contract *See:* **Contract, Unilateral**.

Unilateral Mistake *See:* **Mistake, Unilateral**.

Uniqueness Characteristic of real property that says each piece of land, each building, and each house is a different piece of real estate. Also called **Non-homogeneity**.

Unities, Four The unities of time, title, interest, and possession, required for a joint tenancy. *See:* **Unity of Time; Unity of Title; Unity of Interest;** and **Unity of Possession**.

Unit Owners Association The organization that manages the operation of a condominium, imposing assessments and arranging for the maintenance of the common areas. The association's members are the unit owners and they usually elect a board of directors. Also called a **Condominium Association**.

Unity of Interest Each co-owner having an equal interest (equal share of ownership) in a piece of property.

Unity of Possession Each co-owner being equally entitled to possession of the entire property, because the ownership interests are undivided. *See:* **Interest, Undivided**.

Unity of Time When each co-owner acquired title at the same time.

Unity of Title When each co-owner acquired title through the same instrument (deed, will, or court order).

Universal Agent *See:* **Agent, Universal**.

Unjust Enrichment An unfairly obtained benefit.

Unlawful Detainer Action A summary legal action to regain possession of real property; especially, a lawsuit filed by a landlord to evict a defaulting tenant and regain possession of the property. Also called a **Forcible Detainer Action**.

Unnecessary Hardship Reason for a zoning use variance if permitted uses of the property are not economically feasible and the property cannot be used without the variance.

Untenantable Not fit for occupancy (used to describe rental property).

URAR *See:* **Uniform Residential Appraisal Report**.

Use, Conditional *See:* **Conditional Use**.

Use, Right of *See:* **Right of Use**.

Use Variance *See:* **Variance, Use**.

USPAP *See:* **Uniform Standards of Professional Appraisal Practice.**

Usury Charging an interest rate that exceeds legal limits.

VA *See*: **Veteran's Administration.**

Vacancy and Collection Losses Estimate as to how much future income may be lost when a building isn't fully occupied or tenants don't pay rent.

Valid The legal classification of a contract that is binding and enforceable in a court of law.

Valid Contract *See:* **Contract, Valid.**

Valuable Consideration *See:* **Consideration.**

Valuation *See:* **Appraisal.**

Value Amount of goods or services offered in the marketplace in exchange for something.

Value, Assessed The value placed on property by the taxing authority (e.g., county assessor) for the purposes of taxation. Usually with real estate, this value is only a fraction of the real value.

Value, Fair Market The amount of money a piece of property could bring if placed on the open market for a reasonable period of time, with a buyer willing (but not forced) to buy, and a seller willing (but not forced) to sell, if both buyer and seller were fully informed as to possible use of the land. Also **Market Value.**

Value, Insurance The amount for which property can be insured, usually only representing the replacement costs of the structure and disregarding any value for the land.

Value, Loan The amount of money that a lender is willing to allow someone to borrow to finance a particular piece of property.

Variance A permit obtained from the local zoning authority allowing the holder to use property or build a structure in a way that violates the zoning ordinance. *Compare:* **Conditional Use; Nonconforming Use.**

Variance, Area A variance that permits an owner to build a structure that does not strictly comply with the zoning law's setback requirements, height limits, or other rules affecting the size or placement of buildings.

Variance, Use A variance that permits an owner to use the property in a way that is not ordinarily allowed in that zone; for example, a commercial use in a residential zone.

Vendee A buyer or purchaser; particularly someone buying property under a land contract.

Vendor A seller; particularly, someone selling property by means of a land contract.

Vendor's Lien *See:* **Lien, Vendor's.**

Vested When a person has a present, fixed right or interest in property, even though he or she may not have the right to possession until sometime in the future. For example, a remainderman's interest in property vests when it's granted, not when a life estate ends.

Veto When the president or governor formally rejects a bill that Congress or the legislature has passed. The bill will not become law unless the legislature votes to override the veto.

Veteran's Administration (VA) Government agency that guarantees mortgage loans for eligible veterans.

Void Having no legal force or effect.

Void Contract *See:* **Contract, Void.**

Voidable Contract *See:* **Contract, Voidable.**

Voluntary Alienation *See:* **Alienation, Voluntary.**

Voluntary Conveyance *See:* **Deed in Lieu of Foreclosure.**

Voluntary Lien *See:* **Lien, Voluntary.**

Voluntary Partition *See:* **Partition, Voluntary.**

Waiver The voluntary relinquishment or surrender of a right.

Warranty, Implied A guarantee created by operation of law, whether or not the seller intended to offer it.

Warranty Deed *See:* **Deed, Warranty.**

Warranty of Habitability *See:* **Implied Warranty of Habitability.**

Waste Destruction, damage, or material alteration of property by someone in possession who holds less than a fee estate (such as a life tenant or lessee).

Water Rights The right to use water in or from a river, stream, or lake. *See:* **Appropriative Rights; Littoral Rights; Riparian Rights.**

WCR *See:* **Women's Council of Realtors.**

Wild Deed *See:* **Deed, Wild.**

Wild Document *See:* **Deed, Wild.**

Will A person's legally binding instructions regarding how his or her estate should be disposed of after death. Also called a **Testament**.

Will, Formal A written, witnessed will.

Will, Holographic A will written entirely in the testator or testatrix's handwriting, but which was not witnessed. Not recognized in Ohio because it was not witnessed.

Will, Nuncupative An oral will made on a person's deathbed; can only transfer personal property, not real property.

Witness, Expert A person who has expert knowledge of a subject, either through education or experience, who testifies in a court case.

Witness, Fact A person who witnessed actual events connected with a dispute.

Words of Conveyance A clause in a deed that states that the grantor intends to convey title to the land. Also **Granting Clause**.

Women's Council of Realtors (WCR) An organization devoted to addressing the issues, needs, and concerns of women in the real estate profession. (Now affiliated with the NAR.)

Wraparound Financing When a seller keeps the existing loan and continues to pay on it, while giving the buyer another mortgage.

Wraparound Mortgage *See:* **Mortgage, Wraparound**.

Writ of Execution A court order directing a public officer (often the sheriff or marshal) to seize and/or sell property to regain possession for the owner and/or satisfy a debt.

Writ of Possession A court order issued after an unlawful detainer action, informing a tenant that he or she must vacate the landlord's property within a specified period or be forcibly removed by the sheriff.

Wrongful Eviction *See:* **Eviction, Wrongful**.

Yield The total amount of money that can be made from an investment.

Zoning Government regulation of the uses of property within specified areas. *See:* **Conditional Use; Nonconforming Use; Rezone; Variance**.

Zoning, Exclusionary A zoning law that effectively prevents certain groups (such as minorities or poor people) from living in a community.

Zoning, Spot An illegal rezone that favors (or restricts) a particular property owner (or a small group of owners) without justification.

Zoning Amendment *See:* **Rezone**.

INDEX

A

B

C

M

N

O